ADVANCE PRAISE

"City University of New York has a very long history of making revolu...
was a magnet for students and some faculty who recognized the indivisibility of the
campus and the street, study and struggle. *New York Liberation School* turns to CUNY's
insurgent history to offer lessons for how we might remake higher education and the
world."—**Robin D. G. Kelley**, author of *Freedom Dreams: The Black Radical Imagination*

"This exciting telling of the City University of New York's radical history inspires
us to imagine its future. Despite endless givebacks by administration and pushbacks
from the state, CUNY professors and students contribute to and are influenced by the
larger popular movements at home and around the world. By centering such professors as Audre Lorde, June Jordan, Adrienne Rich, and Toni Cade Bambara; students
like Samuel Delaney and Assata Shakur; and grassroots activists in movements from
Puerto Rican Independence to Palestine Liberation; Conor Tomás Reed makes record
of what a university for poor and working-class people can give to the world. *New York
Liberation School* is a necessary study that enriches our understanding and imagining."
—**Sarah Schulman**, former CUNY student and faculty, and author of *Let the Record
Show: A Political History of ACT UP New York*

"*New York Liberation School* recovers the political organizing led by coalitions of students and educators to decolonize CUNY, the heart of NYC public education. Moving seamlessly between campus and streets, and foregrounding CUNY leaders like
June Jordan and Audre Lorde, this book offers a rich archive of radical experimentation, creativity, and institution-building to a new generation fighting for justice."
—**Robyn C. Spencer**, professor of history at Lehman College, CUNY, and author of
The Revolution Has Come: Black Power, Gender, and the Black Panther Party

"Conor Tomás Reed has gifted us with words that narrate the meaning of struggle of
and for the university. Ranging from early twentieth movements around the university
and militarism, to student and faculty struggles for Black and Puerto Rican Studies, to
the most recent assaults against the neoliberal turn and Occupy, the story of the many
reimaginations of City College, New York are not only a reminder of what the people's
university might be, this book arranges itself as a demand for what it must be. This is
a book for students and organizers, for committed scholars, and for our surrounding
communities. Reed shows us that these are the people who must determine the future
of these spaces. This book listens to the past for instruction, for these forebears have
much to offer. We must thank Reed for allowing their voices space to be heard again.
Now our choices for the future, the future of the university, will be conscious ones."
—**Joshua Myers**, author of *Of Black Study*

"If you don't want to join CUNY in heart and mind after reading this book, check
your pulse. The university re-visioned here as a site of coalitional struggle is, simultaneously, our world in the act of being re-made. To use the author's metaphor, *New York
Liberation School* is a boomerang. Hold on tight to this living history."—**Matt Brim**,
professor of queer studies at the College of Staten Island, CUNY, and author of
Poor Queer Studies: Confronting Elitism in the University

"An electrifying account of social ferment and educational experimentation. Reed constructs a living archive of the campus and street insurgencies that aimed to fulfill the democratic promise of a people's university. From antiracist, feminist, and queer student mobilizations to the emancipatory pedagogies of Toni Cade Bambara, June Jordan, and Adrienne Rich, *New York Liberation School* illuminates the visions of City College radicals who strove to democratize both the production of knowledge and the organization of society. In the age of neoliberal education, we desperately need this history of grassroots efforts to revolutionize learning. *New York Liberation School* is a gift to current and future campus rebels who wish to resist conformity and corporatization, reconstruct social relations, and reimagine what it means to be human."
—**Russell Rickford**, author of *We Are an African People: Independent Education, Black Power, and the Radical Imagination*

"Reed delivers an excellent guidebook for resisting the university from within. This is a story about how we create, with each other, the new worlds we seek; how we write, discuss, teach, and dream collectively in the service of our liberation. By sitting with the groundbreaking written work of intellectuals, cultural workers, students, and activists, and contextualizing it within the movements and political struggles that they were engaged in, Reed illustrates how the production of community organizing and artistic compositions go hand-in-hand to fuel the creation of new social and political possibilities. A must-read for those inside the academy, disillusioned with its limitations, as well as those outside of the academy, curious about its possibilities. Reed makes clear that a learning process occurs through political struggle and that it can transform people, communities, and institutions."—**Amaka Okechukwu**, author of *To Fulfill These Rights: Political Struggle Over Affirmative Action and Open Admissions*

"*New York Liberation School* takes readers on an emotional and fascinating journey through the history of CUNY from the perspective of the world's damned—where social movement and student struggle merge against class society, Eurocentrism, sexism, and the status quo in the production of knowledge. Offering a powerful history of the struggles for a free university with significant content for racialized and impoverished populations, Reed helps us to see clearly the strategies, alliances, internal disputes, achievements, and setbacks in resistance to the consolidation of racial capitalism."—**Yuderkys Espinosa-Miñoso**, coeditor of *Decolonial Feminism in Abya Yala: Caribbean, Meso, and South American Contributions and Challenges*

"With *New York Liberation School*, Conor Tomás Reed tells a fresh story of the revolution that shook college campuses in the late 1960s and 1970s. A deep history of the struggle at CUNY that unfolds through Reed's careful, tender prose, this book chronicles the making of 'Harlem University' in 1969. Reed reveals the startling ways that educators like June Jordan, Toni Cade Bambara, and Audre Lorde; and students like Assata Shakur and Sekou Sundiata; desegregated and decolonized the largest public urban university in the United States. This is an inspiring and thrilling story of radicalism in a time of retrenchment, a story we need now more than ever."—**Erica R. Edwards**, author of *The Other Side of Terror: Black Women and the Culture of U.S. Empire*

"If you want to make a more liberatory university, city, and world, you need to read this book! *New York Liberation School* dives into the oceanic depths of social upheaval at CUNY, inviting us to ride the waves of struggles with intersecting movements that rippled across generations and between the campus and wider city. Rather than abandoning the university as a site of power, students and educators built coalitional power to transform the institution while grappling with counter-insurgencies and recomposing themselves."—**Eli Meyerhoff**, author of *Beyond Education: Radical Studying for Another World*

"Conor Tomás Reed reminds us that education is profoundly liberatory because its best traditions ask the existential questions: who am I and what is my relationship to the nation and world? The protagonists of *New York Liberation School* asked and answered these questions in the largest public university in the country and discovered that who we are, what we're made of, and what we might become, must be answered in conversation with each other and our forebears—in the streets, in the classroom and in our neighborhoods. At a moment of book banning and educational silencing in the United States, this book introduces us to giant teachers like June Jordan, Audre Lorde, Adrienne Rich, and Toni Cade Bambara—and their students who understood that a truly liberatory education travels beyond the university, is dynamic, and is found in poetry, a novel, a song, or a protest that dares to both resist and dream up the best and most egalitarian world imaginable. Reed shows us how *New York Liberation School* came into being and how its revolutionary seeds might blossom in the face of neoliberal adversity." —**Johanna Fernández**, professor of history at Baruch College, CUNY and author of *The Young Lords: A Radical History*

New York Liberation School: Study and Movement for the People's University
Conor Tomás Reed
© 2023 Conor Tomás Reed

ISBN: 978-1-942173-68-7 | eBook ISBN: 978-1-942173-93-9
Library of Congress Number: 2023933972
10 9 8 7 6 5 4 3 2 1

Common Notions
c/o Interference Archive
314 7th St.
Brooklyn, NY 11215

Common Notions
c/o Making Worlds Bookstore
210 S. 45th St.
Philadelphia, PA 19104

www.commonnotions.org
info@commonnotions.org

Discounted bulk quantities of our books are available for organizing, educational, or fundrais-
ing purposes. Please contact Common Notions at the address above for more information.

Cover design by Josh MacPhee
Layout design and typesetting by Graciela "Chela" Vasquez | ChelitasDesign
Printed by union labor in Canada on acid-free paper

New York Liberation School

New York Liberation School
Study and Movement for the
People's University

Conor Tomás Reed

Brooklyn, NY
Philadelphia, PA
commonnotions.org

CONTENTS

Dedication

In their memories we struggle:

Nehanda Abiodun • Shireen Abu Akleh • Aijaz Ahmad • Meena Alexander • Jina Mahsa Amini • Stanley Aronowitz • Jean Anyon • Emilia Baez Concepción • Rosalyn Baxandall • Kathleen McAleer Bogin • Jerry Bogin • Kathy Boudin • John H. Bracey, Jr. • Cacsmy Brutus • Drucilla Cornell • Beni • Mike Davis • Diane di Prima • Lenny Dick • Barbara Ehrenreich • Lawrence Ferlinghetti • Clark Fitzgerald • Michael Gabaldon • Angelica "Titi Leca" Gonzales • David Graeber • Cat Green • Lee "Bird" Harris • Georgina Herrera • Aaron Hess • bell hooks • Austin Hughes • Wadiya Jamal • Miriam Jiménez Román • Mary Norbert Korte • Michael Lardner • Hyun Lee • María Lugones • Thea Hunter • Staughton Lynd • Jane Marcus • Hiram Maristany • Gerald Meyer • Brendan Patrick Molloy • Toni Morrison • Bob Moses • Leith Mullings • Sheryl Nash-Chisholm • Jeffrey Perry • Robert Emmet Reed • Louis Reyes Rivera • Cedric Robinson • Hancy Rodriguez • Zack Rosen • Rosaymi Santos • Elka Schumann • Russell "Maroon" Shoatz • Paul B. Simms • Tomás Soto • Justin Sparks • Betty Lee Sung • Manuel "Tortuguita" Terán • Haunani Kay-Trask • Urvashi Vaid • Jeremy Vanecek • Albert Vann • Ramón Villareal • Jerry Watts • Shatzi Weisberger • Albert Woodfox

INTRODUCTION

The first time I set foot on the City College of New York campus was for a protest. In March 2005, students and workers held a picket in front of a military recruiters' table at a campus career fair. The action was part of a national wave of counter-recruitment efforts responding to the expanding US wars in Afghanistan and Iraq. Three City College students were brutally assaulted by campus police. One had his face smashed into a concrete wall. Another—all five-feet-one-inch of her—was pinned to the ground by several guards and handcuffed. A day later, a staff member who had also participated was escorted from her desk and arrested. Calls for the activists' suspension and job termination ensued.[1]

At the protest I attended soon afterward, students, workers, and neighborhood residents decried the arrests as well as narrowing access to public education, racist recruitment methods, imperialist oil wars, and the violence of policing. They also affirmed the power of collective self-defense. Speakers linked the occupations in Afghanistan, Iraq, and Palestine with repression at home. Many alluded to the City University's long, militant history, through which poor people of colors reshaped their institution and communities.[2] The rally generated an outcry that ultimately rescinded all charges against the "City College Four." My first experience of educational direct action—staged amidst towering neo-Gothic buildings and rolling lawns within the inner-city Harlem neighborhood—was awe-inspiring. I knew instantly that I wanted to make a study and movement home here. One favored chant from that day—"Free CUNY!"—has resounded in my ears ever since, as both a demand and a promise.

Radical social movements at the City University of New York (CUNY) and throughout New York City were already revered in my family before I enrolled at City College in January 2006. In the early 1970s, at the dawn of the Open Admissions policy, my mother studied nursing at Hunter College while my uncle studied criminol-

---

1 *Democracy Now!*, "Campus Resistance: Students Stage Counter-Recruitment Protests Across the Country," March 18, 2005, https://www.democracynow.org/2005/3/18/campus_resistance_students_stage_counter_recruitment/. See also Conor Tomás Reed, "Long Live Said," *The New Inquiry*, October 25, 2013, https://thenewinquiry.com/long-live-said/.

2 The term "people of colors" invites readers to honor the vast array of hues, cultures, and histories of people who identify as African, Asian, Black, Caribbean, Indigenous, Latin American, Middle Eastern, Pacific Islander, mixed, and beyond—across gender, sexuality, and ability spectrums—who cannot be subsumed into one color, as in "people of color," while recognizing that our immense variations entail that no umbrella term will be inclusive enough.

ogy at John Jay College.[3] Their parents had emigrated from Puerto Rico to the Bronx in the early 1950s, and the fact that their kin could now access a free public college education was cause for celebration. My father was also born and raised in the Bronx by his Irish family. In their twenties, my parents were organizers in the Ploughshares movement, a nonviolent direct-action group led by Catholic priests Philip and Daniel Berrigan. Ploughshares militants would enter government offices to pour blood on draft records. They would also hammer dents into weapons found in military silos to render them inoperable.[4]

"Before you were born," my mother would beam at me, "you had been arrested." Shortly after Ronald Reagan's election in November 1980, she joined over two thousand women to surround the Pentagon in resistance to nuclear proliferation and the ever-expanding military budget.[5] She spent ten days in jail while pregnant with me. When this Puerto Rican-Irish coalition kid was born, Philip Berrigan baptized me. My first two homes were the antiwar commune Jonah House in Baltimore, MD and the Catholic Worker–affiliated Bread and Justice House in Bremerton, WA.[6]

Several early years spent in uptown New York City with my parents and siblings first anchored me to a radical sense of home. My mother worked as a nurse at St. Vincent's Hospital in the first and largest HIV/AIDS ward on the East Coast, at the epicenter of the epidemic.[7] My father documented survivors' stories of US-trained death squads in Central America.[8] Even when my family relocated to Texas, I knew that I would return to this city. At a geographic distance for many formative years, New York City radiated as a mythical place. In this book, I have worked to desentimentalize the city while acknowledging its fecundity in the national and global imaginations as a site of concentrated influence and power, both for the wealthy and for working peoples.

The City College antiwar action in 2005—the year I returned to New York—was followed by a three-day strike by the city's Transport Workers Union. These actions demonstrated the impact that both smaller spontaneous and larger coordinated efforts could have on the public university system and on the city at large. As a City College student between 2006 and 2010, I helped to nourish a campus milieu for learning and insurgency along with other students, workers, and community advocates. This included writing for *The Paper*, a longstanding City College newspaper led by Black and Puerto Rican students. I remember City College viscerally—how it felt to enter its imposing gates after trudging up the long slope from Broadway on one side, via the even steeper route up the St. Nicholas Park steps coming from Central Harlem, or by strolling right into campus on sleepy Convent Avenue. During this time I lived in

3 Implemented in Fall 1970, the Open Admissions policy allowed every New York City high school graduate a place in one of CUNY's two- or four-year colleges.

4 Philip Berrigan and Elizabeth McAlister, *The Time's Discipline: The Beatitudes and Nuclear Resistance* (Eugene: Wipf and Stock Publishers, 1989).

5 Howard Zinn, *A People's History of the United States* (New York: Harper, 2017), 603. See also Wesley G. Phelps, "Women's Pentagon Action: The Persistence of Radicalism and Direct-Action Civil Disobedience in the Age of Reagan," *Peace & Change: A Journal of Peace Research* 9, no. 3 (July 2014): 339–365.

6 Dorothy Day-Catholic Worker Collection, Bread and Justice Catholic Worker House (Bremerton, Washington) Records, 1980–1982. Special Collections and University Archives, Marquette University, https://www.marquette.edu/library/archives/Mss/DDCW/DDCW-seriesW29.php/.

7 NYC LGBT Historic Sites Project, "St. Vincent's Hospital Manhattan," February 2021, https://www.nyclgbtsites.org/site/st-vincents-hospital-manhattan/.

8 Thomas F. Reed and Karen Brandow, *The Sky Never Changes: Testimonies from the Guatemalan Labor Movement* (Ithaca: ILR Press, 1996).

Harlem, at 150th and Broadway. Ralph Ellison's historic residence was a block away, on Riverside Drive. Toni Cade Bambara's childhood home was a block in the other direction, on 151st Street.

The iconoclastic socialist feminist Jane Marcus was my first academic mentor.[9] After I researched City College students' involvement in 1930s antifascist struggles and the Spanish Civil War, she urged me to learn about the college's late 1960s upheavals. It was during this period that her longtime colleague Adrienne Rich first collaborated with Bambara, June Jordan, Audre Lorde, and others to teach Black and Puerto Rican students. In 1969, these students took over multiple campus buildings to create "Harlem University," aiming to transform admissions, curricula and governance, and to dismantle the boundaries between neighborhood and school. Over time, I absorbed the radical histories nestled around the campus. I returned to our library's archives frequently, feeling the protest leaflets and student newspapers hum with inherited energy. I spoke eagerly with anyone who had organized, participated in, or recalled these events. This book is the result of my experiences organizing at CUNY, diving into innumerable archives, and holding dialogues with Marcus and many others. It began to take shape seventeen years ago and has been written across multiple waves of struggle. Thousands have coauthored this book.

Coalitions, Compositions, Boomerangs

New York Liberation School chronicles how Black, Puerto Rican, and women educators and students at City College and CUNY revolutionized higher education and US social movements.[10] As New York City became an epicenter of Black, Puerto Rican, and women's militancy, participants produced poetry, fiction, journalism, and communiqués that continue to animate struggles today. These CUNY students and educators rooted themselves in a formal learning institution with the aim of building enduring *counter-institutions*. In the process, they created what Rich once called "a change of world."[11]

This narrative operates on two different registers. First, we present an interpersonal story to recount how several famous cultural workers and organizers shaped their writing and political actions through immersion in City College's Search for Education,

9 Conor Tomás Reed, "Remembering Jane Marcus: CUNY Prof Was a Tenaciously Brilliant Scholar, Activist," *The Indypendent*, June 9, 2015, https://indypendent.org/2015/06/remembering-jane-marcus-cuny-prof-was-a-tenaciously-brilliant-scholar-activist/.

10 This book offers a nonreductive, anti-essentialist, intersectional approach to historically situating these three social groups within and alongside each other. "Black" refers to people of the African diaspora across gender, sexuality, and ability spectrums. "Puerto Rican" refers to people from the island and its diaspora, including Nuyoricans, across gender, sexuality, and ability spectrums. "Women" refers to people who self-identify as this gender across ethnicity, sexuality, and ability spectrums. Our narrative also locates the United States of America within the geographic cosmologies of Turtle Island and Abya Yala. This book focuses on how these identities were composed, culturally expressed, and institutionalized at CUNY and in New York City by enmeshing (or opposing) one's ethnicity, gender, sexuality, abilities, economic position, and historical conjuncture with others around them.

11 Adrienne Rich, *A Change of World: Poems* (New Haven: Yale University Press, 1971).

Elevation, and Knowledge (SEEK) Program.[12] We primarily focus on City College teachers Toni Cade Bambara, David Henderson, June Jordan, Audre Lorde, Adrienne Rich, and Mina P. Shaughnessy; as well as on students Francee Covington, Samuel R. Delany, Guillermo Morales, Louis Reyes Rivera, Assata Shakur, Paul B. Simms, and Sekou Sundiata.[13] Second, we offer an institutional analysis of how public universities like CUNY and the University of Puerto Rico (UPR) became key sites of US state counterinsurgency aimed at suppressing liberation projects in New York City, the United States, and the US-colonized territory of Puerto Rico. These two threads illuminate how, through their *coalitions*, educators and students worked *compositionally* to desegregate and decolonize the largest US public urban university along with its surrounding geographies. *New York Liberation School* is ultimately a historical *boomerang*, a dynamic relation flung across generations to propel our collective energies toward freedom.

Coalitions

In dialogue with feminist scholars of colors, this book encourages a practice of reading these City College figures *coalitionally* across the people and groups that shaped each other's lives.[14] Further, it means recognizing the coalitional identities that comprise our selves. Instead of an individualized, ahistorical approach to self-identification (e.g., Black, woman, queer, working class) that narrows the focus to a sole intersecting point of *being*, thinking coalitionally reveals how identities are historically situated ways of *doing* that radiate outward, bridging and even hurtling over boundaries that claim these social parts are distinct or incommensurable.[15] Coalitional identities are irreducible differences that are manifested and acted upon. People are ongoing, mutually becoming. They are more than solo human forms. As Audre Lorde described herself, beyond the

---

12 Created at City College in 1965, and then extended through community pressure to all CUNY senior colleges in 1967, SEEK prepared Black and Puerto Rican high school students for college by providing noncredit preparatory courses, stipends, and social work counseling, as well as financial support through their time in college. City University of New York, "SEEK & College Discovery," *CUNY History & Mission*, http://www.cuny.edu/academics/programs/notable/seekcd/history-mission.html/.

13 While these teachers and students are the focus of this book, we also wish to honor the vast amount of under-recognized and under-compensated university labor done by office staff, custodians, food workers, groundskeepers, information technology workers, librarians, and beyond, as well as the socially reproductive labor outside of the university that is often unpaid and unvalued.

14 Karma Chavez, *Queer Migration Politics: Activist Rhetoric and Coalitional Possibilities* (Urbana: University of Illinois Press, 2013); María Lugones, *Pilgrimages/Peregrinajes: Theorizing Coalition Against Multiple Oppressions* (Oxford: Rowman and Littlefield, 2003); Linda Luu, "Comment from the Field: Toward Interdisciplinary Coalitions: Eunjung Kim's *Curative Violence* and Jasbir K. Puar's *The Right to Maim*," *Journal of Literary & Cultural Disability Studies* 13, no. 1 (2019): 111–115.

15 While "intersectionality" has come to be recognized as an academic term in the critical race theory discipline that emerged in the mid-1980s, its roots and usage precede that. See, for example, writings and speeches of this period by Gloria E. Anzaldúa, Frances Beal, Patricia Hill Collins, Anna Julia Cooper, Ana Livia Cordero, Kimberlé Crenshaw, Nancy Cunard, Angela Y. Davis, Judy Grahn, Fannie Lou Hamer, bell hooks, Claudia Jones, Yuri Kochiyama, Meridel Le Seuer, Elizabeth "Betita" Martínez, Cherrie Moraga, Tillie Olsen, Lucy Parsons, Ricky Sherover-Marcuse, Barbara Smith, Sojourner Truth, and Ida B. Wells-Barnett, among others.

For more recent key texts, see in particular: Chiara Bottici, *Anarchafeminism* (New York: Bloomsbury, 2022); Eve Mitchell, "I Am a Woman and a Human: A Marxist-Feminist Critique of Intersectionality Theory," *Unity & Struggle*, September 12, 2013, http://www.unityandstruggle.org/2013/09/i-am-a-woman-and-a-human-a-marxist-feminist-critique-of-intersectionality-theory/; Jennifer C. Nash, *Black Feminism Reimagined: After Intersectionality* (Durham: Duke University Press, 2019); Jasbir Puar, *Terrorist Assemblages: Homonationalism in Queer Times* (Durham: Duke University Press, 2007).

constrictions of a single lifetime, "Woman forever. My body, a living representation of other life older longer wiser. The mountains and valleys, trees, rocks. Sand and flowers and water and stone. Made in earth."[16] Attention to coalitional politics shows how these teachers and students integrated differences within themselves and each other, creating a practice of *integrity* that has since become imprinted upon CUNY and within popular cultures more generally.[17]

These coalitional identities brought people into collaboration and offered a method to commit their lives to revolutionary change. The clandestine Black Liberation Army (BLA) invited people from "all walks of life" to join their underground struggle against racial supremacy and capitalism.[18] Similarly, the Puerto Rican underground group Fuerzas Armadas de Liberación Nacional (FALN) enjoined its accomplices to be *for* Puerto Rico even if they weren't *of* Puerto Rican heritage.[19] "I think of being Black not so much as an ethnic category but as an oppositional force or touchstone for looking at situations differently," anarchist Black Panther Ashanti Alston has argued.[20] Considering Asian American movements of the 1960s and '70s, the historian Daryl Maeda has likewise underscored how the "identity that they ultimately advocated was a political marker rather than an ethnic descriptor," one that "represented opposition to racism in the United States and imperialism abroad."[21] For the historian Vijay Prashad, "The Third World was not a place. It was a project."[22]

Movement historians have focused on how Black Power groups forged the political radicalization of other groups. Even when scholars reflect on the Black Panther Party's interaction with China, for example, it becomes a story of Black Power's internationalism rather than one of transrevolutionary cross-pollination. However, the specific record of Black, Puerto Rican, feminist, queer, and disabled coalitional struggles foregrounded in this book reveals that Black political actors were also directly shaped and inspired by their accomplices. For example, Puerto Rican comrades enhanced Black liberation's focus on US colonialism, enabling African and Caribbean decolonization movements to also implicate the US empire and its own colonial subjects. Lesbian women of colors groups like the Combahee River Collective committed to "struggle together with Black men against racism, while we also struggle with Black men about

---

16 Audre Lorde, *Zami: A New Spelling of My Name* (Watertown: Persephone Press, 1982), 7.

17 Lorde often referenced the word "integrity": "In order to make integrated life choices, we must open the sluice gates in our lives, create emotional consistency. This is not to say that we act the same way, or do not change and grow, but that there is an *underlying integrity* that asserts itself in all of our actions." See Audre Lorde, *A Burst of Light: Essays* (Ann Arbor: Firebrand Books, 1988), 5. (Emphasis added.)

18 Assata Shakur, *An Autobiography* (Brooklyn: Lawrence Hill Books, 2001), 52–53.

19 For example, Jewish-American Susan Rosenberg (John Brown Anti-Klan Committee and May 19th Organization member) and Italian Silvia Baraldini (May 19th member) contributed to FALN activities. See Ren Ellis Neyra, *The Cry of the Senses: Listening to Latinx and Caribbean Poetics* (Durham: Duke University Press, 2020), 86.

20 Ashanti Alston, "Black Anarchism," transcript of public talk given at Hunter College, New York City on October 24, 2013, https://archive.org/details/BlackAnarchismAshantiAlston/.

21 Daryl Maeda, *Chains of Babylon: The Rise of Asian America* (Minneapolis: University of Minnesota Press, 2009), 130.

22 Vijay Prashad, *The Darker Nations: A People's History of the Third World* (New York: New Press, 2007), xv.

sexism" and heterosexism.[23] To name this symbiotic empowerment as coalitional underscores how the Black Power movement was also influenced by Asian, Caribbean, Chicanx, European, Indigenous, Latin American, Middle Eastern, Pacific Islander, feminist, queer, and disability liberation movements, which in turn retranslated what Black Power meant in these different encounters.

Compositions

Throughout this book, we draw on the analyses of *class composition* that Autonomist Marxists developed during the urban struggles of the 1960s and '70s, which others have recently embraced to assess the summer 2020 US abolitionist rebellions.[24] Using a polysemic approach, we reflect on the compositions, decompositions, and recompositions of Black, Puerto Rican, and women figures, as well as the institutions and relations in which they acted. Through their practices of writing—daydreaming, journals, class notes, outlines, drafts, revisions, publications, and circulations of words—City College educators and students *rearticulated* themselves and each other.[25] Our task in reading these compositions is not to transpose them onto our own time and places, but to ascertain how they were created so that we might translate their lessons into the present.[26]

At its heart, this book suggests that our New York Liberation School (partly the City College campus, partly the Harlem neighborhood and beyond) became a nucleus of Black–Puerto Rican–Third World–feminist–queer–disabled–revolutionary cultures and politics that has emanated outwards for the last fifty years.[27] Its participants' writings have served as *mobile liberation zones* that spread far beyond the specific context in which they emerged to teach subsequent generations new ways and meanings of strug-

23 Combahee River Collective, "Combahee River Collective Statement," in *How We Get Free: Black Feminism and the Combahee River Collective*, ed. Keeanga-Yamahtta Taylor (Chicago: Haymarket Books, 2017), 19.

24 Anonymous, "The Siege of the Third Precinct in Minneapolis: An Account and Analysis," *CrimethInc.*, June 10, 2020. https://crimethinc.com/2020/06/10/the-siege-of-the-third-precinct-in-minneapolis-an-account-and-analysis/; Mariarosa Dalla Costa and Selma James, *The Power of Women and the Subversion of Community* (Bristol: Falling Wall Press, 1975); Silvia Federici, *Wages Against Housework* (Bristol: Falling Wall Press, 1975); Silvia Federici and Arlen Austin, eds., *Wages for Housework: The New York Committee 1972–1977: History, Theory, Documents* (Brooklyn: Autonomedia, 2017); David P. Palazzo, "The 'Social Factory' in Postwar Italian Radical Thought from Operaismo to Autonomia," PhD diss., CUNY Graduate Center, 2014; Luisa Passerini, *Autobiography of a Generation: Italy, 1968* (Middletown: Wesleyan University Press, 1996); Louise Toupin and Käthe Roth, *Wages for Housework: The History of an International Feminist Movement, 1972–77* (London: Pluto Press, 2018); Steve Wright, *Storming Heaven: Class Composition and Struggle in Italian Autonomous Marxism* (London: Pluto Press, 2002).

25 Stuart Hall notes the entwined meaning of articulation as "both 'joining up' (as in the limbs of the body, or an anatomical structure) and 'giving expression to.'" See Stuart Hall, "Race, Articulation, and Societies Structured in Dominance" (1980), in Hall, *Essential Essays, Volume 1: Foundations of Cultural Studies*, ed. David Morley (Durham: Duke University Press, 2018), 172–221. See also Brent Hayes Edwards, *The Practice of Diaspora: Literature, Translation, and the Rise of Black Internationalism* (Cambridge: Harvard University Press, 2003), 14.

26 Gavin Arnall, "The Many Tasks of the Marxist Translator: Approaching Marxism as/in/with Translation from Antonio Gramsci to the Zapatistas," *Historical Materialism* 30, no. 1 (February 2022): 99–132.

27 Writing about university struggles in 1960s–70s Italy, Sergio Bologna similarly argued, "[T]he best way to distort these University struggles is to pretend that they are only about the University reforms, and therefore only of interest to University workers and students. This is false—because we have seen an entire class composition coming together around the Universities." In Wright, *Storming Heaven*, 203.

gle.[28] Each poem, essay, story, and novel becomes a City College/Harlem University classroom: multicentered, polyvocal, a class both 'in itself' and for itself,' practicing freedom. On this basis, you are also students of our New York Liberation School. This book is a wrested brick, a piece of sustenance from a long-contested institution. Hold it close, then pass it on to others.

Boomerangs

Throughout the book, *boomerang* is used to describe the kinetic power through which actions that appear in one place trigger both inspiration and blowback. Various post-World War II Black radical and anticolonial literatures have emphasized this call-and-response dynamic. In "Everybody's Protest Novel," James Baldwin writes: "Our passion for categorization, life neatly fitted into pegs, has led to an unforeseen, paradoxical distress; confusion, a breakdown of meaning. Those categories which were meant to define and control the world for us have boomeranged us into chaos."[29] Locating the genealogy of European fascism in the horrors of its own colonial histories, Aimé Césaire's *Discourse on Colonialism* recalls how "the bourgeoisie is awakened by a terrific boomerang effect: the gestapos are busy, the prisons fill up, the torturers standing around the racks invent, refine, discuss."[30] In his preface to Frantz Fanon's *The Wretched of the Earth*, Jean-Paul Sartre describes the effect from a different vantage: "In Algeria and Angola, Europeans are massacred at sight. It is the moment of the boomerang; it is the third phase of violence; it comes back on us, it strikes us, and we do not realize . . . that it's we that have launched it."[31] Following President John F. Kennedy's November 1963 assassination, Malcolm X framed the tragedy as "chickens coming home to roost," suggesting that the pervasive social violence that Kennedy failed to stop had ultimately been inflicted upon him.[32]

The boomerang effect resounds as a phenomenon of political retribution against the masters of history.[33] The boomerang alerts us to scores to be settled and expectations to be overturned, from Baldwin's existential disorientation to the vengeance envisioned by Césaire, Sartre, Malcolm X, and others.[34] In conjunction, *New York Liberation School* highlights how the moment of the boomerang also describes when militant

28 Eleanor Traylor, cited in Thabiti Lewis, *"Black People Are My Business": Toni Cade Bambara's Practices of Liberation* (Detroit: Wayne State University Press, 2020), 37.

29 James Baldwin, "Everybody's Protest Novel," in *Notes of a Native Son* (Boston: Beacon Press, 1955), 19.

30 Aimé Césaire, *Discourse on Colonialism*, trans. Joan Pinkham (New York: Monthly Review Press, 1972), 36.

31 Jean-Paul Sartre, "Preface," in Frantz Fanon, *The Wretched of the Earth*, trans. Constance Farrington (New York: Grove Press, 1963), 20.

32 "Malcolm X Scores US and Kennedy: Likens Slaying to 'Chickens Coming Home to Roost,'" *New York Times*, December 2, 1963, https://www.nytimes.com/1963/12/02/archives/malcolm-x-scores-us-and-kennedy-likens-slaying-to-chickens-coming.html/.

33 The term "whirlwind" in Black liberation struggles suggests a broader counter-historiographical cosmology to wield across our movements. See Muhammad Ahmad, *We Will Return in the Whirlwind: Black Radical Organizations, 1960–1975* (Chicago: Charles H. Kerr Publishing Company, 2007); Sekou Odinga, Dhoruba Bin Wahad, and Jamal Joseph, eds., *Look for Me in the Whirlwind: From the Panther 21 to 21st-Century Revolutions* (Oakland: PM Press, 2017); Team Colors Collective, *Uses of a Whirlwind: Movement, Movements, and Contemporary Radical Currents in the United States* (Chico: AK Press, 2010).

34 See Sohail Daulatzi, "Introduction: Fifty Years of the Boomerang," in *Fifty Years of* The Battle of Algiers: *Past as Prologue* (Minneapolis: University of Minnesota Press, 2016).

energies that erupt in one setting can project outward to others, such as when anti-state street uprisings then appear as university revolts. Anticipating this dynamic can allow us to prepare for—and proliferate—polyrhythmic insurgencies across societies, yielding a fertile ecology of movement actions.[35]

Scales of CUNY

This book spans more than a century of City College, CUNY, and New York City history, though our overarching focus is on the years 1960–1980, the last major peak of US social and educational movements. During this period, strikes for school desegregation and curricular change altered the terrain of Black, Puerto Rican, and women's solidarity. Neighborhoods became involved in educational activism through freedom schools. Institutional values were redefined from the kindergartens to the colleges as militants posed visionary challenges around learning strategies, equitable resources, and community control.

The outcomes of various struggles built upon or complicated each other. Energies from the 1963 March on Washington found subsequent expression in the 1964 New York City public school desegregation campaign. The 1968 Columbia University strike and Ocean Hill-Brownsville community control struggles were followed by the 1969 City College strike and Open Admissions policy of 1970. The imposition of tuition at CUNY in 1976 established conditions in 1978 for entry-level reading, writing, and math testing to assign incoming students a score and a place in the university.[36] Put another way, the period between the creation of the SEEK Program at City College in 1965 and the imposition of tuition at CUNY in 1976 coincides with the time between the assassination of Malcolm X (just blocks away from City College) and the 1975 fall of Saigon, the final defeat of the US in Vietnam. The flights of former City College students Guillermo Morales and Assata Shakur to exile in Cuba in 1979 preface the 1980 election of Ronald Reagan and the simultaneous end of several major US left organizations.[37]

Today, US imperialism has restructured and rebranded itself by using neoliberal diversity to mask a counterinsurgency campaign directed at public higher education and cities.[38] By recentering CUNY as one of the major targets identified by neoliberalism and US imperialism, we can see why contemporary CUNY movements are imbued with a spirit of vengeance to settle a fifty-year score. CUNY is but one of many institutions key to our collective liberation that we must learn to claim from below. Comprising twenty-five colleges across five boroughs, CUNY employs over 50,000 campus workers and enrolls more than 270,000 students, mostly women (57 percent) and people of colors (79 percent) who are usually the first in their working-class im-

---

35 A useful caution on the "boomerang effect" can be found in Stuart Schrader, *Badges Without Borders: How Global Counterinsurgency Transformed American Policing* (Oakland: University of California Press, 2019), 43–44; Jeanne Morefield, "Beyond Boomerang," *International Politics Reviews* 8 (2020): 3–10.

36 Ira Shor, interview with the author, January 28, 2022.

37 These organizations included Black Women Organized for Action, Combahee River Collective, National Alliance of Black Feminists, and the Third World Women's Alliance. See Kimberly Springer, *Living for the Revolution: Black Feminist Organizations, 1968–1980* (Durham: Duke University Press, 2005).

38 Roderick A. Ferguson, *The Reorder of Things: The University and its Pedagogies of Minority Difference* (Minneapolis: University of Minnesota Press 2012).

migrant families to attend college.[39] CUNY also includes millions of alumni and our families.

At CUNY, we speak of the different "scales" at which "spatialized politics" are manifested. The body, home, block, community, institutions, city, region, nation, and globe are key co-constitutive sites of transformative change. In pivotal moments, people "jump scales."[40] The interplay between ourselves and each other, our home and our neighborhoods, and the political shake-ups taking place across our city can reconfigure the country and the world (and vice versa). Jumping scales at CUNY, then, means being attentive to how the waves borne of a series of collisions between individual livelihoods, campus and community struggles, the CUNY administration, political and economic elites, a pandemic, and renewed mass uprisings might produce an oceanic transformation.

Institutional Strategies

US universities today are experiencing two divergent lines of flight.[41] Along one arc, popular trends in education movement strategies and scholarship—in particular among some interpretations of Black and Indigenous radical traditions, "Critical University Studies," and "Abolitionist University Studies"—have embraced the terms of escape, fugitivity, marronage, pessimism, and refusal of the university, often questioning it as a locus of transformation.[42] Along the other arc, scholars, administrators, and elite foundations have embraced the call for "public humanities" to reach broader communities outside the campus gates.

Both tendencies were influenced by the university upheavals and freedom learning of the 1950s, '60s, and '70s. These projects were led by Asian, Black, Caribbean, Indigenous, Latinx, and Pacific Islander American communities, with support from European Americans, whose predecessors helped lead a previous wave of educational

---

39 City University of New York, "CUNY Workforce Statistics," https://www.cuny.edu/about/administration/offices/hr/workforce-statistics/; "Student Data Book (Current and Historical)," https://www.cuny.edu/about/administration/offices/oira/institutional/data/.

40 Neil Smith, "Contours of a Spatialized Politics: Homeless Vehicles and the Production of Geographical Scale," *Social Text* 33 (1992): 55–81.

41 An earlier iteration of this writing appears in Conor Tomás Reed, "All Power to the Public Humanities!" *ASAP/Journal*, November 29, 2021, https://asapjournal.com/public-humanities-and-the-arts-of-the-present-all-power-to-the-public-humanities-conor-tomas-reed/.

42 Yulia Gilich and Tony Boardman, "Wildcat Imaginaries: From Abolition University to University Abolition," *Critical Times* 5:1 (April 2022): 109–120; Sandy Grande, "Refusing the University," in *Toward What Justice? Describing Diverse Dreams of Justice in Education*, ed. Eve Tuck and K. Wayne Yang (New York: Routledge, 2018); Pedro Lebrón Ortiz, *Filosofía del cimarronaje* (Toa Baja: Editora Educación Emergente, 2020); Katherine McKittrick, "Freedom is a Secret," in *Black Geographies and the Politics of Place*, ed. Katherine McKittrick and Clyde Woods (Brooklyn: South End Press, 2007); Fred Moten and Stefano Harney, *The Undercommons: Fugitive Planning and Black Study* (Brooklyn and London: Autonomedia and Minor Compositions, 2013); Moten and Harney, *All Incomplete* (London: Minor Compositions, 2021); Moten and Harney, "The University: Last Words," in *Strike MoMA Reader*, 2021, https://www.strikemoma.org/reader/; Madhi Suri Prakash and Gustavo Esteva, *Escaping Education: Living as Learning with Grassroots Cultures* (New York: Peter Lang Publishing, 1998); "Maroon University," Social Justice Initiative, University of Illinois Chicago, Summer 2021, https://sji.uic.edu/maroonu/; Frank Wilderson III, *Afropessimism* (New York: W.W. Norton and Company, 2020).

and social rebellions between the 1910s and the 1940s.[43] From 1960 onward, public college sit-ins and strikes—from Greensboro to Berkeley to the City College of New York to San Francisco State—raised demands to desegregate admissions and neighborhoods while decolonizing curricula. Freedom schools, workshops, direct actions, and other kinds of experimental initiatives redefined learning as a creative, community-rooted process that could prepare people to transform society at large.

Within this context, a *dual-power framework* emerged against the backdrop of anticommunism, Jim Crow racism, domestic counterinsurgency, and imperial war. Activists urged a "long march" to take over social institutions while creating counter-institutions.[44] This approach boomeranged struggles between campuses and communities while melding anarchism, Black/Native/Third World (inter)nationalism, and communism into new ideologies encompassing a vast range of revolutionary initiatives. Although fierce debates about militant strategy and coalitional responsibility abounded, the scale of this liberatory ecosystem compelled the US government to develop a *counter-intelligence* program to undermine it.[45]

Fifty years later, neoliberal colonial-racial-gendered capitalist policies built in the wake of COINTELPRO have prompted mass incarceration, debt, and social inequality that contemporary US social movements have struggled to counteract.[46] In response, some radicals inside the university are developing plans to jettison it. Meanwhile, some liberals and foundations are also seeking to escape campus boundaries using a reformist vision of learning access that erases the liberatory intentions of their forebears. This dynamic portends the conditions for an ideological vacuum in which university-based insurgent teaching and scholarship are replaced by an intellectual retouching of existing models and approaches that are then broadcast outward from campuses to communities under the guise of transformative pedagogies.[47]

Many works in the field of "Critical University Studies" emphasize the theoretical contributions of Louis Althusser, Jacques Derrida, Michel Foucault, and Immanuel

43 Robert Cohen, *When the Old Left Was Young: Student Radicals and America's First Mass Student Movement, 1929–1941* (New York: Oxford University Press, 1993); Eileen Eagen, *Class, Culture, and the Classroom: The Student Peace Movement of the 1930s* (Philadelphia: Temple University Press, 1982); Carol Smith, *The Struggle for Free Speech at CCNY, 1931–42*, https://virtualny.ashp.cuny.edu/gutter/panels/panel1.html/.

44 German student organizer Rudi Dutschke, inspired by the Italian Marxist Antonio Gramsci, mobilized the term "long march through the institutions" for revolutionaries to embed their struggles in social institutions as a long-term strategy toward overthrowing capitalism and creating societies anew. See Dutschke, "On Anti-Authoritarianism," *The New Left Reader*, ed. Carl Oglesby (New York: Grove Press, 1969), 249. See also Rebecca Tarlau, "Prefigurative Politics With, In, and Against the State: The Brazilian Landless Workers Movement and Latin American Philosophies of Education," in *Schooling in the Caribbean and Latin America: Reproduction, Resistance, Revolution, LÁPIZ* 5 (2020), 49–81; Barbara Ehrenreich and John Ehrenreich, *Long March, Short Spring: The Student Uprising at Home and Abroad* (New York: Monthly Review Press, 1969).

45 Ammiel Alcalay, *a little history* (Los Angeles and New York: UpSet Press, 2012).

46 Piya Chatterjee and Sunaina Maira, eds., *The Imperial University: Academic Repression and Scholarly Dissent* (Minneapolis: University of Minnesota Press, 2014); Eleni Schirmer, Jason Wozniak, Dana Morrison, Joanna Gonsalves, and Rich Levy, "Making the Invisible Visible: Organizing against the Instructionally Harmful, Antidemocratic Effects of Institutional Debt," *AAUP Journal of Academic Freedom* 12 (2021), https://www.aaup.org/sites/default/files/Schirmer_et_al_.pdf/.

47 One example of this repackaging is Cathy Davidson, *The New Education: How to Revolutionize the University to Prepare Students for a World in Flux* (New York: Basic Books, 2017).

Kant, often applying their conclusions to conditions quite different from theirs.[48] Likewise, we must ask why the abovementioned appeals to exodus, fugitivity, marronage, pessimism, and refusal are being advanced in this specific moment. These positions are understandable given the embrace of emancipatory visions amidst a heightened state of despair that permeates late capitalism. However, cursorily applying the lessons of fugitivity and marronage from struggles that occurred centuries ago in Brazil, Haiti, Jamaica, and the US South to our own twenty-first-century urban situations risks replicating a "floating tactic," as Salar Mohandesi has observed, "in the hopes of rediscovering the strategy it emerged from."[49] Meanwhile, a pessimistic suspicion of coalitions has emerged alongside wariness about transforming the institutions whose current rulers are bereft of radical consciences.[50] This orientation may suggest that we can't learn to trust each other across differences when confronting the forces that immiserate us, or that we can't distinguish between our systemic oppressors and those who would struggle alongside us to obtain freedom. Anti-institutionality commits this strategic error on a larger scale by rejecting the spaces and resources that could be run collectively by people.

New York Liberation School foregrounds the momentous struggles inside one public university—a battle for control over social infrastructure—to show how we can get free more broadly.[51] CUNY geographer Celeste Winston zeroes in on such possibilities: "The language of fugitivity, in relation to infrastructure, illuminates how everyday survival acts often deemed unlawful can combine into a material basis for struggle."[52] Similarly, CUNY historian Yarimar Bonilla historicizes the role maroons had *in relation to* institutions. Rather than a refusal of engagement, Bonilla highlights how marronage "represents a form of strategic entanglement: a way of crafting and enacting autonomy

48 Aijaz Ahmad identified a contradictory moment after 1968, when many of these intellectuals processing the defeat of the general strike in France turned to a deconstructionist focus on the "death of the subject" and "the end of the social," while in the US, 1968 onwards signaled an escalation by multiple social movements of the possibility of revolutionary change. Even so, the enduring Eurocentrism of the US academy has imposed upon much of our present relationship to universities with this historically and geographically misplaced analysis of defeat. See Ahmad's essay "Literary Theory and 'Third World Literature,'" in *In Theory: Nations, Classes, Literatures* (New York: Verso, 1992), 60–61. A welcome alternative to this trend, drawing analyses from his own experiences teaching at CUNY, is Matt Brim, *Poor Queer Studies: Confronting Elitism in the University* (Durham: Duke University Press, 2020).

49 Salar Mohandesi, "On the Black Bloc," *Viewpoint Magazine*, February 12, 2012, https://viewpointmag.com/2012/02/12/on-the-black-bloc/. For a powerful rejoinder to this critique, read Anonymous, "'We All Float Down Here': RAM's 'Floating Tactics' and the Long Hot Summer of 1967," in *Movement for No Society* (Seattle: Contagion Press, 2018).

50 Kellen Browning and Brian X. Chen, "In Fight Against Violence, Asian and Black Activists Struggle to Agree," *New York Times*, December 19, 2021, https://www.nytimes.com/2021/12/19/us/black-asian-activists-policing-disagreement.html/.

51 George Jackson similarly dedicated attention to creating "autonomous infrastructure" as part of building revolutionary capacities. See George Jackson, *Blood in My Eye* (Baltimore: Black Classics Press, 1990), 69. See also Robin D. G. Kelley, "Black Study, Black Struggle," *Boston Review*, October 24, 2016, https://bostonreview.net/forum/robin-d-g-kelley-black-study-black-struggle/; and Lucien Baskin, "'We Must Learn What We Need to Survive': Making Abolitionist Presence at the City University of New York," *Society and Space*, October 31, 2022, https://www.societyandspace.org/articles/we-must-learn-what-we-need-to-survive-making-abolitionist-presence-at-the-city-university-of-new-york/.

52 Celeste Winston, "Maroon Geographies," *Annals of the American Association of Geographers* 111, no. 7 (2021): 8. See also Celeste Winston, "'How to Lose the Hounds': Tracing the Relevance of Marronage for Contemporary Anti-Police Struggles," PhD diss., CUNY Graduate Center, 2019; Deborah Cowen, "Infrastructures of Empire and Resistance." *Verso* (blog), January 25, 2017, https://www.versobooks.com/blogs/3067-infrastructures-of-empire-and-resistance/.

within a system from which one is unable to fully disentangle."[53] In the following chapters, we will see how CUNY educators like June Jordan, Audre Lorde, and Adrienne Rich studied the relation between the plantation and the university.[54] Following their example, rather than relinquish past insurgent lessons or uncritically transplant them into another time and place, we can update and rearticulate them into our distinct conditions today. In the process, as queer cultural historian José Esteban Muñoz affirms, we can "take our dead with us to the various battles we must wage in their names—and in our names."[55]

There is no *away* toward which we might run. Fleeing our cities and institutions to establish small-scale communal projects in isolation will not guarantee social liberation. In fact, we would be surrendering contested territories and resources to the neocolonial elites who seek to expel us. How, thinking alongside the poet Gil Scott-Heron, can we learn to run together *toward* liberation by refusing to cede ideological and material grounds?[56] What practices could help us reclaim the dual-power tradition of metamorphic collaboration between the university and the universe(s) beyond? Reflecting on the role of education in African decolonization struggles, CUNY people's historian Kazembe Balagun recalls that "the school was not just a physical embodiment." Instead, revolutionaries could "carry the institution in their minds . . . and then rebuild it in any location."[57] Keith Basso writes similarly about a "reciprocal relation in which individuals invest themselves in the landscape while incorporating its meanings into their own most fundamental experience."[58] *New York Liberation School* highlights what happens when people commit to radically reinventing an urban learning institution and its surrounding spaces instead of abandoning them as a lost cause.

Diving into City College and CUNY's histories reveals the university to be an invaluable archive of struggle and world-making, but the lessons of City College and CUNY aren't handily replicable. Instead, this book's immersive attention to an institution—a "militant research" from inside of it—aims to inspire people rooted in other places to conduct your own in-depth studies about the institutions you inhabit and to better understand our particularities as well as how we interrelate across respective sites of movement work.[59] As you read these pages, focus on what makes your homes, neighborhoods, schools, workplaces, hospitals, transit systems, and food resources run.

53 Yarimar Bonilla, *Non-Sovereign Futures: French Caribbean Politics in the Wake of Disenchantment* (Chicago: University of Chicago Press, 2015), 43.

54 See also Craig Steven Wilder, *Ebony and Ivy: Race, Slavery, and the Troubled History of America's Universities* (New York: Bloomsbury Press, 2013); Bianca C. Williams, Dian D. Squire, and Frank A. Tuitt, eds., *Plantation Politics and Campus Rebellions: Power, Diversity, and the Emancipatory Struggle in Higher Education* (Albany: SUNY Press, 2021).

55 José Esteban Muñoz, *Disidentifications: Queers of Color and the Performance of Politics* (Minneapolis: University of Minnesota Press, 1999), 74. See also Tavia Nyong'o, "José Muñoz: Then and There," *The Baffler*, February 10, 2021, https://thebaffler.com/latest/jose-munoz-then-and-there-nyongo/.

56 Gil Scott-Heron, "Running," *I'm New Here*, XL Recordings, 2010, CD and LP.

57 Kazembe Balagun, "The Role of Intellectuals: A Brief History of My Intellectual Development," *Instagram*, April 28, 2021, https://www.instagram.com/tv/COO5CZ2DAhQ/.

58 Keith H. Basso, *Wisdom Sits in Places: Landscape and Language Among the Western Apache* (Albuquerque: University of New Mexico Press, 1996), 102.

59 Natalie Bookchin, Pamela Brown, Suzahn Ebrahimian, Colectivo Enmedio, Alexandra Juhasz, Leónidas Martin, MTL, Nicholas Mirzoeff, Andrew Ross, A. Joan Saab, and Marina Sitrin, *Militant Research Handbook* (New York: New York University, 2013).

Who operates which levers of daily (re)production? What could be done differently? Consider the physicality of these sites, their relationship to the land and to people across generations. Consider their enmeshment with other scales of conflict. Each institution that we transform is a new footing from which to aid others' transformations.

Strategically, schools are among those *seed institutions* most fruitful to collectively claim. Rhythmically consistent semester by semester, they serve as "convergence spaces" for critical thought and action, allowing us to learn how to push and grow through mass direct democratic participation.[60] At the same time, this consistency can mislead. In fact, because of CUNY's mutability, it has been difficult to document its institutional histories. The ruse of institutions is that they are static when in fact they are recreated every day—and can be created anew in different directions. Studying CUNY has allowed us to recognize that the institution is never bound or predictable; struggles to reinvent the university quake beneath our perceived sense of its fixedness.[61] This dynamism is the secret source of the university's power, a built-in contradiction allowing us to create a new university in the shell of the old.

This book therefore focuses on how people worked to construct radically new relations within existing structures—within the same classrooms, buildings, and cities that were built without these changes in mind—while we also navigated the destabilizations that arose from our efforts. This meant overcoming selective notions of prefigurative or insurrectionary politics that assumed we could only create new conditions and spaces by physically tearing down existing ones. Even so, Marx cautions, "the working class cannot simply lay hold of the ready-made state machinery, and wield it for its own purposes."[62] The City College and CUNY experiments recounted in this book confronted the ideological structures and practices of the existing institution, not by burning it down, but by completely rebuilding it. In the process, the university and city we knew were transformed along with their participants.

Living Archives

The dilemma of narrating social histories using the incomplete record of archives has recently been circumvented by a turn toward speculative ways of reading (and writing) within the archival silences. This method has been practiced most strikingly by interpreters of enslavement and emancipation.[63] However, in reconstructing more recent epochs like the one covered in this book, we run the risk of repurposing an imaginative approach suitable to a long-ago era for use in a context for which an ample archive ex-

60 Christina Heatherton, *Arise! Global Radicalism in the Era of the Mexican Revolution* (Oakland: University of California Press, 2022), 16–18.

61 For a discussion about this in the context of Women's Studies, see Sara Ahmed, *Living a Feminist Life* (Durham: Duke University Press, 2017), 112–113.

62 Karl Marx, *The Civil War in France* (New York: International Publishers, 1989 [first published 1871]), https://www.marxists.org/archive/marx/works/1871/civil-war-france/ch05.htm/.

63 See Lucille Clifton, *Generations: A Memoir* (New York: New York Review Books, 2021); Saidiya Hartman, "Venus in Two Acts," *Small Axe* 12, no. 2 (June 2008): 1–14; Saidiya Hartman, *Wayward Lives, Beautiful Experiments: Intimate Histories of Riotous Black Girls, Troublesome Women, and Queer Radicals* (New York: W.W. Norton and Company, 2019); Toni Morrison, "Rememory" and "Memory, Creation, and Fiction," in *The Source of Self-Regard: Selected Essays, Speeches, and Meditations* (New York: Knopf, 2019), 322–325 and 326–333; Christina Sharpe, *In the Wake: On Blackness and Being* (Durham: Duke University Press, 2016). Gratitude to Tanna Tucker for the Morrison citations.

ists but has yet to be plumbed. [64] Little by way of concrete detail is widely known about the lives of the people highlighted in this book, which perhaps indicates the lack of intergenerational connection among and across our movements. We must stay rooted in their material experiences rather than succumbing to nostalgic or melancholic fictions. The 1930s City College organizing veterans passed on long ago, and their legacies are too little known today. The 1960s and '70s militants are closer—a good many are still alive—and they shaped my own generation's struggles to transform CUNY and New York City more broadly.

Despite the abundance of archival records from these earlier movements, we have retained little of these people's lived complexities. What music did they listen to, what comfort foods were shared with loved ones? In which moments did they feel frustrated with the scale of repression they faced from administrators, city elites, and the police? Were they ever overcome with tears in the middle of a busy intersection or in the hushed haven of their beds? When would their classrooms chorus into laughter? So much about their lives is unarchived. As a result, many in the present have a limited understanding of the intricate classroom, campus, and community relationships that led to these strikes and freedom school initiatives. Today, CUNY and citywide movements are likewise insufficiently archived in ways that could inform future upsurges. In revisiting these historical lessons, we welcome current agitators to document your methods for later generations to wield. An emphasis on crowdsourcing CUNY's radical legacies might offer the chance for past and present participants to emerge from the shadows and coauthor these CUNY histories yourselves.

Universities have both absorbed and erased the records of our education movements. The CUNY administration has repeatedly surveilled, seized, and destroyed records of Black, Puerto Rican, and feminist-led struggles. Meanwhile, many movement participants refuse to entrust their records and testimonies to the institution. Throughout the development of this book, such dilemmas were useful for thinking about how to document movements in motion. For example, the April–May 1969 City College campus takeover and the creation of Harlem University was only documented by a handful of participants. Along with interviewing and reading subsequent accounts by the takeover's Black and Puerto Rican student organizers, I filled in interpretive gaps by reflecting on similar encounters that I have experienced firsthand. I wasn't present at the 1969 takeover, but I have been inside and outside of multiple occupied/decolonized campus buildings and urban spaces. In these pages, I try to reenact the anticipation and weight of each moment in which a zone is held; the kinetic power of bodies amassed; the makeshift ways to turn a school into a living room. I was not present in City College classrooms across the twentieth century, but I infuse them with my experiences as a City College student and as a teacher in dozens of CUNY classrooms over the course of seventeen years.

---

64 Various scholars have demonstrated how immersive archival research can recompose lessons from past struggles. For example, Brad Duncan, *Finally Got the News: The Printed Legacy of the U.S. Radical Left, 1970–1979* (Brooklyn: Common Notions, 2017); Johanna Fernández, *The Young Lords: A Radical History* (Chapel Hill: University of North Carolina Press, 2019); Robin D.G. Kelley, *Hammer and Hoe: Alabama Communists During the Great Depression* (Chapel Hill: University of North Carolina Press, 1990); Jorell A. Meléndez-Badillo, *The Lettered Barriada: Workers, Archival Power, and the Politics of Knowledge in Puerto Rico* (Durham: Duke University Press, 2021); Russell Rickford, *We Are an African People: Independent Education, Black Power, and the Radical Imagination* (Oxford: Oxford University Press, 2016); Robyn C. Spencer, *The Revolution Has Come: Black Power, Gender, and the Black Panther Party in Oakland* (Durham: Duke University Press, 2016).

Education, Organization, Metaphor, Labor

Thinking with Paulo Freire and bell hooks, if we view "education as the practice of freedom," then we must assess how contrasting ideas of freedom can yield conflicting modes of learning.[65] To mimic the person who teaches you, to view certain classmates as representatives for the whole group, to recognize everyone in the room as your equal, or to consider no one to be worthy of interaction: these are all political positions from which we learn how to act outside the classroom.[66] We often inherit organizational forms from "dead generations" rather than devising methods suited to our current moment.[67] As these City College educators and students showed us through their pedagogy and political activity, the reciprocal relationship between study and movement can help us rethink questions of revolutionary organization in the present. CUNY educator Ira Shor identifies the task in this way: "the first task of the liberating classroom is to solve the teacher-student contradiction—an ongoing technique, a way of life; not an abstraction—as part of a larger contradiction of working within anti-democratic hierarchical institutions toward democratic anti-hierarchical intentions."[68]

The metaphors our movements have used to describe universities also reveal varying political motives. Many readers will be familiar with the analysis that presents the university as a factory that concentrates people (raw materials), coerces specific repeated behaviors, demands speed-ups and slow-downs, and ultimately churns out finished products.[69] Late-1960s Bay Area struggles imagined places like San Francisco State College as trains: locomotives of history to be commandeered, featuring conductors (teachers) and energy (students), special compartments based on ticket prices, huge vessels engaged in movement.[70] The Baltimore Algebra Project refers to present-day classrooms as laboratories, stages, and "crawl spaces" where different experiments and roles can be tried out covertly to then be practiced in more overt arenas of struggle.[71]

City College poets like Sol Funaroff and Adrienne Rich, writing respectively in the late 1930s and early 1970s, both used the metaphor of the ocean to characterize the classroom and the broader social milieu: our surface familiarity belying unknown depths, the ebbs and flows of waves and shorelines, maritime conflicts between state, commerce, and piracy.[72] Our communities are the sea itself, the rushing and roaring,

---

65 Paulo Freire, *Education: The Practice of Freedom* (London: Writers and Readers Publishing Cooperative, 1976); bell hooks, *Teaching to Transgress: Education as the Practice of Freedom* (London and New York: Routledge, 1994). See also Maggie Nelson, *On Freedom: Four Songs of Care and Constraint* (Minneapolis: Graywolf Press, 2021).

66 Eli Meyerhoff also offers a compelling typology of seven modes of education under capitalism: vertical imaginary, romantic narrative, relations of separation between students and producers and the means of studying, techniques of governance, zero-point epistemology, affective pedagogical economy of credit and debt, and binary figures of educational value and waste. See *Beyond Education*, 15.

67 Karl Marx, *The Eighteenth Brumaire of Louis Bonaparte* (Moscow: Progress Publishers, 1937 [first published 1852]), https://www.marxists.org/archive/marx/works/1852/18th-brumaire/.

68 Ira Shor, interview with the author, January 28, 2022.

69 Edu-Factory Collective, *Toward a Global Autonomous University: Cognitive Labor, The Production of Knowledge, and Exodus from the Education Factory* (Brooklyn: Autonomedia, 2009).

70 Karen Tei Yamashita, *I-Hotel* (Minneapolis: Coffee House Press, 2010).

71 Bob Moses, *Radical Equations: Civil Rights from Mississippi to the Algebra Project* (Boston: Beacon Press, 2002); and Jay Gillen, *Educating for Insurgency: The Roles of Young People in Schools of Poverty* (Chico: AK Press, 2014).

72 This metaphor has been embraced by feminist movements across the Americas and the Caribbean.

the trickling—even the moments of immense stillness. The campus becomes a container for that energy, which then splashes back out to neighborhoods. In turn, each report from a field of struggle is a lighthouse in these churning seas. Inhabiting this metaphor still further, each wave of action contributes to the next by amassing experiential currents or by channeling existing complicities in fresh directions.

Our analyses of organization and study must also address the shifting conditions of labor in the university. The peak moment of upheaval at CUNY occurred at the same time that the university expanded the hiring of low-wage adjunct faculty with little job security. According to Nick Mitchell, "What brought ethnic studies into the university was not only social movements; it was the university itself, [which was] incredibly adept in the absorption, rearticulation, and rerouting of activist desires into forms of institutionalization," including the adjunctification of teaching labors.[73] Adjunct faculty bore the cost of the gains made through the rapid creation and expansion of Ethnic, Gender, and Sexuality Studies departments won through struggle.

These linked phenomena—Black, Third World, and feminist pedagogies and contingent labor—have indelibly shaped CUNY in that these studies and labors are both "adjunct" to the university status quo. At the same time, however, by virtue of their inclusion and containment, they possess the power to transform the university from its margins. The liberatory paradigms developed by CUNY teachers like Toni Cade Bambara, David Henderson, June Jordan, Audre Lorde, and Adrienne Rich (all of whom were first hired as adjuncts) have become deeply woven into our adjunct teaching and learning practices in Ethnic, Gender, and Sexuality Studies and far beyond. They link our livelihoods in the home, community, and classroom; they inspire an inquiry-based humility and warmth in study; they envision writing composition as a way to refashion oneself in relation to others; and they foster struggle across differences for mutual liberation. The long CUNY movement doesn't *have* a pedagogy; it *is* a pedagogy. Despite the ubiquity of such counter-disciplines, however, they often remain unseen, unvalued, and uncompensated. They are a form of care work that the university relies upon but refuses to honor.[74] The feminized labor of adjunct teaching and the pedagogical innovations pioneered in Ethnic, Gender, and Sexuality Studies have become sites both of duress and of *potencia* [power].[75]

Chapters in Our Collective Story

Chapter 1, "Freedom Learning Lineages and Obstacles," reviews the braided origins of Black, Puerto Rican, and Women's Studies and movements in the long twentieth century. It first considers the history of City College in the 1920s and 1930s, when Jewish students mounted desegregation campaigns on campus and fought fascism in Spain. These actions fostered a rebellious campus milieu that enabled the struggles of the 1960s and '70s to emerge into a wave of overlapping liberation movements. Analyzing how coalitions

---

73 Nick Mitchell, "The Fantasy and Fate of Ethnic Studies in an Age of Uprisings: An Interview with Nick Mitchell," *Undercommoning,* July 13, 2016, https://undercommoning.org/nick-mitchell-interview/.

74 Verónica Gago, *Feminist International: How to Change Everything* (New York: Verso, 2020), 27.

75 *Potencia* can be translated from the Spanish as the power *to do* something, rather than the power *over* someone/something [*poder*]. This framing of non-coercive power has been embraced by Latin American and Caribbean struggles since its elaboration in Colectivo Situaciones' *19 and 20: Notes for a New Insurrection* (Brooklyn: Common Notions, 2021).

were forged across differences attends to the schisms between Black, Puerto Rican, and Jewish people in CUNY and New York City. This chapter highlights the 1965 creation of the SEEK Program, the 1969 City College "Harlem University" takeover, the 1970 creation of Open Admissions, the 1976 imposition of tuition, and the 1999 defeat of Open Admissions. On the basis of these events, it establishes CUNY's role in shaping the cultural and political-economic landscape of the United States.

Chapter 2, "Creating the 'Black University,' 'black city,' and 'Life Studies' with Toni Cade Bambara, David Henderson, and June Jordan," explores political identity, institutionality, geographic space, and study through the prism of Black liberation. These three educators brought their experience from New York City neighborhood learning programs into their teaching at City College and, following the 1969 strike, boomeranged these lessons back out into the city.[76] Bambara and Jordan created Black feminist visions for Black Studies, and Henderson developed a disability-centering focus on youth learning and urban reinventions from his work with neighborhood deaf students and with City College's Black and Puerto Rican students.

Chapter 3, "Audre Lorde and Adrienne Rich: Sisters in Struggle," focuses on the entwined interventions that Rich and Lorde made in CUNY and within New York City more broadly.[77] A careful reading across Lorde and Rich's archives and writing situates Lorde's calls to harness fear and eros alongside her poem "Blackstudies" and Rich's calls for counter-institutional *re-vision* alongside her poem "Diving Into the Wreck." Lorde and Rich carried these insights into a wide range of settings that reconfigured public education and social movements. I also consider the contributions made by Mina P. Shaughnessy to extend the SEEK Program's lesson to nationwide educators by exploring her speech "Diving In."

Chapter 4, "The Power of Student Writing and Action," analyzes City College student compositions in the diverse forms they took during the 1960s and '70s. It is an invitation to more fully recognize the central role of youth—and the capacious practice of study—in liberation movements. The chapter explores Samuel R. Delany's early creative writing and memoirs; the "Five Demands" that mobilized the creation of Harlem University; Paul B. Simms, Louis Reyes Rivera, and Sekou Sundiata's work in *Tech News/The Paper*; Francee Covington's writing in Bambara's *The Black Woman* anthology; clandestine compositions by Guillermo Morales and Assata Shakur in the Fuerzas Armadas de Liberación Nacional and the Black Liberation Army; and antifascist interventions by the John Brown Anti-Klan Committee.

76 Some of the archival materials and earlier versions of this text first appeared in *Toni Cade Bambara: "Realizing the Dream of a Black University" & Other Writings (Parts I & II)*, ed. Makeba Lavan and Conor Tomás Reed and *June Jordan: "Life Studies," 1966–1976*, ed. Conor Tomás Reed and Talia Shalev, in *Lost & Found: The CUNY Poetics Document Initiative, Series 7* (New York: The Center for the Humanities, Graduate Center of the City University of New York, 2017).

77 Some of the archival materials and earlier versions of this text first appeared in *Audre Lorde: "I teach myself in outline," Notes, Journals, Syllabi, & an Excerpt from Deotha*, ed. Miriam Atkin and Iemanjá Brown, in *Lost & Found: The CUNY Poetics Document Initiative, Series 7* and *Adrienne Rich: "What we are a part of": Teaching at CUNY, 1968–1974*, ed. Iemanjá Brown, Stefania Heim, erica kaufman, Kristin Moriah, Conor Tomás Reed, Talia Shalev, Wendy Tronrud, and Ammiel Alcalay, in *Lost & Found: The CUNY Poetics Document Initiative, Series 4* (New York: The Center for the Humanities, Graduate Center of the City University of New York, 2014). See also Conor Tomás Reed, "Diving Into SEEK: Adrienne Rich and Social Movements at the City College of New York, 1968–1974," in *Jayne Cortez, Adrienne Rich, and the Feminist Superhero: Voice, Vision, Politics, and Performance in US Contemporary Women's Poetics*, ed. Laura Hinton (Washington, DC: Lexington Books, 2016).

Chapter 5, "Contemporary Struggles for Our Futures," brings these histories to bear on the CUNY movement from 9/11 to the present. Our long resistance to US colonialism and imperialism did not disappear after the end of Open Admissions, but instead grew in opposition to the US wars in Afghanistan and Iraq and the concurrent militarization of CUNY. Multiple waves of struggle—Occupy Wall Street, #BlackLivesMatter, solidarity with Palestine and Puerto Rico—boomeranged through CUNY to nourish a militant cohesion that would address the overlapping crises of COVID-19, neoliberal austerity, resurgent police violence, and erosion of abortion access. The present ecosystem of CUNY movements offers a model for coalitional power that can help us to navigate the uncertainties we now face.

The Coda, "CUNY Will Be Free!," invokes the queer decolonial demand for freedom as a perpetual horizon and vast territory of transformation to create a *People's University*. Celebrating the vast worlds composed and recomposed within CUNY and our surrounding city, we caution against the absorption of our movements into existing power structures. We also critique the practice of top-down, institutional "respectability archiving" and the parasitic appropriation of our struggles for individual gain. Instead, we propose a radical coalitional archival methodology to suggest how we might document our histories while manifesting our futures.

Readers are hereby invited to join the *New York Liberation School* coalition so that we can remake this world.

CHAPTER 1

FREEDOM LEARNING: LINEAGES AND OBSTACLES

The arcs of Black, Puerto Rican, and Women's Studies in New York City are extensive and entwined. Underground freedom learning was practiced between enslaved Africans and then forged in institutions like Catherine Ferguson's School for the Poor (1793) and Myrtilla Miner's Teachers College for Black women (1851).[1] Following the Civil War, Freedmen's Bureau literacy campaigns and post-Reconstruction public education projects proliferated in what W. E. B. Du Bois called "a frenzy for schools."[2] As Angela Y. Davis reports, "Northern white women went South during Reconstruction to assist their Black sisters who were absolutely determined to wipe out illiteracy among the millions of former slaves."[3] By the 1890s, European women comprised 35 percent (56,000) of all college graduates, while only 252 Black women had bachelor's degrees. Nevertheless, Black women's involvement in teacher's colleges was "crucial to the extraordinary growth in basic education and literacy among the southern ex-slave population."[4]

During the early twentieth century, Southern Black and Afro-Caribbean members of the African Blood Brotherhood, Communist Party, Socialist Party, and Universal Negro Improvement Association took turns at the Speaker's Corner on 135th Street and Lenox Avenue, delivering lectures that would sometimes last for hours to massive crowds. Puerto Ricans transported their own freedom learning to the heart of the colonial empire, as they formed alliances with Cuban and Black organizations in New

---

1 Angela Y. Davis, *Women, Race & Class* (New York: Vintage Books, 1981), 102–104. See also Charles M. Payne and Carol Sills Strickland, eds., *Teach Freedom: Education for Liberation in the African-American Tradition* (New York: Teachers College Press, 2008); Heather Andrea Williams, *Self-Taught: African American Education in Slavery and Freedom* (Chapel Hill: University of North Carolina Press, 2005).

2 W. E. B. Du Bois, *Black Reconstruction in America: An Essay Toward a History of the Part Which Black Folk Played in the Attempt to Reconstruct Democracy in America, 1860–1880* (New York: Harcourt, Brace and Company, 1935), 55, 123.

3 Davis, *Women, Race & Class*, 107.

4 Ellen Carol DuBois, "Women's Rights, Suffrage, and Citizenship, 1789–1920," in *The Oxford Handbook of American Women's and Gender History*, ed. Ellen Hartigan-O'Connor and Lisa G. Masterson (Oxfordshire: Oxford University Press, 2018), 450–451.

York.[5] They brought the tradition of *el lector/la lectora*, in which someone would read newspapers, political tracts, and literature to workers as they rolled cigars.[6] Mutual aid organizations were formed, including *La Aurora*, *El Ejemplo*, and *La Razón*. The *Círculo de Tabaqueros* would host events like "Carlos Tresca of *Il Martele* speaking in Italian on 'Anarchism and Darwinian Theory,' Elizabeth Gurley Flynn in English on 'Utopian Communities and Free Will,' Pedro Esteves in Spanish on 'War and Peace and the Role of the Proletariat,' and Catholic anarchist Frank Kelly in Spanish on 'Jesus Christ, The First Communist.'"[7] The most famous Puerto Rican *independentista*, Pedro Albizu Campos (nicknamed *El Maestro* [The Teacher]), contributed to the anticolonial struggles of India and Ireland before committing his life to the liberation of Puerto Rico.

City College Radicalism Emerges

The Ivy League universities in New York City were not hospitable places for such educational experiments. Historian Robert Cohen describes how, well into the 1920s, campuses enshrined "intellectual shallowness and social conformity."[8] Nationwide, many colleges and universities were almost exclusively filled with middle- and upper-class Euro youth lacking the impetus for critical thought and action. The socialist-led educational organization League for Industrial Democracy (LID) gained little traction in this time period. According to one member, a "diluted culture of salesmanship dominates undergraduate life."[9] Historically Black Colleges and Universities (HBCUs) and Women's Colleges confronted different circumstances, from outright racial and sexual terror to meritocratic missions belying limited opportunities.[10] Even the Great Depression did not immediately affect many of the nation's college students since, as Cohen writes, "a majority of undergraduates did not work their way through school." Despite mass unemployment, ubiquitous breadlines, and crisis-induced suicides, most Euro students remained insulated by their families' wealth and even "displayed patronizing or hostile attitudes toward economically disadvantaged collegians."[11]

From its inception, the City College of New York positioned itself as a striking exception to this portrait. During its official opening as the "Free Academy of the City of New York" on January 21, 1849, principal Dr. Horace Webster proclaimed:

---

5 César J. Ayala and Rafael Bernabe, *Puerto Rico in the American Century: A History Since 1898* (Chapel Hill: University of North Carolina Press, 2007). The year 1898 marks both the US seizure of Puerto Rico from Spain and the incorporation of the Bronx, Brooklyn, Manhattan, Queens, and Staten Island into the City of New York.

6 Araceli Tinajero, *El Lector: A History of the Cigar Factory Reader* (Austin: University of Texas Press, 2010). See also Luisa Capetillo, *A Nation of Women: An Early Feminist Speaks Out*, ed. Félix V. Matos-Rodríguez (New York: Penguin Classics, 2021), xv–xviii.

7 Virginia E. Sánchez Korrol, *From Colonia to Community: The History of Puerto Ricans in New York City, 1917–1948* (Westport: Praeger, 1983), 139.

8 Robert Cohen, *When the Old Left Was Young: Student Radicals and America's First Mass Student Movement, 1929–1941* (New York: Oxford University Press, 1993), 9.

9 In Cohen, *When the Old Left Was Young*, 8.

10 See Frank Andre Guridy, *Forging Diaspora: Afro-Cubans and African Americans in a World of Empire and Jim Crow* (Chapel Hill: University of North Carolina Press, 2010); Carmen Kynard, *Vernacular Insurrections: Race, Black Protest, and the New Century in Composition-Literacies Studies* (Albany: SUNY Press, 2014); Margaret A. Nash, *Women's Higher Education in the United States: New Historical Perspectives* (London: Palgrave Macmillan, 2018).

11 Cohen, *When the Old Left Was Young*, 10 and 13.

The experiment is to be tried, whether the highest education can be given to the masses; whether the children of the people, the children of the whole people, can be educated; and whether an institution of learning, of the highest grade, can be successfully controlled by the popular will, not by the privileged few, but by the privileged many.[12]

Even so, City College archivist Sydney Van Nort clarifies: "For the first 60 years, the students studied a curriculum resembling that of the Military Academy at West Point," the alma mater of its first two presidents.[13] In 1866, a year after the end of the US Civil War, the Free Academy changed its name to the College of the City of New York. In 1907, the college moved from its Gramercy Park location to a new site in West Harlem, with neo-Gothic buildings designed by George Browne Post, the architect of the New York Stock Exchange.[14] Most of the students were working- and middle-class English and German immigrants who performed compulsory Reserve Officers' Training Corps (ROTC) military drills on campus while studying curricula that mimicked the Ivy League.

The mass migration of Jewish people to New York City would alter the student composition of City College. Historian James Traub notes that "between 1881 and 1924, approximately 2.8 million Jews left Eastern Europe for the United States as a result of the anti-Semitism and pogroms in Russia and Poland."[15] Many Eastern European refugees, mainly anarchist and socialist Yiddish-speaking Jews, settled in Lower East Side tenements. Discrimination against Jews was common, including compounded racism and anti-Semitism against Afro-Jewish and Puerto Rican-Jewish people concentrated in segregated neighborhoods in Brooklyn, Queens, and West Harlem.[16] The police in New York considered Jews a criminal class alongside Black people. Still, they experienced starkly differing levels of racialized segregation. When Jewish students began entering the City College, they were treated as outsiders and began forming common bonds against oppression. Black students, meanwhile, were almost completely unwelcome at the college.

Jewish students from some of the most impoverished refugee families in the US flocked to City College to obtain a free college education. Over time, they turned the college into a hotbed of antifascism. Robert Cohen conveys how "These New York students ... who had been raised amidst ghettoes as Russian as they were American, were in but not quite yet of America," brought Yiddish radical traditions with them into the college. This cultural dislocation "could be quite radical because it facilitated a certain critical detachment from the American social order, and an awareness of alternative systems of political thought and organization.[17]

---

12 S. Willis Rudy, *The College of the City of New York: A History: 1847–1947* (New York: City College Press, 1949), 29.

13 Sydney Van Nort, *The City College of New York* (Charleston: Arcadia Publishing, 2007), 7.

14 *The City College of New York*, "Our History," https://www.ccny.cuny.edu/about/history/.

15 James Traub, *City on a Hill: Testing the American Dream at City College* (Burlington: Da Capo Press, 1994), 27–28. See also Tony Michels, *Jewish Radicals: A Documentary History* (New York: New York University Press, 2012); Alain Brossart and Sylvie Klingberg, *Revolutionary Yiddishland: A History of Jewish Radicalism* (New York: Verso, 2016).

16 Gratitude to Michael Gould-Wartofsky for this context.

17 Cohen, *When the Old Left Was Young*, 28.

These young radicals had limited options for college. As City College alumnus Nathan Glazer recounts, "the alternative to City in those days was NYU, and the feeling was that was where the kids went who were dumber and had more money."[18] Twenty blocks south of City College, Columbia University saw itself as a training ground for the city's Protestant elite. Faced with growing numbers of qualified Jewish applicants, the school instituted an unofficial Jewish quota. One anonymous administrator explained that such applicants were not "particularly pleasant companions" for Columbia's "natural constituency." Columbia President Nicholas Murray Butler steered the poorer Jews uptown to City College, where elegant buildings obscured the school's impoverishment.[19]

Called the "Citadel on a Hill" or the "Harvard of the Proletariat," City College towered atop a sloping incline along Harlem's west side. The campus gathered together poor, radical Euro immigrant men students and teachers committed to antiracism, antifascism, and intellectual debate (women did not gain full admittance until 1951).[20] A majority of students worked during the day and took night classes with instructors who were only slightly older than them.[21] City College students educated themselves as much as they learned from their teachers. They converged in "vast, gloomy, and pungent" cafeteria alcoves to debate the issues of the day.[22] Alumnus Daniel Bell recounted:

> We'd be reading Engels on street tactics. We'd say, but comrades, there are no paving blocks here, as in Paris. We can't dig up the paving blocks and throw them at the troops. What do we do? Ah! Real problems! And somebody would come up, of course, with a great solution. You'd be surprised how many great military strategists came out of City College! Somebody'd come up and say, well, if you can't get paving blocks and throw them at troops, you barricade each end of the street when the police are in there . . . and the brave revolutionary women go up on top of the roof and throw down hot water![23]

Historian Rodolpho Leslie Schnell notes how by 1916, "the radicalization of students that made City College unique" had begun to influence broader conflicts between administrators and students across the United States.[24] A decade later, in 1926, writes historian Eileen Eagen, student protests at City College achieved the "elimination of compulsory military training."[25]

Frederick C. Robinson, who was president of City College at the time, adhered to

---

18 In Joseph Dorman, *Arguing the World: The New York Intellectuals in Their Own Words* (Chicago: University of Chicago Press, 2001), 43.

19 Dorman, *Arguing the World*, 44.

20 City College of New York Cohen Library Digital Archives, "Women at City College: A Fifty-Year Anniversary Exhibit," http://digitalarchives.ccny.cuny.edu/exhibits/fiftyexhibit/.

21 Eileen Eagen, *Class, Culture, and the Classroom: The Student Peace Movement of the 1930s* (Philadelphia: Temple University Press, 1982), 100.

22 Eagen, *Class, Culture, and the Classroom*, 45.

23 Dorman, *Arguing the World*, 49.

24 Eagan, *Class, Culture and the Classroom*, 38.

25 Eagan, *Class, Culture and the Classroom*, 33.

the traditional mindset of *in loco parentis*—that young people in colleges needed a firm disciplinary hand in the absence of their parents' authority. His repression further activated the students:

> President Robinson and his subordinates violated student free speech rights more often than any other college administration in Depression America. From 1931 to 1934 Robinson's anti-radical campaign resulted in the expulsion of 43 CCNY students, the suspension of 38, and the hauling of hundreds of undergraduates before campus disciplinary boards. . . . Through his abuse of student political rights, CCNY's president inadvertently helped radicalize thousands of students and kept the campus in turmoil.[26]

In response to Robinson's charge that student conduct was "worse than guttersnipes," Eagen reports, "a few days later the campus blossomed with buttons proclaiming, 'I am a Guttersnipe.'"[27]

Throughout the years, coalitions of rowdy students were formed and re-formed, ultimately producing the National Student League (NSL), which "dedicated itself to the goal of radicalizing American college students."[28] With representation at City College and beyond, the NSL marked a significant upswell in student militancy. It created opportunities for other groups like the Student League of Industrial Democracy (SLID) and later the Trotskyist-influenced Young People's Socialist League (YPSL) to gain a footing and stir up campuses. The NSL's rise also marked the first time the US Communist Party (CP) recognized students' role in revolutionary upheaval. Communist student leaders in the NSL—also members of the Young Communist League (YCL, the youth wing of the CP)—were "able to formulate policies that were based more on campus realities than Comintern dogma."[29]

Between 1933 and 1938, many US students took the Oxford Pledge, promising not to participate in foreign wars. At the First National Student Strike Against War on April 13, 1934, 800 City College men and 300 Hunter College women amassed to condemn war, while a mass walkout at Brooklyn College left its classrooms "virtually empty."[30] New York City students comprised 60 percent of those who participated nationwide, and City College was the only campus in the country where police were called.[31] The April Strike Against War became an annual event, growing each year.

As the City College student left grew emboldened to address broader issues on campus, it continued locking horns with Robinson. Students chained themselves to the flagpole in the quad to deliver antifascist speeches and subjected Robinson to mock trials. The cafeteria hosted daily assemblies on world revolution, antiracism, eviction

---

26 Cohen, *When the Old Left Was Young*, 108.

27 Eagen, *Class, Culture, and the Classroom*, 100. See also Philip Kay, "'Guttersnipes' and 'Eliterates': City College in the Popular Imagination," PhD diss., Columbia University, 2011.

28 Cohen, *When the Old Left Was Young*, 30.

29 Cohen, *When the Old Left Was Young*, 38. Robin D. G. Kelley reveals a similar dynamic in Black-led communist organizing among sharecroppers in *Hammer and Hoe*.

30 See Eagen, *Class, Culture, and the Classroom*, 117.

31 Eagen, *Class, Culture, and the Classroom*, 116.

defense, and community relief work. On October 9, 1934, Robinson invited a delegation of young Italian aviators from Mussolini's army to speak on campus. In response,
students organized an antifascist protest both inside and outside of the official meeting
in the Great Hall.

Student Council representative and NSL activist Edwin Alexander was warned not
to stray from a cordial welcome to the university's Italian visitors. He started his Great
Hall address with the words: "I do not intend to be discourteous to our guests. I merely
wish to bring them antifascist greetings from the student body of City College to the
tricked, enslaved student body of Italy." A melee ensued: "Members of the Italian Club
then surrounded and assaulted Alexander. A full-scale riot followed when students from
the audience jumped onto the stage to assist Alexander." More than one hundred students were questioned by the administration following the incident. This intimidation
did not stop the NSL and SLID from organizing a 2,000-strong student strike condemning the administration for opening the school's doors to fascism.[32] On November
20, 1934, they burned a two-headed effigy of President Robinson and Mussolini.[33]

In March 1935, faculty and staff formed the Anti-Fascist Association, the Instruc-
tional Staff Association, and the New York College Teachers Union. Two-thirds of the
faculty at the City's public colleges were adjuncts or tutors who taught for substandard
wages and could be dismissed at will. Most were young graduates of City College and,
like their students, came from poor European immigrant backgrounds. By 1938, the
College Teachers Union won the right of tenure for the lowest paid full-time faculty
and other major reforms. Through these expressions of student and worker power,
City College earned the nickname "the Little Red School House."[34] This escalation
of actions mirrored events that unfolded outside the university. Around New York
City, the Communist Party and other organizations decried Italian aggression against
Ethiopia and the rise of Nazism in Germany. The left watched in horror as govern-
ments around the world refused to address the impending horrors of fascism.

When the Spanish Civil War began in 1936, students from City College joined
an international antifascist defense campaign. Approximately 3,000 volunteers calling
themselves the Abraham Lincoln Brigade deployed from the United States; around
half were from the streets of New York City.[35] At least sixty of these volunteers were
City College students (including the student body president), faculty, and alumni. They
were the largest group representing an academic institution to join the solidarity effort.[36] As historian Eric R. Smith writes, "New York labor unions, anarchists, socialists,
communists, liberals, intellectuals, African Americans, and various immigrant groups
joined the campaigns to aid the Spanish Republic."[37] In this milieu, where "hardly

---

32 Cohen, *When the Old Left Was Young*, 116.

33 See Peter N. Carroll and James D. Fernandez, eds., *Facing Fascism: New York and the Spanish Civil War* (New
York: New York University Press, 2007), 9.

34 Justin Byrne, "From Brooklyn to Belchite: New Yorkers in the Abraham Lincoln Brigade," in *Facing
Fascism*, 78.

35 Robin D.G. Kelley, "'This Ain't Ethiopia, But It'll Do': African Americans in the Spanish Civil War,"
in *Race Rebels: Culture, Politics, and the Black Working Class* (New York: Free Press, 1996), 123–160. See also
Conor Tomás Reed, "Seed Foundations Shakin'": Interwar African Diasporic Responses to Fascism and
the 1936–1939 Spanish Civil War," *The Volunteer: Veterans of the Abraham Lincoln Brigade*, November 22,
2010, https://albavolunteer.org/2010/11/african-responses-to-fascism-the-spanish-civil-war/.

36 Byrne, "From Brooklyn to Belchite," 78.

37 Eric R. Smith, "New York's Aid to the Spanish Republic," in *Facing Fascism*, 44.

a week went by without a benefit event, a rally, or a demonstration," it is difficult to overestimate New Yorkers' support for the Spanish revolution.[38]

The City College Aid Spain Committee held ethnically integrated antifascist dance contests and collected money and clothing. The November 1936 issue of the YCL's pamphlet *Spark* included a fictitious story in which City College is besieged by fascists, the Chemistry Building bombed, and the Great Hall converted into a makeshift hospital while radical students coordinate the resistance. The speculative account noted that many of the "defenders are former officers of the ROTC who persuaded their uniformed comrades to join the anti-fascists." The City College community was stunned to hear that in Spain, thirteen of their sixty *brigadistas* were killed in battle and many more were wounded. In the rotunda of the North Academic Center on campus, you'll find a small plaque honoring those who died in the war. Look for the Guernica lantern held aloft.[39]

This time also witnessed increased Afro-Caribbean and Black American community organizing with their radical European and South Asian neighbors.[40] Formed in 1921 by ten Black students, the Frederick Douglass Society joined forces with the College Teachers Union and the American Student Union to hire Max Yergan—the first Black professor at City College—to teach Black History and Culture in 1937.[41] Bayard Rustin began studying at City College and was briefly a YCL member involved in the fight to free the Scottsboro Boys.[42] Although Hunter College had Black women students as early as 1873, during the 1930s, the Black women student club Toussaint L'Ouverture Society began hosting concerts and lectures. Rising attendance by Black and immigrant women made Hunter College the largest women's college in the world. In the mid-1940s, Black women faculty like Adelaide Cromwell and Mary Huff Diggs were hired, but it wouldn't be until the 1960s that Black women were hired to teach elsewhere at CUNY.[43]

The alphabet soup of organizations at City College—the YCL, the NSL, the SLID, the YPSL—urged students to connect their ideas to tangible struggles during a period of tremendous social upheavals. City College alumnus Sol Funaroff would describe this historic conjuncture as roiling oceanic depths in his poem "The Bellbuoy": "where the cracked heart of the world / sobs through great fissures / whose boiling hells / raise volcanic fires / and tears of stone, / in huge convulsions."

Akin to future City College educator Adrienne Rich's poem "Diving into the Wreck," he drew attention to the sea as a vast metaphoric space in which movements and new social relations can emerge across epochs. Funaroff reached out to the prom-

38 Fraser M. Ottanelli, "The New York City Left and the Spanish Civil War," in *Facing Fascism*, 63.

39 See Wilfred Mendelson, *Let My People Know: The Story of Wilfred Mendelson, "Mendy," August 17, 1915–July 28, 1938*, ed. Joseph Leeds (New York: Manifold, August 2022), https://cuny.manifoldapp.org/projects/let-my-people-know/.

40 Vivek Bald, *Bengali Harlem and the Lost Histories of South Asian America* (Cambridge: Harvard University Press, 2015); Mark Naison, *Communists in Harlem During the Depression* (Champaign: University of Illinois Press, 2004).

41 See "The Struggle for Free Speech at CCNY, 1931–42," https://virtualny.ashp.cuny.edu/gutter/panels/panel17.html.

42 Amaka Okechukwu, *To Fulfill These Rights: Political Struggle Over Affirmative Action and Open Admissions* (New York: Columbia University Press, 2019), 140.

43 Linda M. Perkins, "African-American Women and Hunter College, 1873–1945," *Echo: Journal of the Hunter College Archives* (1995): 23.

ise of liberations yet to come: "I am that exile / from a future time, / from shores of freedom / I may never know, / who hears, sounding in the surf, / tidings from the lips of waves / that meet and kiss / in submarine gardens / of a new Atlantis."[44]

Puerto Rico, COINTELPRO, and McCarthyism's Rise

During the 1930s, as City College students catapulted their campus debates into transnational campaigns, Puerto Rico endured its own eruptions. After the United States assumed colonial control in 1898, the island's diverse agricultural economy was converted into a giant sugar plantation. "Over a 30-year period US corporations came to control the Puerto Rican economy. . . . By 1930 North American monopolies owned 65% of sugar production; three-fifths of all sugar lands were owned by four US companies." During this period, US companies "extracted over $200,000,000 in profit from Puerto Rico."[45] Meanwhile, the average life expectancy for Puerto Ricans was forty-six years.[46] In 1934, a massive sugarcane workers' strike rocked the island, and the Nationalist Party, led by Pedro Albizu Campos, developed the Cadets of the Republic, a popular proto-liberation army.

President Roosevelt appointed a new governor, Blanton D. Winship, who in turn appointed US counterinsurgency expert E. Francis Riggs to become police chief. In October 1935, Winship and Riggs oversaw a massacre at the University of Puerto Rico–Río Piedras campus that killed four Nationalists and wounded forty others.[47] Two Nationalist youths sought vengeance in February 1936 by assassinating Riggs. In retaliation, the government arrested scores of nationalists, charging Albizu Campos with conspiracy to overthrow the US government, and sentencing him to fifteen years in a federal penitentiary. In March 1937, when remaining Nationalist Party members protested Albizu Campos's imprisonment with a march in Ponce, the police retaliated with another massacre that killed 20 and wounded over 150.[48]

As authorities endeavored to stamp out the Puerto Rican anticolonial movement, hundreds of US police officers received training under the leadership of J. Edgar Hoover at the newly formed FBI National Academy on the island. Upon being hired by the FBI in 1919, Hoover's first assignment had been to coordinate the Palmer Raids, which targeted anarchists, Black nationalists, communists, and others in the wake of World War I. Under Hoover's orders, surveillance dossiers—or *carpetas*—were created for over 100,000 Puerto Ricans (15,500 of whom had extensive police files) in a country of four million people. Between 1936 and 1995, the FBI generated 1.8

---

44 Sol Funaroff, "The Bellbuoy," *The Spider and the Clock: Poems* (New York: International Publishers, 1938), 9. Funaroff was born in Beirut, took night classes at City College, worked on the National Student League's *College Students Review*, was friends with Edwin Rolfe and other CCNY *brigadistas*, edited multiple Communist poetry journals, and died at the age of thirty-one.

45 Lincoln Bergman, Gail Dolgin, Robert Gabriner, Maisie McAdoo, and Jonah Raskin, *Puerto Rico: The Flame of Resistance* (San Francisco: Peoples Press, 1977), 40. The present value is estimated at over $3.5 billion.

46 Bergman et al., *Puerto Rico*, 52.

47 Nelson A. Denis, *War Against All Puerto Ricans: Revolution and Terror in America's Colony* (New York: Bold Type Books, 2015), 66.

48 Bergman et al., *Puerto Rico*, 58–59. The Parsley Massacre of Haitians in the US-backed dictatorship of the Dominican Republic occurred months later, in October 1937.

million pages worth of carpetas.[49] These tools for mass surveillance, imprisonment, and murder were developed against nationalists in Puerto Rico before being brought to the United States—first with the Rapp-Coudert hearings, then with the passage of the Smith Act and the rise of McCarthyism, and finally with the creation of Hoover's Counter-Intelligence Program (COINTELPRO), which operated from 1956 to 1971.

Between 1940 and 1942, the Rapp-Coudert Committee investigated "subversive activities" in New York State's schools and colleges. Volunteers who had fought in Spain returned to accusations of "premature anti-fascism." More than 500 public college workers and students were subpoenaed and interrogated about their political activities, including Communist Party membership. Historian Ellen Schrecker writes that although many liberals believed that the committee investigations were "just a facade for an upstate legislative crackdown on the city's school budget," the Rapp-Coudert hearings prompted a wave of anticommunist repression that expanded outward with the HUAC investigations and subsequent rise of McCarthyism.[50] New York Republican Senator Frederic Coudert said of the Committee's purpose, "Now if your dog had rabies you wouldn't clap him into jail after he had bitten a number of persons—you'd put a bullet into his head, if you had that kind of iron in your blood. It is going to require brutal treatment to handle these teachers."[51] Faculty members were denied reappointment, and those who refused to cooperate with the committee, including Max Yergan, were dismissed from their jobs. Others who refused to cooperate, like City College professor Morris U. Schappes, were sentenced to months or even years in The Tombs in lower Manhattan. Ultimately, twenty teachers were fired and eleven others resigned.[52]

In 1949, the New York State Feinberg Law granted power to the Board of Regents to deny employment to any teacher it deemed subversive. As one newspaper reported, "the Regents did not issue a list of 'subversive' groups although it summoned four organizations—the Communist Party, the Socialist Workers Party, the [Industrial] Workers of the World, and the Nationalist Party of Puerto Rico—to a hearing."[53] Even so, that same year, four thousand City College students mounted a five-day general strike and fought police in the streets to combat faculty members' anti-Semitism and dorm-room segregation.[54]

This postwar radicalization would be stifled by Joseph McCarthy's anticommunist witch hunts and the 1950 McCarran Act, which forced Communist Party members to notify the federal government of their affiliation. Across the country, government repression gutted networks of struggle. People were blacklisted from jobs, forced out

---

49 Mireya Navarro, "New Light on Old F.B.I. Fight; Decades of Surveillance of Puerto Rican Groups," *New York Times*, November 28, 2003, www.nytimes.com/2003/11/28/nyregion/new-light-on-old-fbi-fight-decades-of-surveillance-of-puerto-rican-groups.html/.

50 Ellen Schrecker, *No Ivory Tower: McCarthyism and the Universities* (Oxford: Oxford University Press, 1986), 76.

51 See "The Struggle for Free Speech at CCNY, 1931–42," https://virtualny.ashp.cuny.edu/gutter/panels/panel15.html/.

52 Newt Davidson Collective, *Crisis at CUNY* (New York: New Davidson Collective, 1974), 52.

53 *Harvard Crimson*, "N.Y. Courts Ponder Feinberg Law Act Would Bar Teachers Belonging to Groups on Subversive List," April 20, 1950, www.thecrimson.com/article/1950/6/20/ny-courts-ponder-feinberg-law-act/.

54 Daylon Orr, *We Shall Not Be Moved: The CCNY Student Strike of 1949* (Brooklyn: Fugitive Materials, 2022).

of towns, hounded and imprisoned by authorities, estranged from close friends. This vast dissolution of the Left is difficult to fathom today.[55] These conditions amounted to both a political freeze and a pressure cooker for an entire segregated generation. Meanwhile, the college population swelled: in 1930, the number of undergraduate, masters, and doctoral students was 139,800; by 1950, it was 496,800.[56]

During the McCarthy era, activism declined across CUNY. At City College, this coincided with the student body's ethnic makeup changing from Jewish to mostly Irish and Italian.[57] Student clubs were forced to give their membership lists to college administrators, which many feared were then turned over to the FBI. Faculty were pressured to take anticommunist loyalty oaths. By 1958, fifty-seven faculty and staff had been fired, resigned under pressure, or retired after harsh investigations. As Ellen Schrecker recalls, "The Academy's enforcement of McCarthyism silenced an entire generation of radical intellectuals and snuffed out all meaningful opposition."[58]

During this period, a coterie of New York intellectuals would become what sociologist Vilna Bashi Treitler called "interpreters of white America." Among them were "Lionel Trilling, Irving Howe, Philip Rahv, Norman Podhoretz, Daniel Bell, Irving Kristol, Norman Mailer, Sidney Hook, Nathan Glazer, and Martin Peretz. Almost all came from working-class families, almost all were educated at City College or Columbia University," and all were European (including many Ashkenazi Jewish) men.[59] They had emerged essentially unscathed from the anticommunist and anti-Semitic purges of the 1940s and '50s (in part because of their willingness to join the counterinsurgency campaign against militants of colors).[60] Within two decades, this mantle was upended by a cadre of City College educators and students—predominantly Black and Puerto Rican, and also antiracist Jewish, feminist, queer, and anticolonial poets— who served as interpreters of what it means to be humans acting in liberatory relation.

Black and Puerto Rican Migration to New York City

Black and Puerto Rican coalitions would begin to refashion City College, CUNY, and the City of New York through the felicitous timing of their overlapping migrations. During the postwar period, at the height of the massive migration of Black Southerners that recomposed Northern cities like Chicago, Cleveland, Detroit, and New York, Puerto Ricans also began migrating to New York. The 1947 imposition of Operation Bootstrap under Puerto Rican colonial governor Luis Muñoz Marín enticed US corporations to set up tax-free, low-wage factories on the island as they courted Puerto

55 Vivian Gornick, *The Romance of American Communism* (New York: Basic Books, 1979).

56 National Center for Education Statistics, *120 Years of American Education: A Statistical Portrait*, 75, https://nces.ed.gov/pubs93/93442.pdf/.

57 David E. Lavin, Richard A. Silberstein, and Richard Alba, *Right Versus Privilege: The Open-Admissions Experiment at the City University of New York* (New York: Free Press, 1981), 2–4.

58 Schrecker, *No Ivory Tower*, 341.

59 Vilna Bashi Treitler, *The Ethnic Project: Transforming Racial Fiction into Ethnic Factions* (Stanford: Stanford University Press, 2013), 97. See also Joseph Dorman, *Arguing the World: The New York Intellectuals in Their Own Words* (Chicago: University of Chicago Press, 2001).

60 Gratitude to Michael Gould-Wartofsky for this context.

Rican laborers for blue-collar jobs in the US.[61] In 1950, public opposition to this policy precipitated an attempted revolution by Albizu Campos' Nationalist Party.[62] The revolt was crushed, inequalities deepened on the island, and hundreds of thousands of Puerto Ricans brought memories of hardship and insurgency with them to the US. In New York City, Puerto Ricans were huddled alongside Black Americans into overpriced tenements and segregated, under-resourced schools in the Bronx, Brooklyn, the Lower East Side, and Harlem.

So many Puerto Rican children were entering New York City public schools by the early 1950s that the Boards of Education in New York and Puerto Rico began conducting studies together, sending New York schoolteachers to the island to learn about its conditions and learning culture.[63] Even though teachers sought to address illiteracy and alienation in the newly bilingual classroom, the Boards began tracking Puerto Rican students into "special" disability classrooms and segregated schools with Black students.[64] For its part, COINTELPRO worked to demolish the Puerto Rican independence movement with surveillance, imprisonment, and assassination. These two techniques of colonial governance might be called the "research and destroy" methodology.[65] The threat of guerrilla Puerto Ricans entering the United States was not a fantasy: on March 1, 1954, five Puerto Rican *independentistas*—Oscar Collazo, Rafael Cancel Miranda, Andrés Figueroa Cordero, Irving Flores Rodríguez, and Lolita Lebrón—fired guns into the chamber of the US House of Representatives. Mass Puerto Rican migration and visible attacks on the colonial state cracked McCarthyism's seeming impermeability. Together with rising Black freedom struggles, they shifted conditions for a new era of conjoined militancy.

In the public education system of the early 1960s, schools composed of mostly Euro students were afforded ample resources while majority-Black and Puerto Rican schools faced overcrowding, no Black or Puerto Rican history programs, scarce bathrooms and cafeterias, and broken desks and supplies. Meanwhile, colonialist discourse claimed that irresponsible sexual reproduction was the cause of mass migration from Puerto Rico. Working- and middle-class Euro residents began to leave the city en masse, abandoning multiethnic urban centers as they were drawn toward segregated suburban outposts shored up by tax incentives and state subsidies, a phenomenon that came to be known as "white flight."

According to countless media and sociological studies of the time, Black Americans and Puerto Ricans were dangerous, docile, drug addicts, inept, juvenile delinquents,

---

61 Antonio Nadal and Milga Morales Nadal, "Bilingual Education and Puerto Rican Studies: From Vision to Reality," in *Puerto Rican Studies at the City University of New York: The First Fifty Years*, ed. Maria Perez y Gonzalez and Virginia Sánchez Korrol (New York: El Centro Press, 2021), 81.

62 Ayala and Bernabe, *Puerto Rico in the American Century*, 165–168, 179.

63 New York City Board of Education, "Our Children from Puerto Rico: A Report on Their Island Home by the Visiting Puerto Rican Workshop of 1955" (1957), Schomburg Center for Research in Black Culture. See also Madeleine E. López, "Investigating the Investigators: An Analysis of *The Puerto Rican Study*," *CENTRO: Journal of the Center for Puerto Rican Studies Journal* 19, no. 2 (Fall 2007): 61–85.

64 Gerald Markowitz and David Rosner, *Children, Race, and Power: Kenneth and Mamie Clark's Northside Center* (Charlottesville: University of Virginia Press, 1996), 108.

65 See also Jodi Melamed, *Represent and Destroy: Rationalizing Violence in the New Racial Capitalism* (Minneapolis: University of Minnesota Press, 2011).

or mentally handicapped.[66] But their segregation had another effect. Radical traditions were shared as they emerged from the long shadow of McCarthyism and gained distance from racist terror in the South and counterrevolutionary repression on the island. Meanwhile, Afro-Caribbean migration to urban areas in the US Northeast during this time infused Black communities with pan-Caribbean anticolonial energies that made Puerto Rican *independentista* politics kin.[67] Because of Black Americans' and Puerto Ricans' proximity, shared indignation, similar physical features, and involvement in each other's cultural and political activities, notes historian Sonia Song-Ha Lee, this closeness produced an intense affinity for improving each other's lives in a new co-creating paradigm that exceeded the bounds of narrow racialized belonging.[68]

As these lineages coalesced, 1960 surged into a watershed year. Black sit-ins that began in Greensboro, North Carolina, on February 1 soon began to deluge up north. Within a year, more than 50,000 people had performed direct actions in a hundred cities, and more than 3,600 were jailed.[69] Students, faculty, and community members young and elderly joined the sit-ins. On multiple occasions, entire classes would conduct civil disobedience as a cohesive unit. In this way, they converted the classroom into a mobile, directional venue oriented toward praxis. Segregated spaces were recomposed into sites of collective militant study as actors reflected on and changed their surroundings.

Education as direct action reflexively decolonized what studying meant: "Here were the colored students, in coats, white shirts, ties, and one of them was reading Goethe and one was taking notes from a biology text," reported one editorial in a Richmond, Virginia paper. "And here, on the sidewalk outside, was a gang of white boys come to heckle, a ragtail rabble, slack-jawed, black-jacketed, grinning fit to kill, waving the Confederate flag. Eheu! It gives one pause."[70] This contrast was deliberate; the sit-in organizers would remain silent even as they were humiliated, beaten, and arrested. However, the decentralized movement didn't always behave this way. Lorenzo Kom'boa Ervin recalls a major February 1960 rebellion in Chattanooga, Tennessee, during which "we were literally going toe to toe with police and white civilians."[71] Over time, *hegemonic drag*—playing institutional dress-up, bringing the decorum of the "proper" classroom to contested and alternative sites of learning—pushed beyond the politics of respectability.[72] As participants' strategies became more defiant, their styles of dress changed. Movement lessons circulated as crowdsourced scholarship. Freedom

---

66 Sonia Song-Ha Lee, *Building a Latino Civil Rights Movement: Puerto Ricans, African Americans, and the Pursuit of Racial Justice in New York City* (Chapel Hill: University of North Carolina Press, 2014), 52.

67 Winston James, *Holding Aloft the Banner of Ethiopia: Caribbean Radicalism in Early Twentieth Century America* (New York: Verso, 1998).

68 Lee, *Building a Latino Civil Rights Movement*, 4. See also Conor Tomás Reed, "Race," in *Keywords for Radicals: The Contested Vocabulary of Late Capitalist Struggle*, ed. Kelly Fritsch, Clare O'Connor, and A.K. Thompson (Chico: AK Press, 2016).

69 Howard Zinn, *SNCC: The New Abolitionists* (Boston: Beacon Press, 1964), 16.

70 Zinn, *SNCC*, 27.

71 Lorenzo Kom'boa Ervin, *Anarchism and the Black Revolution: The Definitive Edition* (London: Pluto Press, 2021), 2. See also Akinyele Omowale Umoja, *We Will Shoot Back: Armed Resistance in the Mississippi Freedom Movement* (New York: New York University, 2013); Charles E. Cobb, Jr., *This Nonviolent Stuff'll Get You Killed: How Guns Made the Civil Rights Movement Possible* (New York: Basic Books, 2014).

72 See Jason Jules and Graham Marsh, *Black Ivy: A Revolt in Style* (London: Reel Art Press, 2021).

learning spread through teach-ins, freedom rides, sit-ins, and voter registration programs by commandeering buses, churches, homes, businesses, and street corners.

This period also witnessed higher education experts working to contain and neutralize the radical energies arising from the mass influx of working-class students in college classrooms. In his 1960 essay "The 'Cooling Out' Function in Higher Education," sociologist Burton R. Clark wrote, "The conflict between open-door admission and performance of high quality often means a wide discrepancy between the hopes of entering students and the means of their realization. . . . for large numbers[,] failure is inevitable and *structured*.[73] "Cooling out" meant absorbing students into a Eurocentric system that got them into the classrooms and off the streets even as these sites of learning were designed to neglect them. This gambit of inclusion-as-counterinsurgency co-emerged with a fabricated specter of mass dropouts.[74] Within a few years, during the "college panic" deluge of new students called "war babies," the CUNY Board of Higher Education responded with "Operation Shoehorn," an emergency measure to squeeze more students into the university's already overcrowded spaces.[75]

As the Black freedom struggle erupted across Southern campuses and communities, Black women initiated communal learning and mutual aid projects on the East and the West Coasts. The Pat Robinson Group, or The Damned, based in Mount Vernon and New Rochelle, New York, formed in 1960 "to address teen pregnancy, and the group attracted Black women ranging from grandmothers to teenagers, including domestic workers, factory workers, and welfare recipients," writes historian Rosalyn Baxandall.[76] New York City Puerto Rican youth education initiatives emanated with the 1961 formation of ASPIRA under Antonia Pantoja and the 1965 rise of the United Bronx Parents under Evelina Antonetty, both of which offered Puerto Rican students college preparation and their families neighborhood activism skills.[77]

The sweeping impact of the 1963 March on Washington for Jobs and Freedom prompted a movement to desegregate New York City's public schools. March Deputy Director and former City College student Bayard Rustin, along with Reverend Milton Galamison, the Congress of Racial Equality (CORE), and the National Association for the Advancement of Colored People (NAACP), coordinated two massive school boycotts in New York City on February 3 and May 18, 1964, in which almost a million students—mostly Black and Puerto Rican—refused to attend school. On these two dates, over 200 bilingual freedom schools were launched across local churches and community centers—11 in the Bronx, 71 in Brooklyn, 99 in Manhattan (59 of them in Harlem), and 25 in Queens—with some sites equipped to teach more than a thousand

73 Burton R. Clark, "The 'Cooling Out' Function in Higher Education," *American Journal of Sociology* 65, no. 6 (1960): 571 (emphasis in original).

74 Eli Meyerhoff, *Beyond Education: Radical Studying for Another World* (Minneapolis: University of Minnesota Press, 2019), 69.

75 Ruth Landa, "The Birth of a Modern University," *CUNY Matters*, Fall 2011. See also Tahir H. Butt, "Free Tuition and Expansion in New York Public Higher Education," *Theory, Research, and Action in Urban Education* 3, no. 1 (2014), https://traue.commons.gc.cuny.edu/volume-iii-issue-1-fall-2014/free-tuition-expansion-new-york-public-higher-education/.

76 Rosalyn Baxandall, "Re-Visioning the Women's Liberation Movement's Narrative: Early Second Wave African American Feminists," *Feminist Studies* 27, no. 1 (2001): 234.

77 Louis Nuñez, "Reflections on Puerto Rican History: Aspira in the Sixties and the Coming of Age of the Stateside Puerto Rican Community," *CENTRO: Journal of the Center for Puerto Rican Studies Journal* 21, no. 2 (2009): 33–47. See also *Evelina 100: Celebrating the Life and Times of Evelina Antonetty*, https://evelina100.org/.

students a day. Students performed skits about the life of Harriet Tubman and learned about Black abolitionists Frederick Douglass and Mary McLeod Bethune as well as Puerto Rican *independentistas* Ramón Betances and Eugenio María de Hostos. They also sang, did physical exercises, and painted "freedom panorama" murals, exploring questions like. "What did freedom mean to the slaves? What does freedom mean to us today?" At the end of the school day, students received a "Freedom Diploma."[78] These boycotts and freedom schools occurred just before the 1964 Freedom Summer project in Mississippi, in which the Student Nonviolent Coordinating Committee (SNCC) welcomed more than 1,000 students from the North—90 percent Euro, mostly Jewish—to help overturn racial segregation.[79]

This renewed wave of struggles coincided with New York City's public colleges recomposing into a new institution, the City University of New York (CUNY), in 1961. That year, 70 percent of Queens College (QC) students boycotted classes after administrators banned a campus event with Communist Party Secretary Benjamin Davis, Malcolm X, and conservative William F. Buckley. Meanwhile, QC CORE led a recurring integration picket outside of a Manhattan Woolworth's. This period also saw the formation of Friends of SNCC and Friends of SDS (Students for a Democratic Society) chapters at CUNY.[80] In Spring 1963, approximately twenty QC students traveled to Virginia to support freedom schools in Black churches after public schools were shut down in defiance of *Brown v. Board of Education*. In August 1963, the QC student government chartered a bus to the March on Washington. These antiracist initiatives confronted the stakes of violence and death directly. In June 1964, as Freedom Summer began, QC student Andrew Goodman was killed in Mississippi alongside fellow Jewish militant Michael Schwerner (whose wife Rita was also enrolled at QC) and Black freedom fighter James Chaney.[81] That July, the NYPD murder of fifteen-year-old James Powell incited a rebellion in Harlem and Brooklyn led by Black adults and youth.[82]

The Hart-Celler Act (also known as the Immigration and Nationality Act of 1965) would further change the composition of New York, particularly by fostering an influx of Asian Americans—via a kind of Open Admissions immigration policy for the United States. Journalist Jay Caspian Kang underscores, "No single piece of legislation has shaped the demographic and economic history of this country in quite the same way."[83] Like their Black and Puerto Rican counterparts, Asian Americans in New

78 Bayard Rustin Papers, Microfilm reels #11–12, Manuscripts, Archives and Rare Books Division, Schomburg Center for Research in Black Culture, New York Public Library.

79 Daniel Perlstein, "Teaching Freedom: SNCC and the Creation of the Mississippi Freedom Schools," *History of Education Quarterly* 30, no. 3 (Fall 1990): 308.

80 Christopher Gunderson, "The Struggle for CUNY: A History of the CUNY Student Movement, 1969–1999," Master's thesis, Macaulay Honors College, 2014, 3.

81 Queens College Special Collections and Archives, "Campus and Queens Activism of the 1960s," https://www.jstor.org/site/queenscollegearchives/. See also Shomial Ahmad, "Queens College and Civil Rights: Alumni Reflect on Activism 50 Years Ago," *Clarion*, May 2014, https://psc-cuny.org/clarion/2014/may/queens-college-and-civil-rights-alumni-reflect-activism-50-years-ago/.

82 For more on how the 1964 Harlem rebellion shaped US counterinsurgency methods, see Chapter 6, "Riot School," in Schrader, *Badges Without Borders*.

83 Jay Caspian Kang, *The Loneliest Americans* (New York: Crown Publishing, 2021), 22.

York were also co-racialized in relation to cross-ethnic belonging and alienation. Daryl Maeda writes of the coalitional possibilities that would soon surface: "Asian American adaptations of black power's emphasis on race and racial identity not only contributed to the construction of Asian American identity but also provided points of conjunction" around which Black and Asian American struggles co-materialized.[84]

The year 1966 would complicate these prospects of multiethnic solidarity—that July, Stokely Carmichael (later Kwame Ture) demanded "Black Power" from atop a police vehicle in Mississippi, launching a political terminology and strategy that differed from integration and civil rights. Later that year, SNCC urged its Euro members to leave the group and build antiracist political power in their own communities. This framework of "organize your own" persists without revision in many present-day movement spaces.[85]

Riots, Community Control, and Solidarity

In the summer of 1967, riots erupted across the United States. With memories of the 1964 Harlem rebellion still smoldering, Puerto Ricans in East Harlem led a rebellion of their own after two off-duty cops shot Reynaldo Rodriguez during a street altercation. For several days, Puerto Rican New Yorkers swarmed the streets and battled police.[86] Participation was not limited to Puerto Ricans or to Harlemites—with reinforcements from Brooklyn, the South Bronx, and the Lower East Side—Black New Yorkers joined in, helping to erode the boundary between "Black Harlem" and "Spanish Harlem," let alone "Harlem" in general. Preexisting relationships were mobilized when the moment came to strike. As in the 1965 Watts Rebellion, people burned down businesses that refused to hire Black and Puerto Rican residents, blockaded fire trucks, raided liquor stores to get bottles for Molotov cocktails, and shot at police helicopters from rooftops. Meanwhile, religious centers and households coordinated the less visible but equally vital work of food preparation, child and elder care, and medical attention.[87]

After the wave of 1960–66 civil rights actions morphed into calls for Black Power, Black students shifted their focus. Sociologist Harry Edwards notes that during 1967 and 68, more than 90 percent of Black students' sit-ins occurred in universities.[88] In Harlem, Intermediate School (IS) 201 community control organizer Preston Wilcox argued that Black and Puerto Rican schools and communities possessed intrinsic cultural and historical value that could not be grasped by the whitewashed, alienating curriculum of

---

84 Maeda, *Chains of Babylon*, 15.

85 See Daniel Tucker and Anthony Romero, eds., *Organize Your Own: The Politics and Poetics of Self-Determination Movements* (Chicago: Soberscove Press, 2016). Another example of the "floating tactic" noted in this book's Introduction, this approach maintains allegiance to a more than five-decades-old vision of organizational forms in antiracist efforts, even as the current ethnic compositions and social relationships of movement participants have become more multifaceted.

86 Vincent Cannato, *The Ungovernable City: John Lindsay and His Struggle to Save New York* (New York: Basic Books, 2002), 132–137.

87 See Gerald Horne, *Fire This Time: The Watts Uprising and the 1960s* (Burlington: Da Capo Press, 1995); Conor Tomás Reed, "Remembering the Watts Rebellion," *Mask Magazine* (August 2015), archived at https://opencuny.org/conortomasreed/files/2017/01/Remembering-the-Watts-Rebellion.pdf.

88 Harry Edwards, *Black Students* (New York: Free Press, 1970), 61.

Eurocentric schooling.[89] In a meeting with parents, he explained, "If one believes that a segregated white school can be a good school, then one must believe that a segregated Negro and Puerto Rican school, like IS 201, can also be a good school." Another Harlem education advocate, Babette Edwards, put the matter more succinctly: "Our priority is Black community control." IS 201 became a flashpoint for Harlem parents who were outraged that the new school's design was entirely windowless.[90] However, as historian Russell Rickford points out, the community control campaign "never fulfilled demands for academic redemption and self-rule" because in 1969, the city adopted a "'decentralization law' that nominally dispersed the powers of the Board of Education, carving the school system into 'community districts' without genuinely reallocating fiscal, personnel, or curricular functions."[91] Institutional reform designed to stymie rebellion would soon make its way to CUNY.

The 1968 United Federation of Teachers strike against community control in East Harlem, Ocean Hill-Brownsville, and the Lower East Side also sparked divisions. In a shift away from the integrationist demands of the 1964 public school boycotts, Black and Puerto Rican education advocates began to demand autonomous community control of majority-Black and Puerto Rican schools. They wanted a role in hiring and firing teachers and principals, a Black and Puerto Rican Studies curriculum, and deeper connections between each school and its neighborhood. The UFT leadership stoked a racialized conflict so that the strike could be viewed as a (Black) community versus (Euro/Ashkenazi Jewish) labor issue. At the same time, the strike obscured radical Jewish teachers' agreement with Black and Puerto Rican communities' concerns. Lasting thirty-six days, the strike marked a rupture in education struggles. Ordinarily a radical tactic, the strike was in this case reactionary. In retaliation, students, their families, and antiracist teachers mounted a *counterstrike*, an affirmative program to rearticulate direct democratic study as a public good for all.

The strike forced a growing acrimony between Black and Ashkenazi Jewish people into the open and represented a break from their earlier alignment. In the early-to-mid–twentieth century, Black and Jewish residents in New York lived side by side in the Lower East Side, Harlem, the Bronx, and Brooklyn, and groups like the Communist Party actively worked to build antiracist, anticapitalist ties between Black, Jewish, Caribbean, and European immigrants. Black Americans saw in fascism an analogue to American traditions of racial violence and frequently identified with its victims.[92] Although many European Jewish scholars arriving in the US after World War II couldn't get jobs because of anti-Semitic hiring practices, they were welcomed into HBCUs.[93] Many of the Northern

89 In 1966, three months after chanting "Black Power!" in the South, Stokely Carmichael visited IS 201 in Harlem, speaking to parents who converted the Black Power slogan into community control. See Mario D. Fantini, Marilyn Gittell, and Richard Magat, *Community Control and the Urban School* (Westport: Praeger Publishers, 1970), 16.

90 Marta Gutman, "Intermediate School 201: Race, Space, and Modern Architecture in Harlem," in *Educating Harlem: A Century of Schooling and Resistance in a Black Community*, ed. Ansley T. Erickson and Ernest Morrell (New York: Columbia University Press, 2019), 183–209.

91 Russell Rickford, *We Are an African People: Independent Education, Black Power, and the Radical Imagination* (Oxford: Oxford University Press, 2016), 60.

92 See Robin D. G. Kelley, *Race Rebels: Culture, Politics, and the Black Working Class* (New York: Free Press, 1996).

93 See Gabrielle Simon Edgcomb, *From Swastika to Jim Crow: Refugee Scholars at Black Colleges* (Malabar: Krieger Publishing, 1993).

volunteers in the civil rights movement's freedom rides and freedom schools were Jewish.

By the late 1960s, however, politicians, employers, and newspapers were promoting racial divisions between Black and Jewish people. Vilna Bashi Treitler writes of a transformation of American Jewish identities by which certain "Jews took prewar themes in Jewish culture and gave them new postwar assimilationist spins to claim Americanness." In practical terms, this meant stripping away those aspects of Jewish social life that involved the culture of *Yiddishkeit*, labor struggles, and interethnic solidarity.[94] Some Ashkenazi Jewish people assimilating into "whiteness" adopted racist attitudes toward Black and Puerto Rican people in exchange for socioeconomic and psychological benefits.[95]

Jewish communities in urban areas had developed self-determination programs around schools, housing, and food access, and Black Power organizations looked to these as precedents. But since programs of this kind were disrupted when the Black Panther Party for Self Defense tried to implement them, and since Ashkenazi Jewish assimilation into whiteness meant embracing anti-Black racism, Black militants began directing their frustrations at racist Jews along with the racial supremacist structures that accorded Ashkenazi Jews preferential treatment.[96] Groups like the Nation of Islam promoted anti-Semitic views, which were often left unchallenged.[97] In 1967, when members of SNCC critiqued Israel's actions during the Arab–Israeli War, their anti-Zionist stance was spuriously attacked for being anti-Semitic.[98]

By 1968, news flashes documented the My Lai Massacre by US soldiers in Vietnam; Howard University's building occupations; Martin Luther King's assassination and the subsequent mass uprisings in more than a hundred US cities; Black Panther Party battles with the Oakland Police Department; the Columbia University strike and building occupations; the May general strikes in France, and nearby eruptions in Germany, Ireland, Italy, and elsewhere in Europe; and the Catonsville Nine draft card burnings. During the second half of the year, and continuing well into 1969, students at San Francisco State University staged the longest student-led strike in US history. Through their efforts, they won the first School of Ethnic Studies, with Departments of American Indian Studies, Asian American Studies, Black Studies, and La Raza Studies, which inspired movements on the East Coast.[99]

---

94 Treitler, *The Ethnic Project*, 98.

95 See Theodore W. Allen, *The Invention of the White Race* (New York: Verso, 1997); Karen Brodkin, *How Jews Became White Folks: And What That Says about Race in America* (New Brunswick: Rutgers University Press, 2010); George Lipsitz, *The Possessive Investment in Whiteness* (Philadelphia: Temple University Press, 2006); Nell Irvin Painter, *The History of White People* (New York: W.W. Norton and Company, 2011); David R. Roediger, *The Wages of Whiteness: Race and the Making of the American Working Class* (New York: Verso, 2007).

96 For a historical examination of the rise and present manifestations of anti-Semitism, see Jews for Racial and Economic Justice, "Understanding Anti-Semitism: An Offering to Our Movement," 2017, https://www.jfrej.org/assets/uploads/JFREJ-Understanding-Antisemitism-November-2017-v1-3-2.pdf.

97 Robert Reid-Pharr, "Speaking through Anti-Semitism: The Nation of Islam and the Poetics of Black (Counter) Modernity," *Social Text* 49 (1996): 133–147.

98 See Ethel Minor, "Third World Round Up: The Palestine Problem: Test Your Knowledge," *SNCC Newsletter*, June–July 1967, https://snccdigital.org/inside-sncc/policy-statements/palestine; Michael R. Fischbach, *Black Power and Palestine: Transnational Countries of Color* (Stanford: Stanford University Press, 2018); Alex Lubin, *Geographies of Liberation: The Making of an Afro-Arab Political Imaginary* (Chapel Hill: University of North Carolina Press, 2014).

99 Maeda, *Chains of Babylon*, 68–69. See also Kay Boyle, *The Long Walk at San Francisco State and Other Essays* (New York: Grove, 1970); Kang, *Loneliest Americans*; Dikran Karagueuezian, *Blow it Up! The Black Student Revolt at San Francisco State and the Emergence of Dr. Hayakawa* (Boston: Gambit, 1971).

In New York City, the Black Arts Movement began to flourish along with Black and Puerto Rican Studies. Advocates fused poetics and street tactics. In his 1966 poem "Black Art," LeRoi Jones (later Amiri Baraka) demanded "'poems that kill.' / Assassin poems, Poems that shoot / guns. Poems that wrestle cops into alleys / and take their weapons leaving them dead."[100] In the 1967 poem "Black People!," he urged readers to reclaim what capitalism and racial supremacy had stolen from them across centuries: "All the stores will open if you will say the magic words. The magic words are: Up against the wall motherfucker this is a stick up!"[101] At packed readings in the Black Arts Repertory Theater/School in Harlem and the Spirit House in Newark, people would shout these familiar lines with delight. Diane di Prima, an Italian American sister of the Black Arts Movement and a former partner of and publishing collaborator with Baraka, dispatched "Revolutionary Letters" enjoining militant communities to stockpile dry foods, salt, and matches and to fill bathtubs with water in case city officials shut off utilities. She conjured these poems as direct action training so that readers could learn how to anticipate and avoid tear gas, kettling, and unfamiliar areas:

> Everytime you pick the spot for a be-in / a demonstration, a march, a rally, you are choosing the ground / for a potential battle. / You are still calling the shots. / Pick your terrain with that in mind.[102]

Black women were among the most perceptive movement leaders and artists. In 1959, Black lesbian playwright Lorraine Hansberry noted how "the most oppressed group of any oppressed group will be its women, obviously"—but those who are *twice oppressed* can become *twice militant*.[103] By 1970, City College educator Toni Cade Bambara noted that:

> Black women have been forming work-study groups, discussion clubs, co-operative nurseries, cooperative businesses, consumer education groups, women's workshops on the campuses, women's caucuses within existing organizations, Afro-American women's magazines . . . they have begun correspondence with sisters in Vietnam, Guatemala, Algeria, Ghana on the Liberation Struggle and the Woman, formed alliances on a Third World Women plank. They are women who have not, it would seem, been duped by the prevailing notions of 'woman,' but who have maintained a critical stance.[104]

From community control to shifting interethnic alliances to insurgent lessons condensed on poetic lines, radical culture and global politics became a prism of learning,

---

100 LeRoi Jones/Amiri Baraka, "Black Art," *Liberator* 6 (January 1966): 18.

101 LeRoi Jones/Amiri Baraka, "Black People!" *Black Magic: Collected Poetry, 1961–1967* (Indianapolis: Bobbs Merrill Co., 1969).

102 Diane di Prima, "Revolutionary Letter #3" and "Revolutionary Letter #8," *Revolutionary Letters* (San Francisco: City Lights, 1971), 5–6, 13–14.

103 Lorraine Hansberry, "Lorraine Hansberry Discusses Her Play *A Raisin in the Sun*," *The WFMT Studs Terkel Radio Archive*, https://studsterkel.wfmt.com/programs/lorraine-hansberry-discusses-her-play-raisin-sun/.

104 Toni Cade Bambara, "Preface," in *The Black Woman: An Anthology*, ed. Toni Cade Bambara (New York: New American Library, 1970), 9–10.

creativity, and power that would transform City College.

Resisting Empire from the Island to the City to the College

By the mid-1960s, Black and Puerto Rican youth had begun to trickle into a still-segregated CUNY and agitate for change.[105] CUNY historian Johanna Fernández writes of Puerto Rican youth's articulating position in their communities: "These English-speaking children of new migrants became accidental translators—of both language and culture—for the many postwar Puerto Rican newcomers to New York."[106] As CUNY historian Tahir H. Butt argues, they would go up against a "color-blind meritocracy" that "refused to recognize the racial biases embedded within the institution, [which was] typical of northern liberals who perpetuated Jim Crow conditions even as they decried them below the Mason-Dixon Line."[107]

As Black City College educator Barbara Christian noted at the time, City College is located "smack dab in the middle of the largest Black community in the country, and only 9% of its daytime students are Black or Puerto Rican." Moreover, five of that nine percent "came through the [Search for Education, Elevation, and Knowledge] SEEK Program."[108] Within a few years, SEEK would become a nucleus for experimental study that challenged the institutional inequalities entrenched in City College's admissions, curriculum, and relationship to Harlem. With Mina P. Shaughnessy named as program director in 1967, educators and writers like Aijaz Ahmad, Toni Cade Bambara, Barbara Christian, Addison Gayle, David Henderson, June Jordan, Audre Lorde, Larry Neal, Raymond Patterson, and Adrienne Rich engaged these previously excluded students in radical collaborative learning. In the Department of Romance Languages, the Puerto Rican Poet Laureate Diana Ramírez de Arellano also urged Puerto Rican SEEK students to excel.[109]

Campus life in this period was marked by excitement, turmoil, and uncertainty. The Black and Puerto Rican SEEK student population, although tiny, was tremendously active: students invited revolutionaries to speak on campus, screened films like Gillo Pontecorvo's *La battaglia di Algeri* [*The Battle of Algiers*], published pamphlets and newspapers, and collaborated with left-wing faculty and Euro students in SDS. In October 1968, Black Panther Minister of Justice H. Rap Brown, Harry Edwards,

---

105 During the late 1950s and 1960s—before Open Admissions was implemented in 1970—CUNY dramatically expanded its system with the formation of multiple doctoral, four-year, and two-year colleges: Bronx Community College (1957), Queensborough Community College (1958), the CUNY Graduate Center (1961), Manhattan Community College (1963), Kingsborough Community College (1963), John Jay College (1964), York College (1966), LaGuardia Community College (1968), and Lehman College (1968).

106 Fernández, *The Young Lords*, 52.

107 Tahir H. Butt, "'You Are Running a de Facto Segregated University': Racial Segregation and the City University of New York," in *The Strange Careers of the Jim Crow North: Segregation and Struggle Outside of the South*, ed. Brian Purnell, Jeanne Theoharis, and Komozi Woodard (New York: New York University Press, 2019), 187–209.

108 Martha Biondi, *The Black Revolution on Campus* (Berkeley: University of California Press, 2012), 124. See also Jane Maher, *Mina P. Shaughnessy: Her Life and Work* (Urbana: National Council of Teachers of English, 1997), 89–90.

109 Henry Arce, "Oral History Interview with Henry Arce," interview by Douglas Medina, CUNY Digital History Archive, February 26, 2014, https://cdha.cuny.edu/items/show/6842/.

and athlete John Carlos spoke on campus in defense of Carlos and Tommie Smith's Black Power salute at the Mexico City Olympics, a gesture that had come in the wake of mass protests in Mexico City following the massacre of students at Tlatelolco.[110] In November, antiwar students provided AWOL US soldiers Bill Brakefield and David Copp sanctuary at the campus's Finley Ballroom, an action for which almost two hundred students and community members were arrested.[111] And in December, Black Panther Prime Minister Stokely Carmichael (later Kwame Ture) spoke at the City College Great Hall to a massive crowd on a "blueprint for armed struggle against American racism and capitalism."[112] Reviving 1930s City College traditions, these Black and Brown students, along with their Euro student comrades, created a radical intellectual milieu where people could relate experiential lessons from the colonial wars in Algeria, Vietnam, and elsewhere to their own local conditions.

Puerto Rican youth whose families remained on the island also began infusing the University of Puerto Rico with a new wave of anticolonial ferment. At both UPR and City College, the twenty-year US war in Vietnam galvanized student actions. At UPR, students could be drafted and were often sent to the most dangerous war zones even though they were ineligible to vote in US elections. UPR and CUNY students of colors recruited by ROTC were routinely refused officer positions and were instead hurried to the front lines to kill or be killed by Vietnamese people who, like them, were also resisting colonialism.

Puerto Rican students understood the ROTC as a colonial-imperialist presence. At the UPR-Río Piedras campus in San Juan, they began holding protests to expel the ROTC while aligning their strategies with the North Vietnamese student union, with whom they were in correspondence. On Sept 22, 1968, bomb materials were found in the Río Piedras ROTC building as massive rallies were taking place to mark the centennial of *El Grito de Lares*, a September 1868 rebellion against Spanish colonial rule.[113] Rather than simply the culmination of the 1960s or a reaction to McCarthyism, Puerto Rican students saw their movement as part of a much longer insurgent boomerang.

Meanwhile at City College, Euro student antiwar activists would interrupt and ridicule ROTC trainings on campus. In the spring of 1969, they sabotaged an ROTC recruitment event by pouring ox blood on the registration table. "Opposition to the US war on Vietnam was high at CUNY and protests against the war in general and various forms of campus complicity in the war in particular became increasingly militant," CUNY historian Christopher Gunderson notes. "These actions, based largely among white students, established both a mood and a series of tactical precedents . . . that contributed to the atmosphere in which the [1969] Open Admissions strikers were able to win."[114] Black and Puerto Rican youth also organized against the draft, infusing the GI resistance movement with Black Power and anticolonial energies and calling attention to decolonization struggles taking place in Africa, the Caribbean, and elsewhere. At both City College and UPR, campus revolts escalated to contest the very legitimacy of administrators and their state allies.

---

110 Paul Simms, "Black Athletes Defend Olympic Action," *Tech News*, October 30, 1968, 1.

111 Barbara Gutfreund, "Wednesday Night and Thursday Morn," *The Campus*, November 14, 1968, 2.

112 Frederick Douglass Opie, *Upsetting the Apple Cart: Black-Latino Coalitions in New York City from Protest to Public Office* (New York: Columbia University Press, 2014), 78.

113 Miscellaneous, Puerto Rican Collection, University Archives, Río Piedras Campus, University of Puerto Rico.

114 Gunderson, "The Struggle for CUNY," 3.

In campus newspapers, what began as general editorial condemnations of imperialism, colonialism, and police warfare on communities of colors became more precise action reports. As student and faculty organizers composed, revised, and circulated organizing campaigns, their writing became clearer, weaving readers' responses back into their analyses. At the same time, Puerto Rican students lamented the absence of Puerto Rican Studies in the otherwise groundbreaking SEEK program. As Eduardo Cruz reflects: "It was geared for Black students, not Puerto Rican students per se or Latinos. I know that I confronted the SEEK program in not having a Puerto Rican history class, leadership, or staff."[115] An embrace of Afro-Puerto Rican and Afro-Latinx paradigms was still not yet central to student consciousness, but Cruz's argument reveals how SEEK educators were unfamiliar with Puerto Rican Studies.

This process of diving into, excavating, subverting, and critiquing the canon while producing an underground counter-canon: these processes encouraged students to revolutionize the college and demand what they knew was missing. They created groups like the Onyx Society, Puerto Ricans Involved in Student Action (PRISA), the Black and Puerto Rican Students Community (BPRSC) coalition, and the Puerto Rican Student Union (PRSU).[116] Asian American students from City College and Columbia also formed Asian Americans for Action, a radical group that began to organize for Asian American Studies and support community power initiatives in Chinatown.[117]

In Spring 1969, as students and faculty proposed structural changes in admissions, curricula, and campus/community control, they opposed the administration and conservative faculty's deep-seated intransigence. The SEEK Program served as a reciprocal incubator for student and faculty radicalization, but the state budget under Governor Nelson Rockefeller called for slashing its funding while imposing a 20 percent reduction in admissions. Across CUNY, entering first-year students were 13.8 percent Black, 5.9 percent Puerto Rican, 75.9 percent European-American, and 4.4 percent "Other." These figures were disproportionately lower than the Black and Puerto Rican population of traditionally college-aged people.[118]

Black and Puerto Rican students petitioned City College President Buell Gallagher to implement changes, using *The Campus*, *Tech News*, and *Observation Post* student newspapers to publicly debate the issues. Students from the BPRSC, Onyx Society, PRISA, SDS, and the CP's W. E. B. Du Bois Club ultimately co-created a list of Five Demands for the administration:

- A separate degree-granting School of Third World Studies.
- A separate freshman orientation for Black and Puerto Rican students.

---

115 Lillian Jiménez, "Puerto Ricans and Educational Civil Rights: A History of the 1969 City College Takeover (An Interview with Five Participants)," *CENTRO: Journal of the Center for Puerto Rican Studies Journal* 21, no. 2 (Fall 2009): 165.

116 Basilio Serrano, "¡*Rifle, Cañón, y Escopeta!*: A Chronicle of the Puerto Rican Student Union," in *The Puerto Rican Movement: Voices from the Diaspora*, ed. Andrés Torres and José E. Velásquez (Philadelphia: Temple University Press, 1998), 124–143.

117 William Wei, *The Asian American Movement* (Philadelphia: Temple University Press, 1993), 26.

118 Newt Davidson Collective, *Crisis at CUNY*, 65.

- That the SEEK students have a determining voice in the setting of guidelines for the SEEK Program, including the hiring and firing of SEEK personnel.
- That the racial composition of the entering freshman class be reflective of the Black, Puerto Rican, and Asian high school population.
- That all education majors be required to take Black and Puerto Rican history and the Spanish language.[119]

Gallagher tried to quell the mobilization by promising that he would resign if an austere budget was passed. When it did, he kept his promise; and twenty-three of the twenty-seven City College department chairs also tendered their resignations. The future of City College was uncertain.

An act of student, worker, and community composition in April–May 1969 expanded SEEK's mission and altered the course of public higher education nationwide. On April 22, a campus takeover established Harlem University. As participant James Small recounts:

> No one was told of the date of the takeover until the night before. We were all called to a big meeting in the Bronx at the home of a Black professor. People were told to come to spend the night as a security measure. (Then) we came down in three groups. We came at 5 a.m. . . . caught the guards with their pants down. It was raining bloody murder. We took seventeen buildings—the largest takeover in the history of American campus takeovers.[120]

The group of thirty who locked the gates at 5:00 a.m. had become 400 by 11:00 a.m.[121] As a *counter-institution*, Harlem University hosted a walk-in clinic, tutorials, nightly community meetings, and a "free breakfast program for the children in the neighborhood, day care, [and] political education classes."[122] Campus buildings were renamed after Pedro Albizu Campos, Marcus Garvey, Che Guevara, Patrice Lumumba, Huey P. Newton, Mao Tse-Tung, and Malcolm X.[123] Actions spread to other CUNY cam-

119 Black and Puerto Rican Student Community, "Five Demands," CUNY Digital History Archive, https://cdha.cuny.edu/items/show/6952/. See also Paul B. Simms, "What Was Behind the CCNY Takeover?," *Harvard Crimson*, July 7, 1969, https://www.thecrimson.com/article/1969/7/22/what-was-behind-the-ccny-takeover/; Philip Barnett, Judy Connorton, William Gibbons, and Sydney Van Nort, *The Five Demands: The Student Protest and Takeover of 1969*, https://fivedemands.commons.gc.cuny.edu/. The Fall 1968 version of the Five Demands sought Black and Puerto Rican Studies and increased Black and Puerto Rican enrollment, then in Spring 1969 the demands were revised to seek Third World Studies and increased Black, Puerto Rican, and Asian student enrollment.

120 Conrad Dyer, "Protest and the Politics of Open Admissions: The Impact of the Black and Puerto Rican Student Community (of City College)," PhD diss., CUNY Graduate Center, 1990, 1. In various anecdotes and written accounts, the number of occupied buildings ranges from seven to seventeen.

121 Iva Radivojević and Martyna Starosta, dirs., *Are You With Me?: Louis Reyes Rivera 1945–2012* (New York: Occupy CUNY News, 2021), https://vimeo.com/39156555/.

122 Jiménez, "Puerto Ricans and Educational Civil Rights," 165. See also Roderick A. Ferguson, *The Reorder of Things: The University and its Pedagogies of Minority Difference* (Minneapolis: University of Minnesota Press 2012), 76–77.

123 Ken Sasmor and Tom Foty, "It May Not Be the Place You Knew," *The Campus*, May 6, 1969.

puses across four boroughs.[124] Neighborhood residents, students of all ages, and various speakers came to Harlem University's inaugural open house event. They included Betty Shabazz, Kathleen Cleaver, James Foreman, Emory Douglas, H. Rap Brown, and Adam Clayton Powell, who deemed the action "one of the greatest test events" in the history of Black education.

The direct action lasted for two weeks to highlight the Five Demands despite immense counterinsurgent pressure. Puerto Rican City College SEEK students Henry Arce and Eduardo Cruz recall that twenty-five Harlem parents brought "big pots of rice and beans and pork and *pasteles*," and the Lower East Side dispatched "a hundred parents to hold the gates."[125] These community defenders brought nourishment and a sense of home to the college as it underwent a process of decolonization—healthy food that had sustained previous Puerto Rican and diasporic struggles. Parents protecting the gates modeled *cerrar para abrir* [close to open], a process of reclaiming the university familiar in Puerto Rico but new to CUNY.[126]

Shutting down the college demonstrated tactical power, but it also revealed to conservative administrators, students, and teachers what exclusion had felt like for Black and Puerto Rican students and teachers. Closure signaled a different paradigm than integration. Instead of a liberal project of ostensible inclusion, Harlem University understood the need to exclude those who opposed its flourishing so that new forms of freedom learning could arise. In response to criticisms that the strike disrupted regular functioning, one Black City College student said, "so you lose a day, a week, or a semester. We lost generations and damn it, this is what we intend to stop."[127]

While many New Yorkers supported the strike, some condemned it. Puerto Rican student Guillermo Morales recounts a surprise visit by the Zionist paramilitary Jewish Defense League (JDL). He framed the standoff between Black and Puerto Rican students and the JDL:

> [T]he Jewish Defense League was being organized to face us when we marched to the northern field. There they would be waiting for us with pistols in hand. The police, who were present, did nothing to disarm them. . . . [T]hey wanted a dead person to later take the land by force. But they fucked up, we confronted the Zionists and we won the battle. The JDL withdrew their weapons.[128]

This encounter underscores the shift that had occurred from the political allegiances between City College Jewish students and Black and Puerto Rican communities during the 1930s. Historic allies became adversaries as Black and Puerto Rican students demanded entrance to an educational refuge that had long supported Ashkenazi Jewish

---

124 María Pérez y González, "How a Few Students Transformed the Ivory Tower: Puerto Rican Studies and its (R)evolution at Brooklyn College," in *Puerto Rican Studies at the City University of New York*. See also Biondi, *The Black Revolution on Campus*.

125 Jiménez, "Puerto Ricans and Educational Civil Rights," 170.

126 Francisco J. Fortuño Bernier, "'*Cerrar para abrir*': Puerto Rican Student Struggles and the Crisis of Colonial-Capitalism," *Viewpoint Magazine*, April 27, 2017, https://viewpointmag.com/2017/04/27/cerrar-para-abrir-puerto-rican-student-struggles-and-the-crisis-of-colonial-capitalism/.

127 Newt Davidson Collective, *Crisis at CUNY*, 66.

128 William Morales Correa, *Desde la sombra la luz: Pasajes de mi vida* (Scotts Valley: CreateSpace Independent Publishing, 2015), 52. Translation by the author.

students also exiled from elite learning institutions. Meanwhile, campus conservatives abhorred the prospect that more Black and Puerto Rican students might be admitted to the school. For professors and administrators accustomed to a tranquility that belied the upheavals outside the campus gates, the resonance of the Spring 1969 rebellion made them shudder.

Even with these schisms, solidarity between SEEK students, workers, and their families greatly influenced the City College teachers' support for the strike. During the occupation, faculty unanimously voted to approve the Five Demands. By early May, City College's forty Black and Puerto Rican faculty all went on strike in support.[129] Neighborhood pride rippled through Harlem. That summer, at Mount Morris (now Marcus Garvey) Park, the Harlem Cultural Festival gathered thousands of Black and Puerto Rican residents to enjoy music near the institution whose takeover had been supported by many of those in attendance.[130]

Meanwhile, the situation in Puerto Rico was escalating dramatically. At the UPR–Río Piedras campus, students used guerrilla tactics—such as a September 1969 attempt to burn down the ROTC building—against the colonial regime. During a March 4, 1970 riot on campus against the ROTC, police killed a student named Antonia Martínez. On May 4, the US National Guard killed four students at Kent State after students there burned down an ROTC building. The next day, City College students set fire to ROTC equipment as part of a national student strike against war, in which more than 4 million students at over 450 universities and high schools participated. On May 15, police killed two students at Jackson State after they set fire to an ROTC building. As students turned increasingly toward insurgent tactics, US and Puerto Rican campus administrators and government officials shared intelligence tools like a "Checklist on Agitation and Control" and a "Survey of Colleges for the Presidential Commission on Campus Unrest."

These widespread campus rebellions increased the pressure to address the City College strike demands, which flowed directly from the mission and practices of the SEEK program. As the administration dragged its heels to derail the Third World Studies curricular demand, CUNY Chancellor Albert Bowker and the Board of Higher Education revised the admissions demand to create "Open Admissions"—allowing every New York City high school graduate a place in one of CUNY's two- or four-year colleges by Fall 1970.[131]

This post-strike educational policy, today considered a hallmark of CUNY's democratic successes, could also be measured as a calculated form of institutional reform-as-sabotage. CUNY political scientist Conrad Dyer writes that "no major university system had ever moved, almost overnight, from a rigorously selective admissions standard to a policy of guaranteed admission for all high school graduates."[132]

---

129 Newt Davidson Collective, *Crisis at CUNY*, 66.

130 Ahmir "Questlove" Thompson, dir., *Summer of Soul* (Los Angeles: Searchlight Pictures, 2021).

131 Gerald Markowitz writes that CUNY Chancellor Bowker wanted to create avenues for "sub-professional education" after the postwar collapse of New York City's manufacturing economy. See Gerald Markowitz, *Educating for Justice: A History of John Jay College of Criminal Justice* (New York: CUNY Academic Works, 2008), 45. Alexis Pauline Gumbs also notes how CUNY's Open Admissions policy corresponded with an explosion in imprisonment nationwide. See Gumbs, "Nobody Mean More: Black Feminist Pedagogy and Solidarity," in *The Imperial University: Academic Repression and Scholarly Dissent*, eds. Piya Chatterjee and Sunaina Maira (Minneapolis: University of Minnesota Press, 2014), 241.

132 Dyer, "Protest and the Politics of Open Admissions," 146.

CUNY administrators, with city and state government approval, flooded the campuses with new students (the 1970 CUNY freshman class was 75 percent larger than the preceding year) but refused to increase resources.[133] They overwhelmed students and campus workers and, in general, marred the success of free education for New Yorkers of all ethnicities. Still, the profound shift in CUNY's admissions policy meant that many working-class students gained a historic opportunity to go to college, a policy that would be replicated nationwide. The CUNY student body doubled within a year, and within seven years the almost all-Euro student body became majority students of colors, though it still did not meet the strike demand to proportionately enroll Black, Puerto Rican, and Asian students.

Within a year, two additional transformations would impact CUNY and US higher education. First, Black, Puerto Rican, and Women's Studies became institutionalized as departments, programs, or special courses, but often by fighting tooth and nail against the administration.[134] Second, CUNY began relying increasingly on contingent adjunct labor. With 6,000 adjuncts now teaching 40 percent of CUNY's courses, CUNY educators Chloe Smolarski and Irwin Yellowitz write, "Organizers accused CUNY of paying teachers 'sweatshop wages' with the objective of obtaining cheap labor for the Open Admissions program."[135] CUNY's expanded use of adjunct faculty "reflected national trends toward the deprofessionalization of the academic labor force."[136] Increasingly, women adjunct faculty were suddenly tasked with teaching the wave of new CUNY students.[137] This trend particularly impacted women adjunct faculty members at CUNY but was built upon longstanding sexist hiring practices.[138]

As a work of both institutional reform and counterinsurgency, CUNY in 1970 offered many young people new opportunities for education while facilitating their containment.[139] In a 1972 statement to the City College administration, Mina Shaughnessy noted that pre-Open Admissions, "it was common to hear professors, administrators, and even students refer to the arrival of the new students in the metaphors of disease—of debility, decay, paralysis, contagion, even of mortality rates." In one instance, a professor reportedly exclaimed to Shaughnessy, "You've brought the slums to

---

133 Biondi, *The Black Revolution on Campus*, 134.

134 See Conor Tomás Reed, "The Evolution of Puerto Rican Studies at City College," in *Puerto Rican Studies at the City University of New York*, 120–145; Fabio Rojas, *From Black Power to Black Studies: How a Radical Social Movement Became an Academic Discipline* (Baltimore: Johns Hopkins University Press, 2007).

135 The United Federation of College Teachers, "Draft of an Appeal to the City University Community," CUNY Digital History Archive, https://cdha.cuny.edu/items/show/8812/.

136 Chloe Smolarski and Irwin Yellowitz, "CUNY Adjunct Labor," CUNY Digital History Archive, https://cdha.cuny.edu/collections/show/292/.

137 Newt Davidson Collective, *Crisis at CUNY*, 21.

138 Eileen Schell's work reveals that the part-time instructor position emerged when most schools didn't allow women as full professors, and so adjunct positions were usually held by female instructors. These contingent faculty members were referred to as "the housewives of higher education." See Eileen Schell, *Gypsy Academics and Mother-Teachers: Gender, Contingent Labor, and Writing Instruction* (Portsmouth: Heinemann, 1997).

139 Former City College student journalist Albert DeLeon recalls that Open Admissions wasn't rolled out across CUNY. City College and some other schools were amended while other schools' admissions remained largely untouched. [Interview with the author, May 7, 2021.] Sociologist Amaka Okechukwu buttresses this point with statistical evidence that contrasts City College's changing enrollment post-1970 with Hunter College's enrollment, which remained the same in terms of ethnic demographics. See Okechukwu, *To Fulfill These Rights*, 62; Newt Davidson Collective, *Crisis at CUNY*, 42.

my office."[140] In a way, the professor's remark was prescient, albeit misdirected. While the SEEK Program welcomed Black and Puerto Rican youth into CUNY classrooms, the administration mimicked New York's housing policies by increasing admissions while slashing resources and laying off workers. The CUNY administration cynically turned the university into a *slum*.[141] From there, Open Admissions could be attacked by conservative faculty and mainstream media. When tuition was imposed five years later, students were turned into tenants forced to pay for their own immiseration. Not until these conditions were felt by the middle and upper classes did the alarm sound in objection.

This conflicted transition begs a revision to how Open Admissions is often mythologized, providing a lesson for those who advocate for institutional change from below to be wary of unsustainable reforms from above. A critical assessment of this period highlights these braided forms of educational counterinsurgency that impacted the CUNY movement: containment, cooling out, cooptation, and repression.

One, Two, Many Free Universities

History does not swing like a recursive pendulum in which militant disruptions lead to the inevitable rollback of counterinsurgency. Sometimes social containment can serve as a pressure cooker and efforts toward *decontainment* can erupt. Even though the administration and state responded to the strike's demands with a destabilizing counterattack, Open Admissions demonstrated how porous the walls of higher education had become. Historically excluded city residents began to enter CUNY en masse, bringing with them the learning methods and priorities of their communities. Tens of thousands of veterans returning from the US war in Vietnam began studying and organizing opposition to war and racism in the university.[142] CUNY educator Ammiel Alcalay recalled of the time,

> If you wore an army jacket in 1969, 1970, or 1971, it either meant you were a veteran or that you identified with the soldiers and veterans fighting the war against the war in Vietnam. That was still the case when I took classes at City College in New York in the mid-1970s. The draft had passed me by, but a number of the students studying Ancient Greek with me were older and survivors of the war in Vietnam. They were eager to find and lose themselves in texts as archaic and startling as their experiences must have been.[143]

---

140 Maher, *Mina P. Shaughnessy*, 121.

141 The use of this term is neither intended to disparage housing projects nor CUNY, but to establish a comparison between the specific mechanism by which the college administrators, with city and state government support, overcrowded and underfunded the City University in ways similar to landlords' maintenance of New York City's tenements. Indeed, many in CUNY know of the beloved human communities that exist in our resource-starved projects and neighborhoods. See also Saidiya Hartman, "The Terrible Beauty of the Slum," *Brick: A Literary Journal* 99 (July 28, 2017), https://brickmag.com/the-terrible-beauty-of-the-slum/.

142 See *Liberation News Service*, "'Veterans Are Still Experiencing the War at Home': VVAW/WSO Holds Forum on Third World Vets," May–August 1973, https://content.wisconsinhistory.org/digital/collection/p15932coll8/id/75664/; June Svetlovsky and Ben Chitty, "Vietnam Era Ends at the City University of NY," *The Veteran: Vietnam Veterans Against the War* 26 (Fall 1996): 1, 7, 15.

143 Ammiel Alcalay, *a little history* (Los Angeles and New York: UpSet Press, 2012), 125.

Nationally, the college population expanded to levels unseen since after World War II. In 1970, the number of undergraduate, masters, and doctoral students reached 1,561,700.[144]

Around this time, hundreds of Black teachers in New York City pulled out of their unions to form new ones like the Afro-American Teachers Association.[145] Other Black laborers insisted that their unions should align with community control struggles as a workers' matter, arguing that their students' parents were also workers. The pedagogies of Harlem University began to circulate around the city's workplaces and labor halls. Meanwhile, freedom schools, experimental schools, and liberation projects of various kinds continued to flourish even as police and the FBI worked to quash their reach. It can be difficult to conceive the breadth of youth radicalization that the state faced. As historian Max Elbaum recalls,

> A 1971 *New York Times* survey indicated that four out of ten students— nearly 3 million people—thought that a revolution was needed in the United States. Radical sentiment ran even stronger in the African American community and by the early 1970s had penetrated deeply into the Puerto Rican, Chicano, Asian American, and Native American populations. A 1970 survey showed that 30.6 percent of Black enlisted men in the armed forces planned 'to join a militant Black group like the Panthers' when they returned home.[146]

Black autonomous learning projects emerged. *Uhuru Sasa Shule* [Freedom Now School], a Central Brooklyn Afrocentric school serving children ages three to seventeen, was opened in February 1970 by former Ocean Hill-Brownsville teacher Jitu Weusi.[147] The previous year, the Black Panther Party (BPP) held a conference in Oakland where they strategized about how to build Black Studies Departments nationwide. Black and Puerto Rican CUNY students attended this conference and returned with plans to create Black and Puerto Rican Studies Departments at CUNY. The local BPP chapter coordinated free breakfasts and health clinics and offered political education classes for youth and adults, while the *Black Panthers Speak* newspaper offered mobile learning opportunities wherever people gathered to sell and read it.

Puerto Rican community learning also blossomed. The Young Lords, a revolutionary youth group, coordinated neighborhood direct actions in the Lower East Side, Spanish Harlem, and the Bronx to address issues like city disposal services, hospital care, lead-safe housing, and to ensure that community spaces like churches were

---

144 National Center for Education Statistics, *120 Years of American Education*, 75.

145 Mario D. Fantini et al., *Community Control and the Urban School* (Westport: Praeger Publishers, 1970), 245–246.

146 Max Elbaum, *Revolution in the Air: Sixties Radicals Turn to Lenin, Mao, and Che* (New York: Verso, 2002), 18. Max Kleinman also recalls of one May 1970 youth mobilization, "We shut down the whole New York City fucking school system. . . . [Stuyvesant High School students] led a march from Manhattan over the Brooklyn Bridge and met Boys High and all those dudes coming from Brooklyn, and then came back, took over the New School on Fifth Avenue and made that the headquarters. You don't even understand: there were barricades in the street, people were ready for war." See Sean Stewart, ed., *On the Ground: An Illustrated Anecdotal History of the Sixties Underground Press in the U.S.* (Oakland: PM Press, 2011), 90.

147 Rickford, *We Are an African People*, 70–73.

opened to people's needs.[148] For a group whose median age was seventeen, their newspaper, *Pa'lante*, was preternaturally advanced in its attention to Puerto Rican history and the enduring effects of colonialism, racism, and sexism on the island and diaspora. In early 1970, another Puerto Rican group on the Upper West Side named "'El Comité'—made up of Vietnam veterans, factory and construction workers, the unemployed, and former gang members—took over a storefront on 88th Street and Columbus Avenue." By the summer, historian José E. Velásquez writes, they co-coordinated "Operation Move-In." Activists broke into and squatted nine buildings on Columbus Avenue in opposition to the City's "urban renewal" program, which many Black and Puerto Rican neighborhood residents described as "urban removal" of their families.[149] Chris Iijima and JoAnne Miyamoto of the radical Asian American folk group A Grain of Sand supported these efforts, squatting a storefront on 88th Street and Amsterdam Avenue to create a social center for Asian Americans called "'Chickens Come Home to Roost,' after Malcolm X's famous dictum that American violence would return to haunt the nation."[150]

In 1971, the Young Lords collaborated with the Puerto Rican Student Union (PRSU) to hold a conference at Columbia University. One thousand students gathered to create "Free Puerto Rico Now Committees" in high schools and colleges. That October, they coordinated a march of ten thousand people from El Barrio to the United Nations to "demand the end of US colonialism in Puerto Rico, freedom for Puerto Rican political prisoners, and an end to police brutality in our communities."[151] This emerging vision offered models for Puerto Rican Studies that could be formalized in public schools and higher education in New York. Across the country, Puerto Rican Studies programs were concentrated in the East Coast and Midwestern cities where Puerto Ricans had migrated decades earlier. They were limited when compared to the nationwide spread of Black Studies in the early 1970s. In places like New York, however, the intertwined Black and Puerto Rican learning/living/organizing communities were reflected in the implementation of Black and Puerto Rican Studies in universities.

Asian American Studies and Native American Studies also developed through cultural and political initiatives in New York City, the Midwest, and on the West Coast during this time. The revolutionary newspaper *Gidra: The Monthly of the Asian American Experience* was launched in 1969. In 1970, the Basement Workshop formed and began publishing *Bridge: The Magazine of Asians in America*.[152] The communist Red Guard Party transitioned into I Wor Kuen in 1971, shifting from ultra-militancy to

---

148 Fernández, *The Young Lords*; *The Takeover*, dir. Emma Francis-Snyder (Brooklyn: Market Road Films, 2021).

149 José E. Velásquez, "Another West Side Story: An Interview with Members of El Comité-MINP," in *Puerto Rican Movement: Voices from the Diaspora*, 88. See also Oksana Mironova, "'The scythe of progress must move northward': Urban Renewal on the Upper West Side," *Urban Omnibus*, June 10, 2015, https://urbanomnibus.net/2015/06/the-scythe-of-progress-must-move-northward-urban-renewal-on-the-upper-west-side/.

150 Maeda, *Chains of Babylon*, 147.

151 Iris Morales and Denise Oliver-Vélez, "Why Read the Young Lords Today?" in Darrel Enck-Wanzer, ed., *The Young Lords: A Reader* (New York: New York University Press, 2010), ix. See also Meg Starr, "Hit Them Harder: Leadership, Solidarity, and the Puerto Rican Independence Movement," in Dan Berger, ed., *The Hidden 1970s: Histories of Radicalism* (New Brunswick: Rutgers University Press, 2010), 135–154.

152 See Ryan Lee Wong, "Basement Workshop: The Genesis of Asian American Resistance Culture," n.d., https://www.ryanleewong.com/essays-and-criticism/project-five-wwka6/.

community organizing with an explicit focus on women's liberation. A number of I Wor Kuen members were City College students who traveled from Chinatown to Harlem.[153] Asian American activists transformed the politics of the antiwar movement from "bring the troops home" to "stop killing *our* Asian brothers and sisters."[154] Asian American Studies was beginning to coalesce with anthologies like Franklin Odo's *Roots: An Asian American Reader* (1971), Kai-yu Hsu and Helen Palubinskas's *Asian-American Authors* (1972), David Hsin-fu Wand's *Asian-American Heritage* (1974), and the landmark 1974 work *Aiiieeeee! An Anthology of Asian-American Writers*.[155] Native American Studies were inspired by direct actions carried out by the American Indian Movement (AIM), including the occupations of Alcatraz Island, Mount Rushmore, and the Bureau of Indian Affairs, and by confrontations with colonial authorities at Wounded Knee and the proliferation of "survival schools" in the Midwest.[156] The American Indian Community House in New York was formed in 1969.[157] On the West Coast, Jack D. Forbes led the creation of curriculum and infrastructure for D-Q University, a semi-autonomous school of Native American Studies at University of California–Davis.[158]

Women's liberation projects also became institutionally rooted in 1970. In this year, two anthologies—Toni Cade Bambara's *The Black Woman* and Robin Morgan's *Sisterhood is Powerful*—announced that the new decade would center women's militancy. New York City was home to Black, Euro, and Third World women's groups such as Marxist-Feminist Group 1 (MF1), New York Radical Women, Redstockings, Third World Women's Alliance, and the Women's International Terrorist Conspiracy from Hell (WITCH).[159] All told, "the first two women's studies programs were established in 1970, followed by cumulative totals of 15 programs by 1971, 75 by 1973, and 152 by 1975." Several of these programs, like those at like Brooklyn College and City College, were explicitly socialist feminist.[160] The Brooklyn College Women's Organization formed in 1971 successfully implemented a Women's Studies baccalaureate degree in 1974 and won a landmark case against sex discrimination.[161] These efforts at creating new departments and classes sought to reverse the long-standing patriarchal structure of the university.

---

153 Maeda, *Chains of Babylon*, 92–93. Kim Geron, Michael Liu, and Tracy A. M. Lai, *The Snake Dance of Asian American Activism: Community, Vision, and Power* (Washington, DC: Lexington Books, 1994), 84.

154 Maeda, *Chains of Babylon*, 122–123.

155 Hua Hsu, "The Asian-American Canon Breakers," *New Yorker*, December 30, 2019, https://www.newyorker.com/magazine/2020/01/06/the-asian-american-canon-breakers/.

156 Julie L. Davis, *Survival Schools: The American Indian Movement and Community Education in the Twin Cities* (Minneapolis: University of Minnesota Press, 2013).

157 See the "American Indian Community House 50 Winters" project, https://aich50winters.com/.

158 See Jack D. Forbes, *"Yanga Ya," Selected Poems & The Goals of Education* (Parts I & II), in *Lost & Found: The CUNY Poetics Document Initiative*, ed. William Camponovo (New York: The Center for the Humanities, Graduate Center of the City University of New York, 2017).

159 Several Third World Women's Alliance members were CUNY students. See Patricia Romney, *We Were There: The Third World Women's Alliance & The Second Wave* (New York: Feminist Press, 2021).

160 Florence Howe, "New Curricular Focus in Women's Studies Programs," *Women's Studies Newsletter* 4 (Winter 1976): 1–2, 8–11. See also Judith Gardiner, "What Happened to Socialist Feminist Women's Studies?" *Feminist Studies* 34, no. 3 (Fall 2008): 567.

161 "Oral History Interview with Renate Bridenthal," CUNY Digital History Archive, April 21, 2016, https://cdha.cuny.edu/items/show/3112; "Oral History Interview with Lilia Melani," CUNY Digital History Archive, May 22, 2019, https://cdha.cuny.edu/items/show/10642/.

Once embedded in universities, coalitional efforts at creating Black, Puerto Rican, and Women's Studies risked becoming atomized, but also shared tributaries with each other that flowed outwards.[162] At its inception, Women's Studies was easier to institutionalize than Black and Puerto Rican Studies because there were already many more (Euro) women than Black and Puerto Rican educators.[163] However, because Black and Third World insurgencies opened the space for Women's Studies to become formalized, this produced several significant effects. The transition from decentralized affinity-consensus models drawn from early 1960s freedom schools to more "tightened up" hierarchical models influenced the pedagogy of Black and Puerto Rican classrooms. Meanwhile, women's liberation pedagogies (most notably consciousness raising) that had been inspired by the Black freedom struggle often maintained the former decentralized ethos. Consciousness raising, a "major new organizational form, theory of knowledge, and research tool of the women's movement," spread widely in Women's Studies classrooms across the country. Combining the Black Freedom Struggle's church sessions of "telling it like it is" with inspiration from women in the Chinese Revolution "speaking bitterness" in public against their husbands, consciousness raising revealed how Women's Liberation/Studies was nourished by other struggles.[164]

Because Women's Studies' reach exceeded that of isolated and embattled Black and Puerto Rican Studies Departments, its practitioners were able to extend the pedagogical practices of Black and Puerto Rican Studies further into the university, even as Euro women educators became their public face. Still, many Euro Women's Studies educators tried to hire or offer platforms to Black and Puerto Rican women educators as an act of pedagogical solidarity.[165] Black, Puerto Rican, and Third World Women's Studies initiatives in the 1970s thus became a crucial nexus for liberatory forms and contents to entwine, producing some of the most significant breakthroughs in pedagogy, publishing, and organization-building with the Combahee River Collective, The Damned, Kitchen Table: Women of Color Press, and the Third World Women's Alliance.

Ethnic and Gender Studies Divisions

In 1971, Federico Aquino-Bermudez drafted a proposal for a Department of Puerto Rican Studies that envisioned how City College could be a Puerto Rican intellectual and political epicenter. He noted that the college's Education, History, and Romance

---

162 Although a comprehensive narrative of the rise of Asian American, Chicanx, Indigenous, and Pacific Islander Studies is outside the scope of this book, I encourage people to read the 1973 City College Asian American student manifesto and Jack D. Forbes' efforts to create Native American Studies in California as a few examples from these counter-institutional struggles. See Fred Ho, Carolyn Antonio, Diane Fujino, and Steve Yip (eds.), *Legacy to Liberation: Politics and Culture of Revolutionary Asian/Pacific America* (Chico: AK Press, 2000); Jack D. Forbes, "Yanga Ya"; Rodolfo Acuña, *The Making of Chicana/o Studies: In the Trenches of Academe* (New Brunswick: Rutgers University Press, 2011); and Janet Alison Hoskins and Viet Thanh Nguyen, eds., *TransPacific Studies: Framing an Emerging Field* (Honolulu: University of Hawaii Press, 2014).

163 Elaine Showalter, "Introduction: Teaching about Women, 1971," in *Female Studies IV*, ed. Elaine Showalter and Carol Ohmann (Pittsburgh: KNOW, Inc., 1972), iii.

164 Baxandall, "Re-Visioning the Women's Liberation Movement's Narrative," 226 and 233.

165 "Oral History Interview with Tucker Pamella Farley," CUNY Digital History Archive, May 15, 2016, cdha.cuny.edu/items/show/4992/.

Languages Departments refused to offer courses relevant to Puerto Rican Studies and resisted when the Urban and Ethnic Studies (UES) Department tried to initiate them. Even so, the number of students who took courses on Puerto Rico jumped from 90 students in Fall 1969 to 250 in Fall 1970 to 350 in 1971. At the time, Puerto Ricans comprised about 9.3 percent of the city's population—nearly 1 million people—and 12.8 percent of Manhattan's population, but still only 4.6 percent of City College students.[166] In his proposal, Aquino-Bermudez identified some inherent antagonisms of Puerto Rican Studies within settler-colonial US universities, which persist today:

> The department should assume an advocacy role in institutional and so-
> cial change. . . . [A]s the department or its students move into conflict
> roles and conflict issues, the pressures on the part of the University's ad-
> ministration as well as the political establishment will increase to dimin-
> ish these activities. The department, however, has to constantly probe
> and push the limits to which such an activist role can be developed and
> sustained.[167]

As Aquino-Bermudez advocated the creation of a Puerto Rican Studies Department, so too did his colleagues in Afro-American Studies, Asian American Studies, and Jewish Studies.[168] By Spring 1971, UES Chairperson Osborne Scott, who had been hired to deescalate campus dissent, warned that the creation of four distinct depart-ments would increase "competition among the various ethnic groups for resources, fac-ulty lines, and facilities."[169] As UES suffered implementation woes, the Department of Jewish Studies was being fast-tracked for approval, with the potential to grant master's and doctoral degrees in the future.[170] By this time, the 1969 strike's demand for the cre-ation of a School of Black and Puerto Rican Studies had transformed into calls for a School of Third World Studies. Nevertheless, the CUNY Board of Higher Education fractured these coalitional studies into more siloed departments.

In March 1972, a group called "Concerned Asian Students" led a three-day take-over of Goethals Hall at City College, with support from Black and Puerto Rican stu-dents as well as other Asian American students from around the city. Before it ended, the occupation swelled to three hundred people. *Bridge* documented how this action reflected the shifting conditions of Asian American immigration to New York follow-ing passage of the 1965 Hart-Celler Act:

---

166 Within a year, City College would enroll more Puerto Rican students than any other college in the United States. See Meyer Weinberg, *A Chance to Learn: The History of Race and Education in the United States* (Cambridge: Cambridge University Press, 1977), 345–346. Cited in Carmen Kynard, *Vernacular Insur-rections: Race, Black Protest, and the New Century in Composition-Literacies Studies* (Albany: SUNY Press, 2014), 159.

167 Federico Aquino Bermudez, "Proposal for Department of Puerto Rican Studies, 1971–76," 7–8, 36, 37. The City University of New York, City College, Archives and Special Collections, Department of Puerto Rican Studies Papers, Box 1. See also Aquino Bermudez, "Growth and Development of Puerto Rican Studies Departments: A Case Study of Two Departments at the City University of New York," PhD diss., University of Massachusetts Amherst, 1974.

168 City University of New York Board of Higher Education Minutes (1971), 106, https://policy.cuny.edu/policyimport/board_meeting_minutes/1971/document.pdf.

169 Ernest Wu, "Scott Calls Proposal to Disband Dept 'Political Expedient,'" *The Campus*, March 26, 1971, 3. See also "Ethnic Error," *The Campus*, April 16, 1971, 4.

170 "Jewish Studies," *The Paper*, December 17, 1970, 4.

The significance of these events at City College cannot be isolated from the background of the Asian students. In New York City there are perhaps 70,000 Chinese residing on the Lower East Side, including Chinatown proper. There are an additional 50,000 Chinese, Japanese, Filipinos, Koreans and other Asians throughout the rest of the metropolitan area.[171]

CUNY historian Linda Luu foregrounds the "coalitional dimensions of this action, both between students of color on campus, but also between students and community activists. . . . Ethnic studies programs, therefore, are not only borne out of movement struggle, but crucial to maintaining the lifeline of that struggle."[172] The protests resulted in the creation of an Asian American Studies program within the existing Asian Studies Department, a powerful example of how campaigns for Ethnic Studies worked to recompose pre-existing departments to suit their needs.[173] Yuri Kochiyama was one of the first people invited to teach, writes Diane C. Fujino: "Yuri taught about the Vietnam War, the movement to remove US bases in Okinawa, [and] the imposition of martial law in the Philippines."[174] Harlem University was shifting and expanding to include these new liberatory studies.

Perhaps because of this coalescence, City College administrators housed Black Studies and Puerto Rican Studies in the Social Sciences Division, and Asian Studies and Jewish Studies in the Humanities Division, in an apparent effort to create political divisions at the institutional level. It's worth speculating whether these new departments felt compelled to adhere to some disciplinary methodologies over others or to occlude historical links across ethnic lineages. Black Studies courses focused on African, Afro-American, and Anglophonic Afro-Caribbean histories and societies, but gave little space to Afro-Puerto Ricans and other Afro-Caribbean Spanish speakers, or to Afro-Asian, Afro-Indigenous, Afro-Jewish, and Afro-Latin American histories. Similarly, Puerto Rican Studies were not supposed to focus on African, Indigenous, and Jewish connections, though instructors often ignored this constraint.[175] Meanwhile, Asian Studies elided the history of Asian immigration to the Caribbean while Jewish Studies overlooked its long relationship to Black liberation and to the broader ethnic lineages that comprise the Jewish diaspora. The course catalogue for Fall 1972 included a Black Studies course on the Prison and Concentration Camp and a separate Jewish Studies course on the Holocaust and Concentration Camps. Reading across the courses offered in each department reveals connections that were missed or made impossible by the college's imposed restrictions.

Comparing the scene in the 1920s–1930s to this late 1960s–early 1970s period at City College reveals the transition in Jewish intellectual and political life following the

---

171 R. Takashi Yanagida, "Asian Students vs. University Control: The Confrontation at C.C.N.Y.," *Bridge* 1.5 (May/June 1972).

172 Linda Luu, "Resistance Everywhere We Went: The Fight for Asian American Studies at CUNY," in Rose M. Kim, Grace M. Cho, and Robin McGinty, eds., *The Children of the People: Writings by and about CUNY Students on Race and Social Justice* (Lewes: DIO Press, 2022), 175.

173 Wei, *The Asian American Movement*, 134; Geron et al., *The Snake Dance of Asian American Activism*, 71.

174 Diane C. Fujino, *Yuri Kochiyama: Heartbeat of Struggle* (Minneapolis: University of Minnesota Press, 2005), 246.

175 Gabriel Haslip-Viera, email communication with the author, February 4, 2020.

Holocaust and the creation of Israel on the stolen land of historic Palestine. Jewish celebration of Yiddish and Levantine cultures and the cultivation of bonds with other oppressed and colonized peoples was supplanted by an insular focus on Israel. As the settler-colony managed, suppressed, and erased the presence of Mizrahi and Sephardic Jews along with Palestinians, Jewish Studies replicated this project on a disciplinary level.[176] The curriculum adhered to circumscribed definitions of American Jewry and paid selective attention to Israel and the Soviet Union in the diaspora.[177] A narrow focus on Jewish "continuity" fostered by City College Jewish Studies Chairperson Rabbi Irving "Yitz" Greenberg also meant a conscious turn away from Asian American, Black, and Puerto Rican Studies.[178] Like City College literature professor Elie Wiesel, Greenberg was inactive in campus debates about Ethnic Studies. This did not prevent them, however, from vociferously defending Israel from campus newspaper critiques that highlighted the state's dehumanizing treatment of Palestinians and its aid to the South African apartheid regime.[179]

In contrast to the administration's support for Jewish Studies, Puerto Rican Studies were constructed from the ground up, as were Asian American and Black Studies. From its inception, Puerto Rican Studies confronted a preexisting neocolonial canon about a Puerto Rican "culture of poverty." To avoid committing pedagogical violence, Puerto Rican scholars created their own counter-canon.[180] "Everything that we wanted to teach had to be translated from Spanish and mimeographed between 1970 and '74," recounted Edna Acosta-Belén. "We would teach in small groups, and talk about students' experiences themselves as subjects worthy of study."[181] Founded in 1973 at Hunter College, *El Centro de Estudios Puertorriqueños* [The Center for Puerto Rican Studies] produced research task forces, conferences, and *cuadernos* [notebooks] that became the basis for full-length books like *Labor Migration under Capitalism: The Puerto Rican Experience*.[182]

---

176 See Ammiel Alcalay, *After Jews and Arabs: Remaking Levantine Culture* (Minneapolis: University of Minnesota Press, 1993).

177 *The Campus*, "Ethnic Studies Courses," September 3, 1971, 4.

178 Irving "Yitz" Greenberg, "Scholarship and Continuity: Dilemma and Dialectic," *The Teaching of Judaica in American Universities: The Proceedings of a Colloquium* (Association for Jewish Studies, 1970); Shaul Magid, "As Transition Looms, Jewish Studies is Mired in Controversy," *Religion Dispatches*, May 11, 2021, https://religiondispatches.org/as-transition-approaches-jewish-studies-is-mired-in-controversy/.

179 Irving Greenberg and Elie Wiesel, "Letters to the Collective," *The Paper*, December 18, 1975, 4; Alan Kaufman, *Drunken Angel: A Memoir* (Jersey City: Viva Editions, 2013), 48.

180 Carmen Whalen, "Radical Contexts: Puerto Rican Politics in the 1960s and 1970s and the Center for Puerto Rican Studies," *CENTRO: Journal of the Center for Puerto Rican Studies Journal* 21, no. 2 (2009): 229.

181 Edna Acosta-Belén, in Center for Puerto-Rican Studies-Centro, "Afternoon Tertulia: Puerto Rican Studies in CUNY: The First Fifty Years," a conversation with Virginia Sanchez-Korrol, María E. Pérez y Gonzalez, Conor Tomás Reed, and Edna Acosta-Belén, moderated by Ricardo Gabriel, April 7, 2022, https://youtu.be/tbD3YjnbcjE/.

182 History Task Force, *Labor Migration under Capitalism: The Puerto Rican Experience* (New York: Monthly Review Press, 1979).

Fiscal Crises

From the onset of Open Admissions in 1970 to the end of the 1975–76 academic year, CUNY had shifted from being a majority Euro student body to a predominantly Black, Latinx, and Asian student body that now faithfully reflected the ethnic composition of the city at large. Just as this occurred, however, the Board of Higher Education announced plans to implement tuition, a policy demanded by the federal government in exchange for addressing the state's fiscal crisis. Coupled with the city's financial crisis and the US defeat in Vietnam, the racist claim that Open Admissions only benefited poor Blacks and Puerto Ricans paved the way for the CUNY administration to impose tuition on all students. Tuition at CUNY became a nationally recognized issue. Populated by future architects of neoliberal ideology like Chief of Staff Donald Rumsfeld and economic advisor Alan Greenspan, President Ford's cabinet worked to usher in measures that continue to shape our economy today.[183] Ford railed against the "self-indulgent luxury of open admissions and free tuition at City University." His press secretary took the condemnation further by claiming that CUNY's slum conditions fostered Black and Puerto Rican cultures of poverty and addiction. New York City and its public university were likened to "a wayward daughter hooked on heroin"—"You don't give her $100 a day to support her habit. You make her go cold turkey to break her habit."[184] CUNY became a nationwide experiment in the neoliberal privatization of public goods like free college education. This set the stage for sweeping counterinsurgency efforts.

Since 1970, there had been both a liberal and a liberationist vision for Open Admissions, which resulted in an uneven defense when the policy came under fire in the middle of the decade.[185] Despite student walkouts, faculty hunger strikes, campus occupations, and community rallies, a mass campaign to defend free tuition did not emerge. Historian Kim Phillips-Fein stresses that even though imposing tuition to raise $32 million was a "drop in the bucket of what the city needed" to pay off its municipal debt, the Emergency Financial Control Board (EFCB) and Municipal Assistance Corporation (MAC) were convinced that "it wasn't the money that mattered but the symbolism of it." For their part, the city's labor unions became complicit by purchasing MAC bonds with pension funds. The result, according to Phillips-Fein, was "an unexpected commonality between the city's public sector unions and its banks: both were now among New York's largest creditors. . . . With the public and private sector unions both securely on board with business interests, neighborhood groups were left without any coordinated resistance to the city's budget cuts."[186]

The imposition of tuition in Fall 1976 occurred alongside six thousand layoffs (five thousand adjuncts and one thousand full-time staff and tenure-track faculty). Among the axed faculty were many who had helped to usher in Open Admissions. A quarter of the student body disappeared from classrooms.[187] Hostos and John

183 Kim Phillips-Fein, *Fear City: New York's Fiscal Crisis and the Rise of Austerity Politics* (New York: Metropolitan Books, 2017), 2, 40–41.

184 H. Bruce Franklin, *Vietnam & Other American Fantasies* (Amherst: University of Massachusetts Press, 2000), 127.

185 Gunderson, "The Struggle for CUNY," 14.

186 Save Hostos!," CUNY Digital History Archive, https://cdha.cuny.edu/collections/show/172/. See also Phillips-Fein, "The College in the Tire Factory," in *Fear City*.

187 Phillips-Fein, *Fear City*, 139, 207, 253, 263–264.

Jay Colleges were almost shuttered but survived due to massive campus/community campaigns to save them.[188] Medgar Evers and York Colleges resisted being reduced from baccalaureate to associate degree-granting schools.[189] Still, the aggressive economic assault reversed the gains of the 1960s and '70s. It would soon bend the nation's cities and colleges toward privatization and sharpened inequalities.[190]

This setback in educational access was coupled, however, with news of a breakthrough in language justice at City College. In May 1976, Puerto Rican Studies chairperson Aquino-Bermudez announced his receipt of a $25,000 federal grant to implement bilingual education. While thirteen Black professors in the City College English Department—including June Jordan—had been on a three-day hunger strike to protest tuition and major budget cuts, and Hostos College's bilingual education was at risk of elimination, Puerto Rican Studies at City College finally got support for a bilingual education demand dating back to the 1969 strike.[191] The state granted seed money to a specific program rather than addressing resource needs across the institution. Nevertheless, bilingual education prioritized important struggles like translation fluency and language justice.

Meanwhile, historian Meg Starr explains, "As the war in Southeast Asia wound down, activists who had been supporting the Vietnamese National Liberation Front focused greater attention on other liberation movements."[192] This meant that Puerto Rican and Palestinian independence, along with anti-apartheid struggles in South Africa, now became a central focus for the radical left within the US, especially with UPR and Soweto students mounting direct confrontations with police.[193]

City College's various Ethnic Studies departments fared differently in the years following CUNY's implementation of tuition. In Fall 1978, the Jewish Studies Department was reduced to three courses, two faculty members, and only one student majoring in the subject. In contrast, Black Studies had 52 courses, 1,400 students, and 18 faculty members, while Puerto Rican Studies had 23 courses, 535 students, and 8 faculty members. Asian American Studies also had "little problem attracting students."[194]

During the early to mid-1980s, New York City continued to transform as Caribbean and Latin American families (in particular, from the Dominican Republic) as well as Asians and Pacific Islanders continued to migrate to the city. This influx

---

188 "Save Hostos!," CUNY Digital History Archive, https://cdha.cuny.edu/collections/show/172/. See also Phillips-Fein, "The College in the Tire Factory," in *Fear City*, 241–255.

189 "The Founding of Medgar Evers College," CUNY Digital History Archive, https://cdha.cuny.edu/collections/show/111/.

190 See Joshua B. Freeman, *Working-Class New York: Life and Labor Since World War II* (New York: New Press, 2000); Naomi Klein, *The Shock Doctrine: The Rise of Disaster Capitalism* (London: Picador, 2008). The unelected, unaccountable Financial Control Board continues to exist and could again assume sole economic decision-making power if New York were to risk default. See Phillips-Fein, *Fear City*, 312.

191 Pamela Mahabeer, "13 Black Profs Call Hunger Strike to Protest City U 'Resegregation,'" *The Campus*, May 7, 1976.

192 Starr, "Hit Them Harder," 140.

193 Sara Awartani, "In Solidarity: Palestine in the Puerto Rican Political Imaginary," *Radical History Review* 128 (2017): 199–222; Cacimar Cruz Crespo, *Solidaridad Obrero-Estudiantil: las huelgas de 1973 y 1976 en la Universidad de Puerto Rico* (San Juan: Fundación Francisco Manrique Cabrera, 2014); Ann Heffernan and Noor Nieftagodien, *Students Must Rise: Youth Struggle in South Africa Before and Beyond Soweto '76* (Johannesburg: Wits University Press, 2016).

194 Linda Tillman, "Jewish Studies Threatened," *The Campus*, September 29, 1978.

altered the composition of CUNY such that Puerto Ricans were no longer the majority among Caribbean and Latin American students. Meanwhile, a major counterinsurgency-inspired architectural change occurred on the campus. The North Academic Center (NAC), a massive multilevel building that had been under construction since the early 1970s, replaced several buildings on the South Campus that students had occupied in 1969. Designed to look like a ship with a bow, smokestacks, and even a gangplank, NAC was intentionally built with dozens of entrances so that it couldn't be occupied. The architect, John Carl Warnecke, had previously designed prisons.[195] Carol Smith recalled that for the first twenty years of NAC's existence, no hallway signs delineated where classrooms were located. People would wander around, lost, from one area to another, searching for their classes and offices.[196]

By the late 1980s, City College faculty began supporting an emerging wave of students who led protests against tuition increases and budget cuts under Governor Mario Cuomo. These efforts culminated in more than a dozen campus occupations across CUNY in 1989, including at City College's NAC building. Student militants took control of a room on NAC's third floor, close to an entrance at 137th Street and Amsterdam Avenue. There, they created the Guillermo Morales/Assata Shakur Community and Student Center at City College. These actions were followed by another wave of protests against tuition increases and budget cuts in 1991.[197]

Inspired by the Zapatistas in Mexico and by the Intifadas in Palestine, organizers with the CUNY Coalition against the Cuts, Black Student Union, Palestinian Club, Arab Club, and Puerto Rican Club formed the Student Liberation Action Movement (SLAM!) on the heels of a March 23, 1995 25,000-strong protest against tuition increases and the elimination of the SEEK Program.[198] SLAM! sought to recover free tuition and (truly) Open Admissions, but also to oppose US imperialism. They built vibrant campaigns to defend political prisoners, police violence survivors, Palestine, Puerto Rico, and more. As CUNY people's herstorian Suzy Subways recounts, in addition to its main organizing hub at Hunter College, SLAM! also organized at City College to keep the campus "open and accessible to the surrounding

---

195 "North Academic Center & the CCNY Campus," https://www.ccny.cuny.edu/education/about_us_nac_ccny/. See also Sben Korsh, "Brutality," *New York Review of Architecture* 13 (July 15, 2020), https://newyork.substack.com/p/brutality/.

196 Carol Smith, interview with the author, October 12, 2021.

197 James C. McKinley, Jr., "CUNY Protests Spread to More Schools," *New York Times*, April 28, 1989, https://www.nytimes.com/1989/04/28/nyregion/cuny-protests-spread-to-more-schools.html/; Evelyn Nieves, "Protests Are All but Over at CUNY," *New York Times*, April 28, 1991, https://www.nytimes.com/1991/04/28/nyregion/protests-are-all-but-over-at-cuny.html/; Benjamin Schonberger, "Student Protests Over State Budget Cuts Spread to 8 CUNY Campuses," *Chronicle of Higher Education*, April 17, 1991, https://www.chronicle.com/article/Student-Protests-Over-State/86937/; Katherine T. McCaffrey, Christine Kovic, and Charles R. Menzies, "On Strike: Student Activism, CUNY, and Engaged Anthropology," in *Children of the People*, 135–164.

198 Amaka Okechukwu and Suzy Subways (interviewers), "'It Was Electrifying': Organizers Reflect on the March 23, 1995 CUNY Protest 20 Years Later," *SLAM! Herstory Project* (Philadelphia: SLAM! Herstory Project, 2015), https://slamherstory.wordpress.com/2015/03/23/it-was-electrifying-organizers-reflect-on-the-march-23-1995-cuny-protest-20-years-later/. See also *Don't Shoot the Messenger!: Six Years of Struggle by CCNY's Banned, Stolen, Defunded, Defamed, Award-Winning Student Newspaper, 1998-2004, SLAM! Herstory Project* (Philadelphia: SLAM! Herstory Project, 2013), https://slamherstory.wordpress.com/2013/11/08/dont-shoot-the-messenger-download-this-anthology-of-ccnys-activist-newspaper/; Anna Zeemont, "'The Act of the Paper': Literacy, Racial Capitalism, and Student Protest in the 1990s," PhD diss., CUNY Graduate Center, 2022.

neighborhoods."[199]

In 1998, custodial staff at City College informed students that a smoke detector outside the Morales/Shakur Center was actually a surveillance camera aimed at the Center's door. Black Studies educator Herb Boyd reported, "In an adjoining room the students found a television monitor and an apparent listening device that was aimed at the student lounge."[200] Inside the Center, the Pre-University Program, also known as the Free University, gathered "hundreds of high school students from Harlem and Washington Heights to the campus each weekend for events and academic support."[201]

Even prior to the formal termination of Open Admissions as a policy in 1999, the administration had been aiming for years to curb the entrance of Black and Latinx students who led many of the struggles at CUNY. Over time, SEEK's original vision of empowering the excluded to lay claim to the university's future was distorted into sorting and tracking students through a separate and unequal public university.[202] In 1999, Mayor Rudolph Giuliani's office released a report called "The City University of New York: An Institution Adrift" to justify this re-segregation policy. Incoming Chancellor Matthew Goldstein dishonored the struggles that had transformed the university three decades earlier: "The discussion has to move from the ill-preparedness of students and their dropout rates and all the other things that give the perception of CUNY as a *third world university* . . . we need to shift the focus."[203] Goldstein's word choice was not coincidental. In order to erase both the radical legacy of Black, Latinx, and Asian student struggles and the Open Admissions policy that had increased their presence, the new chancellor used colonialist rhetoric to justify renewed racist admissions practices.[204]

City College, CUNY, and New York City remain central reference points for understanding the lineages and obstacles of freedom learning. They reflect how upheavals were infused into pedagogies, the co-evolution of people's identities and coalitional work, and the massive struggles against unsustainable reforms and counterinsurgencies that punctuated the twentieth century. In particular, City College during the 1960s and '70s offers boundless lessons for students, workers, and communities seeking to transform a school and the society around it. The next three chapters address this two-decade period before we turn our attention in Chapter 5 to CUNY

199 Brad Sigal, "Interview by Suzy Subways: Brad Sigal on SLAM! at City College from 1996 to 2000," *SLAM! Herstory Project* (Philadelphia: SLAM! Herstory Project, 2012), https://slamherstory.wordpress.com/2014/04/07/first-audio-segments-from-the-oral-history-interviews/.

200 *Democracy Now!*, "Secret Surveillance of Students," June 4, 1998, https://www.democracynow.org/1998/6/4/secret_surveillance_of_students/.

201 Sigal, "Interview by Suzy Subways: Brad Sigal on SLAM!"

202 Ira Shor, "Our Apartheid: Writing Instruction and Inequality," *Journal of Basic Writing* 16, no. 1 (Spring 1997): 91–104.

203 Mayor's Advisory Task Force on the City University of New York, "The City University of New York: An Institution Adrift" (1999), CUNY Digital History Archive, https://cdha.cuny.edu/items/show/2421/. (Emphasis added.) See also Karen W. Arenson, "Trustees Anoint CUNY Chief with a Pledge Not to Meddle," *The New York Times*, July 23, 1999, https://www.nytimes.com/1999/07/23/nyregion/trustees-anoint-cuny-chief-with-a-pledge-not-to-meddle.html/.

204 This Eurocentric colonial savior rhetoric persists today in some liberal appeals to save the university. For a critique of this trend within "critical university studies," see Abigail Boggs, Eli Meyerhoff, Nick Mitchell, and Zach Schwartz-Weinstein, "Abolitionist University Studies: An Invitation," *Abolition Journal*, August 28, 2019, https://abolitionjournal.org/abolitionist-university-studies-an-invitation/.

post-9/11. First, we will focus upon three Black educators—Toni Cade Bambara, David Henderson, and June Jordan—who infused their City College classrooms with New York City neighborhood pedagogies, nourished the 1969 campus strike, and then transmitted these energies back out into the world.

CHAPTER 2

CREATING THE "BLACK UNIVERSITY," "BLACK CITY," AND "LIFE STUDIES" WITH TONI CADE BAMBARA, DAVID HENDERSON, AND JUNE JORDAN

What makes a university, city, or method of study "Black"? Is it determined by the historical lineages of the people claiming these spaces and practices? Is it contingent upon the political vision they espouse in the process? Are Black institutions, geographies, and ways of learning mobilized in reaction to the Eurocentric-heterosexist-patriarchal institutions that exist, or do they also emerge from a deep "emancipation circuit" of other kinds of relating and infra-structuring—that which is below the surface of dominant perceptions, a "nation under our feet," a "nation on no map"?[1]

This chapter explores three City College of New York educators—Toni Cade Bambara, David Henderson, and June Jordan—all of whom were born in Harlem within several years of each other, and who worked in a place Henderson called "from harlem to lower east side / the space / of a nation."[2] They were involved in various neighborhood learning programs for Black and Puerto Rican youth and coalitions in Brooklyn, Harlem, and the Lower East Side, sometimes laboring alongside each other. A few years before the April–May 1969 City College campus takeover, Bambara, Henderson, and Jordan embedded these lessons from their previous work inside the campus. Then, at this moment of porous institutional rupture, they boomeranged strike strategies back outwards.

To document Bambara, Henderson, and Jordan during this period, we consider a wide arc of their pedagogical efforts. We therefore place Bambara's memoir sketches and campus newspaper editorials alongside Henderson's street-journalism poetics and youth-learning observations as well as Jordan's housing research and public speeches, all with the goal of measuring their collaborative praxis of creating Life Studies and

---

1 William C. Anderson, *The Nation on No Map: Black Anarchism and Abolition* (Chico: AK Press, 2021); Thulani Davis, *The Emancipation Circuit: Black Activism Forging a Culture of Freedom* (Durham: Duke University Press, 2022); and Steven Hahn, *A Nation Under Our Feet: Black Political Struggles in the Rural South from Slavery to the Great Migration* (Cambridge: Harvard University Press, 2003).

2 David Henderson, *Low East* (Berkeley: North Atlantic Books, 1980).

Black Universities across Black Cities. Reading *coalitionally* reveals the intentions between these teachers' interventions for communities to grow together, to advance, to commune. By studying their individual and collective *compositions* both on and off the page, we can recover Toni Cade Bambara and June Jordan as strategic Black feminist scholars who intervened in the formation of Black/Women's Studies while grasping how Henderson enacted an antiformal learning approach with Black and Puerto Rican youth at City College and in New York City.

In this recounting, we can also resituate the college and city as epicenters of Black and Brown radical education and underscore the material conditions from which these three people's expansive legacies emerged in their essays, fiction, letters, poetry, and speeches. Learning through these efforts by Bambara, Henderson, Jordan can help us to critique the City University and the city as a whole while focusing at the same time on what to create instead—how to develop counter-practices from within the very sites and spaces that we intend to overturn.

Toni Cade Bambara: The Making of a Community Scribe

Growing up on 151st Street between Amsterdam and Broadway until the age of ten, Toni Cade Bambara, born in 1939 as Miltona Mirkin Cade, saw Langston Hughes give presentations to children at the local library, absorbed street smarts from elder women neighbors, and stoked her curiosities through an open-door policy for many apartment buildings and local shops in which the concept of private homes and businesses was rejected in favor of communal belonging. Bambara acted as a "community scribe" for adults by drafting verbal agreements and meeting minutes for neighborhood organizers, running tips to local journalists, and transcribing letters to loved ones.[3] This responsibility to document, interpret, and serve a collectivity would ethically anchor her approach to writing.

Throughout her life, Bambara believed in the power of stories to model the conflicts and potential transformations of oppressed people's lives. In answer to the time-honored question—"who set you flowin'?"—that asks from which Black communities emanate individual trajectories, she wrote autobiographical sketches that mined life experiences to reveal creative practices.[4] In the process, Bambara revealed how others could also dedicate themselves to long-term cultural movement work. Two selections from her archive at Spelman College, "Working At It In Five Parts" and "Puerto Ricans," document how during her youth in Harlem, Bambara readily absorbed Black learning practices and a commitment to multiethnic solidarity, an orientation that shaped her mentorship of Black, Puerto Rican, and Third World students in a variety of universities and social movements, and which she would extend to a nationwide "classroom" through her essays, fiction, and films.

In "Working At It In Five Parts," Bambara recalls an extensive network of street educators who shaped the teacher-activist and cultural worker she would become:

---

3 Toni Cade Bambara, *Deep Sightings and Rescue Missions: Fiction, Essays, and Conversations* (New York: Knopf, 1999), 218.

4 Farah Jasmine Griffin, *"Who Set You Flowin'?": The African-American Migration Narrative* (Oxford: Oxford University Press, 1995).

I hung tough with my Daddy in the Apollo and learned how high the community's standards were/are for musical, comic, and flamboyant rap performances. I hung tough with my mother on Speaker's Corner listening to trade unionists, Pan-Africanists, Ida B. Wells Club organizers, Communists, The Temple People as Muslims were then called, Abyssinians as Rastafarians were known as. On the corner of 125th and 7th Avenue in front of Michaux's Book Store, I learned the power of the word and the particularity of the Afro-centric perspective [and] to appreciate the continuity of the community's wisdoms.[5]

Among significant early sites on the timeline elaborated in Chapter 1, Bambara mentions Speaker's Corner and Michaux's Book Store. The "Corner" on 135th Street and Lenox Avenue served as an "outdoor university," teaching people how to deliver incisive arguments, compel audiences across ideological spectrums, make rhetorical room for call-and-response, and above all, be intellectually relevant to others outside oneself.[6] "Professor" Lewis Michaux's National Memorial African Bookstore—a "House of Common Sense and the Home of Proper Propaganda"—cultivated yet another autonomous lecture space outside it, dubbed "Harlem Square" or "African Square," signaling how Black Studies were meant to circulate off the page as much as on it.

Bambara focused on new coalitional experiences, such as the mass migration of Puerto Ricans to New York City, which redefined cultural relations alongside Black Americans and Afro-Caribbeans, making a Black/white paradigm more prismatic and enhanced by a comparative anticolonial analysis. These new neighbors—some who looked different and some "who looked just like us"—arrived without "any winter clothes" and suffered narrow job prospects in a city that retained little of the uplift promised by the US colonial labor migration plan called "Operation Bootstrap." Puerto Rican children who only spoke Spanish were placed in under-resourced, segregated "special education" schools with Black students. Soon, Black and Puerto Rican neighbors began to work together in local organizing campaigns.

> In the beauty parlors, barber shops, and the candy stores where I hung out, grownups would be talking about the rough deal Puerto Ricans were getting from the landlords—overcharging them, not fixing things. Puerto Ricans got active in community tenant organizing—women working in the garment industry were pretty active too—sometimes hooking up with Black workers[,] white workers[,] with the Chinese, until they had enough numbers for an identifiable group.[7]

---

5 Toni Cade Bambara, "Working At It in Five Parts," Part 1, Box 4, Toni Cade Bambara Papers, Spelman College Archives, Atlanta, GA. See also Makeba Lavan and Conor Tomás Reed, eds., *Toni Cade Bambara: "Realizing the Dream of a Black University" & Other Writings*, Part I, in *Lost & Found: The CUNY Poetics Document Initiative, Series 7* (New York: The Center for the Humanities, Graduate Center of the City University of New York, 2017), 13–14.

6 Bambara, *Deep Sightings and Rescue Missions*, 250–251.

7 "Puerto Ricans (Spoken Version)" is composed of notes Bambara assembled for a voice-over in Frances Negrón-Muntaner's 1994 film *Brincando el Charco*. See Toni Cade Bambara, "Puerto Ricans (Spoken version)," Part 1, Box 3, Toni Cade Bambara Papers; Lavan and Reed, eds., *Toni Cade Bambara: "Realizing the Dream of a Black University" & Other Writings*, Part I, 51–53.

Bambara's intimate and firsthand knowledge of these studies on the streets, and her training at the hands of "insubordinates, dissidents, iconoclasts, oppositionists, change agents, radicals, and revolutionaries" propelled the formation of her teaching efforts inside and outside the university.[8] Her attention to the multiethnic dimensions of Harlem helped shape her efforts to create studies that related Black people's histories to those of their neighbors and coworkers who also struggled against institutional and interpersonal racism in the United States and in a global anticapitalist context.

Bambara first entered the university in 1954 as a Queens College undergraduate studying Theater Arts and English Literature. With poet friends Lorenzo Thomas (an early collaborator with the Society of Umbra, a proto-Black Arts Movement group), she contributed to *Spectrum*, the campus literary journal. Upon graduation in 1959, she traveled to Italy to study theatrical performance, and then returned to New York to work as a social worker and occupational therapist. She was a multifaceted artist who learned dance, mime, and writing as she spent time in the Lower East Side and Harlem around the Society of Umbra, the Beats, folk kids, and other countercultural scenes. In 1961, Bambara enrolled in City College for a Master's program in American literature. Bambara's 1964 MA thesis, "The American Adolescent Apprentice Novel," would inform the short fiction she began to write through the late 1960s for *Liberator*, *Negro Digest*, and *Redbook*.[9] Before long, her keen familiarity with the campus as a student would pivot into her assuming a central role in its transformations.

David Henderson: From Umbra to the Classroom

David Henderson was born in Harlem in 1942. He attended school at Bronx Community College, Hunter College, and the New School for Social Research. In 1962, Henderson began to collaborate with fellow Lower East Side Black poets and artists like Lloyd Addison, Tom Dent, Calvin Hernton, Archie Shepp, and Lorenzo Thomas to host workshops for what would become the Society of Umbra.[10] Their antecedents and collaborators included John Henrik Clarke's Harlem Writers Guild, Dan Watts' *Liberator* journal, Calvin Hicks' group On Guard for Freedom, and the Puerto Rican street poetics of Jorge "El Coco" Brandon.

To produce their first issue of *Umbra Magazine* in March 1963, the group cobbled together funds with "two sensational parties" at the Communist Youth Organization's Lower East Side space, at which Bill Dixon and Archie Shepp performed. Henderson cooked black-eyed peas to ensure a prosperous launch. Soon afterwards, the Umbra poets became infamous for spirited group readings which, Tom Dent recalled, "sounded like a well-orchestrated chorus of deeply intimate revelations," extending the workshop's parameters into public interventions that brought "the soul, the *spirit* of what we were into, a kind of presence . . . anywhere we were."[11] Henderson recalls that Umbra was woven into the downtown radical arts and performance scene, including befriending Peter and Elka Schumann and the Bread and Puppet Theater: "They gave us a space for a whole year!"[12] The group also helped to inaugurate the Black Arts

8 Bambara, *Deep Sightings and Rescue Missions*, 174.

9 Linda Janet Holmes, *A Joyous Revolt: Toni Cade Bambara, Writer and Activist* (Westport: Praeger, 2014).

10 Lorenzo Thomas, "The Shadow World: New York's Umbra Workshop & Origins of the Black Arts Movement," *Callaloo* 4 (October 1978): 67.

11 Tom Dent, "Umbra Days," *Black American Literature Forum* 14, no. 3 (Autumn 1980): 107–108.

12 David Henderson, interview with the author, April 2, 2022.

Repertory Theatre/School in April 1965 by reading poems with LeRoi Jones (later, Amiri Baraka).[13] Henderson infused these early poetry readings and coalitional relationships with joy, curiosity, eclectic cultural wellsprings, and communal nourishment, features that would reappear in his classroom practices. As the poet Iris Cushing locates, "The language Henderson was hearing, feeling, and making was that of both the Lower East Side and Harlem of the 1960s. In spite of his youth, Henderson's poetry drew upon a rich life of experience, responding keenly to the complexities of the world he inhabited."[14]

In Spring 1967, Henderson began to teach for the Teachers and Writers Collaborative, a writers-in-the-schools initiative run through Columbia University. In his visits to segregated Black and Puerto Rican seventh-grade classrooms, Henderson would read his poetry, play music like the Beatles' *Sergeant Pepper's Lonely Hearts Club Band* and James Brown's "Money Won't Change You," and prompt student writing on such open questions as exploring what they felt about "uptown" and "downtown."[15] He paid special appreciation to unsanctioned forms of student writing, finding "the students' individual notebook covers [are] more interesting than the subjects discussed in the classrooms."

Henderson criticized how the culture of formal education demanded that "children view school as a game" in which they had to perform or omit aspects of themselves; as a result, "these children hold valuable experiences inside of them which they are prone to downgrade and push out of their consciousness when [they] are supposed to be learning."[16] In contrast, he wrote, "I had tried to be as nonchalant as possible. Sometimes i would disc-jockey, introducing records and talking a bit about the artist. While they wrote i looked thru their yearbook and other magazines. I didn't interrupt when they spoke among themselves. I tried to be the exact opposite of what a teacher is to them."[17] Moreover, Henderson emphasized how Black poetry can activate youth learning:

> The best way to teach black kids to write is to bring in large doses of
> Gwendolyn Brooks, Langston Hughes, Don L. Lee, Sonia Sanchez,
> Nicholas Guillen, Mari Evans. . . . From the particular and familiar of
> contemporary black poets and writers we can capture the enthusiasm of
> the young student and really begin to teach.[18]

From July 29 to August 4 of 1967, Henderson visited the Summer Experimental Program in Deaf Education, hosted by the Gallaudet College for the Deaf and the

---

13 Clayton Riley, "Living Poetry by Black Arts Group," *Liberator* 5, no. 5 (May 1965): n.p.

14 Iris Cushing, *The First Books of David Henderson and Mary Korte: A Research* (New York: Ugly Duckling Presse, 2020), 8.

15 David Henderson, "June 9, 1967—Presentation to the Students" and "June 16, 1967—Presentation to the Class," *Teachers & Writers Collaborative Newsletter* 1, no. 1 (September 1967).

16 Henderson, "May 19, 1967—Class Observation."

17 Henderson, "June 16, 1967—Presentation to the Class."

18 David Henderson, quoted in Phillip Lopate, "Roots and Origins," in *Journal of a Living Experiment: A Documentary History of the First Ten Years of Teachers & Writers Collaborative* (New York: Teachers & Writers Collaborative, 1979), 104–105.

Kendall Elementary School for Deaf Children. In a report on these experiences, Henderson noted that he was the only Black male teacher and thus one who the children were eager to see. He maintained that despite his work as a poet, he wanted to show them that "words, spoken and written, are not the acme of expression." Henderson decided to show them Charlie Chaplin films and attempted some reflection dialogues afterwards. Even though the teacher with whom he was paired demurred when students asked if they could be in films, Henderson suggested that silent films, pantomime theater, and underground experimental theater all used wordless acting. In seeing a Black woman volunteer teaching the students line dances, and then a jazz group performing, Henderson saw the need for acute nonverbal communication.

In an example of antiracist, disability-attuned pedagogy, Henderson argued that frequently punishing grammar mistakes highlighted some teachers' perceptions of ingrained "cultural" deficiencies in their students' thinking, an attitude which precluded a range of learning styles from flourishing. When looking at the students' writing, Henderson reflected, "in these compositions we have the problem of corrections. Before the kids learn what a sentence is, they are being corrected. Their tenses are being spruced up, capitals put in, sentences rounded. With no sense for whatever word rhythms the deaf child might have going in *his* head. . . . Before my eyes I saw language destroyed by the well-meaning teacher who allowed the *book* to come between him and his student." Henderson linked these pedagogical violences to "compare the deaf child to what is commonly known as the 'culturally deprived' (sic) kid, or meaning the ghetto child. Both have communication handicaps; poor reading ability, writing trouble. Both form a sub-culture. . . . In T & W we have found that lifting the correction ax from over the child often spurs him on to a fuller expression in writing. Might not the same tactic be used with deaf children." Anticipating future coalitional disability and antiracist movements and "crip" pedagogies, Henderson concluded his report, "As I would link their educational problem to that of a ghetto child I would also think that the deaf needs a civil rights (human rights) campaign similar to the negro peoples of america."[19]

Henderson was deeply aware of the social forces outside of the classroom that imperiled his students. Henderson's 1967 poem "Keep on Pushing" analyzed the urban warfare that took place during the 1964 Harlem riots. Black and Puerto Rican residents dodged police bullets and set up makeshift care stations after police killed unarmed fifteen-year-old Black boy James Powell and then occupied the neighborhood, mere days after President Johnson signed the Civil Rights Act. In the poem, Henderson warns of the "crude mathematics" of wide avenues that can swallow protest pickets, easily dismantle popular barricades, and "muster five hundred cops in fifteen minutes," but he also suggests how "For Harlem / reinforcements come from the Bronx / just over the three-borough Bridge. / a shot a cry a rumor / can muster five hundred Negroes / from idle and strategic street corners / bars stoops hallways windows." Henderson zeroes in on the city's intense connectivity: a militant whisper in the Bronx dawn could spread to Harlem by morning rush hour, the Lower East Side by midday, and on to Brooklyn and Queens before dinner. Henderson intimately portrays the Harlem community—Alfonso the fish-and-chips counterman who advocates self-defense, children

19 David Henderson, "Some Impressions: Recorded as a Participant-Observer in the Summer Experimental Program in Deaf Education, Gallaudet College for the Deaf, Kendall Elementary School (for Deaf Children), July 29 to August 4, 1967," in *Journal of a Living Experiment*, 76, 79–80. See also Petra Kuppers, "Crip Time," *Tikkun* 29, no. 4 (Fall 2014): 29–30; Robert McRuer, *Crip Theory: Cultural Signs of Queerness and Disability* (New York: New York University Press, 2006); Jasbir K. Puar, *The Right to Maim: Debility, Capacity, Disability* (Durham: Duke University Press, 2017).

dancing on the street at night—with a dignity that contrasts newspaper accounts of "The Face of Violence" and radio announcements urging "law and order."[20]

Here too, we see Henderson seek to lift another "correction ax," this time from a racist power structure upon working-class Black communities. By his late twenties, Henderson's varied occupations as a "union organizer, picket line boss, messenger, carpenter, presser in a cleaning store, grocery clerk, magazine salesman, schoolteacher, front man" informed his poetic accounts of everyday Black life in New York.[21] Henderson's validation of different learning abilities, coupled with a defense of organized revolt, was soon brought into the City College classroom with Black and Puerto Rican students.

June Jordan: Seeing the Streets, Houses, Trees as Schools

June Jordan's immersive radical pedagogy was also formed by her New York City upbringing. Jordan was born in Harlem in 1936 and raised in Brooklyn by Jamaican parents.[22] In early 1960s Harlem, she regularly conversed with Louis Lomax, Malcolm X, *Amsterdam News* reporters, and CORE members, and first began to study architecture in the midtown Donnell Library.[23] During this time, she lived in a Queens housing project, in an interethnic marriage with a young son in public school, and wrote poetry in the hours after her husband and son had gone to bed.[24] She struggled with how her ideas were sometimes misrepresented, such as her April 1964 "Skyrise for Harlem" collaboration with Buckminster Fuller—a utopian housing redesign plan that would feature a series of conical towers and improved access to the Hudson and East Rivers—which infamously ran under the title "Instant Slum Clearance" in *Esquire*.[25] Jordan also documented the July 1964 Harlem riots firsthand from the street-level perspective of residents chafing under police occupation.[26] Within a year, Jordan would be divorced and a single mother scraping—in the words of Alexis Pauline Gumbs—"the bottom of the barrel." Given this position, Gumbs asks, "What does an architect who is accountable

---

20 David Henderson, "Keep on Pushing," in *De Mayor of Harlem* (New York: E.P. Dutton and Co., 1970), 31, 34–35.

21 The list appears on the book jacket biography for Henderson's *De Mayor of Harlem*.

22 June Jordan, *Soldier: A Poet's Childhood* (New York: Basic Books, 2000).

23 As Cheryl J. Fish, Alexis Pauline Gumbs, Charles Davis, and a growing chorus of others remind us, Jordan was an astute environmental critic, urban designer, and architect. See Cheryl J. Fish, "Place, Emotion, and Environmental Justice in Harlem: June Jordan and Buckminster Fuller's 1965 'Architextual' Collaboration," *Discourse: Journal for Theoretical Studies in Media and Culture* 29, no. 2 (2007): 330–345; Alexis Pauline Gumbs, "Nobody Mean More: Black Feminist Pedagogy and Solidarity," in *The Imperial University: Academic Repression and Scholarly Dissent* (Minneapolis: University of Minnesota Press, 2014), 237–259; Charles Davis, "Representing the 'Architextural' Musings of June Jordan," *Race and Architecture*, November 26, 2013, https://raceandarchitecture.wordpress.com/2013/11/26/writing-and-building-black-utopianism-representing-the-architextural-musings-of-june-jordans-his-own-where-1971/; *June Jordan: Pleasures of Perspectives*, Womxn in Design and Architecture Conference, Princeton University, February 24–25, 2022.

24 June Jordan, "One Way of Beginning This Book," in *Civil Wars* (New York: Simon and Schuster, 1981), xvii–xviii.

25 June Jordan, "Instant Slum Clearance," *Esquire* (April 1965), Series VII, Box 58, Folder 24. June Jordan Papers, 1936–2002, Schlesinger Library on the History of Women in America, Radcliffe Institute, Cambridge, MA. See also Jordan, "Letter to R. Buckminster Fuller (1964)," in *Civil Wars*, 23–28.

26 Jordan, "Letter to Michael (1964)," in *Civil Wars*, 16–22.

to the bottom of the barrel, who can give an account of what that rock and hard place space of choosing feels like, what does that architect imagine and build?"[27]

Jordan's writing interwove culture, history, journalism, poetics, politics, and urban design with an acute interdisciplinary focus, even as she was beleaguered by her conditions of getting by. After her friend Malcolm X's February 1965 assassination—which propelled cultural workers like LeRoi Jones (later Amiri Baraka) to reject downtown multiethnic cultural scenes to create a Black Arts mecca in Harlem—Jordan would mourn the state of the neighborhood where the symbiotic casualties of housing and the human body bled together.[28] Jordan's early writings show an engagement with the themes of housing, urban conditions, and youth that served as a prism for social inequities in much Black and Puerto Rican literature of the post-World War II period.

During this period, Jordan also publicly critiqued both the Black positivism of communist historian Herbert Aptheker and the Black pessimism of Jones/Baraka, thus developing a reputation as an unsparing Black feminist critic who acquiesced to no countercultural icons.[29] Jordan rooted her studies of urban lives in their realities of anguish as well as hope and argued that Aptheker's views on Black "superiority" were both sentimental and imprecise: superiority requires political power, which Black people were denied. As a now-single mother of a young multiethnic son, Jordan was also attentive to how calls for Black separatism by such cultural workers as Jones/Baraka (himself a father of multiethnic children) were inapplicable to her own life, as they contributed to an ahistorical elision of how poor Black, German, Irish, Italian, Puerto Rican, and Russian people had lived as families and neighbors—even as they were pitted against each other—in the Lower East Side, where Baraka had previously lived and where she began to do advocacy work.[30]

In 1966, as debates mounted over the continued racial-economic segregation of the city's public schools and neighborhoods, Jordan began to organize with the community action program Mobilization for Youth (MfY) around housing conditions. Although she is absent from the MfY archival collection's finding aids, Jordan was a central analyst and ghostwriter for the organization.[31] Jordan's July 1966 polemic "The Determining Slum," written for MfY's Housing Department, shows how landlords and city officials intentionally created squalid living quarters to disempower residents. Substandard conditions over time became familiar and seemingly permanent for people amassed in these housing structures. Notably, Jordan refers to the dynamics in pedagogical terms:

27 Alexis Pauline Gumbs, "This Instant: June Jordan and a Black Feminist Poetics of Architecture," a four-part meditation on Black feminist architecture as informed by the Black feminist poet and architect June Jordan, July 22, 2013, https://www.scribd.com/document/155271148/This-Instant-June-Jordan-and-a-Black-Feminist-Poetics-of-Architecture/.

28 June Jordan, "Elegy of Place," *American Dialogue*, October–November 1965. Series VII, Box 58, Folder 24. June Jordan Papers.

29 June Jordan, "Comment on Aptheker's 'The Superiority of the Negro,'" *American Dialog*, October–November 1965; "An Opinion: June Meyer on Negro Aims," *Mademoiselle*, April 1966, Series VII, Box 58, Folders 24–25, June Jordan Papers.

30 To be sure, a reductive contrast between multiethnic collaborator LeRoi Jones in the Lower East Side and Black separatist Amiri Baraka in Harlem and Newark is challenged by his relationships with Diane di Prima and Hettie Jones and his longtime friendship with Euro-American poet Ed Dorn. See Diane di Prima, *Recollections of My Life as a Woman* (New York: Viking Press, 2001); Hettie Jones, *How I Became Hettie Jones* (New York: E.P. Dutton and Co., 1990); Claudia Moreno Pisano, *Amiri Baraka and Edward Dorn: The Collected Letters* (Albuquerque: University of New Mexico Press, 2014).

31 Mobilization for Youth Papers, University Archives, Rare Book & Manuscript Library, Columbia University Libraries.

Crowding is a factor commonly associated with slum life. It's commonly known that crowding impedes efforts at cleanliness, discourages home versus street orientation, handicaps the student, and gives rise to a variety of stressful patterns of interaction. . . . Liberation from crowded living quarters usually implies the street. The street functions as cradle, school, and the opportunity for an 'extended kinship system.'[32]

Jordan suggests that after the cramped home becomes unbearable for the student, the street can expand the field of where militant learning is cultivated. The essay's deterministic conclusions about the inevitable stasis of the poor registered Jordan's own doubts at this moment about the collective capacity for people to improve their lives.[33] However, in the years that followed, as Jordan embarked on a teaching career that would carry through the next several decades, she began to articulate a resistance to such deterministic conclusions in her poetry and in the many essays and speeches where she invoked teaching poetry to children. While never shying away from an accurate description of the living conditions that constrain people's lives, she pointed to student writers whose language generated power and led to actions.

Educator Herb Kohl recruited Jordan to work for Teachers & Writers Collaborative (TWC) around the same time that Henderson began. Beginning in Autumn 1967, through their TWC-sponsored program "The Voice of the Children," Jordan and her Euro collaborator Terri Bush gathered over a dozen Black and Puerto Rican teenagers each weekend, in East Harlem and then in Fort Greene, Brooklyn, to read and write poems and newsletters, listen to music, and make field trips.[34] A note to "Visitors and Adult Friends of the Children," dated 1969–1970, prioritizes children's autonomy, as the memo directs adults to give children space as they work and refrain from passing judgment on their writing.[35]

In a December 1967 essay on the state of Harlem's segregated high schools, "You Can't See the Trees for the School," she profiled four young people, including the Puerto Rican poet Victor Hernández Cruz, a student co-teacher for "Voice of the Children" who had dropped out of high school six months before graduation but was already being published by *Evergreen Review* and would go on to develop poetic fusions in Arabic, English, and Spanish.[36] Jordan assessed the perils and promise of Black and Puerto Rican schools within slums, and identified reforms and pedagogical methods that could be implemented by students, teachers, and neighborhood residents, especially those willing to overcome racial supremacist ways of learning and evaluation. She also argued against her TWC colleagues' occasional predilection for "ghetto sensational-

---

32 June Jordan, "The Determining Slum," Paper submitted to the Housing Department, Mobilization for Youth, July 12, 1966. Series XI, Box 75, Folder 2. June Jordan Papers. See also Conor Tomás Reed and Talia Shalev, eds., *June Jordan: "Life Studies," 1966–1976*, in *Lost & Found: The CUNY Poetics Document Initiative, Series 7*, 16–17.

33 In juxtaposition, read Saidiya Hartman's reflections on this social landscape: "The ward, the Bottom, the ghetto—is an urban commons where the poor assemble, improvise the forms of life, experiment with freedom, and refuse the menial existence scripted for them." Hartman, "The Terrible Beauty of the Slum."

34 June Jordan, "The Voice of the Children (1967)," in *Civil Wars*, 29–38.

35 June Jordan, "Visitors and Adult Friends of the Children," Series V, Box 54, Folder 10, June Jordan Papers.

36 June Jordan, "You Can't See the Trees for the School," *Urban Review*, December 1967, Series VII, Box 58, Folder 25, June Jordan Papers.

ism" in accepting the students' writing in more rudimentary forms.[37] She advocated for new definitions of excellence that centered the validity of students' diverse expressions.

During the time she began teaching children, Jordan was recently divorced and the primary caretaker for her son. She began to actively read and cultivate theories of child development. Because she identified the potential power first-person youth writing holds, Jordan saw her advocacy for young poets as a counterforce to public schools' denigration of their lives. Jordan focused especially on the lives of the Black and Puerto Rican students in her weekend workshops and, soon enough, in the college setting.

Black (Community) Studies at City College

The arrival of these three educators to City College signaled a growing cohesion of community-forged Black Studies that sought to transform the college. After completing her master's degree, in 1965 the twenty-six-year-old Bambara began to teach in City College's Search for Education, Elevation, and Knowledge (SEEK) Program. Bambara was one of the first of an outstanding teaching cohort that included Aijaz Ahmad, Barbara Christian, Addison Gayle, Henderson, Jordan, Audre Lorde, Raymond Patterson, Adrienne Rich, and Mina Shaughnessy. Within a few years, SEEK would become a nucleus for counteracting the institutional inequities entrenched in City College's segregated admissions, Eurocentric curriculum and value systems, and colonial relationship to the surrounding Harlem area.

One of Bambara's close colleagues, Barbara Christian, also began teaching in the SEEK program in 1965, while studying for a doctorate at Columbia. She would go on to help establish African American Studies at UC Berkeley, becoming the first African American woman tenured there. While at City College, though still not a full-time member of the faculty, Christian proved instrumental in preparing the ground for the innovative teaching force that would characterize the SEEK Program. In this early period, Bambara and Christian—deeply familiar with CUNY and citywide radical politics—were seen by their colleagues and students as militant yet approachable, younger yet seasoned.

Christian introduced the work of younger Black writers like David Henderson to the faculty. Henderson recalled his summer 1967 hire at the age of twenty-five in the City College SEEK program as a Poet-in-Residence:

> The first meeting I attended was just after, I mean literally, Langston Hughes's funeral that was amazingly just a few blocks away. That was the first time I was meeting all of the folks who would become the core of that SEEK/CCNY faculty group that came together to support the student demands and the overall reforms of the Strike. The people I first got together with were the African Americans and other Blacks and some Puerto Ricans. No one had been on the job that long because the University had literally just opened up to African Americans due to the pressure of the Civil Rights Movement in the south and especially in the north, where urban rioting was often becoming more and more the result of inequality and protest.
> So we had to kind of get our ducks in a row, our signals in order. I immediately fell in with Barbara Christian who had taken on the role of

---

37 Quoted in Phillip Lopate, "Roots and Origins," in *Journal of a Living Experiment*, 113.

explaining my poetry to the English department inquisitors after several requisite introductory readings. And then there were the students to deal with, and the immediate faculty that included those from the English department who acknowledged the long standing policy of consigning African American literature to second class status in the curriculums.[38]

SEEK faculty traversed (and transcended) these differences of institutional and social standing. In Henderson's 1968 pre-baccalaureate summer writing workshop, he never differentiated himself as instructor from the students, consistently referring to "our workshop" and giving assignments that included "interviewing our older relatives, our grandmothers and grandfathers, grand aunts and the like, so as to give us clues to the ways of our clan."[39] In addition, Henderson turned to a non-Western literary source, *The Arabian Nights*, to inspire students to find new tools to activate speech and writing.

Jordan also helped to form new directions in Black Studies and Women's Studies when she began to teach writing at City College in 1967 at the age of thirty-one. Jordan brought to the bustling campus milieu a thorough understanding of urban politics, social aid programs, and neighborhood rebellions in Brooklyn, Harlem, and the Lower East Side. Even so, like Henderson, she was seen as not quite credentialed by the measure of the English Department's traditionalist pedigree. Only one day before the fall semester began, Herb Kohl—who she knew through Teachers & Writers Collaborative—asked her to teach his class so he could write full-time. Bambara made a point to welcome Jordan by walking her to her first day of teaching with the advice, "Anything you have to give, just give it to them. . . . They'll be grateful for it."[40] Such recollections of the generous sensitivity and encouragement between these Black women educators, and the SEEK cohort overall, demonstrate how their pedagogies were animated by emotional support and interpersonal documentation as well as academic rigor. Jordan later recalled, "It was quite amazing. We didn't think of it as amazing. Everybody was just there and we thought that if we could make democracy come to City College that probably we could have an impact on the concept and perhaps even the practice of public education through the country."[41]

During this initial period of SEEK's maturation, Bambara insisted on a form of mentorship and cooperative spirit that was no-bullshit, strategic, visionary, receptive, and jocular. Through departmental reports, newspaper articles, and public letters to students, Bambara scaffolded a long project of political consciousness toward liberation. This approach is seen in a summer 1968 SEEK seminar report that Bambara facilitated at the Alamac Hotel—a CUNY-wide SEEK dormitory on Broadway and 71st Street—in which students collectively chose the course theme: "Colonialism, Neo-Colonialism, and Liberation." Writing in an unceremonious style to her colleagues, Bambara described the stakes of the weekly lessons:

---

38 David Henderson, email communication with Ammiel Alcalay, shared with the author, October 22, 2013.

39 David Henderson, "PRE-BACCALAUREATE PROGRAM CITY COLLEGE: Report on the Summer Seminar." Series XXVII, Carton 9, Folder 385, Adrienne Rich Papers, 1927–1999, Schlesinger Library on the History of Women in America, Radcliffe Institute, Cambridge, MA. See also Hilary Holladay, *The Power of Adrienne Rich: A Biography* (New York: Penguin, 2020), 186–187.

40 June Jordan, "Black Studies: Bringing Back the Person," in *Moving Towards Home: Political Essays* (London: Virago Press, 1989), 20.

41 June Jordan and Peter Erickson, "After Identity," *Transition* 63 (1994): 141.

These were not students boning up for some exam or other, or feverishly taking notes that would guarantee a spotlight in an upcoming course. These were not students approaching subject matter with a critical attitude equipped with Theme, Plot, Technique, and other tools of the trade. These were students painfully aware of the gaps in their education, frantically alert to their need to establish a viable position, a stance in what is for them a daily toe to toe battle with the uglier elements of this country. It was, then, a course with few limits, no specific end, personal, often agonizing—without a doubt the most difficult kind of course to "teach" for there can be no "control" in the usual pedagogic sense, and without a doubt the most worthwhile kind of educational adventure for it lends itself so easily to two-way learning.

Together, Bambara and these students discussed New York City newspaper articles that addressed colonialism and liberation, Jones/Baraka's collection *Home* (including "Cuba Libre," an essay that circulated in multiple SEEK classrooms), Andre Malraux's *Man's Fate*, Alan Paton's *Cry the Beloved Country*, Eldridge Cleaver's *Soul on Ice*, and the Bill Cosby-narrated CBS special "Black History—Lost, Strayed, or Stolen." Bambara reflected on the limits of teaching fiction to students who contended, "I'm tired of living through fiction" and "[i]dentifying with heroes in books is like masturbating." She flexibly intuited materials and activities that could best engage the students. By evaluating their oral, written, and relational work, Bambara distinguished between literacy and competence, an assessment popularized by SEEK educators, which insisted that writing acuity reflected only one facet of students' intelligence.

Similar to Henderson and Jordan's practices in Teachers & Writers Collaborative, Bambara and her SEEK colleagues modeled an anti-authoritarian position as teachers with "very little academic distance" from their students, which provided the interpretive space to explore their curiosities and make demands upon higher education together. In closing her summer report, Bambara noted the significance of SEEK students' interest in autonomous "experimental college" projects such as the Free Universities and Liberation Schools that appeared alongside—or at times within and against—formal universities. She anticipated that these forms of counter-education "now taking place in universities all over the world" could incite the students' visions for alternative learning inside the belly of the beast. After all, to "establish a 'real' college within the mock college" could upend the legitimacy of the preexisting college structure itself.[42]

Meanwhile, Bambara sustained ties with Black radical organizers and journalists in the New York-based *Liberator* journal, who covered the wave of decolonization struggles in Africa and the Caribbean that propelled demands for self-determination and dignity in the United States.[43] Bambara's 1968 story "The Manipulators" features a candid dialogue between two graduate student women teachers, Helen and Sandy, who navigate access to university resources that had been previously unavailable under de

---

42 Toni Cade Bambara, "Summer 1968 SEEK Report." Series IV, Carton 9, Folder 385. Adrienne Rich Papers. See also Lavan and Reed, eds., *Toni Cade Bambara: "Realizing the Dream of a Black University"& Other Writings*, Part II, 1–12.

43 Christopher M. Tinson, *Radical Intellect: Liberator Magazine and Black Activism in the 1960s* (Chapel Hill: University of North Carolina Press, 2017), 115–118.

facto Jim Crow conditions.[44] Helen surmises that she received positive feedback from uncritical Euro professors, but that she would "prefer help to applause." A fellowship allowed her to cease teaching, tutorials, anything but "breeze in and out of the rare book collection and pick up my check." This tender anomaly in *Liberator*'s ordinarily macro-systemic view of Black rebellions offers a rare glimpse of junior Black women college teachers assessing—as they wisecrack over folding laundry—their tokenization by longtime academic practices of racist and sexist paternalism, even as they welcome the financial support suddenly being offered to them.

At the start of the Spring 1969 semester, as student mobilizations began to more directly trouble the administration, Bambara published an essay, "Realizing the Dream of a Black University," in the February 1969 issue of the campus newspaper *Observation Post*. In this under-recognized early blueprint for Black Studies, Bambara predicted that "an explosion is imminent" and urged City College, Harlem, and the city at large to combine forces to desegregate and decolonize the college. She assailed: "A brief glance at the bulletin will reveal that the English Department is still dipping out of the old Anglo-Saxon bag. . . . The infusion of one or two Black literature courses in their curricula does nothing at all to the deeply entrenched notion that Anglo-Saxon literature is THE LITERATURE." In a contrasting vision, Bambara outlined a curriculum on American Justice and the Afro-American, Negritude, Trends in Western Thought, Psychology and Blacks, Eastern Ethics Through Literature, Revolution, and Root Courses. She identified clear policy and institutional reforms, such as the formation of a "Skills Bank":

> The Center would tap the resources in our community and use as instructors those grandmothers, those on the corner hardheads, those students, those instructors, whoever happens to have the knowledge and expertise we desire, regardless of the number of or absence of degrees, publications, titles, honors.
>
> We have already in our student body and on our staff at the College and in SEEK people who know how to teach instruments, dance, lay out magazines, operate radio stations or restaurants, dismantle cars, take over TV stations, read newspapers for slant, handle landlords and cops, organize committees, set up conferences. The Center should begin then, to set up a network of communications so that one person desiring to set up a course in Caribbean cookery, let's say, could be put in touch with chefs, caterers, linguists, anthropologists, etc.[45]

In doing so, she urged campus and community members to transform various studies *now* with what they already have *now*, instead of deferring to an imagined future standoff with distant administrators. Even if the students weren't able to implement her suggestions at that moment, the seeds had been planted.

For Bambara, "Realizing the Dream of a Black University" entailed a more expan-

44 Toni Cade Bambara, "The Manipulators," *Liberator*, August 1968, 14–15. Manuscripts, Archives and Rare Books Division, Schomburg Center for Research in Black Culture, The New York Public Library.

45 Toni Cade Bambara, "Realizing the Dream of a Black University," *Observation Post* Collection, The City University of New York, City College, Archives and Special Collections. See also Lavan and Reed, eds., *Toni Cade Bambara: "Realizing the Dream of a Black University" & Other Writings*, Part II, 13–26.

sive reinvention than simply adding Black students, teachers, and courses. As Joshua Myers notes, "Such dreaming is the province of Black freedom, for us who were never supposed to imagine a reality unstained by the dream of white supremacist Western forms of order." With her position paper, "Bambara was moving from idea to organization, from concept to concrete manifestation. It was a dream that could be real."[46] This meant upending gendered and racialized disciplinary structures, identifying knowledge credentials outside of the academy, and infusing a partisan and liberatory streak to collective study. To realize this dream, a Black University required a physical place of becoming.

Teaching with the Strike

On April 22, 1969, the campaign to both defend and expand access to City College reached a tipping point, when the Black and Puerto Rican student-led campus occupation shut down official business and established Harlem University for two weeks. With the "City College Takeover," students autonomously created short-term changes that they sought to implement as long-term university policies. The SEEK program's educators sympathized deeply with the strike, which was led by many of their students. As Jordan wrote, "In every sense, from faculty petitions to student manifestoes, to the atmosphere in the cafeteria and the bathrooms, City College signified a revolution in progress. Nobody was eating, sleeping, thinking, or moving around anything except the issues at stake."[47]

Bambara, Henderson, and Jordan were actively involved in the strike. One of Bambara's students, Francee Covington (who reappears in Chapter 4), recalls, "She was in the building with us during the takeover, she came after it was claimed. She spent the night. Her presence was reassuring. Looking back, I think she was there to bear witness if anything went terribly awry, then she could say I'm a faculty member, this is what I saw."[48] Bambara hosted community panels on the Black Aesthetic on campus and encouraged her Black and Puerto Rican women students to document their conversations inside the occupation. Henderson served a central role on the City College strike press team, comprised of supportive faculty members. As the students requested, their role was to sustain the campus takeover, while faculty were to focus on disseminating pro-strike perspectives with captivated news media.[49] As detailed later below, Jordan took this time to work with her students while drafting writing that could reach broader audiences around the country.

A peer dialogue between Black and Puerto Rican women students, which later appeared in Bambara's *The Black Woman* anthology, emerged as one of the few recorded student exchanges from within the campus takeover. What began as informal riffs about natural hair, clothing styles, and independence from traditional family constraints moved into strategic feminist critiques of Black and Euro men students wanting to destroy institutions instead of taking them over. As one participant, Dorothy Randall, paraphrased activist men's salvos, "This university is not gonna grant our demands so we're gonna burn the motherfucker down." She lamented: "Who wants

46 Joshua Myers, *Of Black Study* (London: Pluto Press, 2023), 184, 187.

47 June Jordan, "Black Studies: Bringing Back the Person," *Evergreen Review* 17 (October 1969): 21.

48 Francee Covington, interview with the author, May 22, 2021.

49 David Henderson, interview with the author, April 2, 2022.

momentum with no direction. People get all stirred up at a rally and are ready to smash, burn, kill, rape, murder, anything. But when you talk about direction, ask the question 'What can I do?' You get some irrelevant comeback like 'Relate' or 'Get on the case.'" Randall identified a prevailing dilemma in militant struggles outlined in this book's Introduction, namely that sometimes visions for revolutionary change do not surpass the destruction of institutions to strategize counter-constructions using the same physical sites. Another participant, Cenen Moreno, drew anticolonial connections between US struggles and Puerto Rico at a time when University of Puerto Rico students were also fomenting upheavals against the Vietnam War and ROTC presence on their campuses, demonstrating further-reaching intentions to commandeer and transform their university rather than reduce it to rubble.[50] These student rap sessions revealed a glimpse of what City College classrooms could become.

Bambara encouraged these student-led initiatives and wasted no time imploring them to maintain energies after the campus occupation ended. In "Dear Bloods," a memo circulated to student organizers immediately after the strike, she minced few words to affirm that making "something out of nothing is so much better than blowing a fuse." Bambara gave examples and contact information for Black women students initiating "counter-courses" on History, Literature, and Sociology. In the process, she repeated lessons from "Realizing the Dream of a Black University" on self-determination and dual power:

> On the assumptions that all of you mumblers, grumblers, malcontents, workers, designers, etc. are serious about what you've been saying ('A real education—blah, blah, blah'), the Afro-American-Hispanic Studies Center is/was set up. Until it is fully operating (fall '69, *the responsibility of getting that education rests with you in large part.* Jumping up and down, foaming at the mouth, rattling coffee-cups and other weaponry don't get it. If you are serious, set up a counter course in the Experimental College. If you are serious, contact each other.[51]

These dialogues between Bambara and her students reflect contradictions that persist today. Because of her close proximity and the trust built with these students, Bambara could critique their shortcomings while pushing for them to actualize demands directly.

In the immediate aftermath of the strike, Jordan also engaged with the students' Five Demands, deploying the same purposeful care that characterized her youth literacy programs. She quickly wrote two unpublished essays—"The City and City College: An off-campus, off-camera perspective," and "Black Commentary on White Discussion of Black Studies."[52] In them, she addressed the demands for the creation of a school of Third World Studies and for incoming students to proportionally reflect the

---

50 Adele Jones and Group, "Ebony Minds, Black Voices," in *The Black Woman: An Anthology*, ed. Toni Cade Bambara (New York: New American Library, 1970), 231–232, 236–237.

51 Toni Cade Bambara, "Dear Bloods," Buell G. Gallagher Papers, The City University of New York, City College, Archives and Special Collections (emphasis in original). See also Lavan and Reed, eds., *Toni Cade Bambara: "Realizing the Dream of a Black University" & Other Writings*, Part II, 27–28.

52 June Jordan, "Black Commentary on White Discussion of Black Studies," Series XI, Box 75, Folder 9; "The City and City College: an off-campus, off-camera perspective," Series XI, Box 75, Folder 11, both in June Jordan Papers. See also Reed and Shalev, eds., *June Jordan: "Life Studies," 1966–1976*, 44–49.

city's Black, Puerto Rican, and Asian high school student population. She wrote, "For Blacks, there is nothing optional about 'Black Experience' and/or 'Black Studies.' We are that experience, and we must study, must know ourselves."[53] While Jordan proposed study alliances between poor people of all colors, this demand for Black Studies by and for Black people (and, by coalitional extension, Puerto Rican and Third World Studies) built upon the community control paradigm that had heightened over the last several years in New York City. Jordan concluded by introducing the term "Life Studies," which would scaffold her vision for years to come: "Beyond Black or White, there is the search for Life Studies, and therefore, there is this question Universities will have to answer, through radical change, or else perish: How do you provide for the Study of Human Life?"[54] Jordan also highlighted how the admissions demand nurtured solidarity between present and future Black, Puerto Rican, and Asian City College students that "reach[es] outside the University province and into high school habits of student tragedy."[55]

These themes would soon be broadcast nationwide in her landmark essay "Black Studies: Bringing Back the Person," published in the October 1969 issue of *Evergreen Review*. This first major published document on Black Studies by a Black woman educator offered a chronicle of the strike and its aftermath and circulated lessons from the City College rebellion to a mass countercultural audience. Read alongside the archives and published writings of Bambara, Christian, Lorde, and others, these essays by Jordan recover how Black feminist teachers at City College shaped explosive institutional changes when the Black Power movement erupted across campuses, even if they were overlooked in favor of Black and Euro men colleagues' efforts.

"Black Studies: Bringing Back the Person" shone a spotlight on the university's design—both physical and ideological—to upend its legitimacy and point toward new forms of collective control by communities of colors. The college's giant iron and stone campus gates stood as a threshold of plantation governance but also potential reclamation: "It lies there, the university campus, frequently green, and signifying power: power to the people who feed their egos on the grass, inside the gates. . . . At the gates, a temporary freedom plays between the student and the school."[56] This liminal space could guard elitist access to education but could also serve as a first defense for those who decided to take over and transform it. A student newspaper account of the strike similarly described how the South Campus was "ringed by massive stone fences crowned with spikes. Access by only four gates made sealing the campus by an occupation force of about 200 quite effective."[57] Jordan argued that as Black students made use of new educational access, they mustn't become dazzled by evaluation metrics—"the deadly,

---

53 Jordan, "Black Commentary on White Discussion of Black Studies." The essay is a retort to US historian Eugene Genovese's article, "Black Studies: Trouble Ahead," published in the June 1969 issue of *Atlantic Monthly*.

54 Jordan, "Black Commentary on White Discussion of Black Studies." Louis Reyes Rivera would later frame this intention to expand into a "Human Education." See Radivojević and Starosta, dirs., *Are You With Me?*

55 Jordan, "City and City College"; Reed and Shalev, eds., *June Jordan: "Life Studies," 1966–1976*, 47.

56 Jordan, "Black Studies," 22, 25. See also Bianca C. Williams, Dian D. Squire, and Frank A. Tuitt, eds., *Plantation Politics and Campus Rebellions: Power, Diversity, and the Emancipatory Struggle in Higher Education* (Albany: SUNY Press, 2021).

57 "CCNY Shut Down," Special report from *Observation Post*, reprinted in *Liberation News Service* (April 24, 1969), https://archive.org/stream/lns-157/LNS-157_djvu.txt/.

neutral definition" of words like *efficiency* and *competence*—that isolate and reward a miraculous few.[58]

In defense of the Black, Puerto Rican, and Third World Studies demand, Jordan wrote, "Black students, looking for truth, demand teachers least likely to lie, least likely to perpetuate the traditions of lying. . . . We request Black teachers of Black Studies. It is not that we believe only Black people can understand the Black experience. It is, rather, that we acknowledge the difference between reality and criticism as the difference between the Host and the Parasite."[59] Roderick A. Ferguson has inverted this distinction as follows: "Like a parasite, black studies would produce critical formations in numbers that the host would never imagine or suspect. Black studies, in this sense, would exploit the academy for sustenance, residency, and dispersal, imagining ways to be more in the academy than of it."[60] Stefano Harney and Fred Moten have likewise written: "In the face of these conditions one can only sneak into the university and steal what one can. To abuse its hospitality, to spite its mission, to join its refugee colony, its gypsy encampment, to be in but not of—this is the path of the subversive intellectual in the modern university."[61] These contemporary reflections on the role of Black Studies in creating fleeting "undercommons" spaces might signal a circumscribed aim in university struggles. In contrast to Jordan's report on the heels of a major campus/ neighborhood strike that contributed to a broader sea change in higher education, these assessments might only suggest marginal possibilities.

While agreeing with Ferguson, Harney, and Moten's calls to liberate university resources from within, we read Jordan as extending some divergent lessons. To call Black Studies "parasitical" implies that its practitioners are "stealing" what's not theirs. Jordan, however, was waging an opposite claim—that the university feeds upon Black lives while erroneously claiming that these Black lives lack value. Like the colonial metropole, the university is an accumulation of all that subjugated peoples have created, not the other way around. If, as Frantz Fanon asserted, "Europe is literally the creation of the Third World," then we can translate this statement to reveal that that the colonial university is the creation of unsung societies around it and must feast on these societies in order to survive as it works to perpetuate dominant social relations.[62] In order to counteract colonialism's upside-down logic, the demand for Black, Puerto Rican, and Third World Studies at CUNY sought to center our peoples' historic value by emplotting our own educators and students, foregrounding our own methodologies of study, and ultimately wresting control of the institution.

Jordan's argument—that the majority of studies on Black, Puerto Rican, and Third World lives are written not from directly lived realities but are products of well-heeled Euro scholars who make careers out of critically representing them—continues to resound. This dynamic is embedded in much longer histories where enslaved Africans' and colonized people's labor produced social institutions, global trade, and even our

58 Jordan, "Black Studies," 22. See also Erica R. Edwards, "Perfect Grammar: June Jordan and the Intelligence of Empire," in *The Other Side of Terror: Black Women and the Culture of US Empire* (New York: New York University Press, 2021), 236–241.

59 Jordan, "Black Studies," 25–26.

60 Roderick A. Ferguson, *The Reorder of Things: The University and its Pedagogies of Minority Difference* (Minneapolis: University of Minnesota Press 2012), 108.

61 Fred Moten and Stefano Harney, *The Undercommons: Fugitive Planning and Black Study* (Brooklyn and London: Autonomedia and Minor Compositions, 2013), 26.

62 Frantz Fanon, *The Wretched of the Earth*, 102.

fundamental conceptions of humanity, freedom, and material value. And yet, it's possible that Jordan was unnecessarily provincializing Black Studies to affirm that only Black people should teach it. Perhaps, in a way that reflects the actual practices of Jordan and her SEEK colleagues, Black teachers could position themselves at the *forefront* of building Black Studies, while non-Black teacher accomplices of Black Studies could reposition themselves as *students* of Black Studies, in a solidaristic approach that would inform coalitions more broadly.[63] While Jordan elsewhere proposed creating study alliances between poor people of all colors, this unapologetic demand for Black Studies by and for Black people built upon the decolonial community control paradigm that had heightened over the last several years in New York City through public school boycotts, freedom schools, and neighborhood rebellions.

In reflecting upon the demand for CUNY to expand admissions to Black, Puerto Rican, and Asian students, Jordan admired the far-reaching implications of creating bridges between present and future City College students. She pointed out how the failures of public schooling affected all New York City children, while students of colors were the most ignored, as in the case of the nearest high school to City College, which had a 65 percent dropout rate. Jordan proclaimed, "Black and Puerto Rican students at the City College . . . insist upon community. Serving the positive implications of Black Studies (Life Studies), students everywhere must insist on new college admissions policies that will guide and accelerate necessary, radical change, at all levels of education."[64] Ferguson suggests that "As 'life studies,' Black studies, for Jordan, is committed to all possibilities of life and not simply the possibility of black lives."[65] Put another way, the success of public education depends on the maximalist demand that every school—kindergarten through college—and every neighborhood must have abundant resources to thrive.[66]

Bambara and Jordan, alongside Barbara Christian, Audre Lorde, and other City College Black women educators, must be championed as early Black, Black Women's, and Third World Studies field-makers, a status we now grant them in hindsight. Other Black women educators—like Sonia Sanchez, who helped form Black Studies at San Francisco State College and briefly taught at City College—are also a part of these understudied interventions. To be sure, at this time, Bambara and Jordan were writing for prominent publications, but as Black women, they were anomalies in the broader emerging field of Black Studies, which was shepherded by men like Amiri Baraka, John Blassingame, John Bracey, Kenneth Clark, Harold Cruse, St. Clair Drake, Eugene Genovese, Nathan Hare, C. L. R. James, Maulana (Ron) Karenga, Martin Kilson, Thomas Sowell, Ekwueme Michael Thelwell, and C. Vann Woodward. Very rarely were Black women featured in the voluminous Black Studies monographs, anthologies, articles, reports, commissions, and conferences that were

---

63 Consider Aijaz Ahmad's faculty description at Livingston College, where he worked with Bambara after their time at City College. He is described as a "poet, translator, short story writer, and student of Black and Third World literature and culture." Similarly, Bambara's listing reads: "short story writer, critic, community organizer, student of Black literature and history." Rutgers University Archives and Special Collections, 1971–72 course catalog; Andrew Goldstone, "For Aijaz Ahmad," *AndrewGoldstone.com* (blog), March 11, 2022, https://andrewgoldstone.com/blog/ahmad/.

64 Jordan, "Black Studies," 28.

65 Ferguson, *The Reorder of Things*, 109.

66 See Jean Anyon, *Radical Possibilities: Public Policy, Urban Education, and a New Social Movement* (Oxfordshire: Routledge, 2005).

produced at the time. In order to foreground these late 1960s foundations of Black Women's Studies, we must underscore the place-based uniqueness of these City College Black feminists' coalitional contributions to an emerging discipline populated almost entirely by Black heterosexual men.

Strike Reverberations in the City

As the City College strike galvanized a wave of protests across the entire university, so too did it animate support in the neighborhoods from which the Black and Puerto Rican students hailed, namely the Bronx, Brooklyn, Harlem, and the Lower East Side. Meanwhile, these SEEK educators worked to boomerang the strike's visions outwards. For David Henderson and June Jordan, this meant turning to another prominent site of educational transformation: Ocean Hill-Brownsville in Brooklyn. As described in Chapter 1, this neighborhood had been at the center of a highly visible conflict between the largely Black and Puerto Rican community, who were given control of the school district as part of an experimental school decentralization program, and the United Federation of Teachers, who led a strike to resist the community board's decision to reassign a number of Euro teachers and administrators to another district.

In his continued work with Teachers & Writers Collaborative as a Spring 1969 poet-in-residence at Ocean Hill-Brownsville's IS 55, Henderson argued that from grade school to the college level, "Black Literature and culture have been largely kept from the public's eyes and more importantly the eyes of the young student . . . who needs exposure to a culture which deals with him and his problems more than anybody else." Combining his TWC and City College pedagogy with attention to impromptu studies on the street, Henderson highlighted one inspiring instance:

> A couple of students and I went on a sort of field trip to the store to get some sodas. In the candy store the knee-high-to-a-grass-hopper students, 10, 11, 12, 13 were smoking cigarettes and dancing amazing African steps to the juke-box. Such a divergence from the uptight school atmosphere. If there were only a way to make the two worlds meet.[67]

This incident between schooling and hooky stayed with Henderson for years after he left New York City for the West Coast in the 1970s. In a 1975 poem "Alvin Cash / Keep on Dancing," which he dedicated "to the children of intermediate school 55, ocean-hill brownsville," the poet-teacher alludes to the places where autonomous embodied Black Studies appear, flourish, and are then forcibly scattered:

> i be standin' on the corner
> got nowhere to go
> the man in the candystore
> say i can't dance there no more
>
> but i got to keep on dancing
> to stop from going mad
> got to keep on moving
> to win you gotta be bad

---

67 David Henderson, "black literature," *Teachers & Writers Collaborative Newsletter* 2, no. 1 (April 1969): 13–14.

> my bones are tunes
> they jump and jive
> i got to keep on dancing
> to keep up with the steps
> that go before me

In an echo of his earlier poem "Keep on Pushing," which embeds a riotous pedagogical moment in a popular soul song, Henderson describes the unsanctioned energy of Black youth who navigate between the directions of their own movements and those that have been imposed by authority figures above them. The repeated mantra—that despite "nowhere to go . . . *i just got to keep on dancing / i just got to keep on dancing*"—highlights the gulf between Black children's embodied curiosities and the social immobility that his teaching sought to transcend.[68]

During this period, Henderson and Jordan's efforts to expand Black Studies percolated further in letters to each other. In October 1969, Henderson envisioned how Black self-determination could occur on a citywide scale. He presciently anticipated the gutting of urban infrastructure and outlined how a holistic approach to construct a "black city" could animate movements for the 1970s and beyond:

> As far as I'm concerned the cities are dying dying dead. It seems that
> most of the plans of black political organizations are involved with try
> ing to salvage something from and within the dying cities... Instead[,] I
> believe it is time for us to get our own cities. As an unofficial lobbyist/
> worker for black folks it would be in the interest of both the rural and ur
> ban black to realize the city, the black city[,] as a form, as a metaphor[,]
> as a goal to strive for and accomplish.[69]

Henderson's vision corresponded with social-territorial movement strategies laid out by other Black revolutionaries at the time. The Republic of New Afrika, and earlier, the Communist Party in its "Black Belt Thesis," demanded that the US government cede several states in the Southeast to Black people's autonomous self-control. In the North, James and Grace Lee Boggs, Harold Cruse, and the Congress of African People called for Black control of ten cities with significant Black populations.[70] Notably, Henderson was attentive to both urban and rural Black sovereignty—a kind of implicit refusal of salvation in a pastoral past. His appeal entailed not an exodus from urban

---

68 David Henderson, "Alvin Cash / Keep on Dancing," *Low East*, 70. See also Henderson's recollections in "Allen Ginsberg & David Henderson at Naropa 1981 (Part One)," January 1, 1970, *The Allen Ginsberg Project* (blog), https://allenginsberg.org/2015/11/allen-ginsberg-david-henderson-at-naropa-1981-part-one/.

69 David Henderson, Letter to June Jordan, Series IV, Box 35, Folder 5, June Jordan Papers.

70 James and Grace Lee Boggs, "The City is the Black Man's Land," *Monthly Review* (April 1966), https://doi.org/10.14452/MR-017-11-1966-04_4; David Henderson, interview with the author, April 2, 2022; Cedric Johnson, *Revolutionaries to Race Leaders: Black Power and The Making of African American Politics* (Minneapolis: University of Minnesota Press, 2007), 78; Anthony James Ratcliff, "Liberation at the End of a Pen: Writing Pan-African Politics of Cultural Struggle," PhD diss., University of Massachusetts Amherst, 2009, 202.

cities, but a capacious reconfiguration of them into Black cities.[71]

In a kind of public response to Henderson's private call, Jordan delivered a June 1970 graduation speech-poem to the same middle school students with whom Henderson had worked at IS 55 in Ocean Hill-Brownsville. In an invitation to transform public schooling and public life, Jordan urged the middle school students to remember "the truth of your absolute value as a human life":

> [I]nsist that your studies shall become Life Studies: Black Studies. Urban Studies. Environmental Studies. The American evidence of contempt for our Afro-American lives can easily be seen when you realize we who are Black, and we who live in urban centers of the country, and we who poison ourselves simply by breathing the air, and we who swallow soap and worms, and worse than that, when we drink a glass of water—we cannot come into any classroom and learn what we need to know. Where are the central, required courses that will teach us our real heritage of heroes and heroines, rebellion, and loving accomplishment? Where are the central, required courses that will teach us how to design and govern cities so that the cities will function as great temples of life that welcome us inside[,] that welcomes our lives? Where are the central, required courses that teach us how to destroy the enemy, urban situation that threatens all life now dwelling inside our city walls?

Jordan's words resonated in an imperiled context of New York City schooling for Black and Brown youth. As she described it, high school at the time was where "a tragic majority of Black and Puerto Rican children drop out of sight: they leave school: because what happens to them in the classroom annihilates their rightful pride, and meets their earnest, real needs with nothing more than irrelevant and contemptuous instruction." In contrast, Life Studies could teach students what they needed to know to thrive and would honor the particularities of their experiences as a route towards emancipation.

Jordan enjoined these students to graduate from high school and enter CUNY one day, but her words also resonated in a communities-of-colors movement for control of education and entire cities:

> We must make ourselves into a community machine that will eliminate and throw out their political machinery. . . . We must no longer wait for somebody to maybe understand our history and then to maybe teach our children the truth. We must no longer simply tremble when we hear the gunfire of police, or state troopers, or the National Guard. We must take control. We must protect our once-only lives, we have to take apart and then replace the whole political life that has proven deadly to our own lives.

---

71 David Henderson recently expanded on this vision: "City College could be the great beginning of a Black city. Conducting research, training students. We could have districts like Harlem across the US, communities where people could do their work and not be bothered because they angered some big shot from another place. Black folks have been fighting this thing for years. The kids are defiant, and should be." Interview with the author, April 2, 2022.

We have to build a Living structure of our own true human community.[72]

Jordan's Life Studies and community machine analyses exceeded the realm of theoretical musings. In a gesture to break out of the binary between Black Studies and all other (white) studies, Jordan framed Black Studies as not just an elective part of the K–PhD curriculum, but central to the study of all human and ecosystemic experiences. Akin to contemporary radical definitions of study, Life Studies requires going beyond formal classrooms to the street, living room, library, riot, and liberated school building to expand where and how study happens to become fundamentally life-nourishing, life-extending.[73] Community machines can be abolitionist, coalitional, mutual aid, youth-oriented, counterpower structures. Jordan fused the relationship between study and movement on the social terrain of the school as a fecund site for assembling "living structures." "For, what is the purpose of a school," Jordan asked these students and their families, "if it will not prepare you to live your own life of your own choosing in the community of your choice?"[74]

These interventions moved in kinship with Toni Cade Bambara, whose City College experiences continued to shape her after relocating to Livingston College (a semi-autonomous college within Rutgers University in New Jersey) to teach alongside Aijaz Ahmad, Miguel Algarín, Nikki Giovanni, Sonia Sanchez, and A. B. Spellman. Bambara's landmark 1970 anthology *The Black Woman* acted as a new kind of Black, Puerto Rican, and Third World coalitional feminist studies open curriculum.[75] The idea for the anthology began around 1968. After being urged by City College faculty and students to produce an anthology of her work, Bambara instead gathered materials written by Black and Brown women students and teachers from City College and CUNY and placed them alongside analyses by Frances Beal and the Third World Women's Alliance, Grace Lee Boggs, Pat Robinson and The Damned, and more.

Because she wasn't a member of any revolutionary groups at the time, Bambara could interact with a variety of initiatives without having to pledge fealty or close herself off from this or that tendency. However, this doesn't mean she avoided uncomfort-

---

72 June Jordan, "Ocean Hill-Brownsville Graduation Speech for IS 55, June 19, 1970," Series VI, Box 55, Folder 6, June Jordan Papers. See also Reed and Shalev, eds., *June Jordan: "Life Studies," 1966–1976*, 29–34.

73 As Fred Moten puts it in a 2012 interview, "[S]tudy is what you do with other people. It's talking and walking around with other people, working, dancing, suffering, some irreducible convergence of all three, held under the name of speculative practice. The notion of a rehearsal—being in a kind of workshop, playing in a band, in a jam session, or old men sitting on a porch, or people working together in a factory – there are these various modes of activity. The point of calling it 'study' is to mark that the incessant and irreversible intellectuality of these activities was already there." "Studying Through the Undercommons: Stefano Harney & Fred Moten—interviewed by Stevphen Shukaitis," *ClassWarU*, November 12, 2012, https://classwaru.org/2012/11/12/studying-through-the-undercommons-stefano-harney-fred-moten-interviewed-by-stevphen-shukaitis/.

74 June Jordan, "Ocean Hill-Brownsville Graduation Speech for IS 55, June 19, 1970." See also Reed and Shalev, eds., *June Jordan: "Life Studies," 1966–1976*, 33.

75 Bambara, *Black Woman*. See also Cherríe Moraga and Gloria E. Anzaldúa, eds., *This Bridge Called My Back: Writings by Radical Women of Color* (New York: Kitchen Table: Women of Color Press, 1981); Akasha (Gloria T.) Hull, Patricia Bell Scott, and Barbara Smith, eds., *All the Women are White, All the Blacks are Men, But Some of Us Are Brave: Black Women's Studies* (New York: Feminist Press, 1982); Barbara Smith, ed., *Home Girls: A Black Feminist Anthology* (New York: Kitchen Table: Women of Color Press, 1983); Alma Gómez, Cherríe Moraga, and Mariana Romo-Carmona, eds., *Cuentos: Stories by Latinas* (New York: Kitchen Table: Women of Color Press, 1983).

able "in-house" interventions. The anthology encouraged a "crowd-sourcing" method of strategizing women's liberation work across ethnic backgrounds and groups to challenge misogyny in movements, the misappropriation of Third Worldist guerrilla tactics in the US, and the need to understand multiply woven oppressions (an early framing of what would become "intersectionality" discourse). *The Black Woman's* relevance is especially enduring for how it defends reproductive autonomy in a period when some male Black Power leaders equated contraception with genocide. Bambara also had a keen sense of timing to publish with a large press while also supporting independent Black Arts presses, taking advantage of a felicitous moment in which capitalist commodification of Black Arts actually helped the movement reach broad readerships. Bambara's insistence that *The Black Woman* cost under a dollar and be able to fit in one's pocket helped the book reach a second printing in a month.

In one of her two essays for the anthology, "On the Issue of Roles," she lambasted the misogynist elements of campus organizing at the time and redefined how to focus on social change *here* at *home*, anticipating future feminists of colors' analyses of social reproduction, their practices of collective care, and their emphasis on confronting strands of Black nationalism that perpetuate sexism. We can see how the "Dear Bloods" memo's terse mentorship expanded to reach a national audience of Black and Third World students and community radicals:

> Instant coffee is the hallmark of current rhetoric. But we do have time. We'd better take the time to fashion revolutionary selves, revolutionary lives, revolutionary relationships. Mouths don't win the war. It don't even win the people. Neither does haste, urgency, and stretch-out-now insistence. Not all speed is movement. Running off to mimeograph a fuck-whitey leaflet, leaving your mate to brood, is not revolutionary. Hopping a plane to rap to someone else's 'community' while your son struggles alone with the Junior Scholastic assignment on 'The Dark Continent' is not revolutionary. Sitting around murder-mouthing incorrect niggers while your father goes upside your mother's head is not revolutionary. Mapping out a building takeover when your term paper is overdue and your scholarship is under review is not revolutionary. . . . If your house ain't in order, you ain't in order. It is so much easier to be out there than right here. The revolution ain't out there. Yet. But it is here. Should be. And arguing that instant-coffee-ten-minutes-to-midnight alibi to justify hasty-headed dealings with your mate is shit. Ain't no such animal as an instant guerrilla.[76]

Bambara's castigation remains withering. Aiming her critique of sexist movement "roles" in the specific terms of university struggles, she compels Black and Third World men students to embrace Black radical feminism. Anticipating the 1970s shift from externalized to reflexive struggles, Bambara sought new ways to define and articulate being "militant" as an antidote to some chaotic disorganizing tendencies that emerged in social movements by 1969.

Following the *Black Woman* anthology, Bambara published two collections of short stories, *Tales and Stories for Black Folks* and *Gorilla, My Love*, that launched her to promi-

---

76 Bambara, "On the Issue of Roles," in *The Black Woman*, 134–135.

nence. In stories like "My Man Bovanne" and "Raymond's Run," Bambara playfully skewered the ways that some versions of Black nationalism obscured the differently abled and elderly from their vision of a new sturdy Black nation, while "The Lesson" revealed how youth can study commodity fetishism through adventures outside the classroom. Although Bambara was hesitant to call her fiction autobiographical, by reading backwards from the archived memoir sketches she wrote in the '80s and '90s and her City College teaching archives, we can see how she embedded learning experiences in her late '60s and early '70s short fiction. Likewise, these stories' lessons from the '60s were sustained for '70s readers, just as her radical healing novel *The Salt Eaters* bridged '70s lessons for the following decades.

Bambara's timely ability to circulate lessons for readers across generations and spaces is emblematic of the extensive impact of the New York Liberation School curricula detailed throughout this book. Eleanor Traylor suggests that Bambara's creative writing served as mobile "liberation zones" in which characters were "safe to grow and develop consciousness."[77] Thabiti Lewis adds that in these zones, "Bambara's characters fulfill and exceed all of the expectations of Black Nationalists or feminists because they find pathways to freedom that are safe, patient, and make community whole."[78] Farah Jasmine Griffin perhaps best named the stakes of these interventions: "Toni Cade Bambara's extraordinary ordinary people—streetwise, sensitive, and complex— taunt, tease, and haunt: Don't you want to be free? Yes, You. Freedom. What are you going to do to be free?"[79] As readers of Bambara, we can emplot ourselves in these stories and collaborate with her to "make revolution irresistible."[80]

Open Admissions and the Cost of Upheaval

By Fall 1970, when the CUNY Board of Higher Education converted the strike's demand for expanded Black, Puerto Rican, and Asian admissions into a much broader program of Open Admissions, Jordan responded to these shifts with an immensely fruitful period of creativity. Not only did she travel all over the New York area to speak to a wide range of audiences; she also went to Mississippi to research voting rights and land reform with activist Fannie Lou Hamer and writer Alice Walker and visited Rome as the winner of the Prix de Rome in environmental design. Jordan also wrote multiple young-adult novels in Black vernacular English and edited anthologies of African American poetry. Jordan's writings addressed antipoverty legislation, neighborhood safety, language apartheid in schooling, the limits of respectability politics, and more. The SEEK practice of publishing popular anthologies—such as Bambara's *The Black Woman* and Jordan's *Soulscript*, which featured CUNY faculty and student writing—democratized educational resources for a national audience and also worked to decolonize the publishing industry.[81]

---

77 Cited in Thabiti Lewis, *"Black People Are My Business": Toni Cade Bambara's Practices of Liberation* (Detroit: Wayne State University Press, 2020), 37.

78 Lewis, 100.

79 Farah Jasmine Griffin, "Toni Cade Bambara: Free to Be Anywhere in the Universe," *Callaloo: A Journal of African-American and African Arts and Letters* 19, no. 2 (1996): 229.

80 Toni Cade Bambara, "An Interview with Toni Cade Bambara," in Thabiti Lewis, ed., *Conversations with Toni Cade Bambara* (Jackson: University Press of Mississippi, 2012), 35–47.

81 Bambara, *The Black Woman.* June Jordan, *Soulscript: Afro-American Poetry* (New York: Doubleday, 1970).

Meanwhile, the struggle in CUNY to maintain Open Admissions and establish a form of community control that could manifest Bambara's "Black University," Henderson's "black city," and Jordan's "Life Studies" intensified and continued, despite considerable backlash. From 1970 onwards, conservative CUNY faculty and the mainstream media crafted a racist and elitist discourse on "The Death of the University," spinning a tale in which Open Admissions allegedly benefited only poor Black and Puerto Rican students and sent CUNY's standards into a downward spiral while ignoring the ongoing retrenchment that saddled the university with fewer resources and larger classes. As Jordan understood from her housing advocacy days, the long-practiced urban policy of maintaining overcrowded and under-resourced slums in the Bronx, Harlem, Lower East Side, and other impoverished areas became a model for forcibly overcrowding and underfunding CUNY after Open Admissions.

On an everyday, interpersonal level, the impact of these policies exhausted students and workers at City College, even as the institution became nationally recognized as a site of desegregated admissions and writing pedagogies. Nevertheless, these colleagues tenderly looked after each other. For example, after Bambara received Audre Lorde's 1971 poem "Dear Toni Instead of a Letter of Congratulations Upon Your Book and Your Daughter Whom You Are Raising To Be A Correct Little Sister," which celebrates news of her pregnancy and recounts their time at City College, Bambara penned a response that still beams from the archives:

> tryin to think of a really balanced way to say thank you for the stunning poem . . . I mean stunning. So just wow, Audre, it's a fantastic poem.
>
> Overwhelmed,
> Toni[82]

And in a November 1973 letter from Jordan to Lorde, after reading her friend's poem "Movement Song," she wrote:

> I have to report that I am spending these days . . . in the cleaning of my house, and myself, I guess; trying to get ready for winter—a rotten winter like the one last year, when I ran out of everything—food, health—but this time I figure I'd better get the novel written—hell or high water, and then move on. So I am mostly calm, during the day. And gesturing closer and closer to my real work. Maybe god has intervened—to stop all this 'teaching' stuff and 'travelling' stuff so I can/must concentrate on the dream unwritten still, and still a longing for the people of my heart. You keep well, please, and keep in touch, and keep the poem alive.[83]

---

82 Toni Cade Bambara, Letter to Audre Lorde, 1971, Part 1, Box 1, Toni Cade Bambara Papers. See also Audre Lorde, "Dear Toni Instead of a Letter of Congratulations Upon Your Book and Your Daughter Whom You Are Raising To Be A Correct Little Sister," *From a Land Where Other People Live* (Detroit: Broadside Press, 1973), 93–95.

83 Audre Lorde, "Movement Song," *From a Land Where Other People Live*; Jordan, Letter to Audre Lorde, 1973, Series 1, Box 3, Folder 63, Audre Lorde Papers, Spelman College Archives, Atlanta, GA.

After teaching stints at Connecticut College, Sarah Lawrence College, and Yale University, Jordan returned to City College in 1975. At this moment, university austerity measures became a national issue as the US defeat in Vietnam, the rise of neoliberalism, and a fiscal crisis in New York resulted in the end of free education at CUNY.[84]

At a May 5, 1976, CUNY board hearing to establish universal tuition for the first time in its 129-year history, Jordan expressed outrage as one of thirteen City College professors on hunger strike to demand that CUNY remain free.[85] Applying her Mobilization for Youth housing analyses from a decade earlier, she lauded CUNY's historic openness to poor European immigrant students, but noted that once Black and Puerto Rican students began to enter the university in larger numbers, free education was suddenly imperiled. Jordan framed the imposition of tuition in terms of survival—the project of Life Studies was in danger. She warned that ending free education and therefore, truly Open Admissions, would have grave consequences for the city:

> We cannot accept the death of this great, free University because we
> cannot accept the death of the spirit, the death of aspirations, the death
> of the future, that will surely follow for our children, the students. . . . We
> will fast. We will take a cut in salary. We will fight. The possibility that we
> may lose is not a possibility: we have to win. . . . We speak on behalf of
> our children, and our students; we call upon all of the people of the City
> of New York to join with us on behalf of all the children and all of the
> students of the City of New York, to resist this death.[86]

A wildcat strike committee formed within Jordan's union, the Professional Staff Congress (PSC), urging workers to reject tuition costs alongside an austerity labor contract that the PSC leadership argued was the best it could do.[87] As these rank-and-file union organizers feared, the Fall 1976 tuition policy coincided with almost five thousand layoffs of faculty and staff, including many who had helped to usher in Open Admissions and all adjuncts, the erasure of recently won Ethnic Studies classes, and threats to close new CUNY colleges like Hostos and Medgar Evers.[88]

Jordan herself would be laid off from City College for one semester but would return for a final year to mentor and teach poetry to future luminaries like Sekou Sundiata (who reappears in Chapter 4). Even in this tumultuous period, Jordan nurtured a place with her students to create "useful, that is, the usable, criticism of poems"

---

84 H. Bruce Franklin, *Vietnam & Other American Fantasies* (Amherst: University of Massachusetts Press, 2000), 127.

85 *The Paper*, "Resolution by the Black Faculty, Department of English," May 6, 1976: 4; Pamela Mahabeer, "13 Black Profs Call Hunger Strike to Protest City U 'Resegregation,'" *The Campus*, May 7, 1976.

86 June Jordan, "Statement by June Jordan to Board of Higher Ed, on CUNY Retrenchment, End of Open Admissions, Imposition of Tuition; Speaking on behalf of Black Colleagues in English Dept. at CCNY." Series XII, Box 76, Folder 14. June Jordan Papers. See also Reed and Shalev, eds., *June Jordan: "Life Studies," 1966–1976*, 50–53.

87 *Faculty Action*, May 1976, CUNY Digital History Archive, https://cdha.cuny.edu/items/show/1711/.

88 *MCC Strike Committee Bulletin #1*, 1976, CUNY Digital History Archive, https://cdha.cuny.edu/items/show/1691/; CUNY Digital History Archive, "1970–77 Open Admissions – Fiscal Crisis – State Takeover," https://cdha.cuny.edu/coverage/coverage/show/id/33/; "CUNY Adjunct Labor," https://cdha.cuny.edu/collections/show/292/; "Save Hostos!; "MEC for MEC, Albany, 1976," https://cdha.cuny.edu/items/show/3122/.

towards communal goals of artistic expression, which would shape the foundations of her later "Poetry for the People" Program at UC-Berkeley.[89] At the same time, aggressive economic structural adjustments would pave the way for a significant reversal of the social movement aspirations of the preceding decades. The subsequent "retrenchment period" at CUNY saw massive city and state budget cuts, skyrocketing tuition fees, and a shift to relying on adjunct faculty, whose exploitation was enshrined by multiple contract agreements between the PSC and CUNY administration.[90] CUNY and New York City suffered economic shock therapy that would soon be reproduced across the nation's universities and cities.

Continuations

The experiences of Toni Cade Bambara, David Henderson, and June Jordan before, during, and after their time at the City College of New York illustrate how such experimental creative teaching methods could blossom from the SEEK Program at this particular conjuncture in New York City. As detailed in the Introduction, we see why the political and educational elite fought so vociferously to counteract these visions for self-determination in learning. These teacher-writers' forms of movement *composition*—willing clarity and direction through liberatory writing and actions—kept them responsive to an "authenticating audience" of students, peers, and sibling insurgents as members of New York Liberation School's extended intergenerational classroom.[91]

As movement writers, they served as chroniclers and conduits of multiple voices and political events, while regularly publishing and promoting others' work alongside their own. Bambara and Jordan's archives at City College, Radcliffe Institute, and Spelman College brim with the rebellious, loving energy of their teaching, writing, organizing, and friendships. Many letters kept there reflect the enduring value of these City College connections, including between them, Henderson, and their colleagues and students. Only by a *coalitional* reading across these three educators and their archives, interviews, published works, spoken performances, storytelling, and contextual environments does this fuller picture emerge. Reflecting upon them separately below may seem like a re-individualization of their legacies, but the coalescence of their efforts must be understood as indivisible from each other.

As a "community scribe," Bambara's dream of a "Black University" wasn't simply about a place or an institution but about a vision, a form of consciousness, a way of collaborating in this fraught world to actualize future world-shifting alternatives. Her work provides tools to navigate how to get there, but at the same time, she admonishes—with humor and love—the world of "instant coffee" too many of us live in, and makes us remember that "we do have time," that "not all speed is movement." For Bambara, transforming society *out there* and *in here*, according to the wisdom acquired through experience, required a patient and radical vision beyond one protest, communiqué, revolutionary tradition, school, semester, year, decade, even lifetime. Her legacy,

89 June Jordan, "City College Graduate Poetry Workshop Description," Series XII, Box 76, Folder 15, Schlesinger Library on the History of Women in America, Radcliffe Institute, Cambridge, MA. See also Lauren Muller and the Blueprint Collective, *June Jordan's Poetry for the People: A Revolutionary Blueprint* (Oxfordshire: Routledge, 1995).

90 CUNY Digital History Archive, "1978–1992: Retrenchment – Austerity – Tuition," https://cdha.cuny.edu/coverage/coverage/show/id/43/.

91 Louis Massiah, "The Authenticating Audience," *FeministWire*, November 18, 2014, http://www.thefeministwire.com/2014/11/authenticating-audience/.

which expanded from City College to New Jersey, Atlanta, and Philadelphia, endures through an annual conference in her honor at Spelman College and a forthcoming documentary by Louis Massiah, *The TCB School of Organizing.*

Henderson's collaborations in Umbra showed the power of spoken poetry to coalesce and move people, while his written poetry chronicled moments of urban Black lives with an intimate clarity usually absent in journalistic accounts of the time. His attention to Black Studies on the streets and in popular culture inspired a practice of anti-formality in the classroom. Combining curiosity about his students' autonomous activities and an eye for potential coalitions for youth whose traditional schooling and cities underserved, he transformed the role of "poet-in-residence" into movement worker for the young, gifted, and Black and Brown. Henderson still reads at public events, writes, and mentors younger poets. He emphasizes, "I don't want to be listed among a whole bunch of dead Black people because the stuff we're doing is alive."[92] Henderson's dedication to several decades of poetry, study, and community power has kept him attuned to unwritten possibilities in the future. Each time we cross paths, he asks me with an ever-present gleam in his eye, "So what's happening with the CUNY movement?"

Moreover, while the development of Black Studies is often associated with movements in and around colleges and universities, in Jordan's youth literacies program and the speeches she delivered while at City College, we see that the urgency and relevance of Black Studies as Life Studies is rooted in her advocacy for students of all ages in all arenas of living. That Jordan struggled uphill to enact lasting changes against the pressures of colonial-racial-gendered capitalism—during a time of intensified austerity that mirrors our own—indicates that her legacy is still unfinished.[93] Jordan's record of youth-to-university work at CUNY and in New York City shows how she prepared her students to wage critiques across institutions as well as to compose proposals to change them. From university conferences to street vigils for police abolition and women's liberation, Jordan's words continue to resound.

Altogether, these three educators illustrate the power of creating liberatory counterinstitutions within and beyond the institutions where they assembled—not as a claim toward governance, but as a method for undoing the coercions that produce governmentality and subservience—and then radiating these lessons outwards for broader potential complicities across locales and waves of struggles. Their immersive familiarity with the realities of Black, Latinx, and multiethnic neighborhoods; attention to the strategic relationships between sites of housing, education, and conviviality; and dispositions of radical joy and tough love meant that their roles as Black community educators were both earned and embraced. As we will further see in the next chapter on Audre Lorde and Adrienne Rich, these incredible bonds between City College SEEK educators—who many of us now revere as our greatest teachers—were forged in intensive study and movement together. These figures were rooted in the places that transformed them and that they felt a duty to transform.

---

92 David Henderson, interview with the author, April 2, 2022.

93 The Iranian-American poet Solmaz Sharif is currently initiating a "Poetry for the People" Program at the University of Arizona in Jordan's honor. See Rozina Ali, "Poet Laureate of Nowhere: Solmaz Sharif Goes Through Customs," *Lux Magazine* 4 (April 2022), https://lux-magazine.com/article/solmaz-sharif-customs/.

CHAPTER 3

AUDRE LORDE AND ADRIENNE RICH: SISTERS IN STRUGGLE

This chapter conjoins the legacies of two of the most prominent US lesbian feminists of the twentieth century, whose decades-long friendship fundamentally molded each other's lives—and those of countless readers—even as this bond has over time become occluded from how people understand their respective paths to prominence. In the same way that the previous chapter wove together the lives of Toni Cade Bambara, David Henderson, and June Jordan, the narrative below illustrates how Audre Lorde and Adrienne Rich—two teacher–poet–mother–warrior–lesbian–feminist friends—symbiotically forged the dimensions of what a lifelong commitment to radical change across differences and similarities can look like. Lorde and Rich's writing and teaching offer a record of self/mutual reinvention and how one might find the space to practice it. Their movement strategies, poetics, and pedagogy were deliberately entwined in praxis.

Audre Lorde's words are suddenly everywhere—on signs, shirts, and memes, from #Black Lives Matter to reproductive justice demonstrations. *Your silence will not protect you. The master's tools will never dismantle the master's house. Revolution is not a one-time event.* As a result, R.O. Kwon asserts, "Lorde seems prophetic, perhaps alive right now."[1] However, as Nick Mitchell argues, her voluminous legacy is at risk of becoming a series of slogans—"the Audre Lorde that reads like a bumper sticker."[2] Roxane Gay notes how people "parrot Lorde's ideas about dismantling the master's house without taking into account the context from which Lorde crafted those ideas," namely her proposal to not burn bridges with Euro feminists but rather to demand that they do better.[3] Meanwhile, in a contemporary moment marked by treatises against liberal white feminism, we can lift up Rich (among other radical Euro feminists) as an example of a principled

---

1 R.O. Kwon, "Your Silence Will Not Protect You by Audre Lorde review—prophetic and necessary," *The Guardian*, October 4, 2017, https://www.theguardian.com/books/2017/oct/04/your-silence-will-not-protect-you-by-audre-lorder-review/.

2 Nick Mitchell, "On Audre Lorde's Legacy and the "Self" of Self-Care, Part 1 of 3," *Low End Theory*, February 18, 2013, http://www.lowendtheory.org/post/43457761324/on-audre-lordes-legacy-and-the-self-of/.

3 Roxane Gay, "The Legacy of Audre Lorde," *The Paris Review*, September 17, 2020, https://www.theparisreview.org/blog/2020/09/17/the-legacy-of-audre-lorde/.

dedication to intervening in daily political life, especially as her insights now also re-emerge from universities onto the streets.[4]

The distinct yet braided legacies of Lorde and Rich—as lesbian socialist feminists, people's poets, social activists, and innovative educators—altered the landscapes of multiple liberation movements from the late 1960s to the present. They offer a striking example of the possibilities of radical women's intellectual friendship across racialized lines that became increasingly complex in late-twentieth-century New York.[5] While Lorde and Rich were close friends for decades and co-emergent in their writings and actions, their audiences have recently diverged, even as they are being revived in reprints and reviews.[6]

Returning to a vital midlife period, from 1968 through the 1970s, during which Lorde and Rich both taught in the SEEK Program at CUNY, can illuminate their subsequent trajectories. During this germinal moment, Lorde and Rich immersed themselves in the formation of Black, Puerto Rican, and Women's Studies at the City College of New York, and for Lorde, at John Jay College of Criminal Justice. This marked an early entry point for Lorde's teaching, while Rich exchanged her Ivy League classrooms for urban pedagogical trenches. Lorde and Rich's teaching archives at Spelman College and Radcliffe Institute offer a nascent road map of the overlapping themes of liberation and poetics that would become so central to their lives. Reading across their teaching and writing, we can see how Lorde and Rich's commitment to a radical model of education helped precipitate wider social and institutional change while laying the foundations for their lesbian feminist legacies. In particular, Rich's 1972 poem "Diving into the Wreck" and Lorde's 1973 poem "Blackstudies" and autobiomythography *Deotha* remain symbolic records of these experiences.

Through this material excavation of Lorde and Rich's day-to-day teaching lives, we can begin to recover their theoretical interventions in the left, formed through a *compositional* praxis with working-class students of colors who had previously been excluded from the public university. Rich's calls for *re-visioning* women's lives and writings that implicitly challenged the staunch "anti-revisionism" of the US Communist left and Lorde's efforts to weave and analyze contradictions instead of hewing to "easy" identificatory lines contributed to the formation of intersectional analyses.[7] Although it doesn't always appear at the surface of their poetry and essays, Lorde and Rich's attention to the histories of enslavement and racism in their teaching indicate their early role in shaping abolitionist university studies. In connection with this point, this chapter will discuss the decolonial contexts in which the SEEK Program, coordinated

4 Alexis Pauline Gumbs, "Communiqué to White Ally Heaven," *Sinister Wisdom* 87 (Tribute to Adrienne Rich – Fall 2012): 86–100.

5 For a contemporary illustration of this profound kind of bond, see Robyn Maynard and Leanne Betasamosake Simpson, *Rehearsals for Living* (Chicago, Haymarket Books: 2022).

6 Audre Lorde, *Cancer Journals* (New York: Penguin Books, 2020); *Selected Works of Audre Lorde*, ed. Roxane Gay (New York: W.W. Norton and Company, 2020); Adrienne Rich, *Collected Poems: 1950–2012* (New York: W.W. Norton and Company, 2016); *Of Woman Born: Motherhood as Experience & Institution* (New York: W.W. Norton and Company, 2021). Gloria I. Joseph, ed., *The Wind is the Spirit: The Life, Love and Legacy of Audre Lorde* (Villarosa Media, 2016); Wayne Koestenbaum, "Adrienne Rich's Poetry Became Political, but It Remained Rooted in Material Fact," *New York Times*, July 15, 2016, https://www.nytimes.com/2016/07/17/books/review/adrienne-rich-collected-poems-1950-2012.html/.

7 Audre Lorde, "Between Ourselves," *Collected Poems of Audre Lorde* (New York: W.W. Norton & Company, 2000), 224, 324.

by Mina Shaughnessy, contributed to the creation of "basic writing," which would democratize writing instruction across colleges nationwide, even as it would foreground a Euro voice to condense the multiethnic pedagogical lessons of SEEK in the post-Open Admissions era.[8]

Alongside their colleagues and students, Lorde and Rich's participation in the SEEK Program and in Black, Puerto Rican, and Women's Studies would eventually reconfigure CUNY, public life, and social movements while redirecting the course of their own lives and friendship with each other.

Early Years Reaching

Born in 1929, Adrienne Rich was raised in a Baltimore household by a nonobservant Jewish father and a Protestant mother. Her poetry won early renown; her first collection, *A Change of World*, was selected for the 1951 Yale Younger Poets Award.[9] Before arriving at City College, Rich taught writing at the Young Men's/Young Women's Hebrew Association, Swarthmore College, and Columbia University, two subway stops down the street from City College, while parenting three children with her husband Alfred Conrad, a professor in the City College Economics Department. While teaching in the newly formed Graduate Writing Program at Columbia in 1967–68, she immersed herself in the antiwar movements on campus.[10] Her poetry became more politically pronounced, as evident in the collection *Leaflets: Poems 1965–1968*. Rich's attention to the wave of events sweeping the country and the world in 1968 is documented in the collection with the pace of an insurgent advance—two-thirds of the forty-eight poems were written that year, seventeen of them penned in less than a month, right before she began to teach in the City College SEEK program.

For Rich, literature was a necessary though insufficient record of lived experience. She identified with the possibility that language—if connected to action—could undo its own ideological fetters. Her work plumbed the depths between the concrete word and fleeting human responses to it. Her pre-City College poetry weighed material constraints and subjective energies in considering "how we can use what we have / to invent what we need." She critiqued some Columbia men faculty members' disregard of students' ideas as a pedagogical violence, metaphorizing it as sexual assault: "If the mind of the teacher is not in love with the mind of the student, / he is simply practicing rape, and deserves at best our pity." Rich's work urged a dialogue with Black men writers whose revolutionary programs contained misogynist contours: "LeRoi! Eldridge! listen to us, we are ghosts / condemned to haunt the cities where you want to be at home." She also warned of the *conservateur* who carried "illustrated catalogues of all that there is to lose," a prescient image of the harsh reactions to institutional change at City College that she and others in SEEK would endure within a few years.[11]

What stands out in these 1965–68 poems is how Rich demanded an active political use for literature that exceeds its value as a finished product—revered as an inert cultural object or hoisted like a too-tidy banner. She sought to lay bare the stress lines and

---

8 These efforts would become codified in SEEK director Mina P. Shaughnessy's *Errors and Expectations: A Guide for the Teacher of Basic Writing* (Oxford: Oxford University Press, 1977). See also Carmen Kynard, *Vernacular Insurrections: Race, Black Protest, and the New Century in Composition-Literacies Studies* (Albany: SUNY Press, 2014).

9 Adrienne Rich, *A Change of World: Poems* (New Haven: Yale University Press, 1971).

10 Hilary Holladay, *The Power of Adrienne Rich: A Biography* (New York: Penguin, 2020), 174.

11 Rich, *Leaflets: Poems, 1965–1968* (New York: W.W. Norton and Company, 1969), 56, 68, 72.

ardor of creation, circulation, and contact between real people through the written word. Rich's translations of nineteenth-century Indian poet Mirza Ghalib, using the *ghazal* poetry form, in collaboration with her soon-to-be CUNY colleague Aijaz Ahmad, also demonstrated how language can be transmittable, sumptuous, and indeed erotic across linguistic differences.[12] Even though she didn't yet identify as a feminist, Rich's path was intensely altered by this period. She writes in the collection's title poem:

> I want to hand you this
> leaflet streaming with rain or tears
> but the words coming clear
> something you might find crushed into your hand
> after passing a barricade
> and stuff in your raincoat pocket.
> I want this to reach you[13]

Lorde's long relationship to poetry also began in her youth. Born in 1934 and raised in Harlem by Grenadian and Barbadian parents, she recited poems as a way to convey her feelings.[14] In a high school friendship with the Italian-American poet Diane di Prima, Lorde contributed poems to the school literary journal. Several of these poems would later appear in her first collection, *First Cities*, published by di Prima's Poets Press in 1968.[15] One poem, "Generation," addresses Black youth sacrifices in the Southern freedom struggle, lamenting "How the young attempt and are broken" and that "We are more than kin who come to share / Not blood, but the bloodiness of failure." Another poem, "Coal," written in the early 1960s, exemplifies the vexed unmooring that comes with language and communication: "Some words live in my throat / Breeding like adders. Others know sun / Seeking like gypsies over my tongue / To explode through my lips / Like young sparrows bursting from shell. / Some words / Bedevil me."

After working as a nurse's aide, factory worker, social worker, and librarian, Lorde was awarded in 1968 a National Endowment for the Arts teaching residency at Tougaloo College in Jackson, Mississippi. Here she taught poetry to Black students who had been involved in desegregation protests and were eager for creative outlets. In this first teaching experience, Lorde confronted how her Blackness, gender, and sexuality were perceived by others with whom she shared a learning space. Lorde recalls struggling to reveal her interethnic marriage, which by this time was falling apart. In a later interview with Rich, Lorde explained, "it was absolutely necessary for me to declare, as terrified as I was, 'the father of my children is white.' And what that meant in Tougaloo, to those young Black people then, to talk about myself openly and deal with their hostility, their sense of disillusionment . . . was very hard."[16] Nearly all of the poems that comprise her second collection, *Cables to Rage*, would be written during her time at

---

12 Holladay, *The Power of Adrienne Rich*, 196–197.

13 Rich, *Leaflets*, 55–56.

14 Audre Lorde, *Zami: A New Spelling of My Name* (Watertown: Persephone Press, 1982), 31.

15 Poets Press also published fellow SEEK educator David Henderson's first poetry collection in 1967, *Felix of the Silent Forest*, which will be reprinted in 2023 by Pinsapo Press and *Lost & Found: The CUNY Poetics Document Initiative*.

16 Audre Lorde, "An Interview: Adrienne Rich and Audre Lorde," in *Sister Outsider: Essays and Speeches* (Trumansburg: Crossing Press, 1984), 90.

Tougaloo. Upon returning to New York, Lorde was invited by SEEK Program direc-tor Mina Shaughnessy to teach at City College, after Lorde's friend and City College student Yolanda Rios shared *First Cities* with her. Early in the semester, Rich sought out Lorde after buying a copy of *First Cities* at the campus bookstore—the first encounter of what would become a lifelong friendship.[17]

In Autumn 1968, Lorde and Rich—respectively thirty-four and thirty-nine years old and the mothers of two and three children—began to teach writing as adjunct instructors in City College's SEEK Program.[18] Lorde's biographer Alexis De Veaux writes, "although the Tougaloo experience had been successful, this was to be a more formal classroom setting. Responsible for teaching grammar and composition, Lorde entered the classroom fearfully each day, but she relied on her instincts; she admitted her trepidations to her students and taught herself the rudiments of grammar as she taught them to her class."[19] Lorde had been deeply affected by Dr. King's assassina-tion. She confided in her then-partner, Frances Clayton, "If I could go to war, if I could pick up a gun to defend the things I believe, yes—but what am I gonna do in a classroom?" In her first day teaching SEEK students, Lorde confessed to them that "I'm scared too." Like Bambara, Henderson, and Jordan, she transcended the distance usually imposed by faculty as she reveled in learning about composition alongside her students. She recalled, "I'd come into class and say, 'Guess what I found out last night. Tenses are a way of ordering the chaos around time.' I learned that grammar was not arbitrary . . . that it could be freeing as well as restrictive."[20] We see Lorde developing her approach of the teacher as co-learner, an early sign of the vulnerability with which she later shared her thinking and writing process while also inviting readers to express their own breakthroughs.

Rich recalled in her 1972 essay, "Teaching Language in Open Admissions," that Shaughnessy welcomed SEEK faculty to use any relevant materials to keep the stu-dents engaged: "poetry, free association, music, politics, drama, fiction." Curriculum creation was a highly collaborative process, where faculty freely "poached off each oth-er's booklists, methods, essay topics, grammar-teaching exercises."[21] Rich's Fall 1968 class texts included Plato's *Republic*, LeRoi Jones (later Amiri Baraka)'s *Home* and *The Dead Lecturer*, and Paris Leary and Robert Kelly's *A Controversy of Poets*, an example of how SEEK teachers interwove canonical European texts with recently published Black liberation texts and poetry anthologies that assembled both the old guard and new experiments.[22] One writing prompt used a theme in Jones/Baraka's essay "Cuba Libre"—regarding how newspapers lied about the revolution—to encourage students to evaluate how "advertising, political speeches, sermons, movies" bend truths to fit

---

17 Alexis De Veaux, *Warrior Poet: A Biography of Audre Lorde* (New York: W.W. Norton and Company, 2004), 101, 104–105.

18 Rich declined an offer to be a Poet-in-Residence at City College to work in SEEK. Holladay, *The Power of Adrienne Rich*, 184–185.

19 De Veaux, *Warrior Poet*, 102–103.

20 Lorde, "An Interview: Adrienne Rich and Audre Lorde," 94–95.

21 Adrienne Rich, "Teaching Language in Open Admissions (1972)," in *On Lies, Secrets, and Silence: Selected Prose 1966–1978* (New York: W.W. Norton and Company, 1979), 56–57.

22 Adrienne Rich, "Note to Mina Shaughnessy, 18 June 1968." Carton 9, Folder 386. Adrienne Rich Papers. See also Brown, et al., eds., *Adrienne Rich: "What we are part of:" Teaching at CUNY, 1968–1974*, Part I, 12.

specific ideological aims.[23] In her essay, Rich explained these shared horizons of the SEEK program, which became precursors for Ethnic and Gender Studies and college writing composition nationwide:

> Some of the most rudimentary questions we confronted were . . . What are the arguments for and against 'Black English'? . . . Is standard English simply a weapon of colonization? . . . We were dealing not simply with dialect and syntax but with the imagery of lives, the anger and flare of urban youth—how could this be *used*, strengthened, without the lies of artificial polish?

Rich and her Black women colleagues were also attentive to the dearth of published Black women writers in the classroom:

> Ann Petry, Gwendolyn Brooks, June Jordan, Audre Lorde, I came to know and put on my reading lists or copied for classes, but the real crescendo of black women's writing was yet to come . . . integral to the struggle against racism in the literary canon there was another, as yet unarticulated, struggle, against the sexism of black and white male editors, anthologists, critics, and publishers.[24]

SEEK students and teachers stimulated each other through reflexive learning that boomeranged the socially marginalized to the center of a classroom's focus. As Rich wrote: "In this discovery of a *previously submerged culture* we were learning from and with our students as rarely happens in the university . . . we found ourselves reading almost any piece of Western literature through our students' eyes, imagining how this voice, these assumptions, would sound to us if we were they."[25] While some of this came as a revelation for Rich, it was already an assumed practice for Black teachers in SEEK. Carmen Kynard notes, "Rich describes the SEEK students at City College as shaking up *her* own white liberal assumptions, not the academy shaking them with fear . . . students are active agents who are defining themselves *against* the university and redefining the university at the same time."[26]

Campus debates about the future of CUNY began to gain more traction in late 1968 and early 1969. Rich's collection *The Will to Change: Poems 1968–1970* offers a record of her attempts to connect with students in this atmosphere as well as her own shifting self-identity, all through a communicative medium encumbered by existing power relations. In these poems, Rich's speaker grasps for ways to reach her students—"this is the oppressor's language / yet I need it to talk to you"—while they strive to configure a new self: "I need a language to hear myself with / to see myself in / a language like pigment released on the board / blood-black, sexual green, reds

---

23 Adrienne Rich, "We have read and talked about LeRoi Jones' essay." Carton 9, Folder 390. Adrienne Rich Papers. See also Iemanjá Brown, et al., eds., *Adrienne Rich: "What we are part of:" Teaching at CUNY, 1968–1974*, Part II, 9–10.

24 Rich, "Teaching Language in Open Admissions (1972)," 51, 55–56 (emphasis in original).

25 Rich, "Teaching Language in Open Admissions (1972)," 57 (emphasis added).

26 Kynard, *Vernacular Insurrections*, 216.

/ veined with contradictions."[27] These words gesture at the metamorphosis of Rich's own politics, pedagogy, and sexual identity in the context of wider upheavals. The red, black, and green colors of the Black liberation flag—a ubiquitous protest staple at the time—here unfurl and become rewoven as a symbol of solidarity between a Jewish feminist writing teacher and her Black and Puerto Rican students undergoing fundamental changes together. Rich's experiences within the intersectional space of a SEEK classroom were translated into the intimate space of poems that then became circulated in print for others to read and reenact.

Building upon her previous semester's syllabus, Rich's Spring 1969 course included *The Autobiography of Malcolm X*, Julius Lester's *Look Out Whitey!*, Jean-Paul Sartre's *No Exit*, Albert Camus' *The Plague*, Eldridge Cleaver's *Soul on Ice*, and African American poetry. In class discussions, Rich set the *Narrative of the Life of Frederick Douglass* in dialogue with Kenneth M. Stampp's *The Peculiar Institution* and Ulrich Philips' *Life and Labor in the Old South*. She drafted extensive class notes on the etymology and practices of plantations and the development under slavery of racism and legal divisions between poor indentured Euro servants and enslaved Africans from the early seventeenth century onwards. She explored literary techniques and existentialist themes with Richard Wright's "The Man Who Lived Underground." Her writing prompts urged students to examine the Ocean Hill-Brownsville school decentralization struggles, conduct close readings of their neighborhoods, and envision ideal college classes.[28]

When students took over the City College campus in April–May 1969, the carefully knit solidarity between SEEK students, workers, and their extended families invigorated faculty support for the strike.[29] SEEK educator David Henderson recalls that Rich "had an enormous influence with the white faculty who, to our great surprise, came out in support of the strike at crucial moments."[30] Rich's husband, Alfred Conrad, was also an ardent supporter of the Black and Puerto Rican students' struggles, at one point even taking his young teenage son Pablo to visit the occupied campus buildings.[31] While Conrad received much attention in these agitations, Rich was deeply involved in care work with her students and antiracist interventions in the English Department. On April 23, at an emergency City College faculty meeting held the day after the South Campus takeover began, Rich proclaimed:

---

27 Adrienne Rich, "The Burning of Paper Instead of Children," in *The Will to Change: Poems 1968–1970* (New York: W.W. Norton and Company, 1971), 16; Adrienne Rich, "Tear Gas," in *Poems: Selected and New 1950–1974* (New York: W.W. Norton and Company, 1975), 141.

28 Adrienne Rich, "City College SEEK English Course 1.8. April 1969," Carton 9, Folder 388; "Notes for English 1.8," Carton 9, Folder 390; "Assignment from English 1.8," Carton 9, Folder 390; "The Board of Education hearings," Carton 9, Folder 390; "Write an analysis of your neighborhood," Carton 9, Folder 388; "Write a description of a course," Carton 9, Folder 390, all in Adrienne Rich Papers. See also Brown, et al., eds., Adrienne Rich: "What we are part of:" Teaching at CUNY, 1968–1974, Part II, 8–10, 13–20.

29 Carmen Kynard clarifies, "Shaughnessy refused to cancel any of her classes during the turbulent times," believing that her role was "to give them 'the tools to think,' as if the movement was not providing them with that." Even so, "[b]ecause students respected Shaughnessy's devotion to the SEEK Program, they did not destroy her office the way they did [some] other professors' [who also refused to cancel classes]. It is a striking example of students' understanding of Shaughnessy's commitment alongside her limited political compatibility to their social activism." Kynard, *Vernacular Insurrections*, 170.

30 Henderson, email communication with Ammiel Alcalay, shared with the author, October 22, 2013.

31 Pablo Conrad, email communication with the author, May 22, 2022.

I wish to put it on record as a teacher of SEEK students that in admitting ghetto students we are not admitting simply a collection of social and educational problems, remedial problems. We are admitting a wealth of intelligence, tough-mindedness, and motivation. We are admitting minds which, because they have lived, in LeRoi Jones' phrase, as 'suffering intelligences,' have a concern for justice, truth and freedom which many of our better-prepared students unfortunately do not. We must not confuse spoon-fed 'preparedness' with basic intellectual ability. Let's not sell our ghetto students short by imagining that they have everything to gain from the College, and little to give. There is a whole resource of brains, talent and courage which we have hitherto excluded from the American educational system; if we can begin to admit and absorb these gifts, the educational process for both whites and non-whites, teachers and students, will become, in my opinion, vastly more meaningful.[32]

Lorde came out every day to the "University of Harlem" at Intermediate School 201 (a nearby community control epicenter discussed in Chapter 1), where City College classes were relocated during the strike.[33] This satellite learning space was ideologically linked to "Harlem University," the name that students had given City College during the South Campus takeover. However, a later account by Lorde—in a 1985 speech at Medgar Evers College/CUNY—reveals her attempts as a Black lesbian to nourish an expanding university-wide strike despite some participants' unwillingness to transform gender and sexuality roles within Black and Puerto Rican communities:

> When Yoli [Yolanda Rios] and I cooked curried chicken and beans and rice and took our extra blankets and pillows up the hill to the striking students occupying buildings at City College in 1969, demanding open admissions and the right to an education, I was a Black Lesbian. When I walked through the midnight hallways of Lehman College that same year, carrying Midol and Kotex pads for the young Black radical women taking part in the action, and we tried to persuade them that their place in the revolution was not ten paces behind Black men, that spreading their legs to the guys on the tables in the cafeteria was not a revolutionary act no matter what the brothers said, I was a Black Lesbian.[34]

These critical snapshots by Rich and Lorde expose overlapping contradictions within this moment of campus upheavals. Deeply ingrained racist institutional metrics refused to value students of colors' contributions. Meanwhile, exhortations of Black, Puerto Rican, and Third World Power were launched at the expense of Women's and Lesbian Power, so that these 1969 campus occupations harbored conflicting intentions among

---

32 Adrienne Rich, "Statement to C.C.N.Y. Faculty Meeting, Wednesday, April 23 [1969]," Carton 9, Folder 389, Adrienne Rich Papers. See also Brown, et al., eds., *Adrienne Rich: "What we are part of:" Teaching at CUNY, 1968–1974*, Part I, 22–23.

33 De Veaux, *Warrior Poet*, 106.

34 Audre Lorde, "I Am Your Sister: Black Women Organizing Across Sexualities," in Rudolph P. Byrd, Johnnetta Bestch Cole, and Beverly Guy-Sheftall, eds., *I Am Your Sister: Collected and Unpublished Writings of Audre Lorde* (Oxford: Oxford University Press, 2009), 60.

their participants.[35] These issues illustrate how efforts at social change can at times focus on reconstructing institutions without nurturing anti-oppressive mutual respect in the process. Lorde commanded attention to the sexual violence that can occur in movement spaces, including coercive sex that is framed as liberatory. In the swift momentum of these disruptions, it is unclear whether or how these concerns were resolved by SEEK faculty and students. This highlights an enduring dilemma in archiving how radical communities address harm, both internally and publicly, while in motion.

Viewed in general terms, the strike electrified student and faculty relations, transforming the entire university. Critical thinking skills that were honed in SEEK classrooms appeared during the negotiations around the students' Five Demands. Rich recalled that teachers expressed "surprised respect for the students' articulateness, reasoning power, and skill in handling statistics . . . we had known their strength all along: an impatient cutting through of the phony . . . a growing capacity for political analysis which helped counter the low expectations their teachers had always had of them and which many had had of themselves, and more, their knowledge of the naked facts of society."[36] Even though movement participants had a policy of keeping student and faculty organizing meetings separate, the dialogues in classrooms, hallways, open assemblies, and student newspapers demonstrated a community that had undergone a fiery baptism of education as direct action.

However, Open Admissions soon became unsustainable in the face of deepening austerity, and the SEEK Program became inundated, embattled, and under-resourced at the moment that it provided an exceptional new model for what politically focused writing in a nurturing, small-scale environment could look like. A review of SEEK student enrollment statistics demonstrates how quickly the program had to cope with City College's expansion: in its inaugural year of 1965, SEEK enrolled 109 students; by 1967, the number grew to 600; and by Fall 1970, over 3,500 new students were brought into SEEK. One of Open Admissions' most stalwart advocates, Rich's husband Conrad, pivoted in Spring 1970 to criticize the CUNY administration's practice of admitting vast numbers of new students without sufficiently expanding its faculty or resources. As recounted by his colleague Jay Schulman, in a February 1970 campus debate on Open Admissions, Conrad demanded that students "do anything and everything to fight this program" given the unsustainable way that it was being rolled out.[37] During the summer of 1970, Shaughnessy hired and trained more than forty new full- and part-time teachers to prepare for the deluge. Within one year, she would confide to a friend, "I am writing from *under water*—way down deep in a churning, murky, frenzied world full of sentence fragments, and sweet, betrayed students, and memos and suspicious colleagues. . . . I cannot imagine keeping up with the many demands this job makes and I am too busy to contemplate the outcome."[38]

---

35 In Patricia Romney's *We Were There: The Third World Women's Alliance and the Second Wave*, we learn of a student dealing with sexism within SEEK who ended up joining the Third World Women's Alliance. Gratitude to Vani Kannan for this reference.

36 Rich, "Teaching Language in Open Admissions (1972)," 58.

37 Holladay, *The Power of Adrienne Rich*, 204.

38 Jane Maher, *Mina P. Shaughnessy: Her Life and Work* (Urbana: National Council of Teachers of English, 1997), 104–105 (emphasis added).

Re-visioning and Diving into SEEK

Even with these tempestuous transitions, Adrienne Rich continued to welcome her students into vital engagement with the times, as she deepened her focus on writing as a practice of social empowerment. In a May 1970 memo to students before a national student strike, Rich wrote, "Whether or not your classes are meeting as usual, don't stay away from the campus! . . . Come to the campus, talk to people, see what is happening, argue, act. The national student strike is not simply about Cambodia and Kent State, it concerns all political oppression, and the lives of all who live under the US government, here and abroad." The impact of Harlem University persisted. Rich recognized the campus as a staging ground for wider geopolitical interventions, as seen in her poetry-infused teaching notes:

> Classroom as cell—unit—enclosed & enclosing space in which
> teacher & students are alone together
> Can be prison cell commune
> trap junction—place of coming-together
> torture chamber
> But also part of much bigger nationwide cultural revolution[39]

Rich tuned into the classroom's dialectical power, fostering situations in which an array of relations could emerge. Outside the classroom, however, Rich's marriage to Conrad was coming apart. In October 1970, Rich and her sons' lives were profoundly impacted by news of Conrad's suicide. Conrad received a glowing community eulogy at City College, which also honored SEEK counselor Betty Rawls, who had died in a plane crash.[40] Rich's *Will to Change* was published just two months later. It would take Rich more than fifteen years to directly write about her husband's death:

> no person, / trying to take responsibility for her or his identity, should
> have to / be so alone. There must be those among whom we can sit down
> / and weep, and still be counted as warriors. (I make up this strange, an-
> gry packet for you, threaded with love.) I think you thought / there was
> no such place for you, and perhaps there was none then, / and perhaps
> there is none now; but we will have to make it, we who / want an end to
> suffering, who want to change the laws of history, if / we are not to *give*
> *ourselves away.*[41]

These reflections—incalculable grief alchemized into vulnerable bravery—chronicle how far Rich had come in processing Conrad's suicide and suggest that her City College experiences sustained this emotional transfiguration.

In Spring 1971, Rich, who had struggled with physical mobility since being diagnosed with rheumatoid arthritis at the age of twenty-two, including enduring a knee

---

39 Adrienne Rich, "To: ALL Students in English 1.8 B2 and 1.8 C4," Carton 9, Folder 390; "SEEK Notes," Carton 9, Folder 389, both in Adrienne Rich Papers. See also Brown, et al., eds., *Adrienne Rich: "What we are part of." Teaching at CUNY, 1968–1974*, Part I, 10, 15.

40 Holladay, *The Power of Adrienne Rich*, 214, 218.

41 Adrienne Rich, "Sources: XXII," *Your Native Land, Your Life: Poems* (New York: W.W. Norton and Company, 1986), 25 (emphasis in original).

replacement in 1966, took a leave of absence from City College. In late 1969, she had suddenly become terrified to descend staircases, in her sister's home and then in a subway station. At that moment, Rich experienced a phobia "coming on very fast, capable of paralyzing my life," which she had to seek therapy to overcome.[42] Now again beset by knee pain, Rich used crutches and a cane, an outward expression of shifting self-articulation. During this time, she rekindled her friendship with Lorde.[43] When she returned in Fall 1971 as an assistant professor in English, Rich implemented an interdisciplinary, two-semester composition course in which she could work intimately with a writing cohort through readings like Henrik Ibsen's *A Doll's House*, D.H. Lawrence's *Sons and Lovers*, Jerome Rothenberg's *Technicians of the Sacred*, and Piri Thomas's *Down These Mean Streets*. She welcomed the arrival of the new semester with the words, "This class will start from the idea that language—the way we put words together—is a way of acting on reality and eventually gaining more control of one's life."[44]

Rich began to foreground the feminist process of *re-vision* as reinvention, both in writing and lived experiences.[45] She would use another of Ibsen's plays as the title of her 1971 essay "When We Dead Awaken: Writing as Re-Vision," in which she advocated for women's lives and literatures to be revealed and reinterpreted, in part by chronicling her own path as a woman poet.[46] Just as she had reconsidered with SEEK students the racism embedded in canonical texts, she now turned towards the sexism that undergirded most Western literature:

> Re-vision—the act of looking back, of seeing with fresh eyes, of entering an old text from a new critical direction—is for women more than a chapter in cultural history: it is an act of survival. Until we can understand the assumptions in which we are drenched we cannot know ourselves. And this drive to self-knowledge, for women, is more than a search for identity: it is part of our refusal of the self-destructiveness of male-dominated society.[47]

Rich highlighted the political implications of this process, noting that "a change in the concept of sexual identity is essential if we are not going to see the old political order

---

42 Holladay, *The Power of Adrienne Rich*, 169, 206–207, 225, 248. See also Lynn Steger Strong, "How Adrienne Rich Changed Her Mind," *The New Republic*, May 13, 2021, https://newrepublic.com/article/162365/adrienne-rich-changed-mind-biography-review/; Michelle Dean, "Adrienne Rich's Feminist Awakening," *The New Republic*, April 3, 2016, https://newrepublic.com/article/132117/adrienne-richs-feminist-awakening/.

43 Holladay, *The Power of Adrienne Rich*, 221–222.

44 For this semester, Rich shared an office with the poet Gwendolyn Brooks, who was briefly a Poet-in-Residence at City College until she suffered a minor heart attack in December 1971. See Adrienne Rich, "English 1-H Fall 1971," Carton 9, Folder 388, Adrienne Rich Papers. See also Brown, et al., eds., *Adrienne Rich: "What we are part of:" Teaching at CUNY, 1968–1974*, Part II, 22–23.

45 For an elaboration on this theme in Rich's work, see William J. Camponovo, "'An Instrument in the Shape / of a Woman': Reading as Re-Vision in Adrienne Rich," PhD diss., CUNY Graduate Center, 2020.

46 "When We Dead Awaken" was also the title of a poem written by Rich that year and offers a dual textual interpretation for how she activates Ibsen's work in a pedagogical context.

47 Adrienne Rich, "When We Dead Awaken: Writing as Re-Vision (1971)," in *On Lies, Secrets, and Silence: Selected Prose 1966–1978* (New York. W.W. Norton, 1979), 35. See also Claire Schwartz, "Reading Otherwise: On Kinship, Racial Pedagogy, and Reading as Revision," *Jewish Currents*, March 21, 2022, https://jewishcurrents.org/reading-otherwise/.

reassert itself in every new revolution."[48]

By framing re-visioning in *compositional* terms, Rich braided the processes of reading, writing, interpersonal relationships, and liberation strategies in a way that recalls how Italian and US autonomist Marxists of the 1960s and 70s developed the notion of *class composition* as a "conceptual tool for understanding the process whereby the working class is composed, decomposed, and recomposed."[49] With Rich, and indeed with the whole cast of educators, students, and community actors held inside this book's pages, we see a profoundly generative cycle in which their experiences became documented and clarified in their writing, which in turn influenced their actions, which themselves became reinscribed in their writing, as relationships with each other, City College, and New York City reconstituted their shared trajectories. Moreover, in the face of devastating personal, relational, institutional, and social setbacks, these people's senses of self and commitments to each other would decompose, become re-visioned, and re-form. Rich's attention to the material quality of these reinventions resonates with work done in this period by Italian and US Marxist feminists like Mariarosa Dalla Costa, Silvia Federici, and Selma James.[50] At this time, Rich underwent major shifts—frequenting feminist readings, study groups, and community gatherings while reassessing her role as a now-single mother and caretaker of three sons—absorbing lessons in real time from her life.

Rich's injunction to re-vision conflicted with the politics of *anti-revisionism*—a vehement disdain for new or diverging interpretations of Marxist-Leninist-Maoist-Stalinist orthodoxies—that held sway over much of the US "New Communist Movement." In *Revolution in the Air: Sixties Radical Turn to Lenin, Mao, and Che*, Max Elbaum explains[51]:

> Much of the young movement's practical organizing and propaganda work was afflicted by a counterproductive ultraleft tilt. . . . Setting up small, politically pure 'mass organizations' under antirevisionist control was almost always preferred over long-term base building and contention for influence within actually existing mass organizations. . . . Militant rhetoric was regarded as a necessary staple of mass agitation, and a general spirit of 'looking over your left shoulder'—to make sure positions

48 Rich, "When We Dead Awaken," 35.

49 David P. Palazzo, "The 'Social Factory' in Postwar Italian Radical Thought from Operaismo to Autonomia," PhD diss., CUNY Graduate Center, 2014, 125. See also Steve Wright, *Storming Heaven: Class Composition and Struggle in Italian Autonomous Marxism* (London: Pluto Press, 2002).

50 See Mariarosa Dalla Costa and Selma James, *The Power of Women and the Subversion of Community*; Silvia Federici, *Wages Against Housework*; Silvia Federici and Arlen Austin, eds., *Wages for Housework: The New York Committee 1972–1977*.

51 Max Elbaum, *Revolution in the Air: Sixties Radicals Turn to Lenin, Mao, and Che* (New York: Verso, 2002), 118. See also Candace Cohn, "Privilege and the working class," *Socialist Worker*, April 15, 2015, https://socialistworker.org/2015/04/15/privilege-and-the-working-class/. To be sure, not all revolutionaries at the time were of these Stalinist and Maoist persuasions. The Johnson-Forest Tendency and Sojourner Truth Organization are two notable exceptions. See C. L. R. James, Grace C. Lee, and Cornelius Castoriadis, *Facing Reality* (Detroit: Correspondence Publishing Co., 1958); Michael Staudenmaier, *Truth and Revolution: A History of the Sojourner Truth Organization, 1969–1986* (Chico: AK Press, 2012). Anarchists also infused organizing and educational milieus with practices of autonomism, direct democracy, and feminism. See Andrew Cornell, *Unruly Equality: US Anarchism in the Twentieth Century* (Berkeley: University of California Press, 2016); Joel Spring, *A Primer of Libertarian Education* (Montreal: Black Rose Books, 1975); Perspectives Editorial Collective, *Perspectives on Anarchist Theory: Anarcha-Feminisms* 29 (Portland: Institute for Anarchist Studies, 2016).

could not be criticized as insufficiently revolutionary—infused much of the groups' political work.

As evidenced by the newspapers, speeches, and literatures of the time, US communists held onto a relatively narrow range of ossified terms that maintained fealty to perspectives inherited from the Russian and Chinese state revolutions. In contrast, echoing Toni Cade Bambara's "On the Issue of Roles," Rich critiqued: "'Political' poetry by men remains stranded amid the struggles for power among male groups; in condemning US imperialism or the Chilean junta the poet can claim to speak for the oppressed while remaining, as male, part of a system of sexual oppression. The enemy is always outside the self, the struggle somewhere else. . . . As women, we have our work cut out for us."[52]

Rich, meanwhile, saw—within the few years after Open Admissions began—that the Black/white schism of 1960s desegregation battles had recomposed into a broader Third Worldist attention to collaborating across multiple identities in CUNY and New York City. At the conclusion of the Spring 1972 semester, Rich meditated in a department dispatch:

> When we speak the word 'childhood' in a C.C.N.Y. classroom in 1972 we may unconsciously be evoking a period that took place in Puerto Rico, North Carolina, Israel, Cyprus, Hongkong, Queens, Haiti, Germany or 125th Street. The richness of this variety is staggering, the problems it presents complex. I remember when we used to talk, in SEEK, of the problems of being a white teacher in almost all-black classroom; now we are all teachers of whatever race in classrooms where 'identity' is kaleidoscopic.[53]

Publicly, Rich delved into this complex transition period with the essay "Teaching Language in Open Admissions (1972)," which analyzed how the SEEK faculty's experiences with the insurgent Black and Puerto Rican student population before, during, and after the strike catapulted their teaching experiences outward for broader audiences. Rich also waded through the frustrations that she, colleagues, and students endured as the City College administration oversaw a built-for-duress Open Admissions policy while tersely judging "motivation" and "intellectual competency" on an "overcrowded campus where in winter there is often no place to sit between classes. . . with the incessant pressure of time and money driving at them to rush, to get through, to amass the needed credits somehow, to drop out, to stay on with gritted teeth."[54] On a larger level, the state government's insufficient funding hamstrung the promise of Open Admissions, the direct human toll of which the essay recounts. Rich's report remains an

---

52 Rich, "When We Dead Awaken," 49. In her later essays, Rich returned to and expanded Marxism via an engagement with the work of Raya Dunayevskaya, Rosa Luxemburg, and Leon Trotsky. See, for example, "Raya Dunayevskaya's Marx," in *Arts of the Possible: Essays and Conversations* (New York: W.W. Norton and Company, 2001). See also "The muralist," in *What Is Found There: Notebooks on Poetry and Politics* (New York: W.W. Norton and Company, 1993) and "Notes Toward a Politics of Location (1984)," in *Blood, Bread, and Poetry: Selected Prose 1979–1985* (New York: W.W. Norton and Company, 1986).

53 Adrienne Rich, "Final Comments on the Interdisciplinary Program, Spring 1972," Carton 9, Folder 387, Adrienne Rich Papers. See also Brown, et al., eds., *Adrienne Rich: "What we are part of:" Teaching at CUNY, 1968–1974*, Part I, 39.

54 Rich, "Teaching Language in Open Admissions (1972)," 60.

urgent reflection about SEEK's heroic role in the formation of an Open Admissions policy with educational-democratic practices that emanated across the country.

While "Teaching Language in Open Admissions" framed these issues in a clear, prosaic style, Rich also encoded them more subversively in one of her most lauded poems, "Diving into the Wreck." Also written in 1972, this poem offers another written chronicle of Rich's experiences at City College.[55] Since its 1973 publication, the poem has been almost universally interpreted as an allegory of a woman's feminist transformation in reclaiming her own buried past.[56] Several reviews agree on the self-affirming power through which the poem's speaker transcends gender to become androgynous.[57] With affinity for these readings, we can more precisely *locate*—to use a word so important to Rich—"Diving Into the Wreck" within the context of her writing and teaching life at the time.[58] This poem provides a metaphoric view of her experiences in SEEK classrooms, hidden in plain sight. Read this way, the poem becomes a potent document of the SEEK Program's aims to create liberatory education while "under water." It identifies with and explores the depths of the students' "previously submerged culture" as well as how one might learn how to swim through a university transformed in profound but ambivalent ways by the upheavals of the previous years.[59]

Four years into teaching at City College, inundated by administrators' demands for her multiethnic students to climb up a ladder of Eurocentric progress, and only two years after conquering her phobia of descent, Rich describes in "Diving into the Wreck" a lone explorer who climbs down a ladder into an all-encompassing blackness. The speaker must forego plans and pedigree, "learn alone / to turn my body without force / in the deep element," and improvise "among so many who have always / lived here / swaying their crenellated fans / between the reefs / and besides / you breathe differently down here." As the speaker reveals:

> I came to explore the wreck.
> The words are purposes.
> The words are maps.
> I came to see the damage that was done
> and the treasures that prevail.[60]

---

55 Adrienne Rich, *Diving into the Wreck: Poems 1971–1972* (New York: W.W. Norton and Company, 1973), 22–24.

56 Alicia Ostriker, "Her Cargo: Adrienne Rich and the Common Language," *The American Poetry Review* 8.4 (July/August 1979): 8; Christine Stansell, "Review," *Off Our Backs* 4.3 (February 1974): 15; Amy Sickels, *Adrienne Rich* (Philadelphia: Chelsea House Publishers, 2005), 68.

57 Cheri Colby Langdell, *Adrienne Rich: The Moment of Change* (Westport: Praeger, 2004), 113; Grace Schulman, "*Diving into The Wreck: Poems 1971–1972* by Adrienne Rich," *The American Poetry Review* 2.5 (September/October 1973): 11.

58 In "Blood, Bread, and Poetry: The Location of the Poet (1984)," Rich recalled her time at City College: "I felt more and more urgently the dynamic between poetry as language and poetry as a kind of action, probing, burning, stripping, placing itself in dialogue with others out beyond the individual self." In "Notes toward a Politics of Location (1984)," Rich argued: "Begin with the material. Pick up again the long struggle against lofty and privileged abstraction . . . where, when, and under what conditions have women acted and been acted on, as women?" See Rich, *Blood, Bread, and Poetry*, 181, 213.

59 See Conor Tomás Reed, "'Treasures That Prevail': Adrienne Rich, the SEEK Program, and Social Movements at the City College of New York, 1968–1972," in Brown, et al., eds., *Adrienne Rich*, Part II; Reed, "Diving Into SEEK."

60 Rich, "Diving into the Wreck," 23.

Just as Laura (Riding) Jackson asserted that through poetry we can construct ourselves "out of the wreckage which is reality," Rich demonstrates here how a *re-visioned* urban classroom can turn enduring hardships and hidden histories "into this threadbare beauty."[61]

The setting of the ocean for this transformation is vital to measuring Rich and her SEEK students' recompositions. During and since the transatlantic slave trade, people of African descent have recognized the ocean as the figurative and literal site of terror, mourning, mutiny, endurance, and metamorphosis.[62] "Diving into the Wreck" implicitly celebrates this fecundity of African diasporic survival and reinvention. That Rich narrates her own real-time arrival at this revelation indicates how the poem unlearns individualized anguish and evolves into conscientious belonging. By refusing to leave their site of subaqueous duress, the under-resourced classroom space with "foul air or bitter cold, students crowded elbow to elbow, poor acoustics," Rich and her students use what they have to invent what they need.[63] In the process, an outward solidarity with the dark-haired mermaids and armored mermen in her classroom ("I am she: I am he") becomes reborn as a kaleidoscopic we. The poem concludes:

> we are the half-destroyed instruments
> that once held to a course
> the water-eaten log
> the fouled compass . . .
>
> We are, I am, you are
> by cowardice or courage
> the one who find our way
> back to this scene
> carrying a knife, a camera
> a book of myths
> in which
> our names do not appear.[64]

Rich's complicity with SEEK students to critically delve into and write about Western books that contained an abundance of skewed myths about them transformed language into new "maps," purposes, and directions for cross-cultural exhumation. Together, during a period of major institutional and social tumult, they found and composed "treasures that prevail" that otherwise could have been left buried in the wreckage. In an uncanny similarity to City College student Sol Funaroff's 1938 poem "The Bellbuoy," discussed in Chapter 1, Rich and her students were also "exiles from a future time," searching for shores of freedom from within the "cracked heart of the world."

---

61 Laura (Riding) Jackson, *Anarchism is Not Enough*, ed. Lisa Samuels (Berkeley: University of California Press, 2001), 114. Rich, "Diving into the Wreck," 24.

62 See, for example, Dionne Brand, *A Map to the Door of No Return: Notes to Belonging* (Toronto: Doubleday Canada, 2001); Saidiya Hartman, *Lose Your Mother: A Journey Along the Atlantic Slave Route* (New York: Farrar, Straus and Giroux, 2008); M. NourbeSe Phillip, *Zong!* (Middletown: Wesleyan University Press, 2011); Christina Sharpe, *In the Wake: On Blackness and Being* (Durham: Duke University Press, 2016).

63 Rich, "Final Comments on the Interdisciplinary Program, Spring 1972." See also Brown, et al., eds., *Adrienne Rich: "What we are part of:" Teaching at CUNY, 1968–1974*, Part I, 36.

64 Rich, "Diving into the Wreck," 24.

Our interpretation of Rich's experiences during this time flows even further outward from City College, as seen with her family's role in creating the Elizabeth Cleaners Street School, an autonomous high school at West 91st Street and Columbus Avenue about which Rich wrote in a 1972 article, "The Case for a Drop-Out School." Part of this text, and the students' writings (including two of Rich's sons), were published that year in a book called *Starting Your Own High School*. There, Rich explained the genesis of the autonomous school: "in June, 1970, after checking their plans with Operation Move-In, the local squatters organization, about half a dozen parents, two prospective teachers, and about ten students broke open the entrance of the abandoned cleaners and took possession."[65] As the students claimed control over hiring teachers and forming curricular directions, Rich and the other parents learned to turn their bodies "without force in the deep element" of this new autonomous youth education project, lessons which had manifested in Rich's own City College classrooms. She wrote of the Elizabeth Cleaners Street School experiment:

> [T]his is no dream-school, no perfect solution. It's a small, loosely knit, struggling group of people in an unheated, improvised storefront, learning about themselves, each other, community relations, plumbing, politics, how and why structures develop or crumble—all this along with more academic-sounding 'subjects' like Cuba or American history or creative writing or psychology. . . . My children go to school this year to a place where they want to be. They feel deeply involved even when they don't like what's going on. . . . They're learning to improvise, to do things for themselves, to make mistakes and survive them.[66]

"Diving into the Wreck" and these afterlives demonstrate how City College pedagogies radiated outwards for a national audience of educators, even as Open Admissions was under attack. SEEK director Mina Shaughnessy's December 1975 address at the Modern Language Association Conference, "Diving In: An Introduction to Basic Writing," whose title was most likely a reference to Rich's poem, also explores a composition ethos grounded in feminist antiracist student empowerment. Their collaboration across several years is evident in Rich's teaching archives and Shaughnessy's speech, which combines lessons from the City College trenches to transmit SEEK's approach into four steps to decolonize a nation of educators, albeit in language that readopts a colonial paradigm: "GUARDING THE TOWER, CONVERTING THE NATIVES, SOUNDING THE DEPTHS, and DIVING IN." As the essay argues, the teacher must unlearn elitist academic paternalism to become embedded among a diverse working-class student population in a new Open Admissions era. Ultimately, the diver who has "come this far must now make a decision that demands professional courage—the decision to remediate [her/him/their]self, to become a student of new disciplines and of students themselves in order to perceive both their difficulties and their incipient excellence."[67]

---

65 Rich, "Beginnings," in *Starting Your Own High School*, ed. Elizabeth Cleaners Street School People (New York: Random House, 1972), 25.

66 Adrienne Rich, "The Case for a Drop-Out School," *New York Review of Books* (June 15, 1972): 33–34.

67 Mina P. Shaughnessy, "Diving In: An Introduction to Basic Writing," *College Composition and Communication* 27 (October 1976): 238.

At this moment, US higher education was rapidly desegregating admissions, but often with "basic writing" instruction, testing, and literacy requirements that discouraged and suppressed Black and Brown students.[68] Shaughnessy's "Diving In" re-envisioned the long-debased field of "remedial writing" as an urgent project to build cultural democracy through critical literacy, even if her more widely renowned 1977 book *Errors and Expectations* elided much of the City College milieu in which these pedagogies emerged.

From "Blackstudies" to *Deotha*

The Open Admissions wave cascaded unevenly across CUNY, as Lorde discovered while teaching a Fall 1969–Spring 1970 "Race and Education" class in the Lehman College Education Department to "99 percent white" students who refused to fruitfully engage with her lectures or learning materials on how to counteract racism in the classroom and society at large. The paucity of these future public schoolteachers' consciousness on race and colonialism underscored why the City College strike had demanded that all Education majors be required to take Black and Puerto Rican history and learn Spanish. Lorde relocated in Fall 1970 to the rapidly desegregating John Jay College, where she began as the English Department's first Black lecturer, and then in February 1971 joined the newly formed Black and Puerto Rican Studies Department.[69]

Opened in 1965 as the College of Police Science (COPS), and then renamed John Jay College of Criminal Justice in 1967, it was created to grant New York City police officers college degrees and was recognized by the federal government as a site of law enforcement theory and practice. Lorde's experiences at Tougaloo and City College stood in stark contrast to John Jay, where police officer students wore their guns inside classrooms and the ideological direction of teaching was carefully monitored by the administration.[70] As had been the case at City College, the start of Open Admissions in 1970 upended the demographics at John Jay, where a majority Euro middle-class police student body was met with an influx of Black and Puerto Rican working-class students who abhorred police in their neighborhoods. Between 1969 and 1974, the population of Black, Puerto Rican, and "Other" students shifted from 14 percent to 44 percent of the student body.[71] The faculty size doubled in 1970, doubled again in 1971, and then expanded by another 25 percent in 1972. "The number of undergraduates grew from 2,600 (one out of five of whom were "civilians"); to 6,700 in 1972 (over half were civilians); and finally, over 8,600 students in 1973."[72]

Lorde's trajectory was influenced by this moment of teaching writing composition through history, literature, psychology, sociology, and urban studies to a John Jay

68 Annie S. Mendenhall, *Desegregation State: College Writing Programs after the Civil Rights Movement* (Logan: Utah State University Press, 2022).

69 Lorde, "An Interview: Adrienne Rich and Audre Lorde," 95–97.

70 In 1969, the college received a $200,700 federal grant to cover eight hundred police officers' tuition. In Fall 1970, FBI Director J. Edgar Hoover forced fifteen FBI agents to drop out of John Jay after Sociology professor Abraham Blumberg criticized the organization and Hoover himself. See "Timeline of John Jay College History," in the digital exhibition *Fifty Years of Educating for Justice*, https://dc.lib.jjay.cuny.edu/index.php/About/50th#1964/.

71 Gumbs, "Nobody Mean More," 245.

72 See "Timeline of John Jay College History."

student body whose demographics were rapidly reconstituting alongside Lorde's own self-transformations. Alexis Pauline Gumbs argues that the CUNY administration hired Lorde as a *composition* instructor: "in the most cynical sense, the teaching for which [she was] first hired was the mammy labor of the university," insofar as Lorde was "not only hired to teach students to compose coherent essays . . . but also hired to teach the student population how to *be composed*, contained, and conformist in a society in transition."[73] However, Lorde's teaching archives show a different approach, in which she explored, through a critical interdisciplinary Black Women's Studies methodology, the cultural and scientific depths of racism with her Black, Puerto Rican, and Euro students—those policed and policing, suddenly together in the same classroom.

In this instance, we see the disguised power of the composition classroom—an "entry-level" learning space in which Lorde foundationally intervened with a non-self-selecting group replete with differences.[74] As a not-yet-out Black lesbian, Lorde's role as an educator/mediator between her Black and Puerto Rican men students and her Irish, Italian, and Jewish men students forged a rare tenacity that enabled her to speak out later in more public settings across racialized differences between women as well as about divisions in Black communities around sexism and homophobia.[75] As Lorde taught the changing social composition of John Jay students, she too was remade by these pedagogical challenges. As Miriam Atkin and Iemanjá Brown point out, "If scholars tend to separate the poet from the teacher from the human, then Lorde writes them back in as one."[76]

For one academic year, Lorde was instrumental in the formation of the Black and Puerto Rican Studies Department. During this time, she taught "Race and the Urban Situation," with the subtitle "'or Civilization or Death to All American Savages' (Officer's toast, 1779)," in which she and students examined settler colonialism and the enslavement of Native and African peoples as interwoven originating forms of structural racism in the United States. They discussed racism's distinct effects on Black and Euro people, using texts like Joel Kovel's *White Racism*, James and Grace Lee Boggs' *Uprooting Racism and Racists in the United States*, R.D. Laing's *The Politics of Experience*, Toni Cade Bambara's *The Black Woman*, and Florence Kennedy's essay "Institutionalized Oppression vs. The Female." Lorde also included Black, Puerto Rican, and women's fiction such as Nella Larsen's *Quicksand*, Piri Thomas' *Down These Mean Streets*, Gertrude Stein's "Melanctha," and the Black Arts anthology *Amistad*.

Lorde's teaching archives dissect how people enact oppressions through creating targets for violence in others to strip away the recognition of their humanity. In her class notes, Lorde writes: "The 1st primary technique is dehumanization. What is? the

---

73 Gumbs, "Nobody Mean More," 243 (emphasis in original).

74 Bob Moses and Jay Gillen of the Baltimore Algebra Project have written about the strategic space of required "introductory" subjects like composition and mathematics as places where radicals can embed themselves to reach and impact a broader cross section of students. See Bob Moses, *Radical Equations: Civil Rights from Mississippi to the Algebra Project* (Boston: Beacon Press, 2002); Jay Gillen, *Educating for Insurgency: The Roles of Young People in Schools of Poverty* (Chico: AK Press, 2014).

75 Matt Brim, *Poor Queer Studies: Confronting Elitism in the University* (Durham: Duke University Press, 2020), 111.

76 Miriam Atkin and Iemanjá Brown, eds., *Audre Lorde: "I teach myself in outline," Notes, Journals, Syllabi, & an Excerpt from Deotha*, in *Lost & Found: The CUNY Poetics Document Initiative, Series 7* (New York: The Center for the Humanities, Graduate Center of the City University of New York, 2017), 12.

easiest way to justify oppression is to make object just that—object. Not humans in ships—things, slaves, Negroes. The racist must create an image in his mind of something deserving oppression—nonhuman." Instead of seeing colonialism, racism, and whiteness existing across all time, Lorde emphasizes a historical process:

> Institutional racism against Indian could justify wiping them off land. Same development of slavery. First blacks here were not slaves—but indentured servants. But with the growth of tobacco as a cash crop, free labor pool was needed. Not Indians. Blacks.
>
> 1629 rights (?)—Christian
> 1655 English
> 1660 White

Lorde prompts her students to consider: "What are 1. the effects of racism in yourself; 2. what are you doing or prepared to do to alter these attitudes in yourself [and] in your world." Her midterm poses a quotation by Malcolm X on how to confront contemporary racism when equipped with past lessons: "Power steps back only in the face of more power. Do you find this an accurate statement in terms of history of black people in America? Discuss four historical occurrences from before the Mayflower as examples illustrating your answer."[77] Lorde's classroom approach identified interpersonal and structural harms while also urging students to plot how to overcome these conditions.

During this time, Lorde wrote prolifically, publishing *From A Land Where Other People Live* in 1973 and *New York Head Shop and Museum* in 1974. In these collections, she shows how instead of becoming inured to the grind of slow death, people can name the poisons of colonial-racial-gendered capitalism and eject them from both the body and society through a meticulous documentation of their causes and effects. Although only a few of the poems directly address her teaching life, several are dedicated to her City College colleagues. "Movement Song," an intimate plea for recognition between two people, was perhaps written for June Jordan, who wrote of it in a letter to Lorde, "it is mysterious still, to me: dense and beautiful, and nowhere harsh."[78] Lorde's poem to Toni Cade Bambara, "Dear Toni Instead of a Letter of Congratulation Upon Your Book and Your Daughter Whom You Say You Are Raising To Be a Correct Little Sister," enshrines their City College bond backwards and forwards across generations of Black women.

New York Head Shop and Museum conveys the surreal anguish of urban poverty in ways reminiscent of Federico García Lorca's *Poeta en Nueva York* and David Henderson's *De Mayor of Harlem*. Disproportionate cancer rates and sewer plants in Black neighborhoods, young women heroin users on the train, expired goods at the Key Food supermarket—Lorde locates everyday urban violence in the city's infrastructure as a precondition for overturning it. She challenges the assumed solidarities of working-class revolution, as in the poem "May Day Postscript to Karl Marx" about

---

77 Audre Lorde, "Race and the Urban Situation," Series 2.5, Box 46; "Journals; History/lit 210," Series 2.5, Box 46; "Journals; Hist/lit suggested readings," Series 10, Box 82, Folder 25; "Racist society," Series 2.5, Box 46; "Journals," Series 2.5, Box 46; "Journals," Series 10, Box 83, Folder 26, all in Audre Lorde Papers. See also Atkin and Brown, eds., *Audre Lorde: "I teach myself in outline,"* 18–26, 29, 31.

78 June Jordan, Letter to Audre Lorde, Series 1, Box 3, Folder 63, Audre Lorde Papers.

the Hard Hat Riot in May 1970, during which police and construction workers beat up dozens of students on Wall Street who were striking against the expanding war in Vietnam and student massacres at Jackson and Kent State Universities.[79] The poem "Viet-Nam Addenda" (for / Clifford), a prelude to her poem "Power," links the shooting of ten-year-old Black boy Clifford Glover with the indiscriminate US carnage in Vietnam.[80]

Only this collection's concluding poem, "Blackstudies," reveals her acrimonious teaching conditions, dramatized in nightmarish scenes of a teacher and her students in a classroom seventeen stories high.[81] Lorde's archives illuminate how she navigated severe conflicts over the direction of the Black and Puerto Rican Studies Department between the John Jay administration, Chairperson F. Beresford Jones, and its faculty members. This situation was exacerbated when Black students were pitted against her as a lesbian feminist teacher, her office desk was searched, and she and her children received threatening phone calls.[82] Angela Bowen points out how the poem interweaves Lorde's hidden pedagogical injuries from Tougaloo to John Jay:

> 'Blackstudies' is a psycho-sociological study in fear: of being rejected by students as an 'inauthentic' Black woman because of her marriage to a white man; of failing in her attempt to explain her wider vision of the world to students deeply immersed in their 1960s pride of solidarity in 'Blackness'; and of the painful shunning she endures (her defiance notwithstanding) at the hands of the Black Arts Movement hierarchy . . . Lorde's needs were two-fold: to channel her feelings directly into poetry *and* keep the meaning opaque for protection.[83]

Read alongside Rich's "Diving into the Wreck," this poem offers another translucent and mythological account of teaching at CUNY, but it reveals a more trepidatious scenario between a teacher and their students, and is thus an important counterweight to Rich's depiction of transformative survival. The poem candidly portrays the teacher's alienation from students with whom she is supposed to share ethnic/cultural belonging, and which could then become internalized as a failure of pedagogical craft:

> outside my door they are waiting
> with questions that feel like judgements
> when they are unanswered . . .
> I am afraid

---

79 Jefferson Cowie, "The 'Hard Hat Riot' Was a Preview of Today's Political Divisions," *New York Times*, May 11, 2020, https://www.nytimes.com/2020/05/11/nyregion/hard-hat-riot.html/.

80 *Black Main Street*, "Never Forget: 10-Year-Old Clifford Glover Shot In The Back By NYPD," July 22, 2016, https://blackmainstreet.net/never-forget-nypd-officer-killed-10-year-old-clifford-glover/.

81 See Gumbs, "*17th Floor*: A pedagogical oracle from/with Audre Lorde," *Journal of Lesbian Studies* 21, no. 4 (2016): 375–390.

82 Atkin and Brown, eds., *Audre Lorde: "I teach myself in outline,"* 11.

83 Angela Bowen, "Diving into Audre Lorde's 'Blackstudies,'" *Meridians: Feminism, Race, Transnationalism* 4.1 (2003): 114–115. Bowen's title links Lorde and Rich but does not provide the analysis of "Diving into the Wreck" as also a portrait of a CUNY classroom experience.

that the mouths I feed will turn against me
will refuse to swallow in the silence
I am warning them to avoid
I am afraid they will kernel me out like a walnut
extracting the nourishing seed
as my husk stains their lips
with the mixed colors of my pain.

Nevertheless, as a *Blackstudies poem* that mirrors her teaching approach, it offers an interdisciplinary Afro-syncretic symbolism "that knits truth into fable / to leave my story behind." In the process, it differently ritualizes the Eurocentric classroom space, assuming full risk for these kinds of collisions and misconnections.[84]

Alexis Pauline Gumbs identifies this breakthrough in Lorde's poetry at the time that "enables her to create a speaker that can move from subject to subject or, as she will later write in her dream journal, to understand that she is every person in her own nightmare and is also accountable to everyone in her nightmare."[85] Gumbs helps us reconsider that perhaps the students in the poem are externalizations of the various conflicting facets that comprise the internal coalition of Lorde's identity. We can interpret how her actual experiences with students may have been linked to her own self-doubt, an example of how sometimes teachers make fearsome students out of their own anxieties.

It wasn't until the mid-1980s, well after she left John Jay, however, that Lorde would write more transparently about the torment she endured there. After she completed *Zami: A New Spelling of My Name*, Lorde began a second biomythographical work, *Deotha*, about a Black artist named Deotha Chambers who teaches in a Black and Puerto Rican Studies Department at Connors College under an authoritarian chairperson named Cumberbatch Smith.[86] Reading across "Blackstudies," *Deotha*, and Lorde's John Jay teaching archives shows the fraught process whereby Black and Puerto Rican Studies was institutionalized by faculty, students, and an administration with opposing intentions. Lorde recognized how critiquing people within an emerging oppressed institution, organization, or movement may provide ammunition for it to be attacked, but as she later affirmed, "your silence will not protect you" either.[87]

Through the character Deotha, Lorde details the withering effects of toxic leadership; hierarchies between students, teachers, and administrators, exacerbated by petty power plays; and the misogyny and homophobia that roiled behind an empowering Black Studies (of heterosexual men) veneer. These negative forces, to be sure, contrast with the beautiful moments that blossom in the classroom. In one section, Deotha recalls an instance with students that could serve as a classroom journal entry for Lorde:

---

84 Lorde, "Blackstudies," in *Collected Poems of Audre Lorde*, 153–154. Ellipsis mine.

85 Gumbs, "Nobody Mean More," 247.

86 Surprisingly, this revelatory work, whose unfinished vignettes are housed in Lorde's archives, had only been written about in Alexis De Veaux's 2004 biography *Warrior Poet* until the 2017 *Lost & Found* publication of Lorde's CUNY teaching archives, which excerpts the work. See Audre Lorde, "Deotha," Series 2.1, Box 17, Folder 88, Audre Lorde Papers. See also Atkin and Brown, eds., *Audre Lorde: "I teach myself in outline,"* 43–65.

87 Lorde, "The Transformation of Silence into Language and Action," in *Sister Outsider*, 41.

She heard her voice two weeks ago as she'd opened the class—'What goes on in your head has a dignity and value. That's why you learn to write. So you can put it down, save it, share it. And in such a way as you can come back to it later and know what was going on.' Their faces shone like fire in the Connors afternoon sun. Paulo Freire said give them something they care about and they learn to write faster.[88]

Deotha also emphasizes the intimate value of a Black woman educator's self-care within the larger structural and interpersonal college dynamics that necessitate such healing. In a bathtub scene, Deotha narrates her cleansing process to immerse readers in a ritualized practice that renders common household items talismanic. Her self-soothing is interrupted by a phone call: "'Leave our department alone, lezzie!' The young angry voice was abrupt even a shade embarrassed Dee thought and was rapidly followed by a click as the connection was broken. . . . As she calls the neighbor, she wonders if the voice had been one of her own students." This fictionalized account mirrors Lorde's own encounters with harassment in the Black and Puerto Rican Studies Department that she had worked to co-construct. Unlike the aftermath of her poem "Power," in which she fears crossing paths with Thomas J. Shea—the police officer and John Jay student who killed ten-year-old Clifford Glover—in this case, the threat comes from potentially one of her own students.

The archival record remains unclear about whether infighting between Black Studies and Puerto Rican Studies faculty manifested in the ways that Lorde dramatizes, but if so, it's worth inquiring why and how the Black and Puerto Rican coalitional work that emerged in New York City around school desegregation and Ethnic Studies became imperiled once Black and Puerto Rican Studies were institutionalized in this university setting. While at City College, the administration sabotaged the formation of Third World Studies by fragmenting and stratifying the field in different departments, here at John Jay, Black and Puerto Rican faculty vied for limited power in the same department. Nevertheless, speculative possibilities abound on what a Black and Puerto Rican Studies Department led by Lorde could have manifested, as personified by her beloved biomythographical Deotha.[89] Even in hindsight, Lorde emphasized the urgency of the situation: "A relevant Black education. IF NOT NOW, WHEN? The very thought of it was an excitement that percolated through Deotha also, that kept her thinking and dreaming of the possibility for Black students at Connors. She could see the dangers of a limited vision at the same time as she felt her own grave reluctance to implement any broader one."[90]

As members of the John Jay Black and Puerto Rican Studies Department pushed Lorde out, she relocated to the English Department—ironically, cultivating more fruitful space for Black and Puerto Rican Studies by escaping its strictures. In one early interdisciplinary example of Lorde's role in claiming room for Women's Studies, Black Women's Studies, and Black Lesbian Studies in CUNY, she and Blanche Wiesen Cook co-taught a Spring 1972 English class, "American Women in Black and White." They

88 Lorde, "Deotha." See also Atkin and Brown, eds., *Audre Lorde: "I teach myself in outline,"* 15.

89 For Lorde, living with breast cancer which then spread to her liver, this writing project sustained her from the mid-1980s until her death in 1992. At one point, en route to St. Croix to receive medical treatment, she writes, "Make Deotha Chambers' story live." See Audre Lorde, *A Burst of Light* (Ann Arbor: Firebrand Books, 1988), 46.

90 Lorde, "Deotha." See also Atkin and Brown, eds., *Audre Lorde: "I teach myself in outline,"* 50.

discussed gender and racial archetypes, radicalism across suffrage and abolition, and sexual liberation with texts by writers such as Toni Cade Bambara, Mary Beard, Frantz Fanon, Elizabeth Gurley Flynn, Calvin Hernton, and Gerda Lerner. Cook recalls that even though all the course enrollees were "police officers and fire fighters and men, very quickly the women in the bars, in Page Three, and the Sea Colony heard that we were teaching. And they invaded our class, and then very quickly the police students brought their wives and their mothers and their sisters and their friends, and it was the most crowded classroom imaginable."[91] It's possible that in the more general arena of the English Department, rather than in the tightly surveilled Black and Puerto Rican Studies Department, Lorde could tactically convene such disparate students and community members for this rare cross-pollination.

With attention to these radical lesbian interventions, it's no coincidence that in 1973, the newly formed Gay Academic Union held its inaugural conference, "The Universities and the Gay Experience," at John Jay College.[92] This courageous claiming of queer space within a pro-police campus—only a few years after the Stonewall rebellion had fought against the NYPD for several nights—was not exempt from the threat of violence. A bomb scare was announced during the proceedings, and the group had to temporarily relocate outside (into a phalanx of police on the street) before returning to continue the panels.[93] Although no archival evidence verifies that Lorde was present, Cook confirms she was involved in the group.[94] From these all-too-secret campus battles in the early 1970s, Lorde defiantly recomposed herself in the national spotlight as a fear-transcending Black lesbian educator-poet.

Emerging Anger and Eros in Women's Studies

After a year spent at Brandeis University, Rich returned to City College for a final semester in Fall 1974 as a full professor, where she remained one of the few from the initial SEEK faculty cohort before quitting, exhausted, in January 1975.[95] In increasingly diversified classrooms, Rich deepened her radical feminist pedagogy—one that had begun with analyzing Black and existentialist literatures alongside canonical Western works, and then pivoted into explorations of women's liberation and solidarity across different realms of experience. This would come to define Rich's writing, teaching, and politics for the second half of her life and to frame her increasing public status as a fear-transcending Jewish lesbian educator-poet.

Materials from one of Rich's 1974 courses, "Images of Women in Poetry by Men," are emblematic of her interventions in the Women's Studies counter-discipline that

---

91 Blanche Wiesen Cook, "The Lesbian Movement with Blanche Wiesen Cook," interview by Alice Kessler-Harris, April 3, 2017, https://www.youtube.com/watch?v=ew00lc4JwiA/. See also *Lost Womyn's Space* (http://lostwomynsspace.blogspot.com/) and *NYC LGBT Historic Sites Projects* (https://www.ny-clgbtsites.org/) for more examples of lesbian, gay, and queer bars, like Page Three and the Sea Colony, that have disappeared from New York City.

92 Gay Academic Union, "The Universities and the Gay Experience: Proceedings of the Conference Sponsored by the Women and Men of the Gay Academic Union, November 23 and 24, 1973" (New York: Gay Academic Union, 1974). Gratitude to Matt Brim for reviving the historic significance of this conference.

93 Brim, *Poor Queer Studies*, 131–134.

94 De Veaux, *Warrior Poet*, 391 n78.

95 City College had proposed that Rich stay on as an adjunct and teach a class every other semester, which she declined. See Holladay, *The Power of Adrienne Rich*, 434 n2.

had begun to emerge—also seen in her essay "Toward a Woman-Centered University (1973–74)" from that same year.[96] Using poetry by various European and Euro-American men to explore how images of women appear as "persona (voice), myth, emotionally-charged metaphor, and lightning-rod sensibility," the course developed a feminist lens on Du Boisian double consciousness: "not to reduce these poets in terms of their male chauvinism or sexism, but to understand better how women function in men's imaginations and how we have hitherto seen ourselves in man-made mirrors." Her reading list included Virginia Woolf's *Three Guineas*, Simone de Beauvoir's *Second Sex*, Judy Grahn's *A Woman Is Talking to Death*, and the women's poetry anthologies *No More Masks*, *The World Split Open*, and *Rising Tides*. Rich retained attention to how a spectrum of oppressed people can emerge from the wreckage of historical erasure:

> Poetry (all art) connects with politics in that it comes out of a political situation. Who writes, who they write for, how the poet views himself in relation to society, is determined by who has power, who gets educated, who remains illiterate, who can get published. Until very recently for instance homosexuals could not write openly of their sexuality without being banned, censored and treated as obscene—e.g, Whitman; Blacks, especially women, were too busy fighting for survival to write; still, women and minorities have trouble finding recognition in the white male tradition.

Rich's loving dedication to her Black and Puerto Rican City College students' humanity across six years now grew into deeper affinities with women students and strategic collaboration with antipatriarchal men students. As she encapsulated in her class notes, "I want this course to be useful as well as beautiful."[97]

From these early CUNY collaborations, Lorde and Rich continued to fortify each other as sister interlocutors. Lorde's "Love Poem," a famous declaration of lesbian eros, was printed in February of that year in *Ms. Magazine*, which she proudly posted on her John Jay English office door. She had initially read the poem in 1973 at a women-owned bookstore/coffee house on West 72nd Street. Rich was in the audience to witness this "staggering moment."[98] Soon, Rich would also publicly proclaim her love for women, publishing two poems in the 1975 lesbian collection *Amazon Quarterly* and then starting a lifelong relationship with Michelle Cliff, who alongside Lorde actively engaged with Rich on questions of race and sexuality.[99] Alexis De Veaux notes the depth of honest exchange that these two women cultivated with each other, one that implicitly served as a model for interethnic lesbian feminist sisterhood: "The fact that they had a loving, trusting friendship, and respected each other intellectually, made it more possible, as time went by, for them to talk about and confront race."[100]

From the mid-1970s onwards, Lorde turned her pedagogy and writing inside out-

96 Rich, "Toward a Woman-Centered University," in *On Lies, Secrets, and Silence*, 125–155.

97 Adrienne Rich, "English 13.3W Images of Women in Poetry by Men," Carton 9, Folder 391; "Notes on Eng 13.3," Carton 9, Folder 392, both in Adrienne Rich Papers. See also Brown, et al., eds., *Adrienne Rich: "What we are part of:" Teaching at CUNY, 1968–1974*, Part II, 24–32.

98 De Veaux, *Warrior Poet*, 139. See also Kristen Hogan, *The Feminist Bookstore Movement: Lesbian Antiracism and Feminist Accountability* (Durham: Duke University Press, 2016).

99 Sickels, *Adrienne Rich*, 75–77.

100 De Veaux, *Warrior Poet*, 187.

ward to social movements more broadly. Her later 1970s poetry collections, including
Coal, Between Our Selves, and *The Black Unicorn,* continued to embed teaching insights on
the responsibility to name when Black lives are murdered ("Power" and "A Woman/
Dirge for Wasted Children"), imprisoned ("For Assata"), or die early from a lack of
quality healthcare ("Eulogy for Alvin Frost") as well as demonstrating the fecundity
of African orishas and places ("From the House of Yemanja" and "Dahomey") for a
Black/women/lesbian/movement readership. The difficult negotiation between herself and organizations whose entryways were at times fiercely guarded would be transcended in Lorde's famous coalitional self-assertion as a Black lesbian feminist socialist
anarchist warrior poet mother of two multiethnic children.[101]

In 1976, Rich published *Of Woman Born: Motherhood as Experience and Institution,* which
she had developed at an intense conjuncture following her husband's suicide, her embrace of lesbianism, and her choice to leave City College. In the book, Rich focuses on
the contradictory nature of institutionality—centralized and dispersed, concrete and
ideological, radical and repressive—and the varied institutions that women must sabotage, flee, defend, or invent anew.[102] Feminist scholar Haunani Kay-Trask highlights
Rich's use of the phrase *"sexual understructure* of social and political forms," which alerts
our senses to how institutions, usually recognized as brick-and-mortar objects, are as
historically embodied as they are spatial.[103] Rich writes, "[t]o destroy the institution
is not to abolish motherhood," affirming instead, "[i]t is to release the creation and
sustenance of life into the same realm of decision, struggle, surprise, imagination,
and conscious intelligence, as any other difficult, but freely chosen work."[104] Eula Biss
frames how this contrasts institutions as they are with how they can be: "The institution of motherhood, Rich writes, is superimposed over the potential of motherhood.
This is the potential relationship women might have to our reproductive powers and to
children. The institution of motherhood limits the full range of possibilities, and limits
our ability to imagine them."[105] Jennifer C. Nash also highlights how Black feminist
paradigms of motherhood have transcended Rich's analysis toward a more expansive
project of *reproductive justice* to "unite seemingly disparate political issues ranging from
clean drinking water to access to housing, from mass incarceration to transportation,
from the right to contraception to the right to child care."[106]

Drawing a link with previous chapters, we could perhaps hear in Rich's argument an
echo of calls to destroy institutions rather than a vision to transform them. Put more directly,
how do Rich's condemnations of the institution of motherhood relate to the institution of
the university? One way to think alongside Rich is to consider how in the 1986 edition of *Of*

---

101 Lorde, "Age, Race, Class, and Sex: Women Redefining Difference," in *Sister Outsider,* 114. See also
   Audre Lorde, "The Poet as Outsider, Session 4, May 17, 1984," in *dream of europe: Selected Seminars and
   Interviews, 1984–1992* (Chicago: Kenning Editions, 2020), 89; Dorothee Nolte's 1986 interview, "The
   Law is Male and White: Meeting with the Black Author, Audre Lorde," in *Conversations with Audre Lorde,*
   ed. Joan Wylie Hall (Jackson: University of Mississippi Press, 2004), 143.

102 Rich would further pursue this analysis in "Compulsory Heterosexuality and Lesbian Existence
   (1980)," in *Blood, Bread, and Poetry.* See also Amia Srinivasan, *The Right to Sex: Feminism in the 21st Century*
   (New York: Farrar, Straus and Giroux, 2021), 97–98.

103 Haunani Kay-Trask, *Eros and Power: The Promise of Feminist Theory* (Philadelphia: University of Pennsylvania Press, 1981), 2 (emphasis in original).

104 Rich, *Of Woman Born,* 280.

105 Eula Biss, "Of Institution Born," in Adrienne Rich, *Of Woman Born: Motherhood as Experience and Institution* (New York: W.W. Norton and Company, [1976] 2021), xiii.

106 Jennifer C. Nash, "The Political Life of Black Motherhood," *Feminist Studies* 44, no. 3 (2018): 702.

Woman Born, she dedicates ample space to defend abortion access: "The antiabortion move-- ment trivialises women's impulses towards education, independence, self-determination as self-indulgence. Its deepest unwritten text is not about the right to life, but about women's right to be sexual, to separate sexuality from procreation, to have charge over our procreative capacities."[107] Reading across these institutional critiques reveals Rich's insistence upon a range of "freely chosen" experiences—abortion or motherhood, autonomous study or for- mal education, sexual liberation—that allows us to distinguish between institutions *imposed over us* or institutions *directly co-realized by us*. If we hold close her invocation with students to "use what we have to invent what we need," we can further clarify (at least) three positions. Refusing to dismantle any aspects—ideological or material—of an institution is reform- ism. Destroying resources and spaces that could be repurposed by people is insurrectionary wreckage-as-spectacle.[108] With Rich, we can propose a third position that aims for the simul- taneous eradication and recreation of institutions to nourish our lives.[109]

Rich's enduring wish to nurture compositional spaces continued to guide her poetry, such as the 1977 poem "Transcendental Etude" she dedicated to Cliff:

> Such a composition has nothing to do with eternity, / the striving for
> greatness, brilliance / only with the musing of a mind / one with her
> body, experienced fingers quietly pushing / dark against bright, silk
> against roughness, / pulling the tenets of a life together / with no mere
> will to mastery, / only care for the many-lived, / unending forms in
> which she finds herself.[110]

Rich's depiction echoes Lorde's affirmation of internal contradictions, which she em- bedded in three 1978 texts, "A Litany for Survival Number 630," "The Transforma- tion of Silence into Language and Action," and "Uses of the Erotic: The Erotic as

---

107 Rich, *Of Woman Born*, xxxv. Sophie Lewis locates the race-evasive shortcomings in Rich's comparison of forced gestation and enslavement elsewhere in the book. See Sophie Lewis, *Full Surrogacy Now: Femi- nism Against Family* (New York: Verso, 2019), 136.

108 In 2010, near the end of her life, Rich warned of this temptation in her poem "For the Young Anarchists," in *Later Poems: Selected and New, 1971–2012* (New York: W.W. Norton and Company, 2012), 495.

109 Mario Tronti made a similar argument in his 1967 essay "Within and Against": "The working class *within* and *against* capital: this is the premise from which we must begin for any type of general struggle. . . . To make it explode, in other words, one must be there within it. To use it, one must be there within it." See Andrew Anastasi, ed., *The Weapon of Organization: Mario Tronti's Political Revolution in Marxism* (Brooklyn: Common Notions, 2020), 187–188.

110 Adrienne Rich, "Transcendental Etude," *Dreams of a Common Language: Poems 1974–1977* (New York: W.W. Norton and Company, 1978), 77. Brionne Janae extends this vision into present communal compositions of resistance. See "Against Mastery," *The American Poetry Review* 50, no. 6 (November/De- cember 2021), https://aprweb.org/poems/against-mastery/. Gratitude to Julián González Beltrez for sharing this poem.

Power," which were written after Lorde first learned that she had breast cancer.[111] Lorde offers counsel on how to unearth physical, psychic, and social wounds—how to speak their informative pain—in order to heal: "In becoming forcibly and essentially aware of my mortality, and of what I wished and wanted for my life, however short it might be, priorities and omissions became strongly etched in a merciless light, and what I most regretted were my silences. . . . I began to recognize a source of power within myself that comes from the knowledge that while it is most desirable not to be afraid, learning to put fear into a perspective gave me great strength."[112] This call to break out of silences, both externally and internally rendered, runs like a chorus through the rest of her years.

In "The Uses of the Erotic: The Erotic as Power," Lorde thinks beyond both sexual subjection and calls for erotic sublimation by such Marxist thinkers as Herbert Marcuse.[113] Instead, she advocates erotic suffusion: "the open and fearless underlining of my capacity for joy. In the way my body stretches to music and opens into response, hearkening to its deepest rhythms, so every level upon which I sense also opens to the erotically satisfying experience, whether it is dancing, building a bookcase, writing a poem, examining an idea."[114] Contrary to advice that pits self-care against sustained involvement in movements, Lorde urges a kind of "pleasure activism" and "joyful militancy" that weaves ecstasy and commitment to others into a deeper capacity for mutual liberation.[115] Lorde and Rich expanded upon this in a 1979 interview, suggesting that the erotic is a pedagogical force that aligns study and sexuality to evaluate life itself:

> Lorde: This turning away from the erotic on the part of some of our best minds, our most creative and analytic women, is disturbing and destructive. Because we cannot fight old power in old power terms only. The only way we can do it is by creating another whole structure that touches every aspect of our existence, at the same time as we are resisting.

> Rich: And as you were saying about courses, Black studies, women's studies: this is not just a question of being "allowed" to have our history or literature or theory in the old power framework. It is every minute of our

111 While reading this poem in Berlin, in 1989, Lorde revealed: "'A Litany for Survival' is actually 'A Litany for Survival Number 630.' I like to remind myself and the rest of us that the decision for survival is not something you make once, you make it over and over again." In Lorde, *dream of europe*, 224. See also Emily Bernard, "Audre Lorde Broke the Silence," *The New Republic*, March 25, 2021, https://newrepublic.com/article/161595/audre-lorde-warrior-poet-cancer-journals/; Mecca Jamilah Sullivan, *The Poetics of Difference: Queer Feminist Forms in the African Diaspora* (Chicago: University of Illinois Press, 2021), 70–71.

112 Lorde, "The Transformation of Silence into Language and Action," in *Sister Outsider*, 41.

113 For Herbert Marcuse's analyses of eros, see *Eros and Civilization* (Boston: Beacon Press, 1955); *Counterrevolution and Revolt* (Boston: Beacon Press, 1972); and *The Aesthetic Dimension: Toward a Critique of Marxist Aesthetics* (Boston: Beacon Press, 1978).

114 Lorde, "The Uses of the Erotic: The Erotic as Power," in *Sister Outsider*, 56. See also bell hooks, "Eros, Eroticism, and the Pedagogical Process," in *Teaching to Transgress: Education as the Practice of Freedom* (New York and London: Routledge, 1994), 191–200.

115 adrienne marie brown, *Pleasure Activism: The Politics of Feeling Good* (Chico: AK Press, 2019); Carla Bergman and Nick Montgomery, *Joyful Militancy: Building Thriving Resistance in Toxic Times* (Chico: AK Press, 2017).

lives, from our dreams to getting up and brushing our teeth to when we go to teach.[116]

Lorde began to document her life story in prose with the 1980 *Cancer Journals* and 1982 biomythography *Zami: A New Spelling of My Name. Zami* recounts a childhood and sexual awakening that pivoted the trajectory of her life, as it documents the Black and Euro lesbian communities in Harlem and Lower East Side, the factories just north in Hartford, Connecticut, and the expatriate/neocolonial enclaves in Cuernavaca, Mexico. Similarly, Lorde's other writing from these years—including *Audre Lorde: dream of europe*, which collects seminars and speeches from her 1984–92 "Berlin Years," and *A Burst of Light*—chronicle her ecstatic communion with African diasporic, Indigenous, and Third World feminist communities that sustained her as a diasporic educator: the Soweto Sisters, Aboriginal sisters in New Zealand, Caribbean women in Anguilla and St. Croix.[117]

In a 1988 interview, Lorde affirmed, "Survival is not theoretical, it is not something you read about, it is something we take part in every single day. . . . What is it that needs change in your life, in your time, in your street, in your school?" In a striking explanation of how to foster coalitional self-identities in movements, she continues, "We learn by looking at the differences inside ourselves, the contradictions that exist inside me, inside you. How do we not deny pieces of ourselves? How do we avoid using one part of ourselves, the mother, to kill other parts within us—the lover or the warrior. How do we learn to give voice, space, and breath to all of the parts of ourselves without being ripped apart?"[118]

Lorde brought these perspectives back to CUNY at Hunter College, where she taught from 1981 to 1986. Lesbian writer-activist Sarah Schulman, one of her Hunter students at this time, recounted, "Lorde organizing her packed class into one large circle and standing in the center to teach. By the second class, she had learned all the students' names and as she taught, she would make eye contact with specific students, referencing an idea from their papers or from a previous class discussion."[119] Healing full circle from "Blackstudies" and the academic injuries composited in *Deotha*, Lorde's great self-reflexive lesson toward the end of her life was of integrating the different (at times, even conflicting) parts of oneself as a practice for outward coalitional commitments.

When Audre Lorde died in 1992 at the age of fifty-eight, and Adrienne Rich twenty years later at the age of eighty-two, they were widely honored as two of the most influential writers of our time. Lorde's early death was the result of what Ruth Wilson Gilmore has named the entwined "premature death" of racism, sexism, homophobia, ableism, and economic exploitation.[120] As Alexis Pauline Gumbs reminds us, Audre Lorde and her Black feminist colleagues, like Barbara Christian and June Jordan, were refused flexible teaching schedules and medical leave to heal from cancer. Their em-

---

116 Lorde, "An Interview: Adrienne Rich and Audre Lorde," "Interview," in *Sister Outsider*, 102–103.

117 *Audre Lorde: The Berlin Years, 1984 to 1992*, dir. Dagmar Schultz (New York: Newsreel, 2012), http://www.audrelorde-theberlinyears.com; Lorde, *A Burst of Light*.

118 Lorde, *dream of europe*, 140.

119 In Atkin and Brown, eds., *Audre Lorde: "I teach myself in outline,"* 4.

120 Ruth Wilson Gilmore, *Golden Gulag: Prisons, Surplus, Crisis, and Opposition in Globalizing California* (Berkeley: University of California Press, 2007), 28.

ployers—the City University of New York and the University of California—knew that "Black feminists are a trouble more useful as dead invocation than as live troublemakers."[121] Until Rich's own passing in 2012, she foregrounded Lorde's legacy in her writing, speeches, and interviews. In one of Rich's last poems, "Endpapers," she returns to a guiding intention that poetry can sustain radical communities—*I want this to reach you*—even as the words begin to disappear: "The signature to a life requires / the search for a method / rejection of posturing / trust in the witnesses / a vial of invisible ink / a sheet of paper held steady / after the end-stroke / above a deciphering flame."[122]

Continuations

The unfinished metamorphic legacies of Audre Lorde and Adrienne Rich continue to hold lessons on re-visioning and imbuing delight in our relationships and institutions. Lorde and Rich's poetics, seen anew, contain hidden pedagogical depths that can be further explored—just as the movements in which they metaphorically swam can be recognized as huge freedom schools in motion. Instead of understanding intersectionality as an ever-winnowing project of specifying multifaceted identities—a tiny point at which different identities overlap—Lorde instead reached across many different communities from the Venn diagram of her integrated self.[123] Rich, too, pushed back against being "seen too long from too many disconnected angles," instead asserting that her identity was incumbent on sustaining the life force of people who were distinct from her, including Lorde.[124] Their friendship was born of consistent, critical, caring dialogue and debate across decades, and are a model of co-evolution that can show how to relate to each other as colleagues, comrades, teachers, students, friends, lovers, and communities.

Currently, across the Americas, Caribbean, and Europe, Afro-descended and Indigenous women and gender nonbinary people are keeping alive Lorde's work through translation and popular education.[125] Rich's work is also resurging with the reproductive justice movement for free, safe, legal abortion access as well as fully funded childcare, both of which are preconditions for fully consensual parenthood.[126] Lorde

---

121 Alexis Pauline Gumbs, "The Shape of My Impact," *Feminist Wire*, October 29, 2012, https://thefeministwire.com/2012/10/the-shape-of-my-impact/. See also Nick Mitchell, "On Audre Lorde's Legacy and the "Self" of Self-Care, Part 2 of 3," *Low End Theory*, May 14, 2013, https://www.lowendtheory.org/post/50428216600/on-audre-lordes-legacy-and-the-self-of/.

122 Rich, "Endpapers," in *Later Poems: Selected and New, 1971–2012*, 512.

123 Lorde, "Age, Race, Class, and Sex: Women Redefining Difference," in *Sister Outsider*, 114. See also Lorde, "The Poet as Outsider, Session 4, May 17, 1984," in *dream of europe*, 89; Nolte, "The Law is Male and White," 143.

124 Rich, "Split at the Root," in *Blood, Bread, and Poetry*. See also Joyce Antler, *Jewish Radical Feminism: Voices from the Women's Liberation Movement* (New York: New York University Press, 2018).

125 See, for example, Diarenis Calderón Tartabull, AnouchK Ibacka Valiente, A. Tito Mitjans Alayón, and Conor Tomás Reed, "Audre Lorde Now," in *Distributaries*, The Center for the Humanities, CUNY Graduate Center, July 16, 2020, https://www.centerforthehumanities.org/news/audre-lorde-now/; Georgina Jiménez Vidiella, "Audre Lorde y los Encuentros en la casa de la diferencia – Entrevista a la investigadora feminista Georgina Jiménez Vidiella" (2017), http://www.contratiempohistoria.org/?p=6353.

126 See, for example, Jenny Brown, *Birth Strike: The Hidden Fight over Women's Work* (Oakland: PM Press, 2019); Judith Levine, "Hating Motherhood," *Boston Review*, March 3, 2022, https://bostonreview.net/articles/hating-motherhood/; Lewis, *Full Surrogacy Now*.

and Rich understood the power of rooting themselves—and, within each other—for years at CUNY, and then far beyond, in order to enact "a change of world," asking "IF NOT NOW, WHEN?" We now turn to focus on the vast range of student compositions and combat that galvanized these teachers to dedicate their lives to education as the practice of freedom.

CHAPTER 4

THE POWER OF STUDENT WRITING AND ACTION

During the 1960s and '70s, students in the United States were often recognized—even within social movements—as an unconstructed mass, variously spoken of as "raw materials" or proletarians yet to develop class consciousness.[1] Teachers, according to this view, could mold this raw material into elite intellectuals or docile workers, depending on the economic base of the school. These formulations are not surprising. At the time, students comprised one of the most insurgent forces in society. Student power was so dangerous that those in political and economic control needed to obscure or distort it. In part, this meant urging students to practice writing separate from the social contexts in which they could gain power.

The 1977 publication of City College SEEK Director Mina Shaughnessy's *Errors and Expectations: A Guide for the Teacher of Basic Writing*—in which she studied data from 4,000 essays written in exam blue books by City College students during 1970–74—has long served as a primary source for understanding student writing in the period between Open Admissions and the imposition of tuition.[2] Despite Shaughnessy's intentions, however, the social process underlying these students' work has not always been considered within its volatile time and location. At worst, Carmen Kynard cautions, "our continual mapping of *Errors and Expectations* as the response to this historical moment . . . erases the political agitation of African Americans, virtually unmapping their presence and history."[3]

This chapter goes beyond the sentence-level grammatical corrections that Shaughnessy focused on to analyze student compositions before, during, and after the 1969 City

---

1 See Mario Savio, "Mario Savio's Speech before the FSM Sit-in," *Free Speech Movement Archives*, 1964, http://www.fsm-a.org/stacks/mario/mario_speech.html/; James Weaver, "The Student as Worker," in *The University and Revolution*, ed. Gary Weaver and James Weaver (Englewood Cliffs: Prentice-Hall, 1969). An important counterweight is the 1975 pamphlet *Wages for Students*. Originally published without attribution, it was coauthored by graduate students and adjunct teachers George Caffentzis, Monty Neill, and John Willshire-Carrera. See *Wages for Students*, ed. Jakob Jakobsen, María Berríos, and Malav Kanuga (Brooklyn: Common Notions, 2016).

2 Mina Shaughnessy, *Errors and Expectations: A Guide for the Teacher of Basic Writing* (New York and Oxford: Oxford University Press, 1977).

3 Carmen Kynard, *Vernacular Insurrections: Race, Black Protest, and the New Century in Composition-Literacies Studies* (Albany: SUNY Press, 2014), 205.

College campus takeover. The scant record of student writing inside City College classrooms is circumvented by diving into their anthologies, communiqués, demands, journals, and newspapers, which were circulated on and off campus during the 1960s and '70s, as well as students' memoirs written about this period. In this way, we can look toward the vast learning that occurred outside of the City College gates as well as what Black, Puerto Rican, Third World, and antiracist Euro students brought into the college.

For a look at early 1960s student composition, we will consider Samuel R. Delany's work in the *Promethean* student literary journal, his science fiction and personal diaries, and his memoir of this period, *The Motion of Light in Water*. Delany decided to leave the college, twice, so that his writing could flourish outside classroom strictures. During this time, Delany also reflected on the social composition of amassed bodies in urban bathhouses and cruising sites. His attention to the suffused power of the masses, and his related critique of how institutions may obscure our collective strength, helps to situate how students traversed spatial limitations at City College.

We will also assess how the Five Demands animated the April–May 1969 "Harlem University" strike. Cowritten over time by Black, Puerto Rican, Third World, and Euro students, and extending solidarity to high school students who were also in upheaval, these *coalitional* demands became a fulcrum upon which the entire university and city were shifted by student power. Even if they were not fully realized, these demands continue to activate organizers and open imaginative horizons.

Another vehicle for propaganda and agitation was the student newspaper *Tech News/The Paper*. Transformed by the editorial directions of Paul B. Simms, Francee Covington, Louis Reyes Rivera, Sekou Sundiata, and others, this paper chronicled the development of a Black/Puerto Rican/Third World Studies vision at City College amidst decolonization struggles worldwide. Meanwhile, outside City College's gates, Francee Covington's essay in Toni Cade Bambara's anthology *The Black Woman* critiqued simplistic comparisons of revolutionary conditions in Harlem and Algiers. In this way, Covington assumed equal footing with her teacher as contributors to a historic Black feminist intervention.

Finally, while Guillermo Morales and Assata Shakur studied at City College in the early 1970s, their later memoirs, actions, and communiqués with the Fuerzas Armadas de Liberación Nacional (FALN), the Black Panther Party (BPP), and the Black Liberation Army (BLA) are read as student compositions of clandestine revolutionary work reaching backward to their campus experiences. These legacies also point forward to the City College Guillermo Morales/Assata Shakur Community and Student Center—a campus organizing hub for CUNY struggles until 2013, when it was evicted by the CUNY administration. In the same way, the John Brown Anti-Klan Committee's actions to free Morales and Shakur, as well as their efforts to practice principled antiracism at City College, demonstrate the precursors of radical cross-ethnic solidarity manifest in CUNY today.

If we stretch our ideas of what it means to study—insisting that learning takes place both inside and outside of formal institutions, and that we remain students even when composing outside of these institutions—then the basis for student power is much broader than we might otherwise measure.

Samuel Delany: Moving from Institutions to the Masses

Polymath, science fiction author, and chronicler of urban subcultures, Samuel R. Delany was born in Harlem in 1942. His first publication—produced in early adolescence and excerpted in City College educator Kenneth Clark's book *Prejudice and Your Child*—was a piece of queer erotica.[4] By this time, Delany was regularly writing science fiction, poetry, and private journals and had been frequenting Harlem's drag and trans scenes at the Apollo Theater's Jewel Box Revue.[5] He went to Bronx Science High School, where on the first day of class he met Marilyn Hacker, whom he would marry five years later. In Spring 1959, his last year of high school, Delany taught remedial reading and speech to Puerto Rican youth at a community center in the General Ulysses S. Grant Houses. They urged him to streamline and clarify his writing, telling him, "Say what you mean, man." The story "Mike, Jesus, and Me," in which the narrator describes interacting with Puerto Rican youth who are exercising in the Grant Houses, emerged from this challenge.[6] After winning its 1959 prose writers' contest, Delany turned down a full scholarship to New York University, deciding instead to enroll in the City College of New York for Spring 1960.[7]

In his freshman English Composition classroom, Delany recalled that his professor would outline the themes and arguments of a reading ahead of time and then ask the students to read it at home. Student-generated interpretation was not encouraged. "Thus, much of what we would consider learning today, if it occurred, had to take place in the margins," Delany recalled.[8] In contrast, Delany describes Israel E. Drabkin, who taught Elementary Greek, as "one of the best (and one of the most maddening!) teachers I have ever had":

> [Y]ou would go up to the board to write your day's homework for the class to look over, and . . . you'd make a mistake, and the class would titter and someone would start to change and Drabkin would say something like, 'Well, not so fast. I believe I once saw a sixth-century manuscript in a Romanian monastery in which the scribe, for some reason, has written it exactly the way you have there—now, it could have been a mistake; but it could have been a dialectical variant, just as easily.' And a few months later, when I began to read Ferdinand de Saussure's *Course in General Linguistics*, and I got to his primary postulate, 'in language, the sign is arbitrary,' I knew exactly what he meant![9]

Although Delany would leave midway through the following semester, Drabkin's interpretive flexibility would stay with him. In August 1961, Delany and Hacker drove to Detroit to become legally married, during which time they invented a "new language

4 Samuel R. Delany, *The Motion of Light in Water: Sex and Science Fiction Writing in the East Village* (New York: Arbor House/W. Morrow, 1988), 58.

5 Delany, *The Motion of Light in Water*, 102–103.

6 Samuel R. Delany, *In Search of Silence: The Journals of Samuel R. Delany, Volume I, 1957–1969* (Middletown: Wesleyan University Press, 2017), 587–591.

7 Delany, *In Search of Silence*, 130; Delany, *The Motion of Light in Water*, 108.

8 Delany, "Midcentury," *The Jewel-Hinged Jaw: Notes on the Language of Science Fiction* (Elizabethtown: Dragon Press, 1977), 196.

9 Samuel R. Delany, email communication with the author, April 4, 2018.

from scratch; it has its own grammar, vocabulary, and semantic development."[10] He continued to write, publishing four science fiction novels.

Delany decided to reenroll at City College for the Spring 1965 semester, whereupon he joined the *Promethean* as Poetry Editor.[11] The Spring 1965 issue features his poem "Two Dogs Near Death," which remarks: "We come from a tradition assured / of pain or paradise; yet we range."[12] Although Delany was respected by his peers, a journal entry from this period reveals:

> Four years ago, I left school with a distinct image of myself writing. . . . I had publishing and critical success with science fiction . . . . I learned an amazing number of things about action, freedom, commitment—majorly that they exist. At last I decided [to] return to school, discovered my reputation had preceded me, and was smack in the center of the college 'Literary Life' . . . . They haven't quite yet realized that my return, in a way, was a method of coming to terms with outside defeat.[13]

By February 1965, Delany began working on *Babel-17*. Exploring communication and consciousness, the novel charts the adventures of the poet Rydra Wong, who learns a "compressed artificial language" to mediate intergalactic conflict and gain the power of telepathy—"the nexus of old talent and a new way of thinking. It opened worlds of perception, of action."[14] Immersed in the writing process, Delany recalls, "I'd realized the concentration it needed made my college studies almost impossible. 'I'm going to drop school,' I told Bob and Marilyn at dinner, 'again. The book really wants to be written. I know this is what I can do and do well. I've published four others already. It seems silly to write it just for the classes.'"[15] Delany left mid-semester.

During this prolific period, Delany's journals pivot from science fiction sketches to notes on social psychology and desire, from linguistic exercises to erotic fantasies, and back again.[16] In his memoir, *The Motion of Light in Water*, Delany also recounts frequenting the Village's piers and bathhouses to have sex with men, individually and in groups, and attending experimental theater acts in the East Village. "Whether male, female, working or middle class, the first direct sense of political power comes from the apprehension of massed bodies," he wrote. In his view, several dozen men having sex in the back of a large truck was a "highly ordered, highly social, attentive, silent" act, "grounded in a certain care, if not community." He also juxtaposes a night at the bathhouse with a night at the piers in which police arrest eight or nine people, but anywhere from one hundred to two hundred escape.

In the 1950s, homosexuality was framed as an isolated perversion by mainstream society. But these night scenes of massed bodies undermined that image. While official

---

10 Delany, *In Search of Silence*, 299–230.

11 Delany, *The Motion of Light in Water*, 421.

12 Samuel R. Delany, "Two Dogs Near Death," *The Promethean* (January 1965): 112. *The Promethean* Collection, The City University of New York, City College, Archives and Special Collections.

13 Delany, *In Search of Silence*, 308.

14 Samuel Delany, *Babel-17* (New York: Ace Books, 1966), 146.

15 Delany, *The Motion of Light in Water*, 435.

16 Delany, *In Search of Silence*, 260–261.

histories have created "whole galleries of institutions, good and bad, to accommodate our sex," Delany notes, "no one ever got to see its whole."

> These institutions cut it up and made it invisible—certainly much less visible—to the bourgeois world that claimed the phenomenon deviant and dangerous. But, by the same token, they cut it up and thus made any apprehension of its totality all but impossible.[17]

This claim—that bathhouses and experimental art galleries enabled the state to grant permission for queer "deviance" to occur out of sight, thus robbing participants of its collective power—could also be extended to Delany's experiences with schooling. Not only did the structure of City College conceal what was happening inside each class, it also erected a partition between the campus and Harlem. Within a few years, however, student upheavals would push past these barriers.

If Delany had chosen to stay at City College and contribute to the rise of a cohering Black and Puerto Rican student force on campus, how could he have expanded City College and CUNY's transformations? He couldn't have predicted what would occur after he took flight, and staying may have precluded his writing of the works we celebrate today. Still, his infrastructural critique endures: the ways institutions are built often contain and suppress potential mass power.

Student Journalism and Mobilization

In 1965, the same year Delany left City College, the Search for Education, Elevation, and Knowledge (SEEK) Program was launched as a pre-baccalaureate pilot experiment to support 113 Black and Puerto Rican high school students as they entered the segregated campus. Soon, SEEK was permanently approved at City College and spread to other CUNY campuses. Students were selected from specific neighborhoods, which suggests that they arrived with an experiential cohesion built from attending the same schools, neighborhood parks, cultural events, and being mentored by an entwined Black and Puerto Rican urban social life.

Francee Covington arrived at City College in 1966 with 191 incoming SEEK students. She recalls, "I had a lot of experience organizing way before entering City College"—after all, "this was still Jim Crow New York."[18] Covington had been arrested at the age of fourteen when protesting the SUNY Downstate Medical Center's refusal to hire Black and Puerto Rican construction workers, and in 1964 had marched on Washington and attended CORE actions to desegregate public schools.[19] Upon arrival at City College, Covington was housed in the Alamac Hotel—the CUNY-wide SEEK dormitory that remains one of the understudied epicenters of the late-1960s CUNY student movement. It began in 1965 as a "residence experiment," in which SEEK students attended classes in converted rooms in the hotel while also attending classes at the Harlem campus.[20] The Alamac became a cultural and political site for these

17 Delany, *The Motion of Light in Water*, 225–226, 293.

18 Sean Molloy, "A Convenient Myopia: SEEK, Shaughnessy, and the Rise of High-Stakes Testing at CUNY," PhD diss., CUNY Graduate Center, 2016, 29, 82.

19 Francee Covington, interview with the author, May 22, 2021.

20 Robert Marshak, *Academic Renewal in the Seventies: Memoir of a City College President* (Washington, DC: University Press of America, 1982), 107.

students to socialize, talk politics, and uplift each other. Pakistani poet Aijaz Ahmad, a close friend of Adrienne Rich, was the SEEK dorm director, and he encouraged students to cogovern the space.

This was no traditional dorm. According to one student newspaper account:

> The walls blast you with Afro-American culture posters proclaiming, 'Why I Won't Serve Whitey' and 'How Do You Become a Black Revolutionary?' A Dionne Warwick record plays on the stereo and a floating 'bull session' passes through. On the girls' floor, [Black sorority] sisters read James Baldwin and organize projects to aid ghetto children.[21]

"The SEEK students weren't all militants when they arrived at the Alamac Hotel," notes Philip Kay, but the dorm became an insurgent hub in which "residents were reading Malcolm X, Stokely Carmichael, Che Guevara, and Frantz Fanon." Moreover, "Felipe Luciano and Iris Morales, future cofounders of the New York chapter of the Young Lords Party, were SEEK students and Alamac residents during this crucial period."[22] Despite City College's long history of student power, few of these students knew of their 1920s and '30s predecessors detailed in Chapter 1.[23] Were these students limited by this lack of knowledge, or did it offer them flexibility to try new methods of struggle?

In 1968, Covington started a SEEK student newspaper called *The Paper*, with Toni Cade Bambara as the faculty advisor.[24] Although it only lasted one issue, *The Paper* encouraged student writers to practice journalism and host poetry readings at the Alamac.[25] Covington would soon take on a leading role in City College Black and Puerto Rican student agitation. The Alamac would eventually host the formation of Puerto Ricans Involved in Student Action (PRISA) and later became a locus for the coordination of the City College campus takeover and resulting wave of Spring actions across CUNY schools like Brooklyn, Queens, and Lehman College.

Three main City College student newspapers existed during this time—*The Campus, Observation Post*, and *Tech News*, the latter of which had begun in 1942 as a section for science and engineering students inside *The Campus*. a paper for science and engineering students. By the 1960s, however, *Tech News* writers began altering their articles to reflect

21 George Murrell, "SEEK Dorms: Black Culture and Red Carpet," *The Campus*, October 16, 1968, 5. Cited in Philip Kay, "'Guttersnipes' and 'Eliterates': City College in the Popular Imagination." PhD diss., Columbia University, 2011, 221.

22 Kay, "'Guttersnipes' and 'Eliterates,'" 222.

23 Francee Covington, interview with the author, May 22, 2021.

24 Molloy, "A Convenient Myopia," 191.

25 Francee Covington, "Francee Covington: An Oral History of the CCNY 1960s SEEK Program and *The Paper*," interview by Sean Molloy, June 5, 2015, CUNY Digital History Archive, https://cdha.cuny.edu/items/show/7102. See also *The Paper*, "Our Legacy," January 15, 2019, thepaperccny.com/about-us/.

the social ferment around them.[26] Paul B. Simms, who regularly wrote for *Tech News* between 1966 and 1970, recalled that his activism with the Student Nonviolent Coordinating Committee "propelled me to re-channel my contribution."[27] He documented struggles in Harlem, such as the 1966 St. Nicholas Park development plan, the 1968 UFT teachers' strike, and alternative schooling projects. In 1967, Simms conducted interviews with prominent Black leaders like *The Liberator*'s Dan Watts, the Congress of Racial Equality's Floyd McKissick, the Nation of Islam's Louis Farrakhan, the United African American Association's William Wright, and the political comedian Dick Gregory to highlight a spectrum of Black militancy.[28]

By 1968, City College students pursued an accelerated liberatory education amidst citywide strikes, rebellions in hundreds of US cities, and revolts around the world. Black student radicals in the campus group Onyx Society, writes Daniel A. Sherwood, "debated the form such a revolution should take":

> [O]ne student asserted, 'We can't just sit here and be passive and intellectual. People were dying this summer, we have got to get organized. You can't win by throwing bricks.' Another student argued that change would require activists putting their bodies in harm's way. 'You have got to get out there and risk your necks, we have got to be ready to die.' Another student suggested the possible effectiveness of tight organization and economically disruptive action, 'Do you know what one hundred determined, well-trained people can do to the economy of this country? They can wreck it. We should really be thinking about that.'[29]

In November 1968, amidst recurring anti-ROTC actions by the City College Commune, a week-long occupation of Finley's Grand Ballroom to protect AWOL soldiers Bill Brakefield and David Copp resulted in the arrests of 188 predominantly Euro students and community members. Dialogues and debates between Black, Puerto Rican, Asian, and Euro students assessed the level at which they could trust each other's increasingly militant actions. One Onyx organizer, Edwin Fabre, framed it this way: "We recognize that there are common goals which both White and Black people share. However, what we wish to make clear is that White people must not come to us and

26 Limited space precludes us from including the full story of this campus newspaper's transformations and much remains to be written about *Tech News/The Paper*. Gratitude to Maxine Alexander, Diane Anderson, Thomas Bell, Desira Benjamin, Sheryl Bernier, John Bohn, David Calwell, Bob Collazo, Albert DeLeon, Gwen Dixon, Ann Doris, Warren Doris, Eli Dorsey, Faviola Felix, Ted Fleming, Joudon Ford, David Friedlander, Ray Frost, Arlette Hecht, Greg Holder, Steve Holmes, Thomas Holmes, Vicky Hunter, Diane Kearny, Bob Knight, H. Rex Lindsey, Marianita Lopez, Dennis Mack, Tom McDonald, Ayad Mohamed, Jerry Mondesire, Jeff Morgan, Ray Nero, Gwen New, Chris Newton, Brunilda Pabon, Charles Powell, Doroth Randall, Angelita Reyes, Jaime Rivera, Bill Robinson, Cynthia Valentine-Stephens, Tylie Waters, Duane Watts, Eric White, and other participants not highlighted in this book. See also *The Paper*, "Our Legacy," https://www.ccny.cuny.edu/journalism/paper.

27 Paul B. Simms, interview with the author, May 22, 2012.

28 Paul B. Simms, "Black Comic Turned Politician: An Interview with Dick Gregory," *Tech News*, October 31, 1967, 2; "Dan Watts on Powell and on Black Rights and the White Man," *Tech News*, February 14, 1967, 2; "McKissick Accuses Miseducation in Schools," *Tech News*, April 18, 1967, 3. "Minister [Farrakhan]: Black Muslims Don't Exist," *Tech News*, May 9, 1967, 2. "The U.A.A.A.; Black Politics: An Interview with William Wright," *Tech News*, October 3, 1967, 2.

29 Daniel A. Sherwood, "Civic Struggles: Jews, Blacks, and the Question of Inclusion at The City College of New York, 1930–1975," PhD diss., The New School, 2015, 336.

say 'this is the way to improve yourselves.' We must find our own way. We'll build our half of the Brooklyn Bridge, and you (the White Community) build your half, and then we'll meet in the center and work from there."[30]

Months before the April–May 1969 City College strike, Simms described in *Tech News* what a Black Studies curriculum could look like:

> The University would have courses in African History, Afro-American History, Black Culture (both African and Afro-American), Black Contemporary Thought, Asian History, Garveyism, The Lives and Works of Malcolm X, DuBois, Douglass, Fanon and Che, Coalitions with the Left, Revolutionary Actions, American Hypocrisy, American Atrocities, Socialism and its Relevance to Black Nationalism, and other similar courses. Some of these courses could be taught by students, others could be taught by outside teachers. A Black student referendum could determine which courses should be given and which were omitted. It would be expected that every Black student on campus, whether enrolled in the university or not, would contribute to the maintenance of this institution.[31]

The growing demand for City College to alter its admissions to include more Black, Puerto Rican, and Asian students directly alluded to a cross-institutional solidarity with high school student organizers, particularly after the 1968 UFT strike against community control. Neil Philip Buffett writes of a wave of high school student activism by the Black Student Union and other student and community groups, in particular at Ocean Hill-Brownsville in Brooklyn and at IS 201 in Harlem.[32] Jesse Hoffnung-Garskoff writes how Black, Puerto Rican, and Jewish students reopened schools in defiance of the UFT strike, and used free time opened up by the strike to create different social relations.[33] Charlotte "Charlie" Brown, a Black student organizer, recounted, "No amount of organization work could have done what the strike did. It was a racist strike and the kids knew it. The *teachers* were the agitators. The kids saw them in a different light. They weren't adults up there to look at and respect. Wow, the way they acted! We saw Shanker using his ethnic background to raise hate, to pit the Jews against the [B]lacks."[34] Simms also wrote in *Tech News*, "there were many [white] teachers who did not want to strike, and who presently are teaching in the Freedom schools. I personally want to thank them. The Black and Puerto Rican communities know who their friends are."[35]

Two weeks into the UFT teachers' strike, the New York High School Student Union was formed by 200 high school students, in large part through the efforts of

30 Ralph Levinson, "Onyx: Of Black People, by Black People, for Black People," *The Campus*, November 16, 1967, 5. Cited in Sherwood, "Civic Struggles," 339.

31 Paul B. Simms, "From a Black Chair: Institute for Black Students," *Tech News*, December 16, 1968.

32 Neil Philip Buffett, "Crossing the Line: High School Student Activism, the New York High School Student Union, and the 1968 Ocean Hill-Brownsville Teachers' Strike," *Journal of Urban History* 45, no. 6 (November 2019): 1212–1236.

33 Jesse Hoffnung-Garskof, *A Tale of Two Cities: Santo Domingo and New York after 1950* (Princeton: Princeton University Press, 2008), 138.

34 Fred Ferretti, "High School Students of the City, Unite!" *New York Magazine*, April 28, 1969, 43. Cited in Buffett, "Crossing the Line."

35 Paul B. Simms, "From a Black Chair: The Three Lies," *Tech News*, October 23, 1968.

Charlie Brown, Laurie Sandlow, and Howard Swerdloff.[36] Swerdloff was also an editor for the *New York High School Free Press*, a newspaper "of, by, and for liberated high school students." Its printings ranged from 10,000 to 50,000 copies a month.[37] Swerdloff recalls, "We went around the city opening up schools in alliance with the [B]lack student organizations, and we had the newspaper to give out to students who were milling around or in the buildings conducting freedom classes."[38] Nicknamed "Little Lenin" by *The New York Times*, Swerdloff clarified, "We don't want to take over the government. We want to destroy it. I believe people should have power over their own lives, but not over other people's lives."[39] During this time, other high school student newspapers flourished, such as the *New York Herald Tribune* for Stuyvesant High students (50,000 to 60,000 copies a month), and *Sansculottes* for Bronx Science students.[40] In the Lower East Side, Harlem, the Bronx, and around New York City, the Young Lords' newspaper *Palante*, the Black Panthers' *Black Panthers Speak*, and other youth-driven movement compositions also circulated.

Creating Harlem University

By Spring 1969, New York City high schools and CUNY colleges were ready to detonate. The first two months of the semester at City College saw campus escalations involving petitions, mass marches, meetings with the administration, sit-ins at President Gallagher's office, and coordinated disruptions of campus buildings by "sulfur bombs, spray paint, small explosives, and tear gas."[41] Demands were revised by students as their strategies evolved, in a powerful example of the written record being developed in real time along with its writers.

The Five Demands that emerged were a composite of appeals made during the previous years, including those of the Black and Puerto Rican Student Community (BPRSC), the Onyx Society, Puerto Ricans Involved in Student Action (PRISA), the Committee of Ten (formed by the most politically active members of Onyx and PRISA), Students for a Democratic Society (SDS), and the Communist Party's W. E. B. Du Bois Club, composed mostly of Black youth. The demands envisioned:

- A separate degree-granting School of Third World Studies.
- A separate freshman orientation for Black and Puerto Rican students.
- That the SEEK students have a determining voice in the setting of guidelines for the SEEK Program, including the hiring and firing of SEEK personnel.

---

36 Michael Stern, "Teen-Age Revolt: Is It Deeper Today?," *The New York Times*, October 7, 1968, https://timesmachine.nytimes.com/timesmachine/1968/10/07/77180873.pdf/; *The New York Times*, "Teen-agers Form Protest Parade: 200 High School Students of City Form a Union," September 22, 1968, https://timesmachine.nytimes.com/timesmachine/1968/09/22/89345528.pdf/.

37 Ferretti, "High School Students of the City, Unite!," 42.

38 Sean Stewart, ed., *On the Ground: An Illustrated Anecdotal History of the Sixties Underground Press in the U.S.* (Oakland: PM Press, 2011), 36.

39 Stern, "Teen-Age Revolt."

40 See interactive map of New York City's underground presses, "Where the Underground Press Lived," https://www.arcgis.com/apps/MapJournal/index.html?appid=2a21e7dba63b441a-9ca84139a5dd8a93/; Stewart, *On the Ground*, 90.

41 Simms, "What Was Behind the CCNY Takeover?"

- That the racial composition of the entering freshman class be reflective of the Black, Puerto Rican, and Asian high school population.
- That all education majors be required to take Black and Puerto Rican history and the Spanish language.[42]

The Five Demands are notable for their brevity (at Brooklyn College, Black and Puerto Rican student organizers had seventeen demands![43]), which indicates that alternatives sometimes must be condensed into the most crucial structural demands to transform institutions.

In the early morning hours of April 22, 1969, Black and Puerto Rican students braved a torrential downpour to take over several buildings in the City College South Campus.[44] "Families" of trusted student organizers selected by the Committee of Ten organizing group, none over the age of twenty-four, coordinated the rapid takeover. Supportive Euro student radicals, initially taken by surprise at this confidentially planned action, soon occupied another campus building in solidarity. This strike, and the resulting recomposition of City College and CUNY, was a result of insurgent *students'* initiative with workers' and community support.

Immediately, the campus became polarized. Francee Covington recalls, "I was there the whole two weeks (spent two nights away). I would go home, take a shower, fresh clothes and snacks, and then go back to campus. Couldn't get any sleep. Some people would be snoring. I have to be ready for what's coming. We were exhausted. It was two of the longest weeks God created . . . hiding from your mom . . . 'I'm working on a paper!' Press coverage was almost immediate—they were surprised it lasted two weeks. We were on the *Daily News* front page, television cameras each day."[45] Mayoral candidates were forced to weigh in on the takeover. Paul Simms noted that "during the occupation, several thousand dollars was collected from Harlem residents and other Black and Puerto Rican people and now has been placed in a bank for use in the School of Third World Studies."[46] City College and the Harlem community became a bellwether for community control, Third World Studies, and the desegregation and decolonization of CUNY.

Drawing from rhetorical skills honed in SEEK classrooms, students combined writing with disruptive actions to underscore a concrete method of redress. The City College strike occurred within a week of campus actions around the city and country that amplified learning coalitions between educators and students, high schoolers and col-

---

42 Black and Puerto Rican Student Community, "Five Demands," CUNY Digital History Archive, https://cdha.cuny.edu/items/show/6952/. See also Simms, "What Was Behind the CCNY Takeover?" In the Fall 1968 version of demands, it was initially Black and Puerto Rican Studies and increased Black and Puerto Rican student enrollment; in Spring 1969, it became Third World Studies and increased Black, Puerto Rican, and Asian student enrollment.

43 See María Pérez y González, "How a Few Students Transformed the Ivory Tower: Puerto Rican Studies and its (R)evolution at Brooklyn College," in *Puerto Rican Studies at the City University of New York: The First Fifty Years*, ed. María Pérez y González and Virginia Sánchez Korrol (New York: El Centro Press, 2021), 146–180; Martha Biondi, *The Black Revolution on Campus* (Berkeley: University of California Press, 2012); Gisely Colón López, Tami Gold, and Pam Sporn, dirs., *Making the Impossible Possible* (New York: Third World Newsreel, 2021), https://www.gritoproductions.com/making-impossible-possible/.

44 This event is featured in the forthcoming film *The Five Demands*, produced by Tracy Daniels and Andrea Weiss and directed by Greta Schiller, https://thefivedemandsfilm.com/.

45 Francee Covington, interview with the author, May 22, 2021.

46 Simms, "What Was Behind the CCNY Takeover?"

lege-goers, neighborhood and campus organizers. Naming itself "Harlem University," the occupation signaled a reterritorialization through which the entire neighborhood became a place of study and community control.[47] As Samuel R. Delany had presaged, students previously cordoned off inside each classroom were transformed when they amassed as a political force. Study and cohabitation at the Alamac Hotel—which by this time housed 200–300 SEEK students from City College, Brooklyn, Hunter, Lehman, and other CUNY colleges—quickly pivoted to proliferate the specter of Harlem University at other campuses. Philip Kay writes, Black and Puerto Rican student organizers "set up shop off campus, in a storefront on Amsterdam Avenue, and sent a car topped with loudspeakers through the streets to fill people in on what was going on and enlist their support."[48]

The Five Demands aspired to the level of "non-reformist" or revolutionary reforms—students would not be satisfied with paltry concessions, but instead insisted upon monumental changes in CUNY, the city, and beyond.[49] In relation, Tavia Nyong'o writes about the stakes of student demands: "Black studies as a critique of Western civilization teaches us to ask: What do we owe each other for the sacrifices we each are called upon to make to rebuke and repair this world? How can we—those of us who profess to educate—accept the student demand not only as a rebuke, which it certainly is, but also as a gift?"[50] The Harlem University strike helps us to perceive student demands as an invaluable, high-risk, collectivist form of student composition, and one that is more pedagogically noteworthy than the contents of any individual exam blue book.

Even so, Black and Puerto Rican students faced considerable difficulty in sustaining the strike. As City College student journalist Tom Ackerman chronicled, the two-week campus occupation was both intricate and divisive. The college president kept trying to show the Five Demands were being implemented (slowly). Some tenure-track faculty wanted the campus to reopen, while adjuncts advocated for it to stay closed. Black and Puerto Rican students and supportive Euro students did not directly collaborate with one another's building occupations, and the Black and Puerto Rican students attempted to exert militant discipline despite other autonomous actions such as classroom interruptions, fights, and arson.[51]

Paul Simms chronicled the mood on campus during and after the strike:

The following days found classes on strike and the entire campus occu-

47 Raúl Zibechi and Rebecca Tarlau focus on reterritorialization in the context of Latin American social movements. See Raúl Zibechi, *Territories in Resistance: A Cartography of Latin American Social Movements* (Chico: AK Press, 2012); Rebecca Tarlau, *Occupying Schools, Occupying Land: How the Landless Workers Movement Transformed Brazilian Education* (Oxford: Oxford University Press, 2019).

48 Kay, "'Guttersnipes' and 'Eliterates,'" 240.

49 Ruth Wilson Gilmore argues that such "nonreformist reforms" can create social changes that "unravel rather than widen the net of social control through criminalization." See Gilmore, *Golden Gulag*, 242.

50 Tavia Nyong'o, "The Student Demand," *Bully Bloggers*, November 17, 2015, https://bullybloggers.wordpress.com/2015/11/17/the-student-demand/. We can also measure this record of student compositions in a website like *The Demands*, which gathered eighty lists of demands from 2014–2015 #BlackLivesMatter campus mobilizations across the United States, https://web.archive.org/web/20220215002539/https://www.thedemands.org/. See also Roderick A. Ferguson, *We Demand: The University and Student Protests* (Berkeley: University of California Press, 2017).

51 Tom Ackerman, "The South Campus Seizure," *The City College Alumnus* 65, no. 1 (October 1969): 3–32. See also Sherwood, "Civic Struggles," 568–569.

pied by over 1000 cops. Some professors in the [Physics] and Biology Depts. asked Black and Puerto Rican students to come and address their almost all-white classes about the nature of the strike and its implications. Other instructors just gave passing grades to all their students and cancelled classes. A fire was started in one building and totally [destroyed] a music auditorium. A spokesman for the BPRSC stated emphatically that no Black or Puerto Rican student was responsible for destroying part of "the University of Harlem," suggesting that their white radical students or white conservatives started the fire. Directly after the fire, President Gallagher resigned. He explained that he had done all that he could and now it was time for him to go.[52]

Meanwhile, in high schools across the city, a "Spring Offensive" was launched from April 21 to May 19, demonstrating the power of one campus strike to foment a wave of others but also the difficulty of continuing a mass decentralized insurgency. Buffett writes, "While some [schools] experienced sit-in demonstrations, walk-outs, and student-faculty conferences, others experienced property damage from student-set fires and window breakage . . . there were roughly eighty instances of student protest, vandalism, and general disruption at thirty-eight city schools."[53] Eventually across high school and college campuses, the strikes and protests began to dwindle. Direct actions were shut down or forced into the go-slow process of closed-door negotiations with the administration and power elites.

At City College, a conservative Biology professor named Joseph Copeland was appointed interim President by the CUNY Board of Higher Education. At his commencement speech, he reportedly said, "We will have law and order . . . . We will not let the minority upset our institution. They must conform. We will have law and order."[54] The speech was punctuated by standing ovations. This mirrored the crackdown on the West Coast under San Francisco State President S.I. Hayakawa and Governor Ronald Reagan. A counterinsurgent epoch slowly emerged nationwide to justify state violence against social movement gains.

Tech News Becomes The Paper

By September 1969, the strikes had ended, summer had passed, and students had begun a new term—some graduating high school to enter CUNY. Tech News endured as an organizing hub and written record of how students sustained the militant Black, Puerto Rican, and Third World energies that had erupted in the previous semester. Simms brought on incoming SEEK student Louis Reyes Rivera to Tech News, and they began to recruit a dozen Black and Puerto Rican students, including Covington, to help transform the newspaper. In a 2015 interview, Covington recalled of the student-led project:

It's amazing that without the SEEK program there never would have been a Paper, because the three of us who started The Paper, out of those

52 Simms, "What Was Behind the CCNY Takeover?"

53 Buffett, "Crossing the Line," 1228.

54 Simms, "What Was Behind the CCNY Takeover?"

three, two of us were SEEK students. Louis Rivera and I were SEEK students and Paul [Simms] wasn't, but he was the mastermind . . . We didn't have a faculty advisor, we didn't have somebody who was saying 'You can't say this,' 'You gotta do it this way.' So we invented what we thought would work and it worked well.[55]

Rivera's first article with *Tech News*, cowritten with Simms for a September 1969 issue, documented the firing of Wilfred Cartey from his position in the Urban and Ethnic Studies (UES) Department by Joseph Copeland, the new City College president.[56] Cartey, a blind Trinidadian professor of Comparative Literature and Black Studies, had been brought to City College from Columbia University to expand UES (which at the time only offered two courses), and had just published the counter-canonical anthology *Whispers from a Continent: The Literature of Contemporary Black Africa*. During the April–May 1969 strike, he served as a faculty liaison between students, administration, and faculty. Cartey now formally proposed the creation of a distinct school of "Third World Studies," similar to what Bambara and Simms had outlined. His close involvement with the strike was presumably the reason for his dismissal by Copeland, who called the professor "too goddamn shiftless."[57]

Copeland appointed Osborne E. Scott to take Cartey's place as Chairman of the UES Department despite the fact that, by Rivera's account, Scott had "not taught at any college or university anywhere."[58] Rivera, a first-year student just two issues into writing for a campus paper, penned an incisive critique of the institution's reforms from above. A few months later, *Tech News* further assailed Scott and the City College administration's plans for Ethnic Studies by comparing Scott's curriculum proposal with the original one presented by Cartey.[59] The paper's staff and readers were frustrated by how the prospect of meaningful education about their communities' histories was being whittled away. In response, the paper offered Cartey's vision in print as a tangible syllabus from which students and faculty could still shape a more liberatory education, whether it was formally sanctioned for the classroom or not.

The political firing of left-wing professors and the resistance to curriculum reform were not *Tech News*' only beats to cover. In its October 23, 1969 issue, Rivera reported that a federal agent had entered City College's Office of Student Activities, conversed with the secretary, and left with a large manila envelope of student files. When Rivera arrived on the scene, he didn't receive a clear answer about what had transpired from the secretary, who said, "I know why you're here. There was no one here, and he didn't get what he wanted anyway."[60] It's no surprise that the Federal Bureau of Investigation's Counter-Intelligence Program (COINTELPRO) had taken note of this campus insurgency. COINTELPRO used surveillance, sabotage, imprisonment, and assassination to dismantle US liberation groups, but they also targeted the hundreds of uni-

---

55 Francee Covington, "Francee Covington: An Oral History of the CCNY 1960s SEEK Program and *The Paper*."

56 Paul B. Simms and Louis R. Rivera, "Volpe Throws Light on Cartey Mystery, Faculty Cited as the Deciding Factor," *Tech News*, September 25, 1969.

57 *Tech News*, "Copeland Style Moderation," September 25, 1969.

58 Louis Reyes Rivera, "Student-Member of BHE Doubts Scott's Abilities," *Tech News*, October 7, 1969.

59 *Tech News*, "Scott Develops New Courses: Curriculum to be Expanded," October 30, 1969.

60 Louis Reyes Rivera, "Student Files for Federal Agent?," *Tech News*, October 23, 1969; *Tech News*, "Unanswered Questions," October 23, 1969.

versity uprisings that emerged. By this time, the FBI and CIA were collaborating with campus administrators to examine roughly 3,650 student files a year.[61] Although it's unknown how many CUNY students were surveilled, we do know that the New York Police Department's Intelligence Division collected about 520 boxes of records—an estimated 1.1 million pages of documents—on a variety of movements from 1955 to 1972, including local university struggles. CUNY Professor Johanna Fernández's 2014 lawsuit ultimately forced the NYPD, in June 2016, to admit to the existence of these archives, which had been hidden in a Queens warehouse.[62]

At the start of the Spring 1970 semester, the CUNY administration began announcing its plans to implement Open Admissions with a huge influx of new students—but few upgrades in financial and logistical resources. Students and faculty criticized the plan as deliberately structured to overwhelm the colleges and to track students into two- or four-year schools based on their ethnic and class background. Rivera quoted City College professor Alfred Conrad, Adrienne Rich's husband, grilling the school president: "Where do the new students go? Are they going to be isolated in some loft away from the main campus? . . . How can students similar in needs to SEEK students attend full-time with no financial assistance?" Young Lords student activist Carlos Ponte explained how the two-tier "open" university admissions policy would exacerbate race and class stratification: "remedial programs and non-academic courses being taught to Black and Puerto Rican students at the junior college level are primarily geared toward turning out social workers."[63]

A follow-up *Tech News* student survey about the proposed plan noted similar concerns. Student David Caldwell worried that it might be "designed to fail," further adding, "I will not be surprised if the whole thing will be a total fiasco. That will give all the right-wingers a chance to say 'I told you so!'" Another student, James N. Ogunusi, states, "I'm for true open admissions, not the Bullshit that the Board of Higher Education is offering."[64] A *Tech News* editorial lamented the specter of CUNY administrators forcing through deepening precarity masked as reform:

> Open admissions is a necessity—there is no doubt about that. Education[,] similar to Health Care, should be considered a right, not a privilege. . . . We understand that the powers that be, the Board of Higher Education, the Mayor, the Governor, and the people who tell them what to do, had no intention of implementing Open Admissions for the next several years and it was only the initiative taken by the Black and Puerto Rican students here last term that pushed this master plan schedule to this coming fall. But even now, the plan that Board has developed has *built in failures* in not providing remedial assistance for these students, in housing them in lofts and garages and similar edifices not conducive to learning, in granting SEEK students a stipend and offering these new students nothing. And as if this was not enough, the Board has decided

---

61 Seth Rosenfeld, *Subversives: The FBI's War on Student Radicals, and Reagan's Rise to Power* (New York: Farrar, Straus and Giroux, 2012), 386.

62 Nick Pinto, "Under Media Spotlight, City Locates Missing Records of NYPD Political Meddling," *Village Voice*, June 16, 2016, www.villagevoice.com/2016/06/16/under-media-spotlight-city-locates-missing-records-of-nypd-political-meddling/.

63 In Louis Reyes Rivera, "Conrad Attacks Open Admissions Plan," *Tech News*, February 27, 1970.

64 Shirley Brathwaite, "Views in Depth," *Tech News*, April 6, 1970.

to cut the SEEK stipend by over 30% and increase the tuition of Evening Session by considerably more than that, thereby creating a feeling of negativity over the entire plan by both Black and white students. . . . If the Board was really sincere, they would find another plan as well as another means of financing it.[65]

Tech News documented CUNY affairs in a wider milieu of social change amidst state violence. Soon, the paper began to eschew individual bylines for a collectivist analysis by the editorial team, which signaled their recomposition as a multi-author force and also likely protected them from repression.[66] Features highlighted *Tech News'* increasing experimentation with photomontage and other collage techniques that aligned with their collaborative writing ethos. In a visually arresting double-page feature spread on May 15, 1970, the paper mourned the murders of Black students at Texas Southern, Orangeburg, Augusta, Memphis, and Jackson State, and contrasted the public outcry for the four Euro students murdered at Kent State with the more muted response to the cases they highlighted of Black students. At the center of the feature sits an illustration of bullet-riddled Black bodies, while a "KENT"-helmeted National Guardsman grins and shakes the hand of a Southern sheriff. In the background, a silhouette emblazoned with the words "JACKSON STATE" recedes into the darkness of social forgetting. The accompanying text charges CUNY officials with complicit silence:

American racism—you can find it in every single facet of life in these United States. From New York to San Francisco, Birmingham to Maine, white people generally act in patterns that are predicated upon keeping Black people down. Only recently, we have seen how the City College administration and the City University have responded to the deaths of the seven brothers, one by prison guards, and six by the Augusta police. There hasn't been one word out of Copeland or Bowker about the deaths of these Black people.

The *Tech News* editors were increasingly discarding the fiction of journalistic objectivity in favor of a partisan approach. They took calls to direct action out of the editorial pages and splayed them across the publication at large. In keeping with this aim, the article concludes with a section entitled "What Do We Do Now," in which the editors proclaim, "Simply the number of cases of brutality and murder committed on the Black peoples of America by this government should force all Black students and Black people to become actively engaged in the struggle for freedom as an oppressed people."[67]

The practice of identifying threats and untangling contradictions is also seen in Francee Covington's essay "Are the Revolutionary Techniques Employed in *The Battle of Algiers* Applicable to Harlem?" This essay was published in her SEEK teacher Toni Cade Bambara's anthology, *The Black Woman*, after Covington graduated from City

---

65 *Tech News*, "B.H.E. Is Also Dirty," March 5, 1970 (emphasis in original).

66 The Third World Women's Alliance also practiced collective authorship for their newspaper *Triple Jeopardy*. See Patricia Romney, *We Were There: The Third World Women's Alliance & The Second Wave* (New York: Feminist Press, 2021). Gratitude to Vani Kannan for this reference.

67 *Tech News*, "Jackson State, Augusta, Orangeburg, Texas Southern, and on, and on, and on," May 15, 1970.

College in August 1970. Assessing the paradigmatic influence of the Algerian revolution on the US left, especially through the circulation of Frantz Fanon's book *The
Wretched of the Earth* and Gillo Pontecorvo's film *The Battle of Algiers*, Covington dissected
how the successful components of the revolution did not correspond with the possibilities present in Black radical epicenters like "Harlem, Watts, Howard University," and
elsewhere in the United States.[68] The comparison between Algeria and Harlem was
not simply rhetorical: members of the Black and Puerto Rican Student Community
(BPRSC) who coordinated the City College takeover had used the "Committee of
Ten" decentralized underground cell model they learned from watching *The Battle of
Algiers*.[69] According to Covington, however,

> importing the techniques of revolution that were successful in one place
> may prove disastrous in another place . . . the main reasons for the success
> of the Algerian Revolution were (1) religion; (2) a sense of community; (3)
> land base; and (4) outside basis of support . . . none of these elements has
> emerged to any large degree among Black people in this country.

For revolutionaries, she asserts, "knowledge of the area is not enough. Guerrilla warfare
cannot be waged in a laboratory-type setup. It is based on the ability of the guerrillas
to move undetected from one place to another. There must be freedom of movement."
Moreover, Covington noted the dangers of recuperation: "American society is a unique
amoebalike structure that can not only absorb some of the most adverse elements in it
but can also co-opt the ideas of those elements to such an extent as to make it profitable
for the society as a whole."[70] Extending her experience in the SEEK program and *Tech
News* in Harlem to a national audience, Covington advocated for a rigorously place-
based, historically rooted, anticolonial strategy for US urban uprisings, one that drew
inspiration from Algeria but demanded homegrown methods.

Tech News' radical positions were pushed further when Louis Rivera became its editor in chief in the Fall of 1970. The October 6 installment saw *The Paper* appear as
a "special supplement of *Tech News*." One month later, the November 19, 1970 issue
printed *The Paper aka Tech News* across its masthead, proclaiming: "The new banner for
TECH NEWS, THE PAPER, is the culmination of an effort to produce a responsible
Black journal at CCNY. The concept of TECH NEWS has outlived its usefulness. THE
PAPER *aka Tech News*, will fulfill the purpose of projecting the realities of our world
today." The newspaper's transformation provided an example of how an institution
(in this case, a student newspaper) can be overturned from within and reconstructed to
foreground new perspectives that undermine its previous existence. It also maintained
the spirit of the Spring 1969 occupation in written form, even as the university lurched
back into familiar governance. In this way, *The Paper* became an ongoing mobile compo-
nent of Harlem University, passed hand to hand, issuing sparks for future insurgencies.

Employing the skills he honed during his first year with *The Paper*, Rivera used his

---

68 Francee Covington, "Are the Revolutionary Techniques Employed in *The Battle of Algiers* Applicable to
    Harlem?" in *The Black Woman: An Anthology*, ed. Toni Cade Bambara (New York: New American Library,
    1970), 315.

69 See Radivojević and Starosta, *Are You With Me?*

70 Covington, "Are the Revolutionary Techniques Employed in *The Battle of Algiers* Applicable to Har-
    lem?," 314, 317, 322.

editorials to excoriate the administration and rouse the student body. He wove together a variety of writing styles—sarcasm, melodrama, lyricism, and stone-sober brevity.
Simms recalled of Rivera that "he felt the need for a kind of freedom that came from
the crafting of a different set of core values. He was like the glue that really held a lot of
us together." About Rivera's energy and vision, Simms said, "he was connected—there
was a rhythm going on his life, and it came out in his writings and activism."[71] Even so,
Rivera eschewed the spotlight. By February 1971, the production credits section simply
listed him alongside the other members under the collectively held title of "Staff."

After Rivera's year at the helm of the paper, he continued to write incisive articles
on the most pressing issues at CCNY and around the country. The September 30, 1971
issue includes a piece cowritten by Rivera and Bob Feaster (later Sekou Sundiata) about
a City College event mourning the state violence committed during the Attica Prison
uprising.[72] The issue contained another centerfold on the uprising, with a Frederick Douglass quotation underscoring the importance of social struggle: "Those who profess to
favor freedom and yet deprecate agitation are men who want crops without plowing
the ground, rain without thunder and lightning, the ocean without the roar of its many
waters."[73] Also included in the issue is a full-page poem by Feaster, entitled "For Brother George Jackson," the Black Panther who had been murdered one month earlier by
prison guards, and in whose honor the 1971 Attica Uprising had been waged: "Why
Revolution / Why Liberation / from slave-death / subway cemeteries / moving on underground veins / from / machines and ideas that are / foreign and / vulgar to our
/ dreams / life." Feaster's poem doesn't sink into elegiac futility, but concludes with a
rousing call to action: We will not mourn / your death-day / Comrade Brother / we will
take that part of you that can never die. / We will take your / Spirit / your Spirit / your
Spirit to / your Spirit to Struggle / & your Black Love. We will take it / & be something
special / like FREEDOM NOW / like / FREEDOM NOW!"[74]

The Paper's creative, militant, multimodal approach to journalism—its issues now
regularly containing socially charged poems, photographs, illustrations, special features,
and student and faculty interviews—showed its refusal to portray this roiling historical
moment with the nonchalance that is all too common in journalism. In choosing to take
a thematic gamble and redirect its identity as a record of City College political life, *The
Paper* embodied the vision of Black and Puerto Rican students transforming their role in
education and society. While Open Admissions and Ethnic Studies were being sabotaged
from above, this student newspaper seized the opportunity to realize its potential.

Assata Shakur and Guillermo Morales: From CUNY to the Underground

> *It is our duty to fight for our freedom.*
> *It is our duty to win.*

---

71 Paul B. Simms, interview with the author, May 22, 2012.

72 In the mid-1970s, Sundiata would take graduate-level poetry workshops with June Jordan at City
College.

73 David Friedlander, *The Paper*, September 30, 1971.

74 Bob Feaster, "For Brother George Jackson," *The Paper*, September 30, 1971. See also Robin D. G.
Kelley, *Freedom Dreams (Twentieth Anniversary Edition): The Black Radical Imagination* (Boston: Beacon Press,
2022), xxi–xxv.

We must love each other and support each other.
We have nothing to lose but our chains.[75]

These words from Assata Shakur have been repeated by countless crowds in the #Black Lives Matter movement. The phrases fuse Black and Third World feminist calls for revolutionary care with a commitment to class warfare that echoes Marx and Engels' *Communist Manifesto*. "Assata Taught Me" books, shirts, and murals portray her as a godmother to the movement; "Assata Shakur is Welcome Here" posters document the time she was underground and in fugitive flight in the 1970s.[76] However, as with any militant who can be selectively quoted once converted into an icon, we run the risk that her lessons will become tokenized and commodified.

Assata Shakur's autobiography offers a powerful example of how student composition can extend beyond campus walls into broader insurgent interventions. First published in 1987 and reissued in 2001, the book recounts Shakur's revolutionary life, which began with her association with the Black Panther Party (BPP) in the late 1960s. She eventually went underground with the Black Liberation Army (BLA) and survived being shot by the police on the New Jersey Turnpike in 1973. She was incarcerated for several years before escaping prison in 1979 and being granted refuge in Cuba in 1984, where she remains in exile. Her memoir is an invaluable record of becoming a student, community educator, and "unreconstructed insurrectionist," in the words of abolitionist scholar Joy James.[77]

Born on July 16, 1947, in Jamaica, Queens, Shakur spent her teenage and young adulthood years in Harlem, the Lower East Side, Queens, and the Upper West Side. As she became politically involved, Shakur entered Manhattan Community College (MCC)[78] in the late 1960s, as part of a small but growing student force who had benefited from the expansion of public higher education but who focused their efforts on increasing access for others. She became immersed in Black liberation work through Golden Drums, a campus group that created events with Black Studies curricula and activities which they simultaneously demanded that the college formally implement. Through their lectures on Black histories, Shakur learned about Nat Turner and others who resisted enslavement. Golden Drums nurtured a thriving cultural scene, with bridges between higher education, youth, and community knowledge. Along with teaching history, reading, and math, they ran programming that included concerts, plays, poetry readings, dancing, drumming, and more.

Two particular stories about Shakur show how CUNY students and faculty were attentive to educational struggles taking place around the city. In one account from her aunt and lawyer Evelyn Williams, Shakur's first arrest occurred in 1967, along with a hundred other MCC students who had "chained and locked the entrance to a college building to protest curriculum deficiencies in the Black Studies program and

---

75 Assata Shakur, *Autobiography* (Brooklyn: Lawrence Hill Books, 2001), 52.

76 Donna Murch, *Assata Taught Me: State Violence, Mass Incarceration, and the Movement for Black Lives* (Chicago: Haymarket Books, 2020.)

77 Joy James, "Framing the Panther: Assata Shakur and Black Female Agency," in *Want to Start a Revolution?: Radical Women in the Black Freedom Struggle*, ed. Dayo F. Gore, Komozi Woodard, and Jeanne Theoharis (New York: New York University Press, 2009), 144.

78 This CUNY school is now called "the Borough of Manhattan Community College."

the lack of Black faculty."[79] In another instance, she and her MCC friends traveled to a demonstration called by Ocean Hill-Brownsville parents who "wanted a say in what their children were taught, in how their schools were run, and in who was teaching their children." Shakur's group met with City College students and, after the demo had ended, debated how to win full community control. One said, "You can control the social and political institutions, but unless you control the economic and military institutions, you can only go but so far. . . . Fighting for community control is just the first step. It can only go so far. What you need is a revolution."[80]

Shakur graduated from MCC and transferred to City College in 1969. During a short Bay Area trip, she met with Asian, Black, Chicano, and Native American revolutionaries, including members of the Black Panther Party. Back in New York City, she joined the local chapter and became instrumental in the East Harlem free breakfast program and free health clinic. Education was central for the Panthers, and Shakur outlined pedagogical methods in her memoir—practicing culturally empowering children's arts activities, creating movement spaces to foster educational bridges between children and adults, and developing both informal neighborhood programs and formal learning institutions.[81] In an echo of Samuel R. Delany's campus conundrums, Shakur described how she "learned more in one night than i learned in City College in a month" when conversing with Panther 21 members like Dhoruba Bin Wahad, Michael Cetewayo Tabor, and Jamal Joseph, who were out on bail.[82]

Shakur's future comrade Guillermo Morales was born on February 7, 1950, and spent his childhood and adolescence in Spanish Harlem. As a teenager, he picked up odd jobs and visited museums and movie theaters with Black and Puerto Rican friends. In September 1968, Morales arrived at City College and soon began organizing with the Black student group Onyx. As he learned more about Puerto Rican history and independence leader Pedro Albizu Campos, he joined Puerto Ricans Involved in Student Action (PRISA). Morales was involved in campus actions preceding the 1969 strike. In his 2015 memoir, Morales recounted a little-known detail from the strike, an episode in which Black and Puerto Rican students faced off against armed members of the Zionist Jewish Defense League (JDL) on the campus grounds. In another anecdote, he recounted the alliances forged with Black and Brown campus police, who refused to evict the strikers before being replaced by a new repressive security company.

In 1970, Morales transferred to the School of Visual Arts to study filmmaking and joined the Fuerzas Armadas de Liberación Nacional (FALN), an underground guerrilla organization fighting for Puerto Rican independence. During the 1970s, the FALN began organizing on the far left of a larger milieu that included other Puerto Rican independence groups like the Young Lords Party and El Comité and, in Puerto Rico, the Partido Independentista Puertorriqueño (PIP), Partido Socialista Puertorriqueño (PSP), and—by the late 1970s—the Ejército Popular Boricua (also

79 Evelyn Williams, *Inadmissible Evidence: The Story of the African-American Trial Lawyer Who Defended the Black Liberation Army* (Brooklyn: Lawrence Hill Books, 1994), 7.

80 Shakur, *Autobiography*, 181–183.

81 See also Murch, *Living for the City: Migration, Education, and the Rise of the Black Panther Party in Oakland, California* (Chapel Hill: University of North Carolina Press, 2010).

82 Shakur, *Autobiography*, 220. See also Sekou Odinga, Dhoruba Bin Wahad, and Jamal Joseph, eds., *Look for Me in the Whirlwind: From the Panther 21 to 21st-Century Revolutions* (Oakland: PM Press, 2017); Robyn C. Spencer, *The Revolution Has Come: Black Power, Gender, and the Black Panther Party in Oakland* (Durham: Duke University Press, 2016).

known as the Macheteros). In 1973, after completing a senior thesis film on Puerto Rican nationalists, Morales became one of the FALN's primary bomb-makers.[83]

By this time, Shakur had left the Black Panther Party over crises in leadership and direction during a time of vicious state repression. Eventually, she went underground with the Black Liberation Army, an offshoot of the Panthers.[84] After her Spring 1973 arrest, she released the statement "To My People" on July 4 that was broadcast on hundreds of radio stations and published in movement newspapers across the country. The now famous #Black Lives Matter "Assata Chant" is excerpted from this statement:

> Every time a Black Freedom Fighter is murdered or captured, the pigs try to create the impression that they have quashed the movement, destroyed our forces, and put down the Black Revolution. The pigs also try to give the impression that five or ten guerrillas are responsible for every revolutionary action carried out in amerika. That is nonsense. That is absurd. Black revolutionaries do not drop from the moon. We are created by our conditions. Shaped by our oppression. We are being manufactured in droves in the ghetto streets, places like attica, san quentin, bedford hills, leavenworth, and sing sing. They are turning out thousands of us. Many jobless Black veterans and welfare mothers are joining our ranks. Brothers and sisters from all walks of life, who are tired of suffering passively, make up the BLA.
>
> There is, and always will be, until every Black man, woman, and child is free, a Black Liberation Army. The main function of the Black Liberation Army at this time is to create good examples, to struggle for Black freedom, and to prepare for the future. We must defend ourselves and let no one disrespect us. We must gain our liberation by any means necessary.
>
> It is our duty to fight for our freedom.
> It is our duty to win.
> We must love each other and support each other.
> We have nothing to lose but our chains[.]

Shakur then names her friends and comrades murdered by COINTELPRO, police, and prison authorities over the past several years: Ronald Carter, William Christmas, Mark Clark, Mark Essex, Frank "Heavy" Fields, Woodie Changa Olugbala Green, Fred Hampton, Lil' Bobby Hutton, George Jackson, Jonathan Jackson, James McClain, Harold Russell, Zayd Malik Shakur, Anthony Kumu Olugbala White. She ends the address with the words, "We must fight on."[85]

By framing the Black Liberation Army as a perpetual fighting force with members from "all walks of life" that will continue until Black freedom is realized, Shakur defined the group's purpose and participation in the most expansive terms possible. This

---

83 Morales Correa, *Desde la sombra la luz*, 31–45, 52–57, 60–61. See also *Latin American Studies*, "Guillermo Morales Correa: Clandestinidad y exilio," 2004, http://www.latinamericanstudies.org/puertorico/morales-entrevista.htm/.

84 See Odinga et al., *Look for Me in the Whirlwind*.

85 Shakur, *Autobiography*, 52–53.

articulated a strategic pivot for Blackness and revolution that exceeded ethnicity, rooting itself instead in political affiliation. Moreover, as a teacher-organizer writing from prison, she also reminded people that COINTELPRO was a means by which the US government surveilled, disrupted, encaged, and murdered Black teachers and students. The work of state counterintelligence literally meant demolishing the Black Panthers' freedom schools, which had gathered a broad audience among the poor and agitated people of all colors.

Following her imprisonment, Shakur became a major inspiration for movements at CUNY. City College students and workers followed her case closely. In February 1975, City College students hosted an event with Martha Pitts and the National Committee for the Defense of Political Prisoners, where they read a letter that Shakur had written for the occasion:

> Learning can be a beautiful experience and is necessary for the survival and eventual liberation of the people. I doubt that the 'education' that you are receiving is any more relevant or real than it was when I went there. Schools are simply reflections of the systems and societies that govern them. But I hope that the many events that have occurred over the last few years have made it easier to separate relevance from trivia and truth from fiction. Even though it is necessary to attend the system's schools to gain skills that we need, we must never let what we read blind us to what we see.
>
> There is a tremendous revolutionary potential in the colleges of America. And to the problem, working collectively (we) can solve it. There is a great need for a student movement to be built, based not just on students' rights but on human rights. While practice without theory bangs its head against a brick wall, theory without practice lulls itself to sleep.

> Love, Struggle,
> Assata[86]

City College's SEEK educators learned from and advocated on Shakur's behalf. In 1977, June Jordan read at a benefit for Shakur alongside Jayne Cortez. Adrienne Rich compiled notes on Shakur's case in her archives. Audre Lorde kept a poem by Shakur in her archives, and in turn wrote the 1977 poem "For Assata," in which she says, "I dream of your freedom / as my victory / and the victory of all dark women."[87] The most prominent Black Studies journal of the time, *Black Scholar*, featured a 1978 essay that Shakur had written while imprisoned at Rikers Island alongside essays by Angela Y. Davis and Lorde.[88] Still, Shakur's most daring acts of Life Studies—to reference June Jordan—had yet to come.

While Shakur's arrest and subsequent statements made her one of the most infamous US Black women revolutionaries in the 1970s, we know little of Morales' life at this time. His 2015 memoir, *Desde la sombra la luz: Pasajes de mi vida*, obscures the

---

86 Assata Shakur, "Black Liberation: A Reminder," *The Paper*, February 20, 1975.

87 Audre Lorde, "For Assata" (1977), in *The Black Unicorn: Poems* (New York: W.W. Norton and Company, 1978), 28.

88 Assata Shakur, "Women in Prison: How We Are," *The Black Scholar* 9, no. 7 (April 1978).

years between 1974 and 1978. During this time, the FALN conducted more than forty bombings in New York and Chicago, targeting institutions such as federal buildings, banks, insurance companies, police precincts, department stores, hotels, and financial district restaurants.[89] Morales' involvement halted following an incident on July 12, 1978, when a bomb he was constructing in an FALN safe house in East Elmhurst, Queens accidentally exploded, injuring his face and severing nine of his fingers. After flushing sensitive documents down the toilet, Morales was apprehended by the police.[90]

Uptown in Harlem this same year, a new City College student group began organizing in defense of political prisoners and against the encroaching threat of fascism. Calling themselves the John Brown Anti-Klan Committee (JBAKC), the group's leadership was mostly comprised of Euro (including Jewish) lesbians. JBAKC had formed a year earlier "in response to the struggle of Black and Puerto Rican prisoners against KKK organizing among New York State prison guards [with the goal] to combat the growing resurgence of the Ku Klux Klan in the South and elsewhere, and promote the mobilization of white people to fight white supremacy." Soon, the group would form chapters in Austin, Boston, Chicago, and elsewhere.[91] Their newspaper's title proclaimed the group's intentions: *Death to the Klan!* Some had previously helped to form the solidarity group "Friends of Assata and Sundiata" after the 1973 arrests of Shakur and Sundiata Acoli.

JBAKC began distributing leaflets at City College and collaborating with other student groups, including the Arab Student Association and the Black and Puerto Rican Student Community. Some JBAKC members were also in underground groups like the May 19th Communist Organization (M19), which for years had built trust with Black, Puerto Rican, and Third World liberation groups while conducting clandestine efforts to support them. Susan Rosenberg, who had been a member of both JBAKC and M19, had transferred from Barnard College explicitly to do abolitionist campus organizing at City College.[92] Akin to their 1930s predecessors, JBAKC made the campus an epicenter for countering fascism both locally and globally.

One of the group's first major efforts was to support imprisoned militant Khali Siwatu-Odari, who had penned an open letter announcing that the Ku Klux Klan was "infiltrating prisons in the [New York] region, with large numbers of Klansmen holding jobs as guards and prison teachers."[93] JBAKC researched the names and locations of the racial supremacists, conducted legal support, and held campus and community meetings to outline strategies for countering racist attacks by police, the KKK, and neo-Nazi sympathizers. In 1977, the New York High Court ruled that prison guards could join the KKK, after which imprisoned members of NAACP and Latinos Unidos

---

89 Matt Meyer writes: "Between 1974 and 1983, by which time more than a dozen alleged members of the group had been arrested, the FALN claimed responsibility for more than 120 bombings against US corporate or military targets." In *Let Freedom Ring: A Collection of Documents from the Movements to Free US Political Prisoners* (Oakland: PM Press, 2008), 17.

90 Bryan Burrough, *Days of Rage: America's Radical Underground, the FBI, and the Forgotten Age of Revolutionary Violence* (New York: Penguin Press, 2015), 460–465.

91 *Freedom Archives*, "John Brown Anti-Klan Committee" Collection, https://search.freedomarchives.org/search.php?view_collection=7/.

92 William Rosenau, *Tonight We Bombed the US Capitol: The Explosive Story of M19, America's First Female Terrorist Group* (New York: Atria Books, 2020), 31.

93 Hilary Moore and James Tracy, *No Fascist USA!: The John Brown Anti-Klan Committee and Lessons for Today's Movements* (San Francisco: City Lights, 2020), 48.

briefly seized a section of Napanoch Prison in protest.

Within six months of each other in 1979, both Morales and Shakur escaped from custody and went underground again.[94] Although the historical record of these actions is confidential, JBAKC and M19 members, alongside a sister group called "The Family," purportedly aided both escapes.[95] Eventually, Morales and Shakur obtained political exile in Cuba, where they continue to reside today.[96] Their respective memoirs reflect the "strategic silences" that shape the autobiographical writing and journalism of revolutionaries.[97] Like the collectivist bylines used by *Tech News*, these silences indicate another method of self-protection and encourage us to read archival absences more carefully. Between Morales' 1973 graduation from SVA and the 1978 explosion that injured him and his subsequent escape from Bellevue Hospital in 1979, his experiential record remains unstated. Likewise, Shakur obscured how she escaped from New York's Clinton Correctional Facility in 1979 and then relocated to Cuba five years later.

Understandably, these omissions protect the people who co-conspired to free Morales and Shakur, and the underground routes through which they both ultimately fled the United States. However, their methods of escape, hiding out in secret communities, evading police, boarding planes, and fleeing the United States are kept hidden from the state as well as revolutionaries who read their memoirs (and who may have to someday figure out these survival skills). In retrospect, similar to Saidiya Hartman's "critical fabulist" archival counter-reading and Gavin Arnall's focus on "the universalism of the void," reconstructing Morales' and Shakur's hidden lives requires learning *how to read in the underground*.[98]

One way to read absences of this kind is by considering how these former City College students composed their beliefs into being through clandestine actions. This is particularly useful for Morales, whose writing is scanter than Shakur's. His City College writing and SVA thesis film are lost, and the unsigned FALN communiques

---

94 Morales escaped from Bellevue Hospital on May 21, 1979, and Shakur escaped from Clinton Correctional Facility in Dannemora, NY, on November 2, 1979.

95 Regarding Morales' escape, he stated in a 2004 interview, "The only thing that I can tell you is that I did it alone. Inside and outside." [See "Guillermo Morales Correa: Clandestinidad y exilio."] Regarding Shakur, fellow Black Liberation Army member Sekou Odinga was interviewed by historian Robyn C. Spencer in March 2016, revealing that he had been part of a group called "The Family" that aided her escape. Notably, when Spencer "asked Sekou Odinga why the movement freed Shakur, he gave an answer that was not particular to her and her characteristics (i.e., we wanted to free a leader, or we wanted a type of spokesperson) but more that she was positioned in a way/place/situation that made freeing her possible." [Robyn C. Spencer, email communication with the author, September 20, 2017.] Moore and Tracy note that Shakur was freed by Sekou Odinga, Mtayari Sundiata, Winston Patterson, and Silvia Baraldini [*No Fascist USA!*, 97]. Bryan Burrough asserts that both of their escapes were aided by The Family [*Days of Rage*, 474–476]. William Rosenau writes that their escapes were both aided by the May 19th Organization [*Tonight We Bombed the US Capitol*, 65–81].

96 Shakur arrived in Cuba in 1984, and Morales arrived in 1988, after building ties for several years with the Ejército Zapatista de Liberación Nacional (EZLN, also known as the Zapatistas), but then being imprisoned and tortured by Mexican authorities.

97 Margo V. Perkins, *Autobiography as Activism: Three Black Women of the Sixties* (Jackson: University Press of Mississippi, 2000), 19.

98 Saidiya Hartman, "Venus in Two Acts," *Small Axe* 12, no. 2 (June 2008): 1–14; Gavin Arnall, *Subterranean Fanon: An Underground Theory of Radical Change* (New York: Columbia University Press, 2020), 16.

don't confirm his involvement.[99] However, one form of composition that *can* be traced to Morales is his role as the FALN's principal bomb-maker. Stefano Harney and Fred Moten have called for us to extend the realms of study to include a broader range of social interactions—what they call the undercommons—and the compositional practices developed by City College students included their sexual explorations, newspaper projects, and efforts to build Harlem University.[100] By extension, Morales' explosives might also be considered post-college compositions, while his fugitive escape makes his commitment to a life of unshackled study and movement concrete. After all, part of the 1969 college occupation entailed setting fire to the Finley Student Center before the administration ceded to the students' demands. In response to James Baldwin's 1963 query, "Do I really want to be integrated into a burning house?"—perhaps sometimes we must set fire to parts of the house in order to lay claim to it.[101] So then, how can we expand the practice of student composition to include underground acts of decolonization? Where is there room to discuss the Steve Bikos, Leila Khaleds, Ghassan Kanafanis, and Lolita Lebróns, who chose both written and guerrilla warfare forms of resistance?

Another way to practice reading in the underground is by considering the print interventions of the John Brown Anti-Klan Committee. Immediately after Shakur's prison flight in November 1979 (in which at least some JBAKC members assisted) the Madame Binh Graphics Collective and Republic of New Afrika created "Assata Shakur is Welcome Here" posters that JBAKC helped to post around New York City streets—including to cover up FBI Wanted posters.[102] JBAKC's first issue of *Death to the Klan!*, printed that November, honored her freedom on the paper's masthead. The collectively written paper proclaims, "We join all anti-imperialists around the world in celebrating the escape of Assata Shakur, [which] exposes the lies of the government, that tried to paint her as a criminal rather than a leader of her people, and that said the Black Liberation Army had been destroyed." They also celebrated Morales' escape and the September 1979 release of Puerto Rican nationalist political prisoners Oscar Collazo, Rafael Cancel Miranda, Irving Flores Rodriguez, and Lolita Lebrón. JBAKC urged readers to build upon these victories with a renewed struggle for Black and Third World liberation and for self-determination against the growing Klan and other forms of racist terror.[103]

In this inaugural issue of *Death to the Klan!*, JBAKC announced its intention to "fight white supremacy at City College" alongside Black and Third World students threatened with increasing tuition and admissions barriers. They also promised to oppose ad-

---

99 Yale University's archives contain an immense collection of FBI files, which include surveillance of and materials by the FALN. More FALN archives are available at *LatinAmericanStudies.org* (https://www. latinamericanstudies.org/). Cited in Meg Starr, "Hit Them Harder," 152 n44. Virginia Colwell has also assembled several FALN communiques for public view; see http://www.virginiacolwell.com/print/. Cited in Ren Ellis Neyra, *The Cry of the Senses: Listening to Latinx and Caribbean Poetics* (Durham: Duke University Press, 2020), 166, 187 n52.

100 See Stevphen Shukaitis, "Studying Through the Undercommons – An Interview with Stefano Harney and Fred Moten," Class War University archives, http://undercommoning.org/study-ing-through-the-undercommons-stefano-harney-fred-moten-interviewed-by-stevphen-shukaitis/.

101 James Baldwin, *The Fire Next Time* (New York: Dial Press, 1963), 94. See also Jordan, "City and City College"; Simms, "What Was Behind the CCNY Takeover?"

102 Moore and Tracy, *No Fascist USA!*, 97, 100.

103 John Brown Anti-Klan Committee, "Bulletin! Assata Shakur Escapes," *Death to the Klan!* (November 1979): 1, http://freedomarchives.org/Documents/Finder/DOC37_scans/37.dttk.nov79.pdf/.

ministrative censure of the kind experienced by Mike Edwards, a Black student leader threatened with expulsion after challenging a faculty member "who said that Africa had no civilization."[104] JBAKC dedicated special attention in their newspaper—as well as in op-eds sent to *The Paper*—to the implementation of the City College administration's "Operation Snowflake."[105] One editorial explained that, with this program, the administration's "goal is to reestablish City as the 'white citadel on the Hill in Harlem,' a strategic base from which to penetrate and eventually destroy the Black community and re-settle Harlem with white people."[106] A related revolutionary newspaper, *Tip of the Iceberg*, further outlined:

> [S]urrounding buildings are being torn down or gutted and replaced by renovated, middle-income housing; streets are being cordoned off and people will need pass cards to walk through the campus; and, simultaneously, Black and Third World studies programs are being done away with. All told, this produces a city school with a white student body, fortressed in the middle of a Black community, not allowing community residents any access to the campus. . . . In staunch support of this program have been the Zionist forces on campus—led by the [Jewish Defense League] and the Hillel House—who have actively opposed Black students' demands, supported administration programs, and have brought speakers like Meir Kahane to campus in their effort to consolidate the forces of white supremacy and reaction.[107]

JBAKC adopted an explicit framework of following "Third World leadership" to denounce Zionism and the JDL, while also drawing connections between the racial supremacist ideas of the JDL and those of the better-known KKK. In another *Paper* editorial, JBAKC argued,

> On many campuses, zionists have played a particular role in attacking Third World students struggling for their right to education, including in 1969 when the JDL attacked with bats and chains the school takeover by Black and Puerto Rican students demanding open admissions and Third World studies programs.
>
> This is why we say JDL = KKK. And the JDL is cloaked in full legitimacy as it is built at City College through Hillel House and the financial and political backing that zionist organizing receives from the administration, many zionist faculty and students.[108]

---

104 John Brown Anti-Klan Committee, "Fight White Supremacy at City College," *Death to the Klan!* (November 1979): 8–9.

105 John Brown Anti-Klan Committee, "Operation Snowflake: Urban Genocide at CCNY," *The Paper*, February 19, 1980, 4; "Open Forum: Keep Sydenham Open / Stop Operation Snowflake," *The Paper*, September 23, 1980, 5; "Open Forum: Racism at City College," *The Paper*, November 5, 1980, 3. It is unclear whether "Operation Snowflake" was the actual name of the City College administration's policy, or more likely a satirical name given to it by campus organizers.

106 John Brown Anti-Klan Committee, "Defeat Operation Snowflake!," *Death to the Klan!* 1, no. 3 (January/February 1980): 5–6.

107 *Tip of the Iceberg*, "Campus Movement Under COINTELPRO Attack" (February 1981): 3, 12.

108 *The Paper*, "Open Forum: Racism at City College," November 5, 1980, 3.

These debates weren't exclusively localized to City College at CUNY. In 1980, administration and right-wing efforts failed to suppress a Black Solidarity Day at Queens College, which brought together organizers from the Congo, Grenada, Nicaragua, South Africa, and Palestine. JBAKC's predominantly Jewish lesbian leadership suggests that, at this conjuncture of US/Palestinian/Israeli history, Jewish and lesbian politics were bound inextricably with anti-imperialism.[109]

Continuations

The expressive record of City College and New York high school students assembled here suggests that student compositions took myriad forms as they worked to study and transform their daily lives. Still, comparatively little archival record of this activity exists. Although student-operated newspapers like *Tech News/The Paper*, *New York High School Free Press*, and *Death to the Klan!* sought to document and shape movement cultures, behind-the-scenes organizing efforts were kept from the public eye. Indeed, comrades in the Black and Puerto Rican Student Union (BPRSC) and Students for a Democratic Society (SDS) often operated on a "need-to-know" basis in which sensitive information was spread secretly between activist cells (or "families") on campus.

The archival materials of *Tech News/The Paper* are also undervalued and limited. While the City College Cohen Library digitized the entire runs of *The Campus* and *Observation Post* over a decade ago, *Tech News* and *The Paper* have only become digitized within the last few years. For too long, these vibrant pages had been inaccessible to people who couldn't visit the archives in person. Although *The Paper* continues to operate as a politically engaged "Medium for People of African Descent," it has confronted financial difficulties like those that troubled its early-1970s forebears. Even during the late 2000s, when I was a writer and editor for *The Paper*, the school's "Tech Fund" threatened several times to decrease *The Paper*'s operating budget, while *The Campus* newspaper was institutionally buttressed by the Journalism Department. The Harlem University organizers seek to address this inequity with a "Paper Scholarship Fund for Social Justice" to support City College student journalist-activists.[110]

Many of those who were involved with *Tech News/The Paper* during the 1960s and 70s are passing away, and frequently at a younger age than their Euro activist counterparts. SEEK educator David Henderson emphasized this point—that institutional racism can inhibit the archival longevity of historical actors themselves. Compared to many of Columbia University's 1960s and '70s radicals who are still going strong, Black and Puerto Rican activists involved in campus organizing two subway stops north have not fared as well. "A lot of these people are gone . . . some people are well-preserved, and some are still catching hell."[111] Case in point: Wilfred Cartey passed away in 1992 at the age of sixty, receiving a scant *New York Times* obituary that was more of an insult to the Africana scholar's rich memory than a tribute.[112] The lives of his colleagues

---

109 After Assata Shakur's escape, FBI grand juries explicitly targeted lesbians and their organizations. See Moore and Tracy, *No Fascist USA!*, 241–242 n87. See also Emily Hobson, *Lavender and Red: Liberation and Solidarity in the Gay and Lesbian Left* (Berkeley: University of California Press, 2016), 2.

110 *The Paper* Scholarship Fund for Social Justice, https://www.givegab.com/campaigns/the-paper-scholarship-fund/.

111 David Henderson, interview by Ammiel Alcalay, shared with the author, May 21, 2012.

112 *New York Times*, "Wilfred Cartey Dies; A Critic and Poet, 60," March 25, 1992, https://www.nytimes.com/1992/03/25/obituaries/wilfred-cartey-dies-a-critic-and-poet-60.html/.

Barbara Christian, June Jordan, and Audre Lorde were also cut short by institutional neglect and cancer.

Louis Reyes Rivera passed away in 2012 at the age of sixty-seven. He had regularly conducted writing and performance workshops at Sista's Place in Brooklyn, and in Fall 2011 had spoken several times to the CUNY community about the 1969 strike and *The Paper*. Obituaries commemorating Rivera's life and work were published across CUNY newspapers and movement websites.[113] CUNY videographers Martyna Starosta and Iva Radivojević produced the short film *Are You With Me?*, featuring a speech by Rivera interspersed with student and faculty mic-checks from a massive education speak-out of tens of thousands of people during an Occupy Wall Street day of action on November 17, 2011.[114] In a beautiful tribute, *The Paper* dedicated its May 2012 issue to Rivera, including previously unpublished excerpts from the 150-page epic poem he completed just before his death, *Jazz in Jail*:

> Imagine too the lessons we can learn / from all these siblings we comprise / passing torches, moving on / cultivating children yet unborn / teaching each we so embrace / how, just like you & I, they too / are from the seeds / of Medgar & of Martin / of Malcolm & Maurice / of Truth & Tubman / Ida B., Lola & Bracetti, / from Queen Nzinga, Nana too / like them sibs who once belonged / to SNCC & RAM, the BPP & YLO / those Brown Berets & BLA's / Weathermen & women / reared by clearly sought ideals / strident strength so fully striving / to continue what we know / remains so incomplete.[115]

In 2012 and then in 2021, Paul Simms reflected on his collaborations with Rivera as well as what he considered missed opportunities for Black and Puerto Rican students and faculty after the strike. He argued, "Black Studies curriculum should go to the community, not the school where you don't have control. The notion of 'approving' a curriculum has got to do with [being subservient to] a university's limited viewpoint." Simms suggested that CUNY advocates for Black and Puerto Rican-oriented curricula could have also made alternative education links with churches, bookstores, and other community gathering sites.[116] This is what SEEK educators Bambara, Henderson, Jordan, Lorde, and Rich, and some members of the Harlem University takeover crew attempted to do. Simms underscored that people's direct participation in shaping their lives and histories was a matter of "where you put the controlling function—not a set-up of coming back every year to get approval of courses, different programs, when where you were headed was a different way." City College's premeditated failure to create educational change, which arose from limits it dictated regarding the "appropriate" pace of reform, underscores why oppressed people sometimes gravitate toward

---

113 Conor Tomás Reed, "Remembering Louis Reyes Rivera—The People's Poet & a Fighter for a Free and Open CUNY," *Indypendent*, March 15, 2012, https://indypendent.org/2012/03/remembering-louis-reyes-rivera-the-peoples-poet-a-fighter-for-a-free-and-open-cuny/.

114 Radivojević and Starosta, *Are You With Me?*

115 Louis Reyes Rivera, excerpt of *Jazz in Jail*, *The Paper*, May 2012; Louis Reyes Rivera, *Jazz in Jail* (East Elmhurst: Blind Beggar Press, 2016).

116 See also Nikki Giovanni, "I Fell Off the Roof One Day (A View of the Black University)," in *The Black Woman: An Anthology*, ed. Toni Cade Bambara (New York: New American Library, 1970), 165–170.

the politics of separatism, self-determination, and self-management, and why they harbor deep suspicion of the words "be patient."

During our 2012 phone interview, Simms revealed, "if you stand on the post long enough, someone will come by."[117] Simms was telling me that advocates of rebellious student literacies at CUNY need to attend to when and where our living archives are patiently waiting to be heard. When Sean Molloy and I were given the opportunity to interview Simms again in 2021, he and his wife Denise Adams Simms discussed his role at *Tech News/The Paper*, his memories of campus organizing, and how these interventions shaped their lives after City College. Weaving together interviews with Simms that both Sean and I had previously done, we produced an oral history that celebrates the efforts of one actor in this larger ensemble of student militancy.[118] In July 2022, Simms passed away in Loma Linda, California. At his funeral in September, members of *The Paper* joined many in paying tribute to his legacy as a "powerhouse of Black health." Through a brief look at this newspaper's history, we can see that these radical students' engagement with the written word—as part of a larger commitment to social justice—provides a different praxis-oriented lens for studying CUNY students' positions in larger revolutionary struggles.

For Guillermo Morales, Assata Shakur, the Black Liberation Army, Fuerzas Armadas de Liberación Nacional, John Brown Anti-Klan Committee, and May 19th Communist Organization, writing discretion meant the difference between a life underground or a state-inflicted death, even as their legacies continue to be uplifted at City College. I first learned about Morales and Shakur when I began to study at City College in 2006. The Guillermo Morales/Assata Shakur Student and Community Center's red doors—emblazoned with a huge black fist clutching a pencil—were always open to textbook exchanges, campus and neighborhood organizing meetings, a community-led agriculture program, and political study sessions. Morales and Shakur posed an enduring threat to the conservative media, politicians, the police, and right-wing students and administrators, all of whom wanted the Center closed.

In May 2013, the FBI announced that Shakur would be added to the Top 10 Most Wanted List.[119] In October 2013, the City College administration (and, presumably, the NYPD and FBI), seized the Morales/Shakur Center and all of its belongings. A wide array of sensitive archival materials was apprehended, including computers, contact lists, financial records, journals, meeting notes, personal correspondences, phones, and the private property of various members. Police also seized banners, flyers, pamphlets, posters, and other movement ephemera. It is all still in their custody, presuming it has not been destroyed.

Meanwhile, Morales and Shakur are both suspended in a peculiar situation in Cuba. Being a critic of Cuba's authoritarian socialism, Morales has been kept under close watch by the state, even having a Puerto Rican comrade's gift of a video camera seized from him because of suspicions that he may be gathering evidence to fuel his

---

117 Paul B. Simms, interview with the author, May 22, 2012.

118 Paul B. and Denise Adams Simms, "Paul and Denise Adams Simms: An Oral History," interview by Conor Tomás Reed and Sean Molloy, https://www.youtube.com/watch?v=bq5qdE1vd4c/.

119 Immediately afterwards, people made a social media call for "Assata Teach-Ins" to dispel the state's myths about her. Free University of NYC hosted a July 2013 event at Marcus Garvey Park in Harlem called "Assata Shakur's Legacy and Lives of Resistance," where CUNY educator Tony Gronowicz recounted how he had taught Shakur in a CUNY pilot course when she was imprisoned on Rikers Island.

opposition to state policies.[120] While Morales wishes to relocate to his homeland of Puerto Rico, he is stuck on an island approximately two hours from home by airplane. Morales' 2015 memoir, written in Spanish and published by an independent press in Puerto Rico, is his first public opportunity to offer his life story. Shakur's legacy looms even larger, especially after being added to the FBI's Most Wanted List. She has essentially been forced into silent hiding in Cuba. During the Spring of 2015, when words from her "Assata's Chant" had been on the lips of participants in #Black Lives Matter actions across the United States for months, she and Morales were briefly considered as bargaining chips in the "normalization" negotiations between Cuba and the United States.[121] While Cubans would not have been permitted by the state to hold "Hands Off Assata and Guillermo!" demonstrations, and had limited internet access to follow these deliberations, Shakur was being uplifted in the United States as a pedagogical godmother of a new Black Liberation Movement by many who knew little about her present condition as a "twenty-first-century fugitive slave."

This chapter has offered opportunities to reconsider which forms of militant student composition are worthy of our critical recognition. The writing and actions of Delany, Covington, Simms, Rivera, Sundiata, Morales, Shakur, as well as the Black and Puerto Rican Student Community, high school students, and the John Brown Anti-Klan Committee offer incisive records of how students at City College and beyond worked to reinvent their learning conditions through writing and action. Delany opted out of the university in order to focus on his iconoclastic fiction and autobiography. Covington, Rivera, Simms, and Sundiata turned a science and engineering campus newspaper into an epicenter of political analysis and cultural provocation, as Covington expanded her reach to warn against ahistorical anticolonial strategies for a national readership. Morales and Shakur drew on campus organizing experiences to commit their lives to underground revolutionary work. Evaluated alongside their City College educators, we can more thoroughly measure the range and significance of these students' efforts to compose a new university and society into being.

These lessons from the 1960s and '70s took on increasing significance after September 11, 2001. CUNY became an epicenter for confronting both US imperialism and Zionism abroad and increasing social inequities at home. At the same time, new movements for Black, Puerto Rican, feminist, queer, and transnational justice signaled the potential for the entire city to become a freedom school once again. For the CUNY movement, the twenty-first century has revealed the prospects of liberation in our lifetime.

---

120 Anonymous, personal correspondence with the author, March 29, 2018.

121 *The Guardian*, "Cubans to open talks about US fugitives including Assata Shakur as ties warm," April 15, 2015, https://www.theguardian.com/us-news/2015/apr/15/cuban-us-fugitives-open-talks-terror-list-ties-warm/.

CHAPTER 5
CONTEMPORARY STRUGGLES FOR OUR FUTURES

Both the wealthy elite and social movements have long recognized CUNY as a social bellwether. As this book has shown, at various points in the twentieth and twenty-first centuries, CUNY became a primary site of economic, social, and ideological restructuring as well as resistance. Struggles over one university became an epicenter for national, and even global, conflicts.

In the wake of the elimination of Open Admissions in 1999, the enrollment of Black and Latinx youth—who comprise over 65 percent of New York City's public high school students—has steadily declined at several of CUNY's four-year colleges which enjoy disproportionate resources within the system.[1] Black and Latinx students are diverted into the under-resourced four-year CUNY colleges and the two-year colleges, where many become stuck paying for mandatory no-credit remedial classes after their financial aid runs out, ultimately leaving without a degree.[2] While CUNY maintained its diversity post-Open Admissions, it remains intensely segregated and unequal school-by-school. Current reports on New York City public schools argue they are more segregated than in the 1960s, a situation that has propelled the reemergence of independent Afrocentric schools.[3]

Within the last several years, Black and Latinx CUNY students have disproportionately appeared in advertising campaigns that depict both them and the univer-

---

1 New York City Department of Education, "DOE Data at a Glance," https://www.schools.nyc.gov/about-us/reports/doe-data-at-a-glance/; Richard Pérez-Peña, "At CUNY, Stricter Admissions Bring Ethnic Shift," *New York Times*, May 22, 2012, https://www.nytimes.com/2012/05/23/nyregion/at-cunys-top-colleges-black-and-hispanic-freshmen-enrollments-drop.html/. Pérez-Peña estimated Black and Latinx enrollment from 2000 to 2012 had declined from 17 percent to 10 percent.

2 LynNell Hancock and Meredith Kolodner, "When high achievers have no place to go," *The Hechinger Report*, January 13, 2015, https://archive.fo/gU9MM/; Tom Hilliard, "Degrees of Difficulty: Boosting College Success in New York City," *Centers for an Urban Future*, December 2017, https://nycfuture.org/research/degrees-of-difficulty/.

3 Howard Lisnoff, "The Resegregation of New York City Schools," *Counterpunch*, August 3, 2018, https://www.counterpunch.org/2018/08/03/the-resegregation-of-new-york-city-schools/; Eliza Shapiro, "'I Love My Skin!' Why Black Parents Are Turning to Afrocentric Schools," *New York Times*, January 8, 2019, https://www.nytimes.com/2019/01/08/nyregion/afrocentric-schools-segregation-brooklyn.html/.

sity as multiethnic success stories.[4] The actual enrollment and graduation records of these students are distorted to maintain the flow of their tuition funds.[5] Meanwhile, Black, Puerto Rican, and Women's Studies—formed out of entwined liberation movements—have become more isolated from each other and more easily subjugated by the CUNY administration.

Nevertheless, CUNY has once again become a potent incubator of social struggles even as it remains a social movement riddle. Indeed, for quite a long time at CUNY, we have been practicing the art of what Kenyan writer Ngũgĩ wa Thiong'o calls "poor theory"—"maximizing the possibilities inherent in the minimum . . . being extremely creative and experimental in order to survive."[6] Unable to isolate ourselves in seminar-table solipsism, we have pursued a kind of *crowd scholarship* that jettisons "interest" for "involvement." Discussions among crowds of people—in and out of general assemblies, street marches, virtual forums, shared meals, spatial transformations, and jail stints—have assembled critical lessons not yet acknowledged, let alone valued, by scholarly frameworks that emphasize singularly rendered knowledge.

Our conditions of struggle can feel at times insurmountable. Education debt in the United States has surpassed $1.7 trillion.[7] City and state funding recedes, while tuition increases put the squeeze on students and budget cuts devastate whole departments. Three in four available faculty positions promise low-waged contingency. College graduates face unemployment, and the majority of new jobs announced by US companies are for part-time, low-wage service work. Meanwhile, the amount of incarcerated people in the US has skyrocketed from about 250,000 in 1976 (when CUNY imposed universal tuition) to 1.8 million today.[8] According to CUNY professors Steve Brier and Michelle Fine, "three of every four college-bound city high school graduates attend one of CUNY's twenty-four campuses. CUNY's current full-time student body is twenty-six percent African American, thirty percent Latino and thirty-eight percent immigrant. A full fifty-four percent of CUNY students have family incomes below $30,000."[9] In a 2018 poll of 22,000 CUNY students, forty-eight percent had been food insecure within the past thirty days, fifty-five percent were housing insecure in the past year, and fourteen percent were homeless in the previous year.[10]

4 Tyvan Burns, "CUNY recognizes stellar students," *New York Amsterdam News*, June 14, 2018, http://amsterdamnews.com/news/2018/jun/14/cuny-recognizes-stellar-students/.

5 *City University of New York*, "Andrew Mellon Foundation Gifts CUNY $10 Million to Drive Change and Expand a Range of Initiatives Related to Pandemic and Racial Justice," August 13, 2020, https://www1.cuny.edu/mu/forum/2020/08/13/andrew-mellon-foundation-gifts-cuny-10-million-to-drive-change-and-expand-a-range-of-initiatives-related-to-pandemic-and-racial-justice/.

6 Ngũgĩ wa Thiong'o, *Globalectics: Theory and the Politics of Knowing* (New York: Columbia University Press, 2012), 2.

7 Zack Friedman, "Student Loan Debt Statistics In 2022: A Record $1.7 Trillion," *Forbes*, May 16, 2022, https://www.forbes.com/sites/zackfriedman/2022/05/16/student-loan-debt-statistics-in-2022-a-record-17-trillion/.

8 Vera Institute, "People in Jail and Prison in Spring 2021," https://www.vera.org/downloads/publications/people-in-jail-and-prison-in-spring-2021.pdf/.

9 Steve Brier and Michelle Fine, "If Cuomo Is a Progressive He Should Invest in CUNY's Future," *City and State New York*, December 10, 2015, www.cityandstateny.com/articles/opinion/if-cuomo-is-a-progressive-he-should-invest-in-cunys-future.html/.

10 Ben Chapman, "Thousands of CUNY Students Experience Homelessness and Food Insecurity, Report Says," *New York Daily News*, March 26, 2019, https://www.nydailynews.com/new-york/education/ny-cuny-students-experience-homelessness-food-insecurity-20190327-qkilgsntmvbcvgqysz2lni4y7m-story.html/.

CUNY professors Meena Alexander, Michelle Fine, and Nicholas Freudenberg report that "fewer than twenty-five percent of CUNY community college students graduate within three years and fewer than half of four-year college students graduate within six years." But while CUNY could "significantly improve graduation rates with smaller classes, more advising, coordinated support services and financial assistance that enables students to attend school full time . . . the state has not provided CUNY with the resources."[11] A decades-long campaign of disinvestment by New York governors and City mayors has shifted costs onto students and campus workers. Our City University is once again undergoing massive economic restructuring to benefit real estate firms and hedge funds, many of whom employ CUNY Board of Trustees (BoT) members.

As administrators welcome the surveillance, intimidation, and arrest of students and workers who dissent, our campuses become militarized. Still, we gather in living rooms, in union halls, and in the streets because we have no other choice. Despite these grim circumstances, we have witnessed major explosions of education struggles around the world—in Brazil, Quebec, Chile, Puerto Rico, Colombia, South Africa, Spain, England, France, Algeria, and beyond.

From within the besieged university, it can be tempting to limit our targets to the most immediately discernible opponents of free, quality higher education. Nevertheless, struggles at CUNY have continued to address US imperialism, Zionism, neocolonialism in Puerto Rico, abortion access, Black liberation, and anticapitalism. And though CUNY is still undergoing a counterinsurgency campaign, it is also true that it remains a factory for dissent, a locomotive of history, and a wave of insurgent possibility whose effects can reach shores worldwide.

For organizers in CUNY, some significant developments have arisen from our studies, actions, and reflections: to conceive of education itself as a form of direct action, to rethink how we approach the call to strike, and to fuse student/worker campaigns with wider community efforts at social change. The raucous histories of a free CUNY, the 1969 Harlem University strike, and Open Admissions inspire renewed demands for free tuition, desegregated admission, and the liberation of marginalized communities. A CUNY movement that embraces the legacies of Black, Puerto Rican, and feminist studies and actions can also incite other universities toward liberation.

9/11, December 19 and 20, and the Limits of Free Speech on Campus

Following the September 11, 2001 attack on the World Trade Center, CUNY entered a crosshairs of controversy when City College professor Carol Smith and colleagues coordinated an event featuring faculty from across the university to address the historic tragedy as a teachable moment. In his opening remarks, Frank Kirkland shared a message for US institutions: "As the nation's security concerns rise to inordinate levels of paranoia, this is a time for institutions to be more nurturing than the military or police,

11 Meena Alexander, Michelle Fine, and Nicholas Freudenberg, "To Reduce Inequality, Reinvest in CUNY," *Crain's New York Business*, February 25, 2016, www.crainsnewyork.com/article/20160226/OPINION/160229916/to-reduce-inequality-reinvest-in-cuny/.

for institutional arrangements to be more respectful of human life."[12] The next day, the *New York Post* headline ran: "CCNY BASHES AMERICA—STUDENTS, PROFS BLAME ATTACKS ON U.S."[13] The following month, the CUNY Board of Trustees passed a resolution condemning the teach-in—although none of them had been present—declaring that it was "seditious" and "un-American."[14] After three decades of counseling work in the SEEK Program and efforts to promote internationalism on campus through film screenings and other cultural events, Carol Smith was pressured into early retirement by the City College administration.[15]

Following September 11, City College, CUNY, and the Professional Staff Congress (CUNY's faculty and staff union) suffered a reversal of the momentum they had gathered during the previous years of escalating counter-globalization efforts. The US government passed the PATRIOT Act, established the Department of Homeland Security, and initiated wars in Afghanistan in 2002 and Iraq in 2003. Secretary of State and City College alumnus Colin Powell justified the war based on falsehoods about "weapons of mass destruction." In 2002, the PSC began working without a contract, and in 2003 CUNY administrators increased their own salaries.[16]

The year 2001, however, was also emblematized in the Argentinian slogan *"que se vayan todos, que no quede ni uno solo"* [all of them must go, not a single one should remain], after an economic crisis resulted in mass protests and workplace takeovers that began on December 19 and 20.[17] Marina Sitrin reminds us, "People there organized thousands of horizontal neighborhood assemblies (the language of *horizontalidad* was first used at this moment in history in Argentina). . . . Workers took back—recuperated—their workplaces, running them collectively, without hierarchy or bosses."[18]

Then, in 2003, a struggle to oust the US military from the Puerto Rican island of Vieques animated solidarity efforts at City College.[19] This campaign was remarkably successful, and organizing momentum shifted accordingly. As PSC union members began to agitate against the wars in Afghanistan and Iraq, CUNY students held counter-recruitment protests against military personnel who set up at campus career fairs, cafeterias, and entrances to colleges. Students welcomed members of Iraq Veterans Against the War [since renamed About Face] to speak on campus, hosted teach-ins that linked the occupations of Afghanistan and Iraq with Israel's settler-colonial control of Palestine and mobilized for countless antiwar demonstrations.

---

12 "A chance to stop and think," *Clarion*, October 2001, 4, https://archive.psc-cuny.org/PDF/OctClarion.pdf/.

13 Carl Campanile, "CCNY Bashes America—Students, Profs Blame Attacks on U.S.," *New York Post*, October 3, 2001, https://nypost.com/2001/10/03/ccny-bashes-america-students-profs-blame-attacks-on-u-s/.

14 Peter Hogness, "City College teach-in at center of storm," *Clarion*, December 2001, 5, https://archive.psc-cuny.org/PDF/Clarion_Dec_03.pdf/.

15 Carol Smith, interview with the author, October 12, 2021. In 2005, to provide historical context for her being forced out of City College, Smith created an online archive of 1930s and '40s free speech struggles and repression at City College. See *Struggle for Free Speech at CCNY, 1931–1942*, https://virtual-ny.ashp.cuny.edu/gutter/panels/panel1.html/.

16 Peter Hogness, "Union says no to austerity contract," *Clarion*, September 2004, 6, https://archive.psc-cuny.org/PDF/Clarion%20Sept%2004.pdf/.

17 Colectivo Situaciones, *19 & 20: Notes for a New Insurrection* (Brooklyn, Common Notions), 2021.

18 Marina Sitrin, "The Anarchist Spirit," *Dissent Magazine* (Fall 2015), https://www.dissentmagazine.org/article/anarchist-spirit-horizontalism/.

19 Sherrie Baver, interview with the author, September 21, 2019.

By the late 2000s, the CUNY movement began coalescing around anticapitalism, anti-imperialism, antiracism, and aiding other university uprisings in New York City. The 2008 CUNY Social Forum and the *CUNYTime* zine reflected a growing interest in reviving the university's radical histories.[20] During the December 2008 New School occupation and the February 2009 New York University occupation, I experienced firsthand how mass building takeovers with broad outside support could pressure administrations and withstand police repression. I also saw how the April 2009 New School occupation's decision for a small team to coordinate a takeover in secret, with no supportive crowd outside, could be crushed and maligned by campus management. These occupations, like those that swept California in 2009 and 2010, were inspired by the Invisible Committee's *The Coming Insurrection*—with its injunction to "Occupy Everything, Demand Nothing"—as well as by the previous generation's education upheavals.[21] But even as CUNY struggles against racial segregation and privatization were invoked during this period, the historical lessons of 1969, 1975–76, 1989–91, and 1995—in which campus and community upheavals proceeded on the basis of concrete demands—were ignored.

Occupy and the Free University[22]

Occupy Wall Street (OWS) taught us decades' worth of lessons in a matter of months. Many of us in the CUNY community were central to pre-organizing and creating Occupy Wall Street by maintaining a multitude of working groups during the upsurge in citywide revolt. We facilitated thousands-strong public conversations and direct action trainings, built the People's Library, and connected a global art and design community through Occuprint. At the CUNY Graduate Center and then around CUNY, we held regular general assemblies. We claimed campus spaces that had not been used for radical conspiring, and we encouraged deeper collaboration between students, campus workers, and our surrounding communities.

We launched free public education initiatives like Occupy CUNY and the People's University while plotting how to alter our institutions.[23] Students and faculty also ferried direct democracy back into our classrooms. For example, in Spring 2012, several graduate student adjuncts team-taught a course called "Protest and Revolution: Occupy

20 *CUNYTime*, https://cunytime.wordpress.com/.

21 The Invisible Committee, *The Coming Insurrection* (Los Angeles: Semiotext(e), 2007) and "After the Fall: Communiqués from Occupied California," Autumn 2009–February 2010, http://libcom.org/library/after-fall-communiques-occupied-california/. See also Eli Meyerhoff, *Beyond Education: Radical Studying for Another World* (Minneapolis: University of Minnesota Press, 2019), 34; Spencer Beswick, "Living Communism: Theory & Practice of Autonomy & Attack," *Perspectives on Anarchist Theory*, July 29, 2022, https://anarchiststudies.org/living-communism-spencer-beswick/.

22 For earlier versions of this section, see Conor Tomás Reed, "Solid Ground at Occupy Wall Street," *The Indypendent*, September 26, 2011, https://indypendent.org/2011/09/solid-ground-at-occupy-wall-street/; Conor Tomás Reed, "Step One. Occupy Universities. Step Two. Transform Them," *Tidal Magazine* (December 2011), https://www.e-flux.com/legacy/2013/05/TIDAL_occupytheory.pdf?b8c429/; Reed, "On the City as University: Occupy and the Future of Public Education," *Tidal Magazine* (2012)/*The Indypendent*, May 25, 2012, https://indypendent.org/2012/05/the-city-as-university-occupy-and-the-future-of-public-education/.

23 See also David I. Backer, Matthew Bissen, Christopher "Winter" Casuccio, Jacques Laroche, Zane D.R. Mackin, Joe North, Aleksandra Perisic, Chelsea Szendi Schieder, and Jason Wozniak, "What is Horizontal Pedagogy? A Discussion on Dandelions," in *Out of the Ruins: The Emergence of Radical Informal Learning Spaces*, ed. Robert H. Haworth and John M. Elmore (Oakland: PM Press, 2017), 195–222.

Your Education" at Brooklyn College, in which all participants shaped how each class was used. Across CUNY, students and workers began to emphasize practices of anticolonial direct action, horizontal pedagogies, opposition to neoliberalism and debt, and mutual care. Projects that emerged from the lessons of this period include the Bronx Social Center, Crown Heights Tenant Union, Debt Collective, Decolonize This Place, Direct Action Front for Palestine, Free University of NYC, Making Worlds, Occupy Sandy, Red Bloom, and Strike Debt.

After the nationwide eviction of Occupy encampments at the end of 2011, the movement's future was by no means foreseeable. When the call came for a May Day 2012 "General Strike," a schism arose in activist circles about whether to advance the slogan when we knew that it was a tactical impossibility. Students and workers in the CUNY movement decided to embrace the language of striking without setting up picket lines at our schools. In early 2012, several CUNY Graduate Center students published "Five Theses on the Student Strike" in an Occupy Wall Street journal *Tidal*—a kind of response to the call of Harlem University's 1969 Five Demands.[24] This short piece established useful terms for the kind of tactics we sought to proliferate. During the weeks leading up to May 1, we invoked a vision of educational direct action rather than debating whether the day should be called a strike or not.

By the time May Day arrived, we amassed a coalition of students and workers from almost a dozen schools to produce the Free University of NYC: a "collective educational experiment" that assembled 2,000 participants. We drew inspiration from the original 1965–68 Free University of NYC and 1969 Harlem University, and we described our project as an experiment in radical education building on the tradition of movement-based freedom schools. The effort arose from our recognition that the current system was unequal and unsustainable, and that vast sources of knowledge across our communities remained hidden and undervalued. We partook in Zuccotti Park's legacy through the unpermitted reclamation of public space, radical discussion, and free food. Our invitation for anyone to sign up to offer a class, workshop, or skill-share was met with a deluge of submissions. Tuition, ID cards, costly books, security checkpoints, and other obstacles to higher education were erased.

During the five hours we transformed Madison Square Park, educators conducted more than forty workshops, classes, and collective experiences near the historic site of the Free Academy, CUNY's predecessor. More than a dozen faculty members moved their classes into the park in solidarity with the call to strike. Attendees learned about occupying foreclosed housing, student organizing and debate skills, Indigenous environmentalism, open-access academic publishing, and anticapitalist approaches to math and science. Collective poetry readings were held alongside figure drawing classes. Scholars like Drucilla Cornell, David Harvey, Neil Smith, Ruth Wilson Gilmore, and Wayne Koestenbaum (many of them CUNY-affiliated) joined large crowds that gathered and mixed freely.

Our ambition, however, was not to create a utopian enclave, but to catalyze movement activity. At 3:00 p.m., the whole Free U campus marched to the main Union Square rally location before swarming the financial district, book shields and banners in hand. To focus on education as direct action meant transforming public spaces into

---

24 Autonomous Students at the CUNY Graduate Center, "Five Theses on the Student Strike," *Tidal* 2 (March 2012), http://tiny.cc/Tidal2/.

mobile classrooms. Our entire city became the People's University. "The right to the city is far more than the individual liberty to access urban resources," said David Harvey. "It is a right to change ourselves by changing the city."[25]

We boomeranged these efforts back onto our campuses while decentering the university as the sole site where knowledge is made and trafficked.[26] The December 2012 and May–July 2013 Cooper Union occupations to keep the college tuition-free vibrantly evoked visions for why and how CUNY could become free again.[27] More broadly, each academic conference became a space to establish networks and debate militant strategies. Each dissertation became an opportunity for multi-author, multimodal scholarship to be evaluated by a committee of peers. We urged faculty to heed UC-Davis professor Nathan Brown's challenge: "If faculty want to confront the totalitarian conduct of administrations, we will . . . have to organize and participate in occupations and blockades." CUNY workers began meeting this challenge by engaging in direct actions around union contracts. We also learned that we needed to cede intellectual space for community members—the exiles of our current university system—to raise their own critical voices as we confronted the defensive theoretical positions through which flight, fugitivity, marronage, pessimism, and refusal came to hold sway.

Militarism and Surveillance at CUNY[28]

After Occupy, the post-9/11 relationship between CUNY and US imperialism heightened to the point that the university became a central target for military recruitment, counterinsurgency, surveillance, and weapons research. As the United States became mired in its occupations of Iraq and Afghanistan, Arab and Muslim students were increasingly surveilled and military recruiters' presence intensified at CUNY colleges.[29] In November 2011, days after the eviction of Occupy Wall Street from Zuccotti Park, the CUNY administration imposed five years of annual tuition increases. The Board of Trustees assaulted protestors at Baruch College—resulting in dozens of injuries and fifteen arrests (including myself, a Baruch faculty member at the time)—and evacuated an entire campus building a week later as they voted to raise tuition.[30]

In 2013 and 2014, students, workers, and communities organized against the CUNY administration and the US military, for thier plans to use the university as a

25 David Harvey, "The Right to the City," *New Left Review* 53 (September–October 2008), https://newleftreview.org/issues/ii53/articles/david-harvey-the-right-to-the-city/.

26 Conor Tomás Reed, ed., "Occupy CUNY," CUNY Digital History Archive, https://cdha.cuny.edu/collections/show/222/.

27 Free Cooper Union, https://cusos.org/.

28 For an earlier version of this section, see Zoltán Glück, Manissa McCleave Maharawal, Isabelle Nastasia, and Conor Tomás Reed, "Organizing Against Empire: Struggles Over the Militarization of CUNY," *Berkeley Journal of Sociology* 58 (2014): 51–58.

29 John Tarleton, "NYPD Spy Scandal Hits CUNY: Muslim Students Target of Profiling," *Clarion*, November 2011, http://www.psc-cuny.org/clarion/november-2011/nypd-spy-scandal-hits-cuny-muslim-students-target-profiling/.

30 Anthony Alessandrini, "Our University: On Police Violence at CUNY," *Jadaliyya*, November 27, 2011, https://www.jadaliyya.com/Details/24707/Our-University-On-Police-Violence-at-CUNY/; Richard Pérez-Peña, "Amid Protests by Students and Others, CUNY Trustees Vote to Raise Tuition," *New York Times*, November 28, 2011, https://www.nytimes.com/2011/11/29/nyregion/cuny-board-approves-tuition-increases.html/.

testing ground for militarizing public higher education. The appointment of David Petraeus (former head of the Central Intelligence Agency, Iraq War general, and co-author of the *US Army/Marine Corps Counter-Insurgency Field Manual*) to teach at CUNY's Macaulay Honors College, the return of the Reserve Officers Training Corps (ROTC) to undergraduate campuses, and the intensification of campus policing and surveillance were the most visible signs of this trend. As journalist Peter Rugh put it, "America's most diverse university was turned into a war zone."[31]

These developments followed steps outlined by the neoconservative think tank American Enterprise Institute (AEI) in their 2011 report, "Underserved: A Case Study of ROTC in New York City."[32] The report called for a return of ROTC to large urban public universities like CUNY to diversify the military's officer class. It also recommended the appointment of "warrior scholars," naming David Petraeus as an ideal candidate to capture the hearts and minds of potential young recruits and improve the military's public image. CUNY's diverse population might offer the military strategic advantages, AEI argued, as it recruits educated immigrant students from countries where the United States undertakes military operations. Forget, if you will, that students from countries where the US maintains its 1,000-plus foreign military bases may not be predisposed to welcome cheerleaders of empire on their college campuses.

Nationwide, ROTC programs exist at 489 colleges and universities, with further access to 2,469 more colleges, and serve as a college-to-military pipeline for procuring US military officers. In the process, ROTC alters campus life by staging uniformed drill formations. Meanwhile, ROTC professors remain unaccountable to departmental governance procedures. Recruiters often target low-income and working-class US citizens aged 17 to 27, who must serve in the military for up to ten years upon graduation (or pay the "scholarship" money back).[33] Referring to campuses as "hunting grounds," ROTC uses predatory methods to pressure students into military service. At CUNY, ROTC seduced some with free tuition and "job opportunities." However, it also outraged activists, veterans, immigrant communities, and survivors of US imperialism.

Over forty years ago, the CUNY student movement forced the ROTC off campuses through sit-ins, strikes, and arson. In 2012, ROTC suddenly returned. That year, the CUNY administration welcomed the ROTC program to York College, and then in 2013 to City College and Medgar Evers College, where officers were hounded and shamed by students, faculty, staff, alumni, and community activists, who eventually barred them from Medgar Evers and the College of Staten Island (which had been another potential ROTC site). A September 2013 town hall at the College of Staten Island gathered people from across CUNY to hear antiwar veterans and audience

31 Peter Rugh, "The CUNY Wars: How David Petraeus Turned America's Most Diverse University into a War Zone," *Alternet*, December 10, 2013, http://www.alternet.org/education/cuny-wars-how-david-petraeus-turned-americas-most-diverse-university-war-zone/.

32 Cheryl Miller, "Underserved: a case study of ROTC in New York City," *American Enterprise Institute*, May 4, 2011, http://www.aei.org/publication/underserved-a-case-study-of-rotc-in-new-york-city/.

33 As Ann Jones reports, "Army, Air Force, Navy, and Marine JROTC units now flourish in 3,402 high schools nationwide—65% of them in the South—with a total enrollment of 557,129 kids." See Ann Jones, "America's Child Soldiers: JROTC and the Militarizing of America," *TomDispatch*, December 15, 2013, http://www.tomdispatch.com/post/175784/tomgram%3A_ann_jones,_suffer_the_children/. See also Mike Baker, Nicholas Bogel-Burroughs, and Ilana Marcus, "Thousands of Teens Are Being Pushed into Military's Junior R.O.T.C.," *New York Times*, December 11, 2022, https://www.nytimes.com/2022/12/11/us/jrotc-schools-mandatory-automatic-enrollment.html/.

members debate pro-ROTC speakers. This event led to successful resistance against the program and served as a model for a mid-February 2014 town hall at Medgar Evers College. This town hall was timed strategically to occur before a vote by the college's highest governing body, which subsequently decided to remove ROTC from its majority-Black campus. The removal of ROTC from Medgar Evers College marked a huge success for the anti-militarization movement. These campaigns and their town-hall-style political education events provide a template for ousting ROTC at City College and York College.

As former Chancellor Matthew Goldstein brokered a deal to bring Petraeus to CUNY, student activists staged protests to challenge his appointment. In April 2013, Petraeus was appointed as an adjunct at Macaulay Honors College. Initial news articles highlighted blatant wage discrepancies: as a visiting adjunct professor, Petraeus was to be paid $200,000 per year, while adjuncts at the time normally made less than $3,000 per course. In response to popular outrage, Petraeus' salary was eventually reduced to $1, though he still received an undisclosed amount from a private donor.

The administration hoped this pay reduction would quiet the criticism; it did not. By Fall 2013, an Ad-hoc Committee Against the Militarization of CUNY emerged to contest his appointment with a semester-long campaign of direct actions including protests in front of his class each week. Students also followed Petraeus to and from his lectures in a well-orchestrated "bird-dog" tactic. These actions received international attention when Revolutionary Student Coordinating Committee (RSCC) activists disseminated footage of a crowd of students heckling Petraeus for several city blocks calling him a war criminal.[34] Alongside these tactics, the Free University-NYC held "counter-classes" near Macaulay and Baruch Colleges, offering anti-imperialist alternatives to Petraeus' pro-empire spiel.

In response, the CUNY administration condemned the protesters, citing the need to defend Petraeus' "academic freedom." On September 17, 2013, the Monday protests led to the arrest of six students.[35] The brutality of these arrests (video of the incident shows a RSCC member being punched several times in the ribs while being handcuffed) prompted a solidarity letter signed by more than five hundred students and faculty calling for Petraeus' resignation. Despite international media attention, the CUNY administration met both the letter and the police brutality that prompted it with silence.

During this time, activists also took aim at the content of Petraeus' class. The imperialist message was already clear in its title, "The Coming (North) American Decade(s)," and its syllabus included fracking industry-sponsored articles funded and written by oil companies. The course description itself echoed Petraeus' job description at the private equity firm Kohlberg, Kravis, and Roberts, where he works as a consultant. Protesters highlighted these connections, denounced the blatant commercial interests in his curriculum, and challenged the administration's cynical use of "academic freedom" as a protective screen. In addition, City College saw the appearance of weapons

---

34 See Revolutionary Student Coordinating Committee, "CUNY students and RSCC confront David Petraeus," YouTube, September 9, 2013, https://www.youtube.com/watch?v=3HHab-ZCnJw/.

35 These students were charged with multiple offenses, including disorderly conduct, incitement to riot, resisting arrest, and the obstruction of governmental administration.

research and military studies as part of its own curriculum.[36] Despite widespread anger and ongoing demonstrations, Macaulay Honors College announced in April 2014 that Petraeus would remain another academic year to teach the same course.

In the Professional Staff Congress (PSC-CUNY), a newly formed committee against militarization developed to coordinate town halls and governance voting strategies to oust ROTC. The committee also submitted a FOIL request on exchanges between the CUNY administration, the US military, and the American Enterprise Institute to determine how the military funded and influenced the university. The committee's resolution to oppose ROTC at CUNY was passed in May 2014 by the union's executive council and delegate assembly. This set the stage for university-wide faculty and staff pressure against the US military's presence at CUNY and could in turn have further politicized contract negotiations. But this was not the course pursued by the central union leadership.

When actions against Petraeus and ROTC picked up momentum in Fall 2013, the administration responded with a series of repressive blows and surveillance efforts. On October 20, 2013, the Guillermo Morales/Assata Shakur Center was seized by campus police at City College.[37] This educational organizing space—won through a 1989 student strike against tuition increases and serving as a hub for twenty-plus clubs and community organizations—was crucial for students and community members planning the Petraeus protests. Overnight, police dismantled the center, confiscated personal property, and painted over its iconic stenciled door of a pencil-holding fist. In response, campus and community members launched an ongoing campaign to retrieve their belongings and reclaim the space. But while these actions received national media attention and solidarity statements from a variety of social movement organizations, they were ultimately unsuccessful. 2013 became a benchmark for militarization at City College. In May, it renamed its division of Social Sciences "The Colin L. Powell School of Civic and Global Leadership."

With the loss of the Morales/Shakur Center still fresh, the City College community learned in October 2014 that the administration would be closing the Child Development Center for two years while firing all of its workers, shifting children to other centers, and redirecting monies from a $1.6 million grant that had sought to keep it open.[38] The Center was established following the 1969 strike, when student-mothers extended demands to transform the college by taking over a faculty dining room and creating a free childcare cooperative. Several decades later, the Center's walls were adorned with "portraits of civil rights leader Rosa Parks and Puerto Rican independence leader Pedro Albizu Campos, along with leaders from the American Indian movement [which] intended to foster a sense of identification for minority children

36 Glenn Petersen, "Viewpoint: ROTC Revival at CUNY Requires Broad-Based Discussion," *Clarion*, September 2013, http://www.psc-cuny.org/clarion/september-2013/viewpoint-rotc-revival-cuny-requires-broad-based-discussion/.

37 Shawn Carrie, Isabelle Nastasia, and StudentNation, "CUNY Dismantles Community Center, Students Fight Back," *The Nation*, October 25, 2013, http://www.thenation.com/blog/176832/cuny-dismantles-community-center-students-fight-back/.

38 CCNY Parents, "Petition: Please act immediately to look into alternative spaces to house the Childcare Center next year while the current space is being renovated and give us in writing your commitment to keep the Center open permanently," Change.org, https://chng.it/h7dnVz6xFz. See also The Center for the Humanities, "Stories of Struggle: Histories of Childcare Activism at CUNY," seminar, The Center for the Humanities, CUNY Graduate Center, New York, March 4, 2015, https://www.centerforthehumanities.org/programming/stories-of-struggle-histories-of-childcare-activism-at-cuny/.

with figures of Black, Latino, and Indigenous resistance," explains Sujatha Fernandes, a former CUNY educator and parent of a child who attended the Center. A vibrant campaign to save the Center assembled student-parents, children, teachers, and community members to hold rallies, meet with local politicians, and negotiate with evasive administrators. On May 14, 2015, a new Harlem University was born in the form of a "Temporary Childcare Center" established on the City College campus lawn, with "a library center, a family room, a creative art room, and several boards with paintings and drawings by the students." Rows of police surrounded the nearby administration building with metal barricades.[39] City College officials closed the Center on June 30, 2015.

The seizure of radical archives and childcare spaces was not limited to City College. Much less publicity was generated for a January 2012 incident involving CUNY Political Science professor Joseph Wilson, a scholar of 20th-century US Black histories. Amidst a dispute involving allegations of financial misappropriation, eight security guards barged into Wilson's Center for Worker Education office and confiscated his files. Wilson recounts that he and several staff members "were told not to move, that we couldn't make any phone calls or leave the office or speak to anyone." More than thirty years of research on the Brotherhood of Sleeping Car Porters, a death threat against Harlem organizer A. Philip Randolph, a previously undiscovered speech by Martin Luther King, Jr., and correspondences with musician Ray Charles and poet Allen Ginsberg, among other treasures, were seized. James Klein, Wilson's attorney, added, "while indiscriminately discarding and separating the materials and moving them to and from multiple locations without any inventory or chain of custody, CUNY allowed the entire archive to be systematically destroyed, lost, or trashed."[40] After an internal probe involving the Attorney General's office, CUNY fired Wilson in 2016. In 2017, he filed a lawsuit to address professional defamation, Fourth Amendment violations of search and seizure, and property loss of these archives, valued at $12–14 million.[41]

The CUNY student movement has also faced internal challenges around organizing styles and political disagreements. Factionalism, vanguardism, and machismo-ridden styles of militancy have disrupted attempts at coalitional work. This is perhaps captured most poignantly by the fate of the Revolutionary Student Coordinating Committee (RSCC), a Maoist students-of-colors group on several CUNY campuses, which conducted a series of powerful actions in early Fall 2013, including one that yielded the video of members following David Petraeus. In retaliation, CUNY security and the NYPD beat several CUNY activists at protests against Petraeus' hiring. In late October 2013, two RSCC activists were suspended from City College. Before the university's own disciplinary procedures had run their course, CUNY security recommended that these activists be arrested by the NYPD. The New York City District Attorney's office ordered them to turn themselves in to spend a night in jail for attempting to incite a

---

39 Sujatha Fernandes, "Building Child-Centered Social Movements," *Contexts* 15, no. 1 (2016): 58–59.

40 Ginger Adams Otis, "NYC Professor of Black History Says CUNY Illegally Seized $12M Worth of Research Materials—Then Lost Most of It," *Daily News*, February 26, 2019, https://www.nydailynews.com/new-york/ny-metro-black-history-professor-sues-cuny-over-lost-research-20190225-story.html/.

41 Paula Mejía, "Fired Brooklyn College Professor Says CUNY Wrongly Seized Decades of His Research," *Gothamist*, February 27, 2019, https://gothamist.com/news/fired-brooklyn-college-professor-says-cuny-wrongly-seized-decades-of-his-research/.

riot on campus.[42] While they garnered considerable public sympathy for their actions, RSCC went on to alienate their allies, the broader public, and some of their own members through sexism, self-aggrandizing sermons, zealous public denunciations of their would-be allies, and in-fighting. By the end of the semester, their flame was extinguished—but not before causing notable damage along the way.

#BlackLivesMatter and Black Women's Studies on the Streets[43]

> *Tell me something*
> *what you think would happen if*
> *everytime they kill a black boy*
> *then we kill a cop*
> *everytime they kill a black man*
> *then we kill a cop*
> *you think the accident rate would lower subsequently?*

June Jordan's "Poem about Police Violence" was written after sixteen policemen swarmed, beat, and choked Black community leader Arthur Miller to death in Crown Heights on June 14, 1978.[44] This same lynching method, the "chokehold," would later be used to kill Anthony Baez in 1994 and Eric Garner in 2014.[45]

Jordan's poem highlighted how the "diction of the powerful" construes police brutality as "justifiable accidents," while community defense efforts are framed as "resisting arrest" and "incitement to riot." Jordan's question flows from the long lineage of the Black Arts Movement and Black Women's Studies at CUNY, where poetry and performance test ideas that can be enacted, and where conflicts are shared across spoken words. Jordan called for retribution against police violence, revealed the dignity in rioting, and illuminated new directions for Black lives not just to matter, but to articulate the furthest horizons of liberation.

In December of 2014 and into the new year, demonstrators took to the streets in protest of the NYPD's longstanding racial violence. Peter Liang's February 11 grand jury indictment for the murder of Akai Gurley created a rare opportunity to argue in favor of community control, defend rioting, advance abolitionist alternatives to polic-

---

42 Anna Merlan, "City College Lifts Suspensions Against Two Student Protesters, But Criminal Charges Still Stand," *The Village Voice*, November 25, 2013, http://www.villagevoice.com/news/city-college-lifts-suspensions-against-two-student-protesters-but-criminal-charges-still-stand-6681234/.

43 For an earlier version of this section, see Conor Tomás Reed, "Black Arts Boomerang," *The New Inquiry*, February 18, 2015, https://thenewinquiry.com/black-arts-boomerang/.

44 June Jordan, "Poem about Police Violence," in *Directed by Desire: The Collected Poems of June Jordan* (Port Townsend: Copper Canyon Press, 2007), 272. A year later, at a march in Brooklyn against the state murder of Puerto Rican man Luis Baez, Jordan narrowly evaded being attacked by police. See Erica R. Edwards, *The Other Side of Terror: Black Women and the Culture of US Empire* (New York: New York University Press, 2021), 236–241.

45 Errol Louis, "Police Brutality: A Backstory," *NY1*, June 5, 2020, https://www.ny1.com/nyc/all-boroughs/news/2020/06/05/police-brutality--a-backstory-new-york-city/.

ing, and recognize queer Black women's creation of the #BlackLivesMatter meme.[46] Films and television shows centering Black lives and movements—*Atlanta*, *Concerning Violence*, *Dear White People*, *Fruitvale Station*, *I Am Not Your Negro*, *Moonlight*, *Random Acts of Flyness*, *Selma*, *Sorry to Bother You*, *The Throwaways*—started to proliferate. Claudia Rankine's 2014 poetry collection *Citizen: An American Lyric* offered rhythmic meditations on Black people ensnared by police stop and frisks, coworkers, sports, cultures, each other, themselves: "you are not the guy and still you fit the description because there is only one guy who is always the guy fitting the description."[47]

In December 2014, the streets of New York swelled with direct action poetics and the resounding words of Black Arts cultural critic Larry Neal from 1970: "A realistic movement among the black arts community should be about the *extension* of the *remembered* and a *resurrection* of the *unremembered*."[48] During the December 2014 Millions March NYC, Eric Garner's stare was held aloft in a public art performance by a surging body of thousands, as Michael Brown's walk down the middle of the street was reenacted by entire families. "Hands up, don't shoot" became "Fists up, fight back." Marches stretched up to Harlem proclaiming, "No struggle, no progress" and "By any means necessary" on Frederick Douglass and Malcolm X Boulevards. Final words became incantations of endurance: *I can't breathe. I can't breathe. I can't breathe.*

Lyrical eulogies were fashioned on the spot: "Turn up, don't turn down: we do this for Mike Brown." "Push back, now push harder: we do this for Eric Garner. "Hands up to the sky: we do this for Akai." "This is why we're here: justice for Tamir." Remixes, layered one after another, wove improvisations and pop references: "No cop zone, no cop zone! They know better, they know better!" (after Rae Sremmurd's "No Flex Zone") . . . "Turn down for what?" (DJ Snake and Lil Jon) . . . "All I wanna say is they don't really care about us!" (Michael Jackson). Protestors ridiculed police budgets and uniforms: "Why you dressed in riot gear? I don't see no riot here." Double Dutch swarms cleverly shut down intersections: "They think it's a game. They think it's a joke." New strategies were tested on the tongues of those about to enact them: "Community control, it's our demand. Can we do it? Yes we can!"

Interventionist theater played out on bridges, highways, squares, parks, stations, and markets, as helicopters crisscrossed the sky and cop cars trailed behind. Brooklyn Bridge, Manhattan Bridge, Triborough Bridge, Verrazano Bridge, FDR Drive, West Side Highway, Foley Square, Times Square, Union Square, Washington Square, Bryant Park, Columbus Circle, Grand Central Station, Macy's Parade, Rockefeller Tree Lighting, Saks Fifth Avenue—all clogged with the thick boil of intergenerational blood. #BlackBrunch's 4.5-minute Sunday interruptions in posh restaurants lay the realities of bullet-riddled Black lives on the table. Like the direct action lessons from CUNY, these wildcat tactics inherited from anticolonial liberation movements prac-

46 See Alicia Garza, "A Herstory of the #BlackLivesMatter Movement," *Feminist Wire*, October 7, 2014, https://thefeministwire.com/2014/10/blacklivesmatter-2/; Michael Gould-Wartofsky, "When Rioting is Rational," *Jacobin Magazine*, January 2, 2015, https://www.jacobinmag.com/2015/01/when-rioting-is-rational-ferguson/; José Martín, "Policing is a Dirty Job, But Nobody's Gotta Do It: 6 Ideas for a Cop-Free World," *Rolling Stone*, December 16, 2014, https://www.rollingstone.com/politics/politics-news/policing-is-a-dirty-job-but-nobodys-gotta-do-it-6-ideas-for-a-cop-free-world-199465/; Vicky Osterweil, *In Defense of Looting: A Riotous History of Uncivil Action* (New York: Bold Type Books, 2020).

47 Claudia Rankine, *Citizen: An American Lyric* (Minneapolis: Graywolf Press, 2014) 106.

48 Larry Neal, "Ellison's Zoot Suit: Politics as Ritual," *Black World* (December 1970): 31–52. (Emphasis in original).

ticed the "war of the flea"—urban guerrilla methods of swarm-strike-fade-repeat to disrupt multiple places at once while avoiding "hard lock" occupations that can result in mass arrests.

In this moment, the slow work of propaganda (many ideas to few people) shifted to new fields of agitation (few ideas to many people).[49] These "few ideas" emerged from centuries-deep analyses and experiences suddenly condensed and made portable. Direct Action Front for Palestine's keffiyeh-trimmed banner, "When we breathe, we breathe together," revealed the long history of Black–Palestinian solidarity underscored by CUNY professor Robyn C. Spencer's *BlackonPalestine* Tumblr and the 2014 trip to Palestine taken by a delegation of Dream Defenders, #BlackLivesMatter, and Ferguson organizers.[50] Links were also being made between Black and Asian communities. These efforts included #AsiansforBlackLives and, at CUNY, the Coalition for the Revitalization of Asian American Studies at Hunter College (CRAASH) and the Coalition of Brooklyn College Radical Asians (COBRA), which resisted anti-Black, anti-Asian, and anti-Palestinian racism while championing Ethnic Studies. Can't Touch This NYC's 2014–2015 street action principles also articulated methods of solidarity that could oppose police repression and foster space for self-critiques.[51]

The movements of the 2014–2015 era condensed the struggles of the past. Attention to movement compositions and archiving from below decentered Eurocentric narratives in order to share lessons of the dispossessed. But while many alumni from the CUNY movements of the twentieth century created the conditions for a mass racial justice movement to bloom, the city government, nonprofit industrial complex, and cultural elite responded by installing a moderate, tokenizing leadership.[52] But as the movement journalist Messiah Rhodes argues, "freedom may mean that the alienated, the mis-educated, the thugs, the orphans will be your equals."[53]

Palestine, Free Speech, and Labor[54]

During the post-9/11 period, CUNY dramatically shifted in terms of solidarity with Palestine and opposition to the surveillance of Muslim students. Critiques of Israel's unchecked military aggression against Gaza heightened during its carpet-bombing campaigns in 2008, 2012, and 2014. While receiving $8.5 million a day in US military aid, Israel destroyed hospitals, schools, electricity, and water supplies in Gaza, killed

49 Duncan Hallas, "Agitation and Propaganda," *Socialist Worker Review* 68 (September 1984): 10, www. marxists.org/archive/hallas/works/1984/09/agitprop.htm/.

50 Kristian Davis Bailey, "Dream Defenders, Black Lives Matter & Ferguson Reps Take Historic Trip to Palestine," *Ebony Magazine*, January 9, 2015, https://www.ebony.com/news/dream-defenders-black-lives-matter-ferguson-reps-take-historic-trip-to-palestine/#ixzz3ORwS2gdM/.

51 Can't Touch This: NYC Anti-Repression Committee, "5 Principles for the Anti-Police Brutality Movement," n.d., https://canttouchthisnyc.wordpress.com/5-principles-for-the-anti-police-brutality-movement/.

52 Jacob Siegel, "Eric Garner Protesters Have a Direct Line to City Hall," *Daily Beast*, January 11, 2014, https://www.thedailybeast.com/eric-garner-protesters-have-a-direct-line-to-city-hall/.

53 Messiah Rhodes, "The Lumpen Blacks," {*Young*}*ist*, December 4, 2014, https://youngist.github.io/clean-blog/the-lumpen-blacks#.YmWStPvMLrc/.

54 For an earlier version of this section, see Conor Tomás Reed, "Intersecting Picket Lines: Free Speech, Palestine, and the CUNY Contract," *Viewpoint Magazine*, June 23, 2016, https://viewpointmag.com/2016/06/23/intersecting-picket-lines-free-speech-palestine-and-the-cuny-contract/.

3,900 Palestinians, and left many more wounded in these three campaigns.

The CUNY movement linked up with the international Boycott, Divestment, Sanctions (BDS) campaign to oppose Israeli apartheid.[55] Inspired by the boycotts passed by multiple academic associations and the divestments initiated throughout the University of California system, chapters of Students for Justice in Palestine (SJP) at CUNY organized teach-ins, speaking tours, and street theater performances during Israeli Apartheid Weeks. Eventually, we formed CUNY for Palestine to organize students and workers together. CUNY Graduate Center students called for academic solidarity with Palestinian students, workers, and their families living under Israeli occupation. After a two-year campaign, the Graduate Center's student government passed an academic boycott in April 2016.[56]

The realities of the occupation might have felt distant were it not for Zionist organizations, college administrators, and government officials' attempts at repression on CUNY campuses.[57] Instead of being silenced, however, Palestinians and their accomplices at CUNY began sharing stories more insistently about what people in Gaza and the West Bank endure under the US-backed Israeli military. The wars against Arabs and Muslims abroad and surveillance at home were connected. In 2011, journalists exposed NYPD surveillance of Muslim student groups at eight CUNY schools between 2003 to 2006.[58] A similar operation had also occurred from 2011 to 2015 at Brooklyn College. An informant named "Mel" embedded herself in Muslim friendship circles, in Students for Justice in Palestine (SJP), and in a "Unity Coalition," which organized SJP, the Black Student Union, Puerto Rican Alliance, Dominican Student Movement, and other left student groups.[59]

In Fall 2015, as the PSC mobilized for a strike authorization vote, Governor Andrew Cuomo and state legislators proposed a $500 million cut to CUNY's budget (harkening back to its 1976 emergency status). He also threatened a tuition hike of $1,500 or more over the next five years, this coming on the heels of a 30.4 percent hike spread across the five-year period that began in 2011. But while these actions received national media attention and solidarity statements from a variety of social movement organizations, they were ultimately unsuccessful. Based on a letter by the Zionist Organization of America citing a series of "anti-Semitic" events at CUNY (defined only with regard to Jewish students, not to Arab students who are also Semitic, while also ignoring recurring anti-Arab and Islamophobic incidents), the New York State Senate announced in March 2016 that it would "deny additional funding for CUNY senior schools until it is satisfied that the administration has developed a plan to guarantee the

55 In 2005, hundreds of Palestinian civil society organizations issued a global call for boycott, divestment, and sanctions (BDS) against Israel until it complied with international law and universal principles of human rights. See BDS Movement, https://bdsmovement.net/.

56 Academic Boycott of Israel at CUNY, https://cunyboycott.wordpress.com/.

57 PSC-CUNY, "Kristofer Petersen-Overton Gets His Job Back," October 2, 2015, www.psc-cuny.org/about-us/kristofer-petersen-overton-gets-his-job-back/; NYC Students for Justice in Palestine, "The Real Story: The New McCarthyism and Repression of Palestine Activism at CUNY," February 26, 2016, nycsjp.wordpress.com/2016/02/24/the-real-story-the-new-mccarthyism-and-repression-of-palestine-activism-at-cuny/.

58 John Tarleton, "NYPD Spy Scandal Hits CUNY."

59 Jeanne Theoharis, "'I Feel Like a Despised Insect': Coming of Age Under Surveillance in New York," *The Intercept*, February 18, 2016, https://theintercept.com/2016/02/18/coming-of-age-under-surveillance-in-new-york/; Katie Mitchell, dir., *Watched* (Portland: Collective Eye Films, 2017).

safety of students of all faiths."[60] A CUNY task force on anti-Semitism called professor Sarah Schulman and SJP student leaders into closed-door disciplinary meetings reminiscent of the 1940s Rapp-Coudert Committee, which presaged the rise of McCarthyism, underscoring that there exists a "Palestine exception" to the principles of free speech.[61] In the summer of 2016, Cuomo introduced a bill to attack people and institutions that advocate BDS,[62] Even though state funding was ultimately restored to CUNY, the irony, of course, was that this massive gash in the budget would have also hurt Jewish students, faculty, and staff.

On June 20, 2016, five days after the PSC reached a contract agreement with CUNY, the Board of Trustees convened a public hearing to propose a "Freedom of Expression and Expressive Conduct" policy.[63] This policy would impose a rule requiring students to receive advance permission from CUNY security to hold organizing meetings, public assemblies, or even to distribute flyers. By the CUNY lawyer's own admission, the policy was tailored to counter recent #BlackLivesMatter and Palestine solidarity actions. At the hearing, three dozen students, workers, and alumni railed against the BoT, demanding that the proposed policy be scrapped.

Even though the 2016 contract was brokered only after the PSC threatened to strike, it was by no means a radical agreement. The 10.41 percent salary increase (compounded for 2010–2017) didn't surpass inflation, and the three-year adjunct appointment system (instead of reappointments each semester) wouldn't apply to most adjuncts. Management was empowered to hire new star faculty with exorbitant salaries (call it the Paul Krugmanization of CUNY), thus wrenching wage disparities even wider.[64] The administration delayed negotiations so that the PSC vote to ratify the new contract and the BoT vote to curtail free speech would both occur when most of the CUNY community was dispersed for the summer. However, in the face of escalating political crises at CUNY—labor austerity, free speech, US militarism, and solidarity with Palestine—the union leadership struggled to mount a broad, multifaceted opposition to a policy that would inhibit the right to amass a picket line.

The government and administration have fused economic crises and ideological attacks into a new political economy at CUNY. The PSC repeatedly voices its defense of CUNY's mission to provide quality education to working-class people of all colors

60 NYC Students for Justice in Palestine, "The Real Story"; David Howard King, "New York City Interests Given Varied Priority in Three Albany Budget Plans," *Gotham Gazette*, March 16, 2016, www.gothamgazette.com/city/6226-new-york-city-interests-given-varied-priority-in-three-albany-budget-plans/.

61 Sarah Schulman, "Today I Testified Before the CUNY Task Force on Anti-Semitism," *Jadaliyya*, March 24, 2016, http://jadaliyya.com/Details/33117/Today-I-Testified-Before-the-CUNY-Task-Force-on-Anti-Semitism/; Center for Constitutional Rights, "Brooklyn College Students Cleared at Controversial Disciplinary Hearing," *Common Dreams*, May 31, 2016, www.commondreams.org/newswire/2016/05/31/brooklyn-college-students-cleared-controversial-disciplinary-hearing/; Palestine Legal, "The Palestine Exception to Free Speech: A Movement Under Attack in the US," https://palestinelegal.org/the-palestine-exception/.

62 *Democracy Now!*, "Debate: Is Cuomo's Crackdown on BDS Unconstitutional McCarthyism or a Stand Against Anti-Semitism?," June 9, 2016, www.democracynow.org/2016/6/9/debate_is_cuomos_crackdown_on_bds/.

63 Maxine Joselow, "CUNY Considers Free Speech Policy," *Inside Higher Ed*, June 20, 2016, www.insidehighered.com/news/2016/06/20/cuny-considers-free-speech-policy/; Ariel Kaminer, "Two New York City Colleges Draft Rules That Restrict Protests," *New York Times*, December 10, 2018, http://www.nytimes.com/2013/12/11/education/2-new-york-city-colleges-draft-rules-that-restrict-protests.html/.

64 James Hoff, "The Economics of Prestige," *Inside Higher Ed*, April 21, 2014, www.insidehighered.com/views/2014/04/21/essay-what-hiring-paul-krugman-says-about-values-public-higher-education/.

and backgrounds. However, it has maintained its limited contracts without taking a public stand against the administration's exploitation of adjunct faculty, anti-BDS bills, McCarthyistic hearings, student surveillance, and "Freedom of Expression and Expressive Conduct" policy. Even with a landslide 92 percent vote in favor of strike action in Spring 2016, it continued fighting with one arm tied behind its back.

This situation demands that we rethink the strategies that guide labor organizing on college campuses, especially CUNY. Since 9/11, the CUNY administration and New York government have entwined the languages of antiracism, law and order, and fiscal responsibility to enforce structural underfunding and repression. But if a defense of free speech and anti-imperialism is fused with the struggles of organized labor, a new opening for struggle can emerge. If CUNY's movements are to reverse this assault, we'll have to force the union to move past the economism of their contract campaigns and embrace struggles that speak to people's lives in their entirety.

Labor movements are always at risk of eliding concurrent struggles that affect their most marginalized workers and support bases. But these issues are a part of our picket line, and indeed have become a central means by which many of us organize as laborers, which then shifts the terrain of "university" struggles. A class recomposition is taking place to gather various kinds of workers—athletes, artists, dockworkers, educators, healthcare workers, journalists, retail workers, scientists, students, and beyond—under the "one big union" of BDS, police abolition, abortion access, and beyond to coordinate rank-and-file cross-industry actions that link apartheid and imperialism abroad with austerity, policing, and draconian attacks on reproductive justice at home. Only through intersecting picket lines can we address labor contract campaigns within larger struggles to transform CUNY and beyond. In the words of *Tidal Magazine*, an anticolonial movement journal created by militants who later formed Decolonize This Place:

> Boycott is a necessary yet limited tactic. Each 'win' is but a small part of a coordinated exertion and intensification of pressure. The value of Boycott lies as much in the economic damage it could do to the target as it does in the conversations, bonds, and spaces that are formed in the process of organizing. These are the foundations of any future liberation, beyond Boycott and beyond BDS itself.[65]

CUNY students and workers, like the US labor movement more broadly, are stuck between two forms of social composition: one that is bound by parochial bread-and-butter demands and one in which our actions can reverberate around the world as they transform our working and learning conditions. When we strike at the heart of the empire, we redirect the course toward liberatory unionism. Defending access to—and livelihoods within—the nation's largest public urban university means opposing a half-century business-class assault on our schools, workplaces, and communities. As was true fifty years ago, we are not alone in facing this neoliberal assault.

---

65 Some of *Tidal*'s back issues are available on New York University's Hemispheric Institute website, http://archive.hemisphericinstitute.org/hemi/en/occupy-tidal/.

Counter-Institutional Models in the University of Puerto Rico and CUNY

In 2010 and 2011, University of Puerto Rico (UPR) students coordinated two massive student strikes that were precursors to the Arab Spring that began in January 2011, the Chilean student uprisings in May 2011, the Occupy movement in Fall 2011, and the Quebec student strike in May 2012. Against neocolonial austerity policies and the privatization of public education, students were able to confront the administration and rally support around the island.[66] At CUNY, we followed and supported these UPR strikes, holding fundraisers and educational events with strike leaders who then came to study at CUNY.

Smaller UPR strikes also occurred between 2014 and 2016. UPR student militants emphasized mutual aid programs to build relationships while directly supporting each other's day-to-day needs. Beginning in 2013, *Comedores Sociales* [Community Kitchens] of Puerto Rico provided meals in exchange for resources, cooking labor, and organizing space. That June, the US government passed the Puerto Rico Oversight, Management, and Economic Stability Act (PROMESA), which imposed a fiscal control board to reclaim Puerto Rico's public "debt" and gut the UPR budget by $450 million (half its total, and almost identical to the amount that Cuomo threatened to cut from CUNY at the time). As Puerto Ricans protested this decree, an October 2016 gathering converted the crisis into a radical realignment of strategies. Many *"agri-ecologia"* groups, who had been running social kitchens and sustainable farms both in rural towns and in cities like Carolina, Cayey, Mayagüez, Ponce, San Juan, and Utuado, devised strategies that could outlast the PROMESA crisis. They discussed reterritorialization, community defense, and transforming land to sustain movement work.

In Spring 2017, UPR–Río Piedras students in San Juan went on strike. By April 5, all eleven UPR campuses and 58,000 students were on strike. All but one campus was occupied. The Social Kitchens fed students at various UPR campuses while veterans from the 2010–2011 UPR strike shared perspectives over food. Some created autonomous gardens, like UPR-Cayey's *huerto resiliencia* [resilience garden]. Through their general assemblies, action committees, and plenary meetings, the UPR students advanced demands that weren't limited to university issues. They called for an audit of the national debt, knowing that challenging the debt's legitimacy might save UPR, the healthcare system, and people's pensions from billions in austerity cuts.

One difficulty was that, unlike student struggles fifty years ago with campus administrators and the ROTC, the enemies on the PROMESA board were now far away. The urban Río Piedras campus was the most highlighted and vocal, and thus during the 2017 strike, their occupation got more attention than, for example, the agricultural campus at Utuado, where undergraduates maintained five acres of land—literally plowing fields with oxen and milking cows—while also coordinating their own occupation.

Once again, CUNY students closely followed and supported the strike, which now involved CUNY graduates who had gone back to UPR to mentor the new wave of strikers. In May, CUNY–UPR Solidarity hosted a video dialogue with strikers. In June, a delegation of CUNY scholar-organizers went to Puerto Rico to interview over a dozen strike participants in Cayey, San Juan, and Utuado. We shared strategies on resisting

---

66 Marisol LeBrón, *Policing Life and Death: Race, Violence, and Resistance in Puerto Rico* (Berkeley: University of California Press, 2019).

debt-austerity across both public university systems and discussed plans to bring UPR students to do a speaking tour in the US Northeast.

On September 20, 2017, however, these visions were dramatically halted when Hurricane Maria pummeled the island. The official death toll was 64 but the actual number may have been as high as 4,645 people.[67] Millions were left without electricity or phone access. The US military set up recovery stations with FEMA and the private sector, and immediately the bidding began for which companies would get contracts for cleanup, food and water distribution, and repairing the electricity grid. Meanwhile, thousands of containers of recovery supplies were stranded at the ports because of a colonial policy that restricted which ships could deliver materials to Puerto Rico. Since 2017, recurring electrical outages have knocked out power on the entire island for up to 48 hours at a time.[68]

In contrast to this colonial relief operation, the Social Kitchens formed *Centros de Apoyo Mutuo* [Mutual Aid Centers] (CAMs) across the island. People expanded the mutual support they had practiced during the 2010–2011 UPR campus occupations and food exchanges to create health clinics, telephone sharing, and housing and energy reconstruction. Groups like Papel Machete performed community theater around the island, linking the hurricane with the colonial debt crisis. These projects took a long-term recovery perspective to challenge the state's efforts to privatize schools and energy, and to rewrite labor laws. The proto-mutual aid disaster relief network that developed during the UPR strikes was reactivated after Hurricane Maria and inspired CUNY and UPR *compas* to build new decolonial solidarities. We can strategize more across these two public universities, which gather people in the Puerto Rican diaspora alongside Indigenous people, Palestinians, and other survivors of neocolonialism.

In Puerto Rico, the conditions for a 21st century decolonization struggle have emerged through recurring strikes at its public university; outrage at PROMESA; Hurricanes Fiona, Irma, and María; the ouster of Governor Ricardo Rosselló and the arrest of his successor, Wanda Vázquez, on corruption charges; multiple earthquakes, LUMA's privatization of electricity, and an ongoing pandemic. The disgraced government has confronted a populace that increasingly turns to the Mutual Aid Centers (CAMs), abandoned school reclamations like La Conde, militant feminist groups like La Colectiva Feminista en Construcción, Afro-Boricua queer and trans initiatives like Espicy Nipples, cultural organizations like Agitarte and Papel Machete, and direct action formations like Se Acabaron Las Promesas as a new ecosystem of Puerto Rican democracy and liberation.[69] Post-Maria Puerto Rico has its fair share of villains—a neocolonial government, cryptocurrency false prophets, Airbnb parasites. In opposition, a wave of insurgencies is rising—for women and trans people, teachers' pensions, mutual aid, against colonial debt, and more. Puerto Rico is still one of our best movement schools. It also needs our support in the epicenter of global capitalism.

67 George Washington University's Milken Institute School of Public Health and University of Puerto Rico Graduate School of Public Health, "Project Report: Ascertainment of the Estimated Excess Mortality from Hurricane María in Puerto Rico," GW Milken Institute SPH, August 27, 2018, http://prstudy.publichealth.gwu.edu/releases-reports.

68 Patricia Mazzei, "'Why Don't We Have Electricity?': Outages Plague Puerto Rico," *New York Times*, November 10, 2021, https://www.nytimes.com/2021/10/19/us/puerto-rico-electricity-protest.html/.

69 Jorge Díaz Ortíz, "Organizing Mutual Solidarity Projects as an Act of Resistance in Puerto Rico," *A Blade of Grass*, June 16, 2020, https://abladeofgrass.org/articles/organizing-mutual-solidarity-projects-act-resistance-puerto-rico/. See also Juan Carlos Dávila Santiago, dir., *Simulacros de liberación* [*Drills of Liberation*] (Aguada: Républica 21 Media, 2021).

These questions of solidarity were central to "Ourselves and the Academy: Ethnic Studies in CUNY," a December 2019 event hosted by Free CUNY at City College in which professors Iris López, Maria Romo-Carmona, and Vanessa Valdés spoke with a roomful of undergraduate student organizers. Reflecting on the 1969 Harlem University campus takeover, Valdés framed the current moment as Black Studies and Latin American and Latino Studies respecting each other's autonomy—a notably different framing than how City College students and movements fifty years ago fought for Black, Puerto Rican, Third World, and Women's Studies and liberation.

This distinction opens up whether the politics of coalition-building in the university have transitioned into the politics of autonomy, which may risk continued erosion in an institutional context of struggling with scarce resources. Ethnic Studies departments were formed out of entwined liberation movements, but then became isolated as embattled vestiges within hostile universities. However, as Brooklyn College Puerto Rican and Latino Studies educator María Pérez y González (former Chairperson of Puerto Rican and Latino Studies at Brooklyn College) warns, in times of austerity administrators may wish to merge (and further downsize) these distinct programs or departments into "Ethnic Studies." Consequently, "independence/departmental autonomy with strong solidarity among these ethnic studies groups and allies is more desirable and effective."[70] Their future survival—and further, liberation—will be nourished through comparative studies and actions in conjunction with each other as well as among larger coalitions like those that had established them. We will need to reconsolidate power across our differences to defend the studies that were created back then. At the same time, we must insist that a Third World University and a broader liberated society is not only possible, but an intergenerational promise that we intend to keep.

On May 1, 2019, Puerto Rican scholar Félix "Felo" Matos Rodríguez was appointed the first Chancellor of color in the university's history. Unlike many in the CUNY Board of Trustees, Matos Rodríguez is a longtime educator—a historian on the lives and work of Puerto Rican women—who previously served as President of Hostos Community College, Director of El Centro, and President of Queens College. He got his first teaching job at age twenty-three in Puerto Rican Studies at City College. Those who knew Matos Rodríguez's record of service and scholarship hoped that his leadership could restore and broaden Ethnic Studies across the university.

However, since becoming Chancellor, Matos Rodríguez has presided over additional tuition increases that predominantly affect students who take the Ethnic Studies classes he once taught. This situation is worsened by a $13 billion New York State budget deficit and a refusal by the legislature to prioritize public higher education. However, Matos Rodríguez has inherited the leadership mantle at a moment when CUNY's students, workers, alumni, and supporters in the city of New York are striving to decolonize and transform the university. CUNY communities have repeatedly amassed at the Chancellor's Westchester home and CUNY's Midtown NYC headquarters to

---

70 María Pérez y González, email communication with the author, February 2, 2020.

invoke the specter of a "communiversity."[71]

CUNY Faces COVID-19, Welcomes BLM 2.0, and Defends Abortion Access[72]

In 2020, the global COVID-19 pandemic killed more people at CUNY than at any other university in the country, and many of New York City's forty-three thousand deaths are within a few degrees of proximity to our university, including alumni.[73] Frontline workers—mainly women of colors—were "martyred against [their] will," while those imprisoned and detained were left to die in dense high-contagion cages.[74] At the same time, the murders of Ahmaud Arbery, Rayshard Brooks, Raymond Chaluisant, George Floyd, Mario Gonzalez, Tony McDade, Sean Reed, Oluwatoyin Salau, Breonna Taylor, Neida Tijerina, Jayland Walker, Daunte Wright, and so many more confirm that the inherent brutality of policing will endanger any attempts at social healing and that fighting for our lives means sabotaging state violence in myriad material ways.[75]

That summer, #BlackLivesMatter 2.0 mobilizations boomeranged across cities and then universities.[76] By one estimate, between 15 and 26 million people were involved in uprisings that shook almost 550 cities and towns across the country.[77] In New York, uproarious protests swarmed streets, confronted police, set dozens of cop cruisers and vans on fire, evaded and sustained arrests, redistributed goods, resisted curfews, and recomposed into a massive freedom school, studying itself while in motion. The Fall 2019 FTP (Fuck the Police/Free the People/Fight the Power) protests to resist increased policing in the New York City transit system had built up a strong current of defiant

71 Jenna Gaudino, "CUNY Adjuncts Dish Out Demands at 'Brunch with Felo,'" *The Indypendent*, February 14, 2022, https://indypendent.org/2022/02/cuny-adjuncts-dish-out-demands-at-brunch-with-felo/. See also, the "Communiversity" radical learning project that emerged from the 2022 New School adjunct strike, https://www.instagram.com/communiversitynyc/.

72 For an earlier version of this section, see Conor Tomás Reed, "Realizing the Dream of a Liberation University," *Verso* (blog), September 8, 2020, https://www.versobooks.com/blogs/4848-hot-city-realizing-the-dream-of-a-liberation-university; Conor Tomás Reed, "All Power to the Public Humanities!" *ASAP/Journal*, November 29, 2021, https://asapjournal.com/public-humanities-and-the-arts-of-the-present-all-power-to-the-public-humanities-conor-tomas-reed/.

73 Marjorie Valburn, "Lives and Livelihoods," *Inside Higher Ed*, June 23, 2020, https://www.insidehighered.com/news/2020/06/23/cuny-system-suffers-more-coronavirus-deaths-any-other-higher-ed-system-us/.

74 See Hanna Wallis, "Nurses Say They Don't Want to Be Called Heroes During the Coronavirus Pandemic," *Teen Vogue*, April 28, 2020, https://www.teenvogue.com/story/nurses-dont-want-to-be-called-heroes; Jillian Primiano, "From One Essential Worker to Another: Demanding Safe Working Conditions Could Save My Life," *Left Voice*, April 30, 2020, https://www.leftvoice.org/from-one-essential-worker-to-another-demanding-safe-working-conditions-could-save-my-life/; Left Voice, "Please don't call me a hero. I am being martyred against my will," Instagram, May 10, 2020, https://www.instagram.com/p/CAA0WRaJCH3/.

75 Mapping Police Violence, https://mappingpoliceviolence.org/; *Washington Post*, "Fatal Force: Police Shootings Database," last updated March 21, 2023 [originally published May 30, 2015], https://www.washingtonpost.com/graphics/investigations/police-shootings-database/.

76 Unity and Struggle, "Big Brick Energy: A Multi-city Study of the 2020 George Floyd Uprising," July 20, 2022, http://www.unityandstruggle.org/2022/07/big-brick-energy-a-multi-city-study-of-the-2020-george-floyd-uprising/.

77 Larry Buchanan, Quoctrung Bui, and Jugal K. Patel, "Black Lives Matter May Be the Largest Movement in U.S. History," *New York Times*, July 3, 2020, https://www.nytimes.com/interactive/2020/07/03/us/george-floyd-protests-crowd-size.html.

street actions, with crowds hopping turnstiles, secretly signaling to change locations and evade police, creating protest trains, and mounting mass outdoor teach-ins. FTP was a continuation and advancement of earlier city-wide campaigns led by Decolonize This Place, Take Back the Bronx, Why Accountability, Swipe It Forward, Cop Watch NYC, NYC Shut it Down, Comité Boricua En La Diáspora, and others. Several years of targeting city museum boards, monuments, landlords, politicians, and cops while fostering electrified movement spaces then pivoted to wresting control over transit—our ability to freely move—a *logistical institution* that is central to all working-class New Yorkers. As these abolitionist subway actions grew, a brutal police assault and mass kettling arrest of the fourth FTP convergence occurred on June 4, 2020, several days into the city's eruption after George Floyd's murder.[78] The state sought to suppress FTP as ringleaders, but whole neighborhoods were becoming ungovernable while learning to keep each other safe. The summer 2020 uprisings, like those in the earlier 2010s, targeted the *logistical institutions* of the state—including police precincts—along with major nodes of commerce and traffic. Combined outrage from the health crisis, police terror, and mass unemployment were recomposed into rowdy public assembly, although over time these uprisings became rote marches without targets and depleted in number.

In these overlapping waves of action that poured onto campus, Indigenous and anticolonial participants dedicated closer attention to the land underneath these institutions and the ecological histories with which they're enmeshed. As Roderick A. Ferguson frames it,

> The recent record of protests on U.S. college campuses confirms the ancestral presence of the subjugated and our need to respond to that presence. In this way we can think of colleges and universities as contested ancestral grounds, ones in which dominant and subjugated ancestors vie for ideological authority.[79]

At CUNY, calls by Black, Indigenous, and People of Colors (BIPoC) faculty, staff, and students to create antiracist campuses abounded at Brooklyn College, CUNY Law School, Hunter College, Lehman College, and elsewhere. These were preceded by a Fall 2019 Latinx Student Alliance campaign to decolonize the Lehman English curriculum, as well as Spring 2020 Puerto Rican Alliance demands to confront structural racism at Brooklyn, which evolved into the formation of the Anti-Racist Coalition (ARC).[80] ARC organizer Rhea Rahman explained,

> Recognizing the profound connection between austerity measures and systemic racism, and that any broad-based financial cuts will always impact those already most severely marginalized, activists called on admin-

---

78 Human Rights Watch, "'Kettling' Protesters in the Bronx," September 30, 2020, https://www.hrw.org/report/2020/09/30/kettling-protesters-bronx/systemic-police-brutality-and-its-costs-united-states/. See also "Kettled in Mott Haven," *Spirit of May 28*, November 29, 2022, https://www.sm28.org/articles/kettled-in-mott-haven/.

79 Roderick A. Ferguson, "On the Subject of Roots: The Ancestor as Institutional Foundation," *Radical Philosophy* 2, no. 10 (Summer 2021), https://www.radicalphilosophy.com/article/on-the-subject-of-roots/.

80 Brooklyn College Anti-Racist Coalition, https://antiracistcoalitionbc.wordpress.com/.

istrators, as well as the broader Brooklyn College community, to imagine what a Black-life affirming campus might look like.[81]

Further initiatives by Free CUNY, the People's Cultural Plan, and Rank and File Action (RAFA) emerged to kick cops out of CUNY, K–12 schools, and the labor movement.[82] Meanwhile, the social media campaign #DreamCUNY stoked our imaginative visions by asking "what would the CUNY of your dreams be like?" while students asserted that, once and for all, "it's time for CUNY to say goodbye to cops."[83]

During the summer of 2020, the CUNY administration laid off three thousand adjuncts, causing hundreds to lose their healthcare coverage, and terminated countless other campus workers while hoarding federal CARES Act money that could have been used to retain them.[84] As CUNY faculty affirmed, these low-paid campus workers and students are "heroes"—they have the power to "resurrect," reclaim, and transform the university anew.[85] It's remarkable how CUNY adjuncts navigated 2020, weaving in themes of austerity, #BlackLivesMatter and abolition, and COVID-19, all while honing accessibility and care skills for students who were devastated by these overlapping crises.[86] Our already food- and housing-insecure CUNY students suffered increased unemployment and danger of eviction, while a thriving urban farm at Kingsborough Community College was shuttered and then reopened with bottom-level wages.[87] These conditions were abhorrent given the city's immense wealth, with education,

81 Anthony Alessandrini, Zahra Ali, Kylie Broderick, Juan Doe, Nadim El Kak, Rhea Rahman, and Ghiwa Sayegh, "Roundtable: Protest and Social Mobilization in the Time of COVID-19," *Jadaliyya*, August 20, 2020, https://www.jadaliyya.com/Details/41574/Roundtable-Protest-and-Social-Mobilization-in-the-Time-of-COVID-19/.

82 Hakim Bishara and Valentina Di Liscia, "NYC High School and College Students Demand 'Cops Out!' of Schools," *Hyperallergic*, January 30, 2020, https://hyperallergic.com/540230/nyc-high-school-and-college-students-demand-cops-out-of-schools/.

83 Teona Pagan, Daniel Vazquez, Elizabeth Bazile, Hailey Lam, and Diana Kennedy, "It's Time for CUNY to Say Goodbye to Cops: Fighting for a Free University," *Radical History Review*, November 17, 2020, https://www.radicalhistoryreview.org/abusablepast/its-time-for-cuny-to-say-goodbye-to-cops-fighting-for-a-free-university/. See also David Klassen, "Cops Off Campus and Out of Our Unions!: A Report from PSC-CUNY"'s Rank-and-File," *Spectre Journal*, July 1, 2020, https://spectrejournal.com/cops-out-of-our-unions/.

84 Ben Brachfeld, "Faculty Union Sues CUNY, Demands Injunction To Rehire Laid-Off Adjuncts," *Gothamist*, July 3, 2020, https://gothamist.com/news/faculty-union-sues-cuny-demands-injunction-rehire-laid-adjuncts/. See also Michael Fabricant and Steve Brier, "Racialized Austerity: The Case of CUNY," *Gotham Gazette*, August 20, 2020, https://www.gothamgazette.com/opinion/9691-racialized-austerity-case-of-cuny-funding-new-york-public-college/.

85 Jeanne Theoharis, Alan Aja, and Joseph Entin, "Spare CUNY, and Save the Education our Heroes Deserve," *City Limits*, May 13, 2020, https://citylimits.org/2020/05/13/opinion-spare-cuny-and-save-the-education-our-heroes-deserve/. See also Corey Robin, "The Pandemic is the Time to Resurrect the Public University," *New Yorker*, May 7, 2020, https://www.newyorker.com/culture/cultural-comment/the-pandemic-is-the-time-to-resurrect-the-public-university/.

86 Sami Disu, Joanna Dressel, Jamila Hammami, Marianne Madoré, and Conor Tomás Reed, *"The amount of labor we do for free" and other contradictions: A collective inquiry into the pedagogical choices of CUNY adjunct and graduate student instructors who taught with free of charge materials during the year 2020*, Manifold, April 2022, https://cuny.manifoldapp.org/projects/the-amount-of-labor-we-do-for-free-and-other-contradictions/.

87 Save KCC Urban Farm, "Say NO to budget cuts at the urban farm!," *The Action Network*, https://actionnetwork.org/petitions/say-no-to-proposed-budget-cuts-to-kingsborough-community-colleges-urban-farm/.

health, and housing being cut while the NYPD nets $6 billion in each budget cycle.[88]

If, as Marx and Engels argue, the ruling class creates its own gravediggers, and if, by extension, the university is both a spatial concentration of exploitation and the latent site of its overcoming, what happens in a pandemic when the entire city becomes a graveyard?[89] Taking inspiration from nationwide university tuition strikes and the UC-Santa Cruz grade strikes, organizers in Free CUNY and Rank and File Action realized that the CUNY machine cannot function without students paying tuition, staff maintaining campus functions, and faculty submitting grades.[90] Beyond these functions, the rest of the semester is, as Louis Althusser argued, ideological exchange, or, as la paperson more recently detailed, settler-colonial control of university grounds.[91] Throughout 2020, Free CUNY laid plans for a potential tuition-strike campaign as RAFA generated support for a potential grade strike while urging the PSC to coordinate a broader strike campaign.

However, the PSC's leadership failed to turn the crisis into an organizing wave. Although the last few years have seen more teacher's strikes than the last few decades, the PSC leadership's theory of labor mobilization argued that it was necessary for every single union member to be reached by phone before it could utter the word "strike." In this way, it froze up in the face of the largest crisis since 1976.[92] In contrast, rank-and-file organizers took inspiration from the likes of the Combahee River Collective, who wrote, "We might use our position at the bottom . . . to make a clear leap into revolutionary action."[93]

Alongside the upsurge of militant antiracist organizing there exists in the PSC an entrenched liberal current that tokenizes BIPoC workers and students while admonishing more insurgent complicities.[94] This "woke white liberalism" emerged during the last twenty years of CUNY's accelerated neoliberal shift following the end of Open Admissions.[95] Euro faculty advanced in their tenured positions by producing progressive (enough) scholarship and virtue-signaling, while poor multiethnic coworkers and

88 Kelsey Chatlosh, "CUNY, Public Colleges Face Mass Budget Cuts Under the Shock of COVID-19," *Teen Vogue*, September 8, 2020, https://www.teenvogue.com/story/cuny-budget-cuts/.

89 Karl Marx and Friedrich Engels, "Manifesto of the Communist Party," in *Marx/Engels Selected Works, Vol. One* (Moscow: Progress Publishers, 1969 [first published February 1848]), https://www.marxists.org/archive/marx/works/1848/communist-manifesto/.

90 Mary Retta, "Students Across the Country Are Going on Strike," *The Nation*, April 24, 2020, https://www.thenation.com/article/activism/students-across-the-country-are-going-on-strike/. See also UCSC COLA Agitation Committee, "Time to Strike: Academic Workers and the Tactic of Withholding Grades," *Jadaliyya*, August 20, 2020, https://www.jadaliyya.com/Details/41578/Time-to-Strike-Academic-Workers-and-the-Tactic-of-Withholding-Grades/.

91 Louis Althusser, "Ideology and Ideological State Apparatuses (Notes Towards an Investigation)," in *Lenin and Philosophy and Other Essays* (New York: Monthly Review Press, 1971). See also la paperson, *A Third University Is Possible* (Minneapolis: University of Minnesota Press, 2017).

92 Eric Blanc, *Red State Revolt: The Teachers' Strike Wave and Working-Class Politics* (New York: Verso, 2019).

93 Combahee River Collective, "Combahee River Collective Statement." See also Daniel Bensaïd, "'Leaps, Leaps, Leaps': Lenin and Politics," *International Socialism* 2, no. 95 (July 2002): 148–163.

94 See M., "A Critique of Ally Politics," in *Taking Sides: Revolutionary Solidarity and the Poverty of Liberalism*, ed. Cindy Milstein (Chico: AK Press, 2015).

95 Asma Khalid, "How White Liberals Became Woke, Radically Changing Their Outlook on Race," *NPR.org*, October 1, 2019, https://www.npr.org/2019/10/01/763383478/how-white-liberals-became-woke-radically-changing-their-outlook-on-race/.

students were squeezed by adjunctification and rising tuition.[96] Within the last few years, as abolitionist antiracist projects have taken flight, a bureaucratized version of racial justice has also appeared at the top ranks. CUNY hired Matos Rodríguez as Chancellor, who in turn appointed the university's first presidents of Asian and Dominican descent, who promptly oversaw austerity measures and educational redlining.

Under such conditions, stern warnings by Euro tenured faculty to uncritically support Black leadership may undermine political debates about which strategies and tactics are most effective, or be used to prioritize fighting select instances of racism and sexism at the expense of broadly improving our learning and laboring conditions. City College alumnus Keeanga-Yamahtta Taylor warns that the "unspoken promise of racial representation is that social, economic, and political dynamics can change when someone from a marginalized group is at the helm. Too often, however, in Black politics, symbolism has stood in for making a meaningful difference in the lives of Black people."[97] The ambiguous call to follow Black leadership could allow neoliberal Black leaders (like Medgar Evers College's now-resigned president Rudy Crew) to be protected in a moment when they're being forced out by multiethnic, feminist, queer CUNY students and workers.[98] Our politics cannot be reduced to burdening Black people with the sole responsibility of setting the movement's direction and expecting others merely to follow. Instead, they should consist of active collaborations across differences to produce changes that were unthinkable even a short time ago. In the words of Audre Lorde, "There is no such thing as a single-issue struggle because we do not live single-issue lives."[99]

A prevailing difficulty in overcoming both the CUNY administration and our union's mis-leadership can be found in the fleeting compositions of our counterpower structures. During the last several years, grassroots formations like CUNY Struggle and campaigns like "$7K or Strike" offered inspiring examples of how CUNY could be revitalized through direct action and ambitious demands to counteract austerity and galvanize the union's sense of its power using defiant pickets and agit-prop.[100] A proto-counterleadership milieu arose in Rank and File Action from these efforts but has yet to form a caucus to oust the existing PSC leadership. Partly, this owes to ongoing debates about whether it makes more sense to lay claim to existing union structures or to create direct democratic processes instead. These questions have evolved since the times when we would occupy spaces without making specific demands. Still, the answer remains uncertain. In this case, we did forge concrete demands but were unable to occupy the institutional spaces (the union hall, campus buildings) through which they might be realized.

Embracing lessons from Harlem University, one way to expand counterpower could be to orient our university demands with those of surrounding neighborhoods:

96 City University of New York University Human Resources, "Statistics and Reports," https://www.cuny.edu/about/administration/offices/hr/recruitment-diversity/statistics-and-reports/.

97 Keeanga-Yamahtta Taylor, "Joe Biden, Kamala Harris, and the Limits of Representation," *The New Yorker*, August 24, 2020, https://www.newyorker.com/news/our-columnists/joe-biden-kamala-harris-and-the-limits-of-representation/. See also Olúfẹ́mi O. Táíwò, *Elite Capture: How the Powerful Took Over Identity Politics (And Everything Else)* (Chicago: Haymarket Books, 2022).

98 Owen Brown, "Rudy Crew Must Resign: A Medgar Evers Professor Says He Has Failed to Meet the Moment," *New York Daily News*, August 9, 2020, https://www.nydailynews.com/opinion/ny-oped-rudy-crew-must-resign-20200809-54a3igbljjgq5csadiizxpp57q-story.html/.

99 Audre Lorde, "Learning from the 60s," in *Sister Outsider: Essays and Speeches* (Trumansburg: Crossing Press, 1984), 138.

100 CUNY Struggle, *CUNY at the Crossroads: a history of the mess we're in and how to get out of it*, Fall 2016, https://cunystruggle.org/cuny-at-the-crossroads/.

housing, care, food, and other essentials. The labor movement has recently embraced the language of "Bargaining for the Common Good."[101] This strategy was powerfully embodied by the Chicago Teachers Union, who in a 2019 contract renegotiation demanded affordable housing for students and that the government fund schools by diverting debt payments from banks.[102] Similarly, a contract negotiated in 2019 at Rutgers redistributed salary gains to women and/or tenurable faculty of colors (although adjuncts were left out of these gains).[103]

What if PSC officials as well as management became caught in the undertow of antiracist feminist demands that continue to surge across CUNY? Even within the PSC's own Anti-Racism Committee, several abolitionists stymied by the liberalism embedded in the union's "leadership" resigned en masse in March 2023, but are still connecting with others committed to liberatory unionism nationwide. If we heeded this vision, we could co-activate struggles instead of siloing issues of "economic justice," "gender justice," and "racial justice."[104] CUNY movements can expand to include free, safe, and legal abortion access; cancellation of rent and evictions; decriminalization of sex work; abolishing the police, ICE, and imprisonment; universal free healthcare; increasing wages and protections for all workers; and expanding unemployment resources. These victories can provide footholds for larger anticapitalist transformations.

A bevy of such projects has blossomed around CUNY and the city at large in an emerging ecosystem of community-oriented arts/pedagogies/actions that are essential preconditions to deeper uprisings. A November 2020–Jan 2021 online residency, "Radiating Black~Puerto Rican~Feminist Studies from the City University of New York to the Americas and the Caribbean," that I curated with Wendy's Subway and several CUNY institutions featured public dialogues on the lives of Toni Cade Bambara, June Jordan, and Audre Lorde; stories of how CUNY movements created Open Admissions and Ethnic Studies; and present efforts to decolonize CUNY and New York City.[105]

On April 15, 2021, Debt Collective and Labor Notes' Public Higher Education Workers (PHEW), along with the CUNY Adjunct Project and a PSC union chapter, launched a national "Debt Reveal" Day to show how the university pays off debts by

101 Bargaining for the Common Good, https://www.bargainingforthecommongood.org/.

102 Sara Freund, "Chicago teachers fight for affordable housing in contract negotiations," *Curbed*, October 16, 2019 https://chicago.curbed.com/2019/10/10/20908479/chicago-teachers-strike-affordable-housing/; Rebecca Burns, "How Chicago Teachers are Taking on Wall Street," *The Intercept*, October 25, 2019, https://theintercept.com/2019/10/25/chicago-teachers-strike-wall-street/.

103 Astra Taylor and Todd Wolfson, "Beyond the Neoliberal University," *Boston Review*, August 4, 2020, http://bostonreview.net/class-inequality/todd-wolfson-astra-taylor-beyond-neoliberal-university/. See also Rutgers Adjuncts Caucus (@RUExploited), https://twitter.com/ruexploited/.

104 Wilson Sherwin and Douglas Young, two CUNY alums, respectively model this symbiotic method across abolition and antiwork movements, and across university adjunctification and gig economy struggles. See Wilson Sherwin, "Working for Abolition Means Abolishing Work," *Spectre Journal*, June 1, 2022, https://spectrejournal.com/working-for-abolition-means-abolishing-work; Douglas Young, "Working Alone: Atomized and Desocialized Production as an Obstacle to Power," *Spectre Journal*, April 21, 2022, https://spectrejournal.com/atomized-and-desocialized-production-as-an-obstacle-to-power.

105 Conor Tomás Reed, "Radiating Black~Puerto Rican~Feminist Studies from the City University of New York to the Americas and the Caribbean," event series, The Center for the Humanities, https://www.centerforthehumanities.org/programming/radiating-black-puerto-rican-feminist-studies-from-the-city-university-of-new-york-to-the-americas-and-the-caribbean/.

raising tuition and expanding adjunct labor.[106] Then on May 14, CUNY and New York City groups held a "Cops Out of CUNY!" tour through multiple campuses, Central Park, and the CUNY Police headquarters. Testimonies by the Bronx Student Strike Committee, Brooklyn College Anti-Racist Coalition, CUNY for Abolition and Safety, Free CUNY, North Bronx Collective, NYC 4 Abortion Rights, Rank and File Action, and Save Center for Puerto Rican Studies "Centro" Coalition called for campus policing to be abolished and for its multimillion budget to be reinvested in free tuition; Ethnic, Gender, and Sexuality Studies; childcare; housing; and food.[107] That May, during Israel's renewed bombing of Gaza, a flurry of CUNY statements responded in solidarity with Palestine and the BDS movement.[108] In Fall 2021, the Cross-CUNY Working Group Against Racism and Colonialism held an exceptional teach-in series to link CUNY to broader transnational struggles.[109] Food and land sovereignty initiatives by CUNY and community organizers took root, such as "Archives in Common," which spotlighted undocumented immigrant health and mutual aid efforts, and the "Land Back" zine by the North Bronx Collective, which interviewed multiple participants in community gardens who were locked out during the pandemic.[110] Meanwhile, CUNY adjuncts reflexively analyzed how abolitionist pedagogies can also undo the system of grading as we know it.[111]

In 2022, CUNY struggles continued to erupt. An anti-HBCU bomb threat at York College and anti-Black graffiti found near the SEEK offices at Queens College aligned students and workers against the CUNY administration's tepid response.[112] The announcement of the Supreme Court's revocation of legal abortion protections spurred the formation of CUNY for Abortion Rights (CUNYFAR), which coordinated a defiant march on June 24 where 20,000 people flooded lower Manhattan, then hosted a Fall strategy convergence, and joined ongoing clinic defenses led by NYC for Abortion

106 CUNY Adjunct Project, "CUNY Debt Reveal," https://cunyadjunctproject.org/peoples-budget/cuny-debt-reveal/; Debt Collective, https://debtcollective.org/; Labor Notes, https://labornotes.org/.

107 Cops Off Campus Coalition, https://copsoffcampuscoalition.com/abolition-may/; see Free CUNY! [@cuny_free], "Show up for our co-organized cross-CUNY/city Abolition May event: COPS OUT OF CUNY!," Twitter, May, 13, 2021, https://twitter.com/cuny_free/status/1392834032392544272.

108 CUNY for Palestine, https://linktr.ee/cuny4palestine/.

109 Cross-CUNY Working Group Against Racism and Colonialism, https://linktr.ee/CUNYAgainstRacismColonialism/.

110 Ángeles Donoso Macaya, "Archives in Common," event series, The Center for the Humanities, https://www.centerforthehumanities.org/public-engagement/seminars/archives-in-common/; North Bronx Collective, https://linktr.ee/northbxcollective/.

111 Joaly Burgos, Jane Guskin, Hailey Lam, Marianne Madoré, Andréa Stella, and Anna Zeemont, "Resisting Surveillance, Practicing/Imagining the End of Grading," The Journal of Interactive Technology and Pedagogy, December 10, 2021, https://jitp.commons.gc.cuny.edu/resisting-surveillance-practicing-imagining-the-end-of-grading/.

112 Ariana Purisic, "York College Evacuates After Bomb Threat Hoax," The Ticker, March 25, 2022, https://theticker.org/6907/news/york-college-evacuates-after-bomb-threat-hoax/; Sarah Weissman, "HBCU Bomb Threats Take a Toll on Mental Health," Inside Higher Ed, April 8, 2022, https://www.insidehighered.com/news/2022/04/08/hbcu-bomb-threats-take-toll-mental-health/; Weissman, "Racist Graffiti Creates Months of Tension at Queens College," Inside Higher Ed, May 25, 2022, https://www.insidehighered.com/news/2022/05/25/racist-graffiti-creates-months-tensions-queens-college/.

Rights.[113] This coalition draws upon *marea verde* [green wave] abortion access victories from Argentina, Chile, Colombia, Ireland, Mexico, Poland, Puerto Rico, and beyond, which understand *struggles as school*—"more than just the achievement of women to exercise rights over their own bodies: they are a binding force [across] far-flung parts of the world."[114] CUNYFAR is now teaming up with other schools in New York City and across the country to insist upon the continuation of abortion training at their medical programs, to expand campus reproductive services for all, and to establish scholarships and reduced tuition for people coming from states with abortion restrictions.

Furthermore, as this book goes to press, a "Reclaim the Commons" campaign at the CUNY Graduate Center has opened up the Dining Commons to CUNY- and NYC-wide communities, and established an autonomous "People's Pantry," as its students and workers also push to re-open cafeteria services, expand Childcare Center access and affordability, halt college housing rent hikes, and oust the GC President and Provost.

Continuations

Within these multiple entwined crises, the New York Liberation School serves as both a lifeline and a guide to action. We must reach for each other—across our fears of mortality, through acute and chronic illnesses—both on and off the insurgent streets. We must devote attention to the suffering that impacted our health before the pandemic—particularly that of Black, Indigenous, and Global South/Third World communities, LGBTQ and gender non-conforming communities, and disabled and chronically ill communities, most of whom are among the working poor.[115] Claiming power over and across our different lives means refusing a separation between those living with chronic illness, who cannot attend physical protests, and those who protest in the streets. Nascent care networks can offer both the method and the structure for coordinating movement during crises.[116]

To realize the dream of a New York Liberation School, we must expand the visions and actions of these City College legacies by synergizing economic, gender, and racial justice efforts, and fostering the scale and intensity of collective involvement that reshaped our university and city fifty years ago. A strike wave at CUNY could activate 250,000 students, over 50,000 PSC faculty and staff, millions of alumni, twenty-five

113 See CUNY for Abortion Rights, https://www.instagram.com/cunyforabortionrights/; "All Out for Abortion Access!: Organizing at CUNY and Beyond," PublicsLab, https://publicslab.gc.cuny.edu/events/all-out-for-abortion-access-organizing-at-cuny-and-beyond/; NYC for Abortion Rights, https://www.instagram.com/nycforabortionrights/.

114 Susana Draper and Verónica Gago, "Struggles as School: Reproductive Justice, a Cross-Border Reflection," *Verso* (blog), August 5, 2022, https://www.versobooks.com/blogs/5396-struggles-as-school-reproductive-justice-a-cross-border-reflection/.

115 Linda Villarosa, "'A Terrible Price': The Deadly Racial Disparities of COVID-19 in America," *The New York Times*, April 29, 2020, https://www.nytimes.com/2020/04/29/magazine/racial-dispari-ties-COVID-19.html/. See also Petruce Jean-Charles, "LGBTQ Americans are getting coronavirus, losing jobs. Anti-gay bias is making it worse for them," *USA Today*, May 9, 2020, https://www.usatoday.com/story/news/nation/2020/05/09/discrimination-racism-fuel-COVID-19-woes-lgbtq-ameri-cans/3070036001/.

116 New York City residents developed and expanded a wave of mutual aid projects, such as Collective Focus (https://collectivefocus.site), Woodbine (https://www.woodbine.nyc), and "friendly fridges" (https://nycfridge.com). For one example of how these infrastructural efforts could become linked to each other, see Woodbine, "Urgent Pedagogies and Autonomous Infrastructure with Sandi Hilal and Pelin Tan," September 22, 2021, https://www.patreon.com/posts/56492881/.

campuses, and almost nine million of our neighbors across the five boroughs. Dozens of unions and workers' centers, hundreds of community organizations, and thousands of nascent sites of militancy can co-choreograph with us how to refuse one form of living and enact another.

Combining the lessons of pandemic mutual care, #BlackLivesMatter's resistance to colonial-racial-gendered capitalism, feminist movements' insistence on reproductive autonomy, and the overall reprioritization of society that blossomed over these last few years, CUNY could become one of many strategic epicenters for creating fundamental social change. Despite tremendous obstacles, a growing base of militant coalitions, deepening relationships, and organizing skills are converging to advance a revolutionary vision that can be reached through decisive strikes and the development of counter-institutional power. If we want to create the university, city, and world of our dreams, we must arise to our already-existing powers to transform it.

CODA

CUNY WILL BE FREE!

CUNY is not yet a people's university. We have not yet made the city a college, a vast field of purposeful learning and transformation. Across the decades, two favored chants at CUNY demonstrations have been "Free CUNY!" and "CUNY Will Be Free!" These collectively sung intentions are a refusal of elites' desire to impose a price tag on our education, making it more inaccessible and enshrining it with the aura of a commodity, making learning into a property relationship. The chants also articulate freedom beyond cost, pointing toward the fullest expression of shared liberation. Admittedly, reaching toward this future can sometimes feel like an ongoing horizon that we will never reach. Some militants caution us not to embed our political investments in the "future," which they consider a temporal ruse, wielded by the wealthy, that distorts our sense of the past and present.[1] Others warn instead that we have to learn how to *survive* the future.[2] We live in an ecological moment in which food and water scarcity, mass migrations due to climate change and war, and the threat of capitalist states and markets converting to neofascist rule are fundamentally restructuring our world.

But even while holding attention to this existing fraught historical moment, comrades, we must look ahead to what we can forge. Opposing a broad swath of immiserations and rehearsing other kinds of sociality into existence entails queering our relationship to times and spaces.[3] Radical queering can translate our sense of the situated past through our present conjuncture into a future we can't predict but that our collective wills can fundamentally shape. This is an act that could also be described as coalitions composing transitional revolutionary programs through study and movement. Let us remember, after all, that the name of the experiment that gathered these extraordinary people together at City College—SEEK—is a verb that is persistently future-reaching.

1 Marcello Tarì, *There is No Unhappy Revolution: The Communism of Destitution*, trans. Richard Braude (Brooklyn: Common Notions, 2021).

2 Scott Branson, Raven Hudson, and Bry Reed, eds., *Surviving the Future: Abolitionist Queer Strategies* (Oakland: PM Press, 2023).

3 This creative practice is demonstrated in M.E. O'Brien and Eman Abdelhadi's *Everything for Everyone*, a speculative future narrative where CUNY movements fit into a larger account of revolutionary upheavals and counter-social institutions. See M.E. O'Brien and Eman Abdelhadi, *Everything for Everyone: An Oral History of the New York Commune, 2052–2072* (Brooklyn: Common Notions, 2022). See also Robin D. G. Kelley, "'When History Wakes': A New Beginning, Fall 2021," in *Freedom Dreams: The Black Radical Imagination*, Twentieth Anniversary Edition (Boston: Beacon Press, 2022), 195–226.

José Esteban Muñoz focused on this subjunctive power of queerness in his book *Cruising Utopia: The Then and There of Queer Futurity*:

> Queerness is not yet here. Queerness is an ideality. Put another way, we are not yet queer, but we can feel it as the warm illumination of a horizon imbued with potentiality. We have never been queer, yet queerness exists for us as an ideality that can be distilled from the past and used to imagine a future. The future is queerness's domain.[4]

A people's university in a city run collectively as a freedom school would be a queer sociality indeed. We have not yet queered CUNY and the city of New York, but the lessons laid out in this book suggest an abundance of methods for how we could.

The ever-evolving character of CUNY movements is diasporic, transhemispheric, a worlds-making endeavor. Ultimately, this is a story of how the largest public urban university in the United States has come to be composed of communities who survived displacement by colonialism, enslavement, and imperialism. To borrow the words of Sri Lankan-British Marxist A. Sivanandan: "We are here because you were there."[5] People from the colonized territories of Palestine, Puerto Rico, Hawaii, the Philippines, Guam, Indigenous lands in the Americas and Caribbean, along with all of our siblings from Africa, Asia, the Levant, Pacific Islands, and across the Third World/Global South are the majority at CUNY and in this city. We also have principled antiracist European and Jewish accomplices who struggle alongside us. When we turn our focus to the multifaceted potential of our university and city as a model for broader transnational resistance, and together develop strategies and organizational power, then we can move from reckoning with colonial-racial-gendered capitalism to celebrating the end of it.

The timing for reconfiguring the condition of our lives is, counterintuitively, the best it could be. Three years ago, when the global COVID-19 health crisis imposed physical distance between us, our institutions, and each other, the entire status quo was called into question, including how and why we structure social relations and practice education. The US government distributed pandemic funds, paused collections on rent and debt, and temporarily halted evictions and executions. These sweeping actions would previously have been unthinkable within the terms of the neoliberal order. At the same time, community control of our schools and cities is not an immediately foreseeable future. It's critical to practice and prepare for a sustained negation of institutions as they currently are and a simultaneous creation of what they should be. Diverse urban freedom movements that oppose colonial/state recognition will not succeed by envisioning lines of ambiguous escape or incompatibility with each other.

4 José Esteban Muñoz, *Cruising Utopia: The Then and There of Queer Futurity* (New York: New York University Press, 2009), 1. See also Yarimar Bonilla, "Postdisaster Futures: Hopeful Pessimism, Imperial Ruination, and La futura cuir," *Small Axe* 62 (July 2020): 147–162; Jigna Desai and Kevin P. Murphy, "Subjunctively Inhabiting the University," *Critical Ethnic Studies* 4, no. 1 (Spring 2018): 21–43; Linda Luu, "Resistance Everywhere We Went: The Fight for Asian American Studies at CUNY," in Rose M. Kim, Grace M. Cho, and Robin McGinty, eds., *The Children of the People: Writings by and about CUNY Students on Race and Social Justice* (Lewes: DIO Press, 2022), 171–187.

5 A. Sivanandan, *Catching History on the Wing: Race, Culture and Globalisation* (London: Pluto Press, 2008), xi. See also Virou Srilangarajah, "We Are Here Because You Were With Us: Remembering A. Sivanandan (1923–2018)," *Verso* (blog), February 7, 2018, https://www.versobooks.com/blogs/3608-we-are-here-because-you-were-with-us-remembering-a-sivanandan-1923-2018/.

Rather, we have the chance to succeed by mapping out and taking over the institutions and living spaces where our power is already concentrated. This is not a call for governance from above, but to recompose our relations so that none represent another, so that all can contribute to the daily purpose and functioning of our lives.

Liberating Education

This book's intention has been to highlight an expansive ensemble of people in a particular university and city ecosystem—one among many sites of institutional power that can be studied and remade. During CUNY's upheavals, living rooms, classrooms, departments, colleges, neighborhoods, and the entire city composed the field of struggle: each classroom a potential coalition, each department a counter-disciplinary foothold, each neighborhood a social-territorial force to defend and organize with others. The unfinished freedom school legacies of Black, Puerto Rican, and Women's Studies, which existed simultaneously as educational projects and social movements, continue to hold insights for New York City and beyond. In this sense, it's no surprise that many of these City College teachers and students have become the "godparents" of our contemporary movements.

Solidarity means studying each other's contexts to build trust and take risks to transform our schools and societies, and in the process, to change ourselves. Consider the words of June Jordan: "I was born a Black woman / and now / I am become a Palestinian / against the relentless laughter of evil / there is less and less living room / and where are my loved ones? // It is time to make our way home."[6] Or recall Adrienne Rich: "I am she: I am he [. . .] We are, I am, you are."[7] How familiar are we with each other's living rooms? Who are our loved ones? With whom do we become recomposed? This intimate pedagogical work can be done openly, patiently, to expand our interlocking power.

Even if you have been inspired by the accounts in these pages, some readers may look askance at the idea that the contemporary university can be a locus of social reconstruction. Indeed, the university as we know it has become a sweatshop and a warehouse of "predatory inclusion."[8] Nearly 80 percent of faculty members were tenured or tenure-track in 1969. Now roughly 75 percent of faculty are nontenured. These numbers are exacerbated by ongoing colonial-gendered-racist hiring practices of adjunct faculty of colors who become entrapped in academia's growing underclass and the treatment of tenure-track faculty of colors who bear the representative burden

6 June Jordan, "Moving Toward Home," *Living Room: New Poems* (New York: Thunder's Mouth Press, 1985), 134.

7 Adrienne Rich, "Diving into the Wreck," in *Diving into the Wreck: Poems 1971–1972* (New York: W.W. Norton and Company, 1973), 24.

8 Louise Seamster and Raphaël Charron-Chénier, "Predatory Inclusion and Education Debt: Rethinking the Racial Wealth Gap," *Social Currents* 4, no. 3 (2017): 199–207. See also Keeanga-Yamahtta Taylor, *Race for Profit: How Banks and the Real Estate Industry Undermined Black Homeownership* (Chapel Hill: University of North Carolina Press, 2019), 5.

of providing inclusive diversity to the institution.[9] Adam Harris writes, "From 1993 to 2013, the percentage of underrepresented minorities in [adjunct faculty] positions grew by 230 percent, and those receiving "tenure-track positions grew by just 30 percent."[10]

Insurgent intellectual work within the university has thus had to navigate a road filled with contradictions. As Nick Mitchell argues, "the institutional project of Black studies . . . [has] functioned both to bring the university to crisis and to supply the university with an instrument of crisis management."[11] As we work to take over and recreate the university within our respective disciplines, we must also never assent to the mirage of solid institutional ground. It is when our familiarized processes of intellectual work become shaky, contested, unmoored, upended, reconstituted, that we can overcome the university as it's currently structured.[12] In this way, we must undo even our own disciplinary groundings as we rebuild the university, so that we don't become absorbed into its administration's team of crisis managers.

Archiving in Ethical Motion

All of these interrelated dynamics described in the book—liberation movements, counterinsurgency operations, the formal university archive and the informal movement archive, the myth and materiality of our lives at CUNY—have now mostly been reabsorbed back into academia where they can be tokenized and policed. As discussed across the book, universities legitimize only select traces of these movements—call it "respectability archiving"—while forcing other parts of our movement histories into anonymity, even to the point of making repository sites disappear. Our CUNY story remains incomplete. What gets allowed in and what is erased? To my knowledge, only a few print archives exist of the two weeks inside Harlem University, and the Finley Building fire on the campus that precipitated Open Admissions has been mostly scrubbed from the record. No finding aids exist for the contents of the now-evicted Morales/Shakur Center—twenty-four years of movement materials confiscated by the CUNY administration and NYPD—in part because the record of these belongings contained the potential for endangering its creators.

The university has enshrined a paradigm of archiving and publishing that replicates these colonial relations of smash, grab, scoop, mine, co-opt, distort, or destroy—a

---

9 See Lorgia García Peña, *Community as Rebellion: A Syllabus for Surviving Academia as a Woman of Color* (Chicago: Haymarket Books, 2022); Gabriella Gutiérrez y Muhs, Yolanda Flores Niemann, Carmen G. González, and Angela P. Harris, eds., *Presumed Incompetent: The Intersections of Race and Class for Women in Academia* (Logan: Utah State University Press, 2012); Yolanda Flores Niemann, Gabriella Gutiérrez y Muhs, and Carmen G. González, eds., *Presumed Incompetent II: Race, Class, Power, and Resistance of Women in Academia* (Logan: Utah State University Press, 2020).

10 Adam Harris, "The Death of an Adjunct," *The Atlantic*, April 8, 2019, https://www.theatlantic.com/education/archive/2019/04/adjunct-professors-higher-education-thea-hunter/586168/.

11 Nick Mitchell, "(Critical Ethnic Studies) Intellectual," *Critical Ethnic Studies* 1, no. 1 (Spring 2015): 88.

12 See Eli B. Liechtenstein and Dave Mesing, "Notes on Contemporary University Struggles: A Dossier," *Viewpoint Magazine*, January 19, 2022, https://viewpointmag.com/2022/01/19/notes-on-contemporary-university-struggles-a-dossier/; *Abolish the University?*, Abolitionist University Studies, 2023, https://drive.google.com/file/d/17d-_Wx-B9rhunCu_4q36YEmApbP_AOZP/view.

scholastic parasitism about which June Jordan warned us half a century ago.[13] In a subtle gesture at these power relations, the copyright page in university press books will often list the university (or even its trustees) as bearing ownership of the work. All too often, social movement participants are not the main decision-makers around our archives and stories. Building relationships through archival research, creation, and protection—narrating our struggles as a vehicle for community empowerment, popular education, intergenerational care, and new organizing formations—is suppressed or undervalued in exchange for single, unaccountable authorships. As we practice a radical politics of citation with each other in CUNY and New York City, we also witness our histories, lived experiences, written work, and collaborative projects appropriated. Not even the beloved CUNY stories herein are immune from the dynamics of exploitation and usurpation that are condoned in academia.

Kimberly Springer, a historian of 1960s and '70s US Black feminist organizations, draws attention to these contradictions of movement archival practices in order to highlight whether intellectual production should take place in radical coalition or professional self-serving isolation. Springer explains how institutional archives all too often manufacture incomplete and biased evidence of these movements, an unstated racial and gendered supremacist practice that impacts how our lessons are transmitted across time. She appeals to present and future archivists and historians,

> [H]ow do we archivists and preservationists convey to those struggling, in this fast-paced moment, the importance of organizing archives? Those of us who care about preserving our organizing past for use in the future need to convey that an archive isn't a dead entity—archives are a living repository. Maintaining our own records is the best chance we have of shaping *our* reality.[14]

If we want to radically eschew the counterinsurgent archiving that Springer warns about, we can practice the radical coalitional methodologies being generated at places like the Spelman College Archives, Freedom Archives, Highlander Folk Center, Interference Archive, Lesbian Herstory Archives, and Weeksville Heritage Center; at CUNY sites and projects like the Brooklyn College students' "Friends of the TENTS," "El Centro" Center for Puerto Rican Studies, CUNY Digital History Archive, the Dominican Studies Institute, and *Lost & Found: The CUNY Poetics Document Initiative* at the Center for the Humanities; and in libraries like the Schomburg Center for Research in Black Culture. We must also reflect upon the spaces that have been stolen from us. Multiple New York City movement centers were shuttered over the last decade, including 16 Beaver Street (2014), Brecht Forum (2014), Bronx Social Center (2019), Brooklyn Commons (2020), 5Pointz

---

13 June Jordan, "Black Studies: Bringing Back the Person," in *Moving Towards Home: Political Essays* (London: Virago Press, 1989), 20. Silvia Rivera Cusicanqui also spotlights this knowledge usurpation from the Global South to North: "*Ch'ixinakax utxiwa*: A Reflection on the Practices and Discourses of Decolonization," in *Ch'ixinakax utxiwa: On Practices and Discourses of Decolonization* (Cambridge: Polity Press, 2020), 46–70.

14 Kimberly Springer, "Radical Archives and the New Cycles of Contention," *Viewpoint Magazine*, October 31, 2015, https://viewpointmag.com/2015/10/31/radical-archives-and-the-new-cycles-of-contention/.

(2014), Gathering of the Tribes (2014), and Rebel Diaz Artists Collective (2013).[15]

The fate of CUNY, New York City, and the world is once again at a crossroads. Campaigns to reconstruct universities and societies are escalating again in the wake of the nation erupting in the most vibrant struggles for abolitionist and anticolonial liberation, reproductive justice, workers' power, antifascism, and other social exigencies seen in two generations. Over fifty years ago, a coalition of Black, Puerto Rican, Asian, and Euro students and teachers, feminists, queers, disabled, multigenerational, interfaith, newly arrived immigrants and longtime residents succeeded in reinventing the largest public urban university in the nation while altering a city situated as one of the world's epicenters of power.

By continuing to invoke the demand and promise that "CUNY Will Be Free!"—a perpetual horizon and not a single outcome; a vast territory of transformation and not a single university; a commune as expansive and intricate as our lives—we can reclaim these vibrant histories to recompose our movements today. If education is the practice of freedom, then where, how, and with whom we study and move is of the most profound significance. We invite New York Liberation School accomplices to be nourished by these extraordinary lessons as we strategize and realize our liberatory futures together.

---

15 Gratitude to Matt Peterson and Mary Taylor for confirming dates for this context.

ACKNOWLEDGMENTS

Immeasurable tributaries of care—by families, comrades and accomplices, colleagues and collaborators, co-students and co-workers, friends and lovers, across multiple waves of social movements—sustained the creation of this book. The single name printed on its cover is indeed inaccurate: thousands of us composed *New York Liberation School*. The potent cycles of living, relating, and growing together—the ebbs and flows of radical involvement and personal attachments—has made writing this acknowledgments section a sensitive undertaking. While limited space doesn't permit me to thank everyone, I wish to honor many without whom it would have been impossible to realize this dream.

I celebrate my Puerto Rican/Irish/Nigerian family, the original inspiration source: *mi madre revolucionaria* Iris, my sage sister Genevieve, my tenacious brother Ernesto, Joseph, Maroof, Gina, my brilliant and hilarious niblings—Aurora, Mariam, Adeena, Idris, Eliana; *m'athair stócach* Tom, Dawn; *tía* Bruni and *primxs* Fernando y Yanis; *tío* Carlos; aunt Kathy and cousins Robert, Brendan, Declan; first cousin Kathleen; and others.

I celebrate Texas comrades—the tricksters, iconoclasts, abolitionists, anarchists, and socialists who first taught me how to evolve and delight in study and struggle: Anthony, Audrey, Brian, Lynnea, Felix, Chris, Katie, Johanna, Gabe, Lewis, Lauren C, Iris, Owen, Justin I., Alecia, Jones, July, David, Bree, Glenn, Janelle, Meredith, Priya, Marta, Anu, Patrick, Justin S., Jeremy, Karen, Joules, Katie F., Thomas Manfred, Meghann, Hugo, Diego, Skot!, Andi, Lauren R., Ashley, Elizabeth and Sarah H., Mrs. Bohrer, Roni, Margaret, Shantelle, Brian, Sam, Kelly, Lily, Mike, Mark, Jeff, Sarah M., Amarin, Kim S, Nick, Deblina, Cindy, Matt K, Matt B., Derek, Jeff S., Lizzie, BookPeople, Inside Books Project, and others.

I celebrate the last three tumultuous years' life doulas, ride-or-die friends, and soul siblings who cheered and sustained me in limitless profound ways throughout the process of birthing this book: Gavin Arnall, Iemanjá Brown, Johnny Cruz McCullough, Ginger Ging-Dwan Boyd, Taqiyya Haden, Michele Hardesty, Vani Kannan, Tre Kwon, Makeba Lavan, Marianne Madoré, Meliça McIntyre, Lark Omura, Dina Shirin, Wilson Sherwin, AK Thompson, Tanna Tucker, Jason Wozniak, and Layla Zami.

I celebrate my love Jess, without whose vibrant supportive energies this book might not have been completed. It has been a gift to nurture the slow process of co-creating a relationship home with you ever since we first met at a neighborhood eviction defense. Your pedagogical grace, organizing vision of localized militant care, boundless curiosity, nimble pivots between serious and silly, and shared desire to experience and transform our lives together has recomposed what I thought *amor* could be. It's finally time to really celebrate, snuggo!

I celebrate the Herculean efforts and abundant patience of Common Notions in shepherding this book into being while fostering a communist ethos in book publishing: Malav Kanuga for first inviting me to conjure it; Erika Biddle-Stavrakos and Andy Battle for your luminous, line-by-line, invaluable feedback that honed its shape and substance; Josh MacPhee for the radiant cover design; Stella Becerril for the publicity panache, and Graciela "Chela" Vasquez, Alexander Dwinell, Nicki Kattoura, and Aparajita Basu for further production and marketing support. Effusive accolades again to Malav and Erika for your steady accompaniment through the book's final whirlwind of becoming.

I celebrate the families, friends, and archival hearths of these CUNY and New York City figures and movements: Pablo Conrad, Christoph Keller, Jan Heller Levi, Louis Massiah, Walter Naegle, Beth Rollins, Karma Bambara Smith, Brooklyn College Library, City College Cohen Library, CUNY Digital History Archive, CUNY Graduate Center Mina Rees Library, "El Centro" Center for Puerto Rican Studies Library, Freedom Archives, Interference Archive, Lesbian Herstory Archives, Schlesinger Library on the History of Women in America at Radcliffe Institute, Schomburg Center for Research in Black Culture, SLAM! Herstory Project, and Spelman College.

I celebrate the movement elders who were interviewed for this book and its earlier iterations: Sherry Baver, Francee Covington, Albert DeLeon, Samuel R. Delany, Gabriel Haslip-Viera, David Henderson, Iris Lopez, Ira Shor, Paul B. Simms, and Carol Smith.

I celebrate the rowdy *Lost & Found: CUNY Poetics Document Initiative* crews who first collaboratively nourished these CUNY teachers' archives into flight: Ammiel Alcalay, Miriam Atkin, Iemanjá Brown, Stefania Heim, erica kaufman, Makeba Lavan, Kristin Moriah, Talia Shalev, and Wendy Tronrud.

I celebrate the brilliant readers who gave substantial feedback on earlier versions and sections of the book, including my dissertation committee—Ammiel Alcalay, Carmen Kynard, Robyn C. Spencer, and Ira Shor—as well as Gavin Arnall, Brent Hayes Edwards, Michael Gould-Wartofsky, Vani Kannan, Mark McBeth, Robert Reid-Pharr, Tanna Tucker, Jason Wozniak, and Layla Zami. A hearty mention to AK Thompson, whose astute editorial eye strengthened several chapters. Advance praise from movement writers who I revere was a stunning culmination to this project. For your words and work, gratitude to Robin D.G. Kelley, Sarah Schulman, Robyn C. Spencer, Joshua Myers, Matt Brim, Russell Rickford, Amaka Okechukwu, Yuderkys Espinosa-Miñoso, Erica R. Edwards, Eli Meyerhoff, and Johanna Fernández.

I celebrate the vivacious, versatile, courageous, intricate, inventive CUNY students with whom I have had the tremendous honor to co-learn and co-teach for over a decade at Baruch College, Brooklyn College, the Graduate Center, Kingsborough Community College, LaGuardia Community College, and Medgar Evers College. I hope you saw your power and promise in these pages of our legacy.

I celebrate Kensington, Flatbush, Sunset Park, and Crown Heights housemates and comrades, including: Johnny, Diana, Andy, Quentin, Desiree, Andrew, Otis, Devon, Stan, Whitney, Michele, Matt, Morgan, Maya, Layla, Oxana, Iemanjá, Mona, Kaz, Aarushi, Ash, John, Jillian, Josiah, Tuffy, Aria, Fox, Belit, Lauren, Joél, Kate, Nika, Aleks, Jacques, Smaran, Mara, Ostap, Hazel, Obi Wan "Chonkers" Catnobi, Amadi, Marguerite, Rohit, and Zara.

I celebrate the steadfast writing crews who urged me along step-by-step: Spencer Beswick, Vanessa Lynn, Marianne Madoré, Wilson Sherwin, Zohre Soltani, Kimberly Sue, Zoey Thill, and AK Thompson.

I celebrate the healers who lit a path for emergence: Stephen Anen, Amber Eden, Orion Johnstone, Carlos Padrón, Dulcinea Pitagora, Rachel Rampil, Patricia Yoon.

I celebrate the Audre Lorde reading group, including: Nimo Ali, Spencer Garcia, Lorraine Githiora, Joy Gutierrez, Suzanne Herrera Li Puma, Zahra Khalid, Ana

Malagon, Poppie Mphuthing, Sughey Ramírez, Jillian Lane White, and T Wilkins. I celebrate the co-editors of the *Black Feminist Studies in the Americas and the Caribbean* anthology-in-process: Diarenis Calderón Tartabull, Makeba Lavan, A. Tito Mitjans Alayón, Violeta Orozco Barrera, and Layla Zami.

I celebrate Latin American Philosophy of Education Society (LAPES) *compas*, including: Dave Backer, Miguel Angel Blanco Martinez, Veronica Brownstone, Ana Cecilia Galindo Diego, Ariana González Stokas, Ginger Guin, Stephanie Huezo, D. Bret Leraul, David Morales, Aleksandra Perisic, Tomas de Rezende Rocha, Sheeva Sabati, and Jason Wozniak.

I celebrate the publishing platforms that circulated earlier versions of these words: *ASAP/Journal, Berkeley Journal of Sociology, The Indypendent, Lost & Found: The CUNY Poetics Document Initiative, Mask Magazine, New Inquiry, Tidal Magazine, Verso* blog, and *Viewpoint Magazine*.

I celebrate Free University of New York City comrades, including: Andrew Adair, Elizabeth Adams, Susan Naomi Bernstein, Lila Carpenter, Russell Chou, Nara Roberta da Silva, Adelaide Dicken, Rayya El Zein, Mike Friedman, Beatrice Glow, Zoltán Glück, Anna Hillary, Erika Houle, Ken Lin, Manissa Maharawal, Darragh Martin, Thea Martinez, Melissa Marturano, Melica McIntyre, Ada Newman-Plotnick, Christine Nyland, Irene Osorio, Emma Pliskin, Matt Presto, Gregory Samantha Rosenthal, Kiran Samuel, Jessica Santos Lopez, Stina Soderling, Andrew Stark, Fern Thompsett, Matt Tinker, Babak Tofighi, Laura Trager, Brad Young, and Vanessa Zettler.

I celebrate Free CUNY comrades, including: Olivia Asher, Lucien Baskin, Briana Calderón-Navarro, Mel Corning, Moll Daniels, Erik Forman, Sarah Gafur, Petra Gregory, Josip Hugo, Alexandria James, Yasmine Kamel, Vani Kannan, Ericka Labrada, Hailey Lam, Chris LaSasso, Robin Marshall, Chris Mejia, Enrique Peña Oropeza, Yashkumar Shah, Khalil Sulker, Kana Tateishi, Anna Tsomo, Amy Vera, and Meghan Williams.

I celebrate Rank and File Action comrades, including: Mariel Acosta, Sofya Aptekar, Robert Balun, Hyunjeong Renee Bell, Giacomo Bianchino, Karanja Keita Carroll, Stuart Chen-Hayes, Erin Cully, Sami Disu, Ángeles Donoso Macaya, Angela Dunne, Jane Guskin, James Hoff, Zoe Hu, Boyda Johnstone, Jeremey Kane, David Klassen, Carol Lang, Gerry Martini, Corinna Mullin, Chris Natoli, Nicodemis Nicoludis, Nathan Nikolic, Alycia Sellie, Rebecca Smart, Alexander Pau Soria, Pamela Stemberg, Travis Sweatte, Reiko Tahara, Olivia Wood, Tom Watters, and Alex Wolf.

I celebrate City College/Harlem University comrades, including: Raja Abdulhaq, Lindsie Augustin, Carter Barnwell, Nick Bergreen, Susan Besse, Brother Shep, Diana Carolina Sierra, Lyric Croy, Jennifer DeBoer, Gregory Downs, Alberto Duarte, Megan Foster, Meir Gal, Dulce Garcia, William Gibbons, Dave Gonzalez, Maciej Grebowicz, Fadila Habchi, Taqiyya Haden, Rosa Haire, Deon Hamer, JoAnn Hamilton, Michele Hehn, Laura Hinton, Aaron Hess, Ian Kavuma, Yusef Khalil, Sam Kimball, Jake Kornegay, Chet Kozlowski, John Krinsky, Whitney Leeds, Christy Mag Uidhir, Jane Marcus, Sonny Obhan, Alyssia Osorio, Emily Parson, Tiffany Paul, Emma Pinkerton, Jared Rodriguez, Justino Rodriguez, Yarisbel Rodriguez, Jessica Rothenberg, Roberto Rosario, Emmanuel Santos, James Savio, Elizabeth Starcevic, Fidel Tavarez, Keeanga-Yamahtta Taylor, Vanessa Valdés, Michelle Valladares, Sydney Van Nort, Harold Veeser, Luis Villagran, Diane Watford, and Hank Williams.

I celebrate CUNY Graduate Center comrades, including: Reclaim the Commons and the People's Pantry, PublicsLab, the Center for Place, Culture, and Politics (Ruth Wilson Gilmore, David Harvey, Peter Hitchcock, Mary Taylor); the Institute for Research in the African Diaspora in the Americas and the Caribbean (Zee Dempster, Robert Reid-Pharr); *Lost & Found: The CUNY Poetics Document Initiative* at the Center for the Humanities (Ammiel Alcalay, Miriam Atkin, Alisa Besher, Ana Božičević, Iemanjá Brown, William Camponovo, Emily Claman, Iris Cushing, Anne Donlon, Stefania Heim, David Henderson, erica kaufman, Mary Catherine Kinniburgh, Kai Krienke, Makeba Lavan, Stephon Lawrence, Jordan Lorde, Claudia Moreno Parsons, Kate Tarlow Morgan, Kristin Moriah, Megan Paslawski, Alexander Pau Soria, Zohra Saed, Talia Shalev, Mariana Soto, Kendra Sullivan, Sampson Starkweather, Michael Seth Stewart, Öykü Tekten, Wendy Tronrud, and Kyle Waugh); the Graduate Center General Assembly, $7K or Strike, CUNY Adjunct Project, CUNY Struggle, Mariel Acosta, Fikreab Admasu, Hector Agredano, Sara Deniz Akant, Khaled Al Hilli, Andrew Anastasi, Denisse Andrade, Jess Applebaum, Colin Ashley, Hilarie Ashton, Chloe Asselin, Daisy Atterbury, Elvis Bakaitis, Gordon Barnes, Elvira Basevich, Justin Beauchamp, Marimer Berberena, Matthew Bissen, Carwil Bjork-James, Sophie Bjork-James, Matt Block, Natascia Boeri, C. Ray Borck, Sonia Vaz Borges, Marnie Brady, Ari Brostoff, Rachel Brown, Tahir Butt, Claire Cahen, Katherine Carl, Christina Chaise, Elena Chavez Goycochea, Rachel Chapman, Anita Cheng, Martin Cobian, Tatiana Cozzarelli, Juan Cruz Ferre, Erin Cully, Ashley Dawson, Lyn DiIorio, Rashel Dorleans, LeiLani Dowell, Deshonay Dozier, Emily Drabinski, Joanna Dressel, Rayya El Zein, Katie Entigar, Paola Evangelista, Mohammed Ezzeldin, Leanne Fan, Amelia Fortunato, Francisco Fortuño Bernier, Tonya Foster, Rebecca Fullan, Cori Gabbard, Ricardo Gabriel, Margaret Galvan, Nick Gamso, Ally Ganster, Aidah Gil, Bruno Giuliani, Erin Glass, Nick Glastonbury, Liz Goetz, Jesse Goldstein, Seth Graves, Timothy Griffiths, Jamila Hammami, Maya Harakawa, Stacy Hartman, Christina Heatherton, Rasheed Hinds, Joey Hirsh, Mohamad Hodeib, Kristina Huang, Tristan Husby, Pete Ikeler, Stef Jones, Malav Kanuga, Rakhee Kewada, Aurash Khawarzad, Liz Knafo, Wayne Koestenbaum, Brad Krumholz, Eero Laine, Sakina Laksimi, Alexis Larsson, Khan Le, Karen Lepri, Antonia Levy, Rachel Liebert, Shaun Lin, Cihan Tekay Liu, Elliot Liu, Siwin Lo, Linsey Ly, Manissa McCleave Maharawal, Laura Malhotra, Amanda Matles, Simone Martin, Dadland Maye, Mark McBeth, Steve McFarland, Robin McGinty, Tsedale Melaku, Sarah Molinari, Sean Molloy, Sheehan Moore, Sandra Moyano, Britt Munro, Rafael Mutis, Guarav Narasimha, Chris Natoli, Jason Nielsen, Itsue Nakaya Pérez, Sobukwe Odinga, Yasemin Ozer, Maryam Parhizkar, Lindsay Parme, Jeremiah Perez-Torres, Kristofer Petersen-Overton, Janelle Poe, Saira Rafiee, Marlene Nava Ramos, Patricia Cipoletti Rodríguez, Anick Rolland, Daniel Schneider, Christian Seiner, Alycia Sellie, Kate Sheese, Roxanne Shirazi, Ira Shor, Noah Shuster, Elizabeth Sibilia, Nancy Silverman, Hamad Sindhi, Doug Singsen, Marina Sitrin, Shibanee Sivanayagam, Shawn(ta) Smith-Cruz, Fabienne Snowden, David Spataro, Chy Sprauve, Alyson Spurgas, Samuel Stein, Sara Jane Stoner, Tristan Striker, Celina Su, Chris Sula, Jen Tang, Polly Thistlewaite, Joseph Torres-Gonzalez, Anh Tran, Lynne Turner, Erik Wallenberg, Jerry Watts, Barbara Webb, Simone White, Hilary Wilson, and Anna Zeemont.

I celebrate CUNY comrades, including: CUNY for Abolition and Safety and CUNY for Abortion Rights, CUNY for Palestine, Cross-CUNY Working Group

Against Racism and Colonialism, New York Students Rising, Occupy CUNY, Save El Centro for Puerto Rican Studies Campaign, Students for Educational Rights, Students United for a Free CUNY, Brooklyn College (BC) Student Union, BC Africana Studies Department, BC American Studies Program, BC Puerto Rican and Latinx Studies Department, BC Wolfe Institute, Veronica Agard, Ashley Ngozi Agbasoga, Rabia Ahsin Tarar, Tony Alessandrini, Sarah Aly, Matt Arnold, Kazembe Balagun, Adam Bangser, John Bolger, Renate Bridenthal, Matt Brim, Tashawn Brown, Michael Busch, Steve Cerulli, Victoria Chevalier, Samir Chopra, Dan Cione, Kwami Coleman, Lizette Colón, Adriano Contreras, Beth Cooper, Melissa Correa, Kevin Cortez, Todd Craig, Prudence Cumberbatch, Sara Beth Curtis, Jackie DiSalvo, Raura Doreste, Katherine Duckworth, Joseph Entin, Miriam Gabriel, Brenda Greene, Johanna Fernández, Sujatha Fernandes, Ashley Foster, Denise Romero Franco, Emma Francis-Snyder, Jess Freeman, Becca Glaser, Jeremy Glick, Natalie Goncharov, Julian González Beltrez, Savannah Gordon, Julian Guerrero, Natalie Havlin, Owen Hill, Sharmin Hossain, Tiffany Huan, Timothy Hunter, Russell Irwin, Lillian Jiménez, Lawrence "Jahi" Joseph, Rachel Kauder Nalebuff, Rosamond King, Glenn Kissack, Nerdeen Kiswani, Zach LaMalfa, John Lawrence, Shayhan Lewis, Chris Lopez, Derek Ludovici, Linda Luu, Esperanza Martell, Linda Martín Alcoff, Jezra Matthews, Miles McAfee, Hoda Mitwally, Clau O'Brien Moscoso, Tony O'Brien, Amaka Okechukwu, Philip Ording, Rupal Oza, María Perez y González, Rosalind Petchesky, Drew Pham, Caterina Pierre, Karen Pitt, Iva Radivojevic, Sabrina Rahmouk, Heather Ramirez, Anne Rice, Zulai Romero, Jean-Eddy Saint Jean, Julieta Salgado, Virginia Sánchez Korrol, Sarah Schulman, Ramsey Scott, Yael Shafritz, Alexi Shalom, Uruj Sheikh, Saar Shemesh, Arden Sherman, Heather Simon, Carly Smith, Debbie Sonu, Ripley Soprano, Robyn C. Spencer. Heather Squire, Martyna Starosta, Julia Steiner, Chris Stone, Laura Tanenbaum, Shay Thompson, Suzy Subways, Cynthia Tobar, Saadia Toor, Bart Van Steirteghem, Blanca Vasquez, Daniel Vasquez, Phoenix Velasquez, Jocelyn Wills, and James Wilson.

I celebrate comrades in New York City and beyond, including: AgitArte, Centros de Apoyo Mutuo, Debt Collective, Decolonize This Place, Direct Action Front for Palestine, Free University of New York City, Labor for Black Lives, Labor for Palestine, *LÁPIZ* Journal, Mayday Space, Making Worlds, Motivito, Nosotrxs, Observatorio Critico, Occupy Sandy, Occupy Wall Street, Papel Machete, Proyecto Arcoiris, El Rebozo, Rude Mechanical Orchestra, Strike Debt, Strike MoMA, Student Bloc, Tinta Limón, Wendy's Subway, Eman Abdelhadi, Rabab Abdulhadi, Desiree Abu-Odeh, Suzanne Adely, Salomé Aguilera Skvirsky, LoriKim Alexander, Siraj Ali, Genji Amino, Raquel de Anda, Sérgio Andrade, Tsipe Angelson, Aru Apaza, Sofia Arias, Toivo Asheeke, Hagar Aviram, Kristian Davis Bailey, Davarian Baldwin, Cesar Barros Arteaga, Stella Becerril, Adolfo Bejar Lara, Javiera Benavente, Mark Bergfeld, Jeff Berryhill, Tauno Biltsted, Matt Binetti, Rahel Biru, Sy Biswas, Sarah Blust, Leina Bocar, Jez Bold, Gina Bonilla, Dan Boscov-Ellen, Ginger Ging-Dwan Boyd, Mark Bray, Ronald Briggs, Michelle Brotman, Samuel Lang Budin, Harry Burke, Ximena Bustamante, George Caffentzis, Altaira Caldarella, Kalin Callaghan, Kevin Caplicki, Rocio Natasha Cancel, Roosbelinda Cardenas, Daphne Carr, Josh Carrera, Mario Castillo, Chris "Winter" Casuccio, James Cersonsky, Margaret Cerullo, Vanissa Chan, Logan Chappe, Stefan Christoff, Max Cohen, Alicia Coleman, Desiree Colón, Claude Copeland, Rachel Corbman, Shadia and Cheese Luis Crespo, Kique Cubero García, Christina Daniel, Yasmina Dardari, Juan Carlos Dávila Santiago,

Lamis Deek, Lisa DePiano, Elae DeSilva-Johnson, Sam Desire, Nitasha Dhillon, Oscar Diaz, Jorge "Cano" Díaz Ortiz, Isbel Diaz Torres, Paul Dill, Ali Dineen, Sarah Dowd, Susana Draper, Sascha Altman DuBrul, Paulie Anne Duke, Todd Eaton, Basma Eid, Anna Ekros, Tobi Erner, Yuderkys Espinosa Miñoso, Wes Ettinger, Helia Faezipour, Silvia Federici, Isa Figueroa, William Figueroa, Lisa Fithian, Adrián Pío Flores, Anton Ford, Severin Fowles Andrew Francis, Eddie Fukui, Noah Fuller, Paul Funkhouser, Olivia Michiko Gagnon, David Galarza Santa, Sofia Gallisa Muriente, Laleña Garcia, Ezequiel Gatto, Olivia Geiger, Michael George-Strom, Jasmine Gibson, Kyle Goen, Thomas Gokey, Ash Goh Hua, Suzanne Goldenberg, Joey Gonzalez, Mirelis Gonzalez, Silvia Gonzalez, Jerry Goralnick, Andrea Gordillo, Laura Gottesdiener, Michael Gould-Wartofsky, David Graeber, Elia Gran, Maylin Grant, Priscilla Grim, Cristobal Guerra, Alicia Grullón, Austin Guest, Sid Gurung, Rigoberto Lara Guzmán, Akua Gyamerah, Kim Hall, Hajra Hafeez-ur-Rahman, Zyad Hammad, Lani Hanna, Laura Hanna, Crystal Hans, Natasha Hargovan, Tag Harmon, Tom Haviv, Mary Annaise Heglar, Victor Hernandez Cruz, Claudia Heske, Ryan Hickey, Jason Hicks, Andy Hines, Linda Janet Holmes, Marisa Holmes, Colby Hopkins, Abeer Hoque, Jen Hoyer, Sarah Hughes, Amar Husain, Amin Husain, AnouchK Ibacka Valiente, Sanjana "Sunny" Iyer, Aaron Jaffe, Jakob Jakobson, Vida James, Lea Johnson, Monica Johnson, Beck Jordan-Young, Skanda Kadirgamar, Manu Karuka, Jennie Kassanoff, Nozomi Kato, Robin D.G. Kelley, Jina Kim, Ohyoon Kim, Sarah Koshar, Jess Kulikowski, Arun Kundnani, Bassam Kurdali, Stacy Lanyon, Philippe Lapointe, Ann Larson, Arielle Lawson, Vicky Le, Caryn Lederer, Michael Letwin, Rozsa Daniel Lang Levitsky, Thabiti Lewis, Bleue Liverpool, Peter LoRe, Amanda Lotspike, Susana and Sebastian Loza, Kara Lynch, Ben Mabie, Rebecca Manski, Jenny Marion, Yotam Marom, Jose Martín, Elena Martinez, Alicia Martinson, Nomaduma Masilela, Liz Mason-Deese, Natalie Matos, Natalie McClellan, Erik McGregor, Yates McKee, Andrew Meeker, Nina Mehta, Aisha Mershani, Eli Meyerhoff, Ben Meyers, Crystal Migwans, Mamie Minch, Debra Minkoff, Magally Miranda Alcázar, Nick Mirzoeff, Eve Mitchell, Salar Mohandesi, Nastaran Mohit, Manijeh Moradian, Hanakyle Moranz, Luis Moreno-Caballud, Luigi Morris, Blair Mosner, Adam Mumford, Agustin Muñoz Ríos, Rob Murray, Indra Murti, Namanda Musoke, Lenina Nadal, Premilla Nadasen, Eli Nadeau, Eva Nidzeeva, Vaimoana Litia Makakaufaki Niumeitolu, Celia Naylor, Frances Negrón-Muntaner, Lauren No Land, Ana Nogueira, Sandra Nurse, Keegan O'Brien, Michelle O'Brien, Clare O'Connor, Anika Paris, Lucy Parks, Leigh Patel, Lily Paulina, Luke Peace Poet, Jeffrey Perry, Khury Petersen-Smith, Matt Peterson, Nick Pinto, Sandy Placido, Jive Poetic, Jackson Polys, Lana Povitz, Sarah Quinter, Graciela Razo, Sarah Raymundo, Jessie Reilly, Messiah Rhodes, Patrick Robbins, Giovanni Roberto, Amy Roberts, Rob Robinson, Andrés Rodríguez, Pati Rodriguez, Shellyne Rodriguez, Sugeily Rodriguez Lebrón, Deyanira Rojas-Sosa, Jimmy Roque Martinez, Raquel Rosario, Jordy Rosenberg, Andrew Ross, Sary Rottenberg, Aiko Roudette, Vicente Rubio, Peter Rugh, Ra Ruiz, Sahar Sadjadi, Marz Saffore, Radhika Sainath, Begonia Santa-Cecilia, Cinthya Santos Briones, Carol Schaeffer, Erin Schell, Stuart Schrader, Chris Schroth, Red Schulte, Sarah Seidman, Antonio Serna, Lucas Shapiro, Lindsey Shilleh, Maya Shoukri, Wally Showman, Etienne Simard, Stacy Skolnik, Fateh Slavitskaya, Holly Smith, "Pirate" Jenny Smith, Victoria Sobel, Zak Solomon, Daniel Solon, Nelini Stamp, Jean Stevens, Zelene Pineda Suchilt, Elise Swain, John Tarleton, Todd Tavares, Astra Taylor, Charles Theonia, Chris Tinson, Christy

Thornton, Steven Thrasher, Katy Tosh, Wilson Valentin, Rachel Valinsky, Carina del Valle Schorske, Madison Van Oort, Lissa Vanderbeck, Gina Velasco, Jimena Vergara, Mitchell Verter, Jaime Veve, Geo Vidiella, Yves Voltaire, Mette Loulou Von Kohl, Neha Vora, Jamara Wakefield, Devin Brahja Waldman, Bronte Walker, Kassandra Ware, Kirsten Weisbeck, Marina Weiss, Bryan Welton, Amy Weng, Kimberly White, Sophia Williams, Michelle Woods, Anastasia Usinowicz, Tracy Yoder, Quito Ziegler, and Or Zublasky.

I express gratitude for the financial support I received along the way from the American Council of Learned Societies, Davis-Putter Scholarship, Institute for Citizens Scholars; Mellon Mays Undergraduate Fellowship; Schlesinger Library on the History of Women in America; Schomburg Center for Research in Black Culture; Social Science Research Council; CUNY Graduate Center (GC) Advanced Research Collaborative; GC Center for the Humanities; GC Center for Latin American, Caribbean, and Latino Studies; GC Dean K. Harrison Fellowship; GC Doctoral Student Research Grant; and GC *Lost & Found: The CUNY Poetics Document Initiative*. I hope this book makes use of these resources to help activate our movements to ultimately overturn all systems of exclusivity and deprivation. Everything for everyone!

WORKS INCITED

Abolish the University? Abolitionist University Studies, 2023. Available at https://drive.google.com/file/d/17d-_Wx-B9rhunCu_4q36YEmApbP_AOZP/view.

Ackerman, Tom. "The South Campus Seizure." *The City College Alumnus* 65, no. 1 (October 1969): 3–32.

Acuña, Rodolfo. *The Making of Chicana/o Studies: In the Trenches of Academe.* New Brunswick: Rutgers University Press, 2011.

"After the Fall: Communiqués from Occupied California." Pamphlet series. Occupy California, 2009–2010. Available at http://libcom.org/library/after-fall-communiques-occupied-california/.

Ahmad, Aijaz. *In Theory: Nations, Classes, Literatures.* New York: Verso, 1992.

Ahmad, Muhammad. *We Will Return in the Whirlwind: Black Radical Organizations 1960–1975.* Chicago: Charles H. Kerr Publishing Company, 2007.

Ahmad, Shomial. "Queens College and Civil Rights: Alumni Reflect on Activism 50 Years Ago." *Clarion,* May 2014. https://psc-cuny.org/clarion/2014/may/queens-college-and-civil-rights-alumni-reflect-activism-50-years-ago/.

Ahmed, Sara. *Living a Feminist Life.* Durham: Duke University Press, 2017.

Alcalay, Ammiel. *a little history.* Los Angeles and New York: UpSet Press, 2012.

———. *After Jews and Arabs: Remaking Levantine Culture.* Minneapolis: University of Minnesota Press, 1993.

Alessandrini, Anthony. "Our University: On Police Violence at CUNY." *Jadaliyya,* November 27, 2011. https://www.jadaliyya.com/Details/24707/Our-University-On-Police-Violence-at-CUNY/.

———, Zahra Ali, Kylie Broderick, Juan Doe, Nadim El Kak, Rhea Rahman, and Ghiwa Sayegh. "Roundtable: Protest and Social Mobilization in the Time of COVID-19." *Jadaliyya,* August 20, 2020. https://www.jadaliyya.com/Details/41574/Roundtable-Protest-and-Social-Mobilization-in-the-Time-of-COVID-19/.

Alexander, Meena, Michelle Fine, and Nicholas Freudenberg. "To Reduce Inequality, Reinvest in CUNY." *Crain's New York Business,* February 25, 2016. https://www.crainsnewyork.com/article/20160226/OPINION/160229916/to-reduce-inequality-reinvest-in-cuny/.

Ali, Rozina. "Poet Laureate of Nowhere: Solmaz Sharif Goes Through Customs." *Lux Magazine* 4 (April 2022). https://lux-magazine.com/article/solmaz-sharif-customs/.

Allen, Theodore W. *The Invention of the White Race.* New York: Verso, 1997.

Alston, Ashanti. "Black Anarchism." Transcript of public talk given at Hunter College, New York City, October 24, 2013. https://archive.org/details/BlackAnarchismAshantiAlston/.

Althusser, Louis. "Ideology and Ideological State Apparatuses (Notes Towards an Investigation)." *Lenin and Philosophy and Other Essays.* New York: Monthly Review Press, 1971.

Anastasi, Andrew, ed. *The Weapon of Organization: Mario Tronti's Political Revolution in Marxism.* Brooklyn: Common Notions, 2020.

Anderson, William C. *The Nation on No Map: Black Anarchism and Abolition.* Chico: AK Press, 2021.

Anonymous. Personal correspondence with the author. March 29, 2018.

Antler, Joyce. *Jewish Radical Feminism: Voices from the Women's Liberation Movement.* New York: New York University Press, 2018.

Anyon, Jean. *Radical Possibilities: Public Policy, Urban Education, and a New Social Movement.* Oxfordshire: Routledge, 2005.

Aptekar, Sofya. *Green Card Soldier: Between Model Immigrant and Security Threat.* Cambridge: MIT Press, 2023.

Aquino Bermudez, Federico. "Proposal for Department of Puerto Rican Studies, 1971–76." The City University of New York, City College, Archives and Special Collections, Department of Puerto Rican Studies Papers, Box 1.

———. "Growth and Development of Puerto Rican Studies Departments: A Case Study of Two Departments at the City University of New York." PhD diss., University of Massachusetts Amherst, 1974.

Arce, Henry. "Oral History Interview with Henry Arce." Interview by Douglas Medina. February 26, 2014. CUNY Digital History Archive. https://cdha.cuny.edu/items/show/6842/.

Arenson, Karen W. "Trustees Anoint CUNY Chief with a Pledge Not to Meddle." *New York Times,* July 23, 1999. https://www.nytimes.com/1999/07/23/nyregion/trustees-anoint-cuny-chief-with-a-pledge-not-to-meddle.html/.

Arnall, Gavin. "The Many Tasks of the Marxist Translator: Approaching Marxism as/in/with Translation from Antonio Gramsci to the Zapatistas." *Historical Materialism* 30, no. 1 (February 2022): 99–132.

———. *Subterranean Fanon: An Underground Theory of Radical Change.* New York: Columbia University Press, 2020.

Autonomous Students at the CUNY Graduate Center. "Five Theses on the Student Strike." *Tidal* 2 (March 2012). Archived at https://docs.google.com/file/d/0B8k8g5Bb3BxdMko3Y1NkdUVRd0t-nUFdpUmpWckJ2dw/edit?resourcekey=0-GtG3pfvlwIvmprXoaSpfSQ/.

Awartani, Sara. "In Solidarity: *Palestine* in the Puerto Rican Political Imaginary." *Radical History Review* 128 (2017): 199–222.

Ayala, César J., and Rafael Bernabe. *Puerto Rico in the American Century: A History Since 1898.* Chapel Hill: University of North Carolina Press, 2007.

Backer, David I., Matthew Bissen, Christopher "Winter" Casuccio, Jacques Laroche, Zane D.R. Mackin, Joe North, Aleksandra Perisic, Chelsea Szendi Schieder, and Jason Wozniak. "What is Horizontal Pedagogy? A Discussion on Dandelions." In *Out of the Ruins: The Emergence of Radical Informal Learning Spaces,* edited by Robert H. Haworth and John M. Elmore, 195–222. Oakland: PM Press, 2017.

Bailey, Kristian Davis. "Dream Defenders, Black Lives Matter & Ferguson Reps Take Historic Trip to Palestine." *Ebony Magazine,* January 9, 2015. https://www.ebony.com/news/dream-defenders-black-lives-matter-ferguson-reps-take-historic-trip-to-palestine/#ixzz3ORwS2gdM/.

Baker, Mike, Nicholas Bogel-Burroughs, and Ilana Marcus. "Thousands of Teens Are Being Pushed into Military's Junior R.O.T.C." *New York Times,* December 11, 2022. https://www.nytimes.com/2022/12/11/us/jrotc-schools-mandatory-automatic-enrollment.html/.

Balagun, Kazembe. "The Role of Intellectuals: A brief history of my intellectual development." Instagram, April 28, 2021. https://www.instagram.com/tv/COO5CZ2DAhQ/.

Bald, Vivek. *Bengali Harlem and the Lost Histories of South Asian America.* Cambridge: Harvard University Press, 2015.

Baldwin, James. "Everybody's Protest Novel." In *Notes of a Native Son,* 13–23. Boston: Beacon Press, 1955.

———. *The Fire Next Time.* New York: Dial Press, 1963.

Bambara, Toni Cade. "Dear Bloods." Buell G. Gallagher Papers, The City University of New York, City College, Archives and Special Collections.

———. *Deep Sightings and Rescue Missions: Fiction, Essays, and Conversations.* New York: Knopf, 1999.

———. "An Interview with Toni Cade Bambara." In *Conversations with Toni Cade Bambara,* edited by Thabiti Lewis, 35–47. Jackson: University Press of Mississippi, 2012.

———. Letter to Audre Lorde. 1971. Part 1, Box 1, Toni Cade Bambara Papers, Spelman College Archives, Atlanta, GA.

———. "The Manipulators." *Liberator* (August 1968). Manuscripts, Archives and Rare Books Division, Schomburg Center for Research in Black Culture, The New York Public Library.

———. "Realizing the Dream of a Black University." *Observation Post* Collection, The City University of New York, City College, Archives and Special Collections.

———. *Toni Cade Bambara: "Realizing the Dream of a Black University" & Other Writings (Parts I & II).* In *Lost & Found: The CUNY Poetics Document Initiative, Series 7,* edited by Makeba Lavan and Conor Tomás Reed. The Center for the Humanities, Graduate Center of the City University of New York, 2017.

———. *The Black Woman: An Anthology.* New York: New American Library, 1970.

———. "Puerto Ricans (Spoken version)." Part 1, Box 3, Toni Cade Bambara Papers, Spelman College Archives, Atlanta, GA.

———. "Summer 1968 SEEK Report." Series IV, Carton 9, Folder 385. Adrienne Rich Papers, 1927–1999. Schlesinger Library on the History of Women in America, Radcliffe Institute, Cambridge, MA.

———. "Working At It in Five Parts." Part 1, Box 4, Toni Cade Bambara Papers, Spelman College Archives, Atlanta, GA.

Barger, Keith D. "Hearing the Cry of the Poor: The Catholic Worker Communities in Oregon and Washington 1940 to the Present." Master's Thesis, University of Portland, 1992.

Barnett, Philip, Judy Connorton, William Gibbons, and Sydney Van Nort, eds. "The Five Demands: The Student Protest and Takeover of 1969," n.d. CUNY Academic Commons. https://fivedemands.commons.gc.cuny.edu/.

Baskin, Lucien. "'We Must Learn What We Need to Survive': Making Abolitionist Presence at the City University of New York." *Society and Space,* October 31, 2022. https://www.societyandspace.org/articles/we-must-learn-what-we-need-to-survive-making-abolitionist-presence-at-the-city-university-of-new-york/

Basso, Keith H. *Wisdom Sits in Places: Landscape and Language Among the Western Apache.* Albuquerque: University of New Mexico Press, 1996.

Baver, Sherrie. Interview with the author. September 21, 2019.

Baxandall, Rosalyn. "Re-Visioning the Women's Liberation Movement's Narrative: Early Second Wave African American Feminists." *Feminist Studies* 27, no. 1 (2001): 225–245.

Bensaïd, Daniel. "'Leaps, Leaps, Leaps': Lenin and Politics." In *Lenin Reloaded: Toward a Politics of Truth,* edited by Sebastian Budgen, Stathis Kouvelakis, and Slavoj Zizek, 148–163. Durham: Duke University Press, 2007.

Bergman, Carla, and Nick Montgomery. *Joyful Militancy: Building Thriving Resistance in Toxic Times*. Chico: AK Press, 2017.

Bergman, Lincoln, Gail Dolgin, Robert Gabriner, Maisie McAdoo, and Jonah Raskin. *Puerto Rico: The Flame of Resistance*. San Francisco: Peoples Press, 1977.

Bernard, Emily. "Audre Lorde Broke the Silence." *The New Republic*, March 25, 2021. https://newrepublic.com/article/161595/audre-lorde-warrior-poet-cancer-journals/.

Berrigan, Philip, and Elizabeth McAlister. *The Time's Discipline: The Beatitudes and Nuclear Resistance*. Eugene: Wipf and Stock Publishers, 1989.

Beswick, Spencer. "Living Communism: Theory & Practice of Autonomy & Attack." *Perspectives on Anarchist Theory*, July 29, 2022. https://anarchiststudies.org/living-communism-spencer-beswick/.

Biondi, Martha. *The Black Revolution on Campus*. Berkeley: University of California Press, 2012.

Bishara, Hakim, and Valentina Di Liscia. "NYC High School and College Students Demand 'Cops Out!' of Schools." *Hyperallergic*, January 30, 2020. https://hyperallergic.com/540230/nyc-high-school-and-college-students-demand-cops-out-of-schools/.

Biss, Eula. "Of Institution Born." In Adrienne Rich, *Of Woman Born: Motherhood as Experience and Institution*, xi–xx. New York: W.W. Norton, [1976] 2021.

Black and Puerto Rican Student Community. "Five Demands." CUNY Digital History Archive. May 1969. https://cdha.cuny.edu/items/show/6952/.

Blanc, Eric. *Red State Revolt: The Teachers' Strike Wave and Working-Class Politics*. New York: Verso, 2019.

Boggs, Abigail, Eli Meyerhoff, Nick Mitchell, and Zach Schwartz-Weinstein. "Abolitionist University Studies: An Invitation." *Abolition Journal*, August 28, 2019. https://abolitionjournal.org/abolitionist-university-studies-an-invitation/.

Boggs, James and Grace Lee. "The City Is the Black Man's Land." *Monthly Review* (April 1966). https://doi.org/10.14452/MR-017-11-1966-04_4.

Bonilla, Yarimar. *Non-Sovereign Futures: French Caribbean Politics in the Wake of Disenchantment*. Chicago: University of Chicago Press, 2015.

———. "Postdisaster Futures: Hopeful Pessimism, Imperial Ruination, and La futura cuir." *Small Axe* 62 (July 2020): 147–162.

Bonus, Rick. *The Ocean in the School: Pacific Islander Students Transforming Their University*. Durham: Duke University Press, 2020.

Bookchin, Natalie, Pamela Brown, Suzahn Ebrahimian, Colectivo Enmedio, Alexandra Juhasz, Leónidas Martin, MTL, Nicholas Mirzoeff, Andrew Ross, A. Joan Saab, and Marina Sitrin. *Militant Research Handbook*. New York: New York University, 2013.

Bottici, Chiara. *Anarchafeminism*. New York: Bloomsbury, 2022.

Bowen, Angela. "Diving into Audre Lorde's 'Blackstudies.'" *Meridians: Feminism, Race, Transnationalism* 4.1 (2003): 109–129.

Boyle, Kay. *The Long Walk at San Francisco State and Other Essays*. New York: Grove, 1970.

Brachfeld, Ben. "Faculty Union Sues CUNY, Demands Injunction to Rehire Laid-Off Adjuncts." *Gothamist*, July 3, 2020. https://gothamist.com/news/faculty-union-sues-cuny-demands-injunction-rehire-laid-adjuncts/.

Brand, Dionne. *A Map to the Door of No Return: Notes to Belonging*. Toronto: Doubleday Canada, 2001.

Branson, Scott, Raven Hudson, and Bry Reed, eds. *Surviving the Future: Abolitionist Queer Strategies*. Oakland: PM Press, 2022.

Brathwaite, Shirley. "Views in Depth." *Tech News*, April 6, 1970.

Bridenthal, Renate. "Oral History Interview with Renate Bridenthal." April 21, 2016. CUNY Digital History Archive. https://cdha.cuny.edu/items/show/3112/.

Brier, Steve, and Michelle Fine. "If Cuomo Is a Progressive He Should Invest in CUNY's Future." *City and State New York*, December 10, 2015. www.cityandstateny.com/articles/opinion/if-cuomo-is-a-progressive-he-should-invest-in-cunys-future.html/.

Brim, Matt. *Poor Queer Studies: Confronting Elitism in the University*. Durham: Duke University Press, 2020.

Brodkin, Karen. *How Jews Became White Folks: And What That Says about Race in America*. New Brunswick: Rutgers University Press, 2010.

Brossart, Alain, and Sylvie Klingberg. *Revolutionary Yiddishland: A History of Jewish Radicalism*. New York: Verso, 2016.

brown, adrienne marie. *Pleasure Activism: The Politics of Feeling Good*. Chico: AK Press, 2019.

Brown, Jenny. *Birth Strike: The Hidden Fight over Women's Work*. Oakland: PM Press, 2019.

Brown, Owen. "Rudy Crew must resign: A Medgar Evers professor says he has failed to meet the moment." *New York Daily News*, August 9, 2020. https://www.nydailynews.com/opinion/ny-oped-rudy-crew-must-resign-20200809-54a3igbljjgq5csadiizxpp57q-story.html/.

Browning, Kellen, and Brian X. Chen. "In Fight Against Violence, Asian and Black Activists Struggle to Agree." *New York Times*, December 19, 2021. https://www.nytimes.com/2021/12/19/us/black-asian-activists-policing-disagreement.html/.

Buchanan, Larry, Quoctrung Bui, and Jugal K. Patel. "Black Lives Matter May Be the Largest Movement in U.S. History." *New York Times*, July 3, 2020. https://www.nytimes.com/interactive/2020/07/03/us/george-floyd-protests-crowd-size.html/.

Buttett, Neil Philip. "Crossing the Line: High School Student Activism, the New York High School Student Union, and the 1968 Ocean Hill-Brownsville Teachers' Strike." *Journal of Urban History* 45, no. 6 (November 2019): 1212–1236.

Burgos, Joaly, Jane Guskin, Hailey Lam, Marianne Madoré, Andréa Stella, and Anna Zeemont. "Resisting Surveillance, Practicing/Imagining the End of Grading." *The Journal of Interactive Technology and Pedagogy*, December 10, 2021. https://jitp.commons.gc.cuny.edu/resisting-surveillance-practicing-imagining-the-end-of-grading/.

Burns, Rebecca. "How Chicago Teachers are Taking on Wall Street." *The Intercept*, October 25, 2019. https://theintercept.com/2019/10/25/chicago-teachers-strike-wall-street/.

Burrough, Bryan. *Days of Rage: America's Radical Underground, the FBI, and the Forgotten Age of Revolutionary Violence*. New York: Penguin Press, 2015.

Butt, Tahir H. "Free Tuition and Expansion in New York Public Higher Education." *Theory, Research, and Action in Urban Education* 3, no. 1 (Fall 2014). https://traue.commons.gc.cuny.edu/volume-iii-issue-1-fall-2014/free-tuition-expansion-new-york-public-higher-education/.

———. "'You Are Running a de Facto Segregated University': Racial Segregation and the City University of New York." In *The Strange Careers of the Jim Crow North: Segregation and Struggle Outside of the South*, edited by Brian Purnell, Jeanne Theoharis, and Komozi Woodard, 187–209. New York: New York University Press, 2019.

Byrne, Justin. "From Brooklyn to Belchite: New Yorkers in the Abraham Lincoln Brigade." In *Facing Fascism: New York and the Spanish Civil War*, edited by Peter N. Carroll and James D. Fernandez, 70–83. New York: New York University Press, 2007.

Cabán, Pedro. "Remaking Puerto Rican Studies at 50 Years." In *Puerto Rican Studies at the City University of New York: The First Fifty Years*, edited by María Pérez y González and Virginia Sánchez Korrol, 16–42. New York: El Centro Press, 2021.

Caffentzis, George, Monty Neill, and John Willshire-Carrera. *Wages for Students*. Edited by Jakob Jakobsen, María Berríos, and Malav Kanuga. Brooklyn: Common Notions, 2016.

Calderón Tartabull, Diarenis, AnouchK Ibacka Valiente, A. Tito Mitjans Alayón, and Conor Tomás Reed. "Audre Lorde Now." *Distributaries*, July 16, 2020. https://www.centerforthehumanities.org/news/audre-lorde-now/.

Campanile, Carl. "CCNY Bashes America—Students, Profs Blame Attacks on U.S." *New York Post*, October 3, 2001. https://nypost.com/2001/10/03/ccny-bashes-america-students-profs-blame-attacks-on-u-s/.

Camponovo, William J. "'An Instrument in the Shape / of a Woman': Reading as Re-Vision in Adrienne Rich." PhD diss., CUNY Graduate Center, 2020.

The Campus. "Ethnic Error." April 16, 1971.

———. "Ethnic Studies Courses." September 3, 1971.

Cannato, Vincent. *The Ungovernable City: John Lindsay and His Struggle to Save New York*. New York: Basic Books, 2002.

Can't Touch This: NYC Anti-Repression Committee. "5 Principles for the Anti-Police Brutality Movement," n.d. https://canttouchthisnyc.wordpress.com/5-principles-for-the-anti-police-brutality-movement/.

Capetillo, Luisa. *A Nation of Women: An Early Feminist Speaks Out*. Edited by Félix V. Matos-Rodríguez. New York: Penguin Classics, 2021.

Carrie, Shawn, Isabelle Nastasia, and StudentNation. "CUNY Dismantles Community Center, Students Fight Back." *The Nation*, October 25, 2013. http://www.thenation.com/blog/176832/cuny-dismantles-community-center-students-fight-back/.

Carroll, Peter N., and James D. Fernandez, eds. *Facing Fascism: New York and the Spanish Civil War*. New York: New York University Press, 2007.

Carson, Clayborne. *In Struggle: SNCC and the Black Awakening of the 1960s*. Cambridge: Harvard University Press, 1981.

"CCNY Shut Down." Special report from *Observation Post*. *Liberation News Service* 157 (April 24, 1969): 3–4. Available at https://archive.org/stream/lns-157/LNS-157_djvu.txt/.

Center for Constitutional Rights. "Brooklyn College Students Cleared at Controversial Disciplinary Hearing." *Common Dreams*, May 31, 2016. www.commondreams.org/newswire/2016/05/31/brooklyn-college-students-cleared-controversial-disciplinary-hearing/.

Center for the Humanities. "Stories of Struggle: Histories of Childcare Activism at CUNY." Seminar, Center for the Humanities, City University of New York Graduate Center, New York, March 4, 2015. https://www.centerforthehumanities.org/programming/stories-of-struggle-histories-of-childcare-activism-at-cuny/.

Center for Puerto Rican Studies-Centro. "Afternoon Tertulia: Puerto Rican Studies in CUNY 50 Years." Conversation with Virginia Sanchez-Korrol, and María E. Pérez y Gonzalez, Conor Tomás Reed, and Edna Acosta-Belén, moderated by Ricardo Gabriel. YouTube, April 7, 2022. https://youtu.be/tbD3YjnbcjE.

Césaire, Aimé. *Discourse on Colonialism*. Translated by Joan Pinkham. New York: Monthly Review Press, 1972.

Chapman, Ben. "Thousands of CUNY Students Experience Homelessness and Food Insecurity, Report Says." *New York Daily News*, March 26, 2019. https://www.nydailynews.com/new-york/education/ny-cuny-students-experience-homelessness-food-insecurity-20190327-qkilgsntmvbcvgqysz2lni-4y7m-story.html/.

Chatlosh, Kelsey. "CUNY, Public Colleges Face Mass Budget Cuts Under the Shock of COVID-19." *Teen Vogue*, September 8, 2020. https://www.teenvogue.com/story/cuny-budget-cuts/.

Chatterjee, Piya, and Sunaina Maira, eds. *The Imperial University: Academic Repression and Scholarly Dissent*. Minneapolis: University of Minnesota Press, 2014.

Chavez, Karma. *Queer Migration Politics: Activist Rhetoric and Coalitional Possibilities*. Urbana: University of Illinois Press, 2013.

City College of New York, Cohen Library Digital Archives. "Women at City College: A Fifty-Year Anniversary Exhibit." http://digital-archives.ccny.cuny.edu/exhibits/fiftyexhibit/.

City University of New York. "Andrew Mellon Foundation Gifts CUNY $10 Million to Drive Change and Expand a Range of Initiatives Related to Pandemic and Racial Justice," August 13, 2020. https://www1.cuny.edu/mu/forum/2020/08/13/andrew-mellon-foundation-gifts-cuny-10-million-to-drive-change-and-expand-a-range-of-initiatives-related-to-pandemic-and-racial-justice/.

———. "Interactive Student Data Book," n.d. https://insights.cuny.edu/t/CUNYGuest/views/Student-DataBook/Enrollment./

City University of New York, Board of Higher Education Minutes. 1971. http://policy.cuny.edu/minutes/.

Clarion. "A chance to stop and think." October 2001. https://archive.psc-cuny.org/PDF/OctClarion.pdf/.

Clark, Burton R. "The 'Cooling Out' Function in Higher Education." *American Journal of Sociology* 65, no. 6 (1960): 569–576.

Clifton, Lucille. *Generations: A Memoir*. New York: New York Review Books, 2021.

Cobb, Jr., Charles E. *This Nonviolent Stuff'll Get You Killed: How Guns Made the Civil Rights Movement Possible*. New York: Basic Books, 2014.

Cohen, Robert. *When the Old Left Was Young: Student Radicals and America's First Mass Student Movement, 1929–1941*. New York: Oxford University Press, 1993.

Cohn, Candace. "Privilege and the working class." *Socialist Worker*, April 15, 2015. https://socialistworker.org/2015/04/15/privilege-and-the-working-class/.

Colectivo Situaciones. *19 & 20: Notes for a New Insurrection*. Brooklyn: Common Notions, 2021.

Colón López, Gisely, Tami Gold, and Pam Sporn, dirs. *Making the Impossible Possible*. 2021; New York: Third World Newsreel.

Combahee River Collective, "Combahee River Collective Statement." In *How We Get Free: Black Feminism and the Combahee River Collective*, edited by Keeanga-Yamahtta Taylor, 15–27. Chicago: Haymarket Books, 2017.

Conrad, Pablo. Email communication with the author. May 22, 2022.

Cook, Blanche Wiesen. "The Lesbian Movement with Blanche Wiesen Cook." Interview by Alice Kessler-Harris. YouTube, April 3, 2017. https://www.youtube.com/watch?v=ew00Ic4JwiA/.

Cornell, Andrew. *Unruly Equality: US Anarchism in the Twentieth Century*. Berkeley: University of California Press, 2016.

Covington, Francee. "Are the Revolutionary Techniques Employed in *The Battle of Algiers* Applicable to Harlem?" In *The Black Woman: An Anthology*, edited by Toni Cade Bambara, 313–321. New York: New American Library, 1970.

———. "Francee Covington: An Oral History of the CCNY 1960s SEEK Program and *The Paper*." Interview by Sean Molloy. June 5, 2015. CUNY Digital History Archive. https://cdha.cuny.edu/items/show/7102.

———. Interview with the author. May 22, 2021.

Cowen, Deborah. "Infrastructures of Empire and Resistance." *Verso* (blog), January 25, 2017. https://www.versobooks.com/blogs/3067-infrastructures-of-empire-and-resistance/.

Cowie, Jefferson. "The 'Hard Hat Riot' Was a Preview of Today's Political Divisions." *New York Times*, May 11, 2020. https://www.nytimes.com/2020/05/11/nyregion/hard-hat-riot.html/.

Cruz Crespo, Cacimar. *Solidaridad Obrero-Estudiantil: las huelgas de 1973 y 1976 en la Universidad de Puerto Rico.* San Juan: Fundación Francisco Manrique Cabrera, 2014.

CUNY Digital History Archive. "1970-77 Open Admissions – Fiscal Crisis – State Takeover." https://dha.cuny.edu/coverage/coverage/show/id/33/.

———. "1978-1992: Retrenchment – Austerity – Tuition." https://cdha.cuny.edu/coverage/coverage/show/id/43/.

———. "CUNY Adjunct Labor." https://cdha.cuny.edu/collections/show/292/.

———. *Faculty Action.* May 1976. CUNY Digital History Archive. https://cdha.cuny.edu/items/show/1711/.

———. "The Founding of Medgar Evers College." https://cdha.cuny.edu/collections/show/111/.

———. "MEC for MEC, Albany, 1976." https://cdha.cuny.edu/items/show/3122/.

———. "Occupy CUNY." Edited by Conor Tómas Reed. October 12, 2017. https://cdha.cuny.edu/collections/show/222/.

———. "Save Hostos!" https://cdha.cuny.edu/collections/show/172/.

CUNY Struggle. *CUNY at the Crossroads: a history of the mess we're in and how to get out of it.* Fall 2016. https://cunystruggle.org/cuny-at-the-crossroads/.

Cushing, Iris. *The First Books of David Henderson and Mary Korte: A Research.* New York: Ugly Duckling Presse, 2020.

Dalla Costa, Mariarosa, and Selma James. *The Power of Women and the Subversion of Community.* Bristol: Falling Wall Press, 1975.

Daniels, Tracy, Greta Schiller, and Andrea Weiss, dirs. *The Five Demands.* 2023; New York: Jezebel Productions.

Daulatzi, Sohail. *Fifty Years of* The Battle of Algiers: *Past as Prologue.* Minneapolis: University of Minnesota Press, 2016.

Davidson, Cathy. *The New Education: How to Revolutionize the University to Prepare Students for a World in Flux.* New York: Basic Books, 2017.

Dávila Santiago, Juan Carlos, dir. *Simulacros de liberación [Drills of Liberation].* 2021; Aguada, Puerto Rico: República 21 Media.

Davis, Angela Y. *Women, Race & Class.* New York: Vintage Books, 1981.

Davis, Charles. "Representing the 'Architextural' Musings of June Jordan." *Race and Architecture*, November 26, 2013. https://raceandarchitecture.wordpress.com/2013/11/26/writing-and-building-black-utopianism-representing-the-architextural-musings-of-june-jordans-his-own-where-1971/.

Davis, Julie L. *Survival Schools: The American Indian Movement and Community Education in the Twin Cities.* Minneapolis: University of Minnesota Press, 2013.

Davis, Thulani. *The Emancipation Circuit: Black Activism Forging a Culture of Freedom.* Durham: Duke University Press, 2022.

De Veaux, Alexis. *Warrior Poet: A Biography of Audre Lorde.* New York: W.W. Norton, 2004.

Dean, Michelle. "Adrienne Rich's Feminist Awakening." *The New Republic*, April 3, 2016. https://newrepublic.com/article/132117/adrienne-richs-feminist-awakening/.

Delany, Samuel R. *Babel-17.* New York: Ace Books, 1966.

———. Email communication with the author. April 4, 2018.

———. *In Search of Silence: The Journals of Samuel R. Delany, Volume I, 1957–1969.* Middletown: Wesleyan University Press, 2017.

———. "Midcentury." In *The Jewel-Hinged Jaw: Notes on the Language of Science Fiction*, 187–226. Elizabethtown: Dragon Press, 1977.

———. *The Motion of Light in Water: Sex and Science Fiction Writing in the East Village.* New York: Arbor House/W. Morrow, 1988.

———. "Two Dogs Near Death." *The Promethean* (January 1965). *The Promethean* Collection, The City University of New York, City College, Archives and Special Collections.

DeLeon, Albert. Interview with the author. May 7, 2021.

Democracy Now! "Campus Resistance: Students Stage Counter-Recruitment Protests Across the Country." Host Amy Goodman in conversation with City College protestors/arrestees Chris Duga, Hadas Their, and Carol Lang. *Democracy Now!*, March 18, 2005. https://www.democracynow.org/2005/3/18/campus_resistance_students_stage_counter_recruitment/.

———. "Debate: Is Cuomo's Crackdown on BDS Unconstitutional McCarthyism or a Stand Against Anti-Semitism?" June 9, 2016. www.democracynow.org/2016/6/9/debate_is_cuomos_crackdown_on_bds/.

———. "Secret Surveillance of Students." June 4, 1998. https://www.democracynow.org/1998/6/4/

secret_surveillance_of_students/.

Denis, Nelson A. *War Against All Puerto Ricans: Revolution and Terror in America's Colony.* New York: Bold Type Books, 2015.

Dent, Tom. "Umbra Days." *Black American Literature Forum* 14, no. 3 (Autumn 1980): 107–108.

Desai, Jigna, and Kevin P. Murphy. "Subjunctively Inhabiting the University." *Critical Ethnic Studies* 4, no. 1 (Spring 2018): 21–43.

di Prima, Diane. *Recollections of My Life as a Woman.* New York: Viking Press, 2001.

———. "Revolutionary Letter #3," "Revolutionary Letter #8." In *Revolutionary Letters*, 9–10, 17. San Francisco: City Lights, 1971.

Díaz Ortíz, Jorge. "Organizing Mutual Solidarity Projects as an Act of Resistance in Puerto Rico." *A Blade of Grass*, June 16, 2020. https://abladeofgrass.org/articles/organizing-mutual-solidarity-proj-ects-act-resistance-puerto-rico/.

Disu, Sami, Joanna Dressel, Jamila Hammami, Marianne Madoré, and Conor Tomás Reed. *"The amount of labor we do for free" and other contradictions: A collective inquiry into the pedagogical choices of CUNY adjunct and graduate student instructors who taught with free of charge materials during the year 2020. Manifold.* April 2022. https://cuny.manifoldapp.org/projects/the-amount-of-labor-we-do-for-free-and-other-contradic-tions/.

Donoso Macaya, Ángeles. "Archives in Common: Migrant Practices/Knowledges/Memory." Event series, Center for the Humanities, City University of New York Graduate Center, New York, 2002. https://www.centerforthehumanities.org/public-engagement/seminars/archives-in-common/.

Dorman, Joseph. *Arguing the World: The New York Intellectuals in Their Own Words.* Chicago: University of Chicago Press, 2001.

Dorothy Day-Catholic Worker Collection, Bread and Justice Catholic Worker House (Bremerton, Wash-ington) Records, 1980–1982. Special Collections and University Archives, Marquette University. https://www.marquette.edu/library/archives/Mss/DDCW/DDCW-seriesW29.php/.

Draper, Susana, and Verónica Gago. "Struggles as School: Reproductive Justice, a Cross-Border Reflec-tion." *Verso* (blog), August 5, 2022. https://www.versobooks.com/blogs/5396-struggles-as-school-re-productive-justice-a-cross-border-reflection/.

Du Bois, W. E. B. *Black Reconstruction in America: An Essay Toward a History of the Part Which Black Folk Played in the Attempt to Reconstruct Democracy in America, 1860–1880.* New York: Harcourt, Brace and Company, 1935.

DuBois, Ellen Carol. "Women's Rights, Suffrage, and Citizenship, 1789–1920." In *The Oxford Handbook of American Women's and Gender History*, edited by Ellen Hartigan-O'Connor and Lisa G. Masterson, 443–462. Oxfordshire: Oxford University Press, 2018.

Duncan, Brad. *Finally Got the News: The Printed Legacy of the U.S. Radical Left, 1970–1979.* Brooklyn: Com-mon Notions, 2017.

Dutschke, Rudi. "On Anti-Authoritarianism." In *The New Left Reader*, edited by Carl Oglesby, 243–253. New York: Grove Press, 1969.

Dyer, Conrad. "Protest and the Politics of Open Admissions: The Impact of the Black and Puerto Rican Student Community (of City College)." PhD diss., CUNY Graduate Center, 1990.

Eagen, Eileen. *Class, Culture, and the Classroom: The Student Peace Movement of the 1930s.* Philadelphia: Temple University Press, 1982.

Edgcomb, Gabrielle Simon. *From Swastika to Jim Crow: Refugee Scholars at Black Colleges.* Malabar: Krieger Publishing, 1993.

Edu-Factory Collective. *Toward a Global Autonomous University: Cognitive Labor, The Production of Knowledge, and Exodus from the Education Factory.* Brooklyn: Autonomedia, 2009.

Edwards, Brent Hayes. *The Practice of Diaspora: Literature, Translation, and the Rise of Black Internationalism.* Cambridge: Harvard University Press, 2003.

Edwards, Erica R. *The Other Side of Terror: Black Women and the Culture of US Empire.* New York: New York University Press, 2021.

Edwards, Harry. *Black Students.* New York: Free Press, 1970.

Ehrenreich, Barbara and John Ehrenreich. *Long March, Short Spring: The Student Uprising at Home and Abroad.* New York: Monthly Review Press, 1969.

Elbaum, Max. *Revolution in the Air: Sixties Radicals Turn to Lenin, Mao, and Che.* New York: Verso, 2002.

Ervin, Lorenzo Kom'boa. *Anarchism and the Black Revolution: The Definitive Edition.* London: Pluto Press, 2021.

Espinosa-Miñoso, Yuderkys, María Lugones, and Nelson Maldonado-Torres, eds. *Decolonial Feminism in Abya Yala: Caribbean, Meso, and South American Contributions and Challenges.* Oxford: Rowman and Littlefield, 2022.

Fabricant, Michael, and Steve Brier. "Racialized Austerity: The Case of CUNY." *Gotham Gazette*, August 20, 2020. https://www.gothamgazette.com/opinion/9691-racialized-austerity-case-of-cuny-funding-new-york-public-college/.

Fanon, Frantz. *The Wretched of the Earth*. Translated by Constance Farrington. New York: Grove Press, 1963.

Fantini, Mario D., Marilyn Gittell, and Richard Magat. *Community Control and the Urban School*. Westport: Praeger Publishers, 1970.

Farley, Tucker Pamela. "Oral History Interview with Tucker Pamela Farley." May 15, 2016. CUNY Digital History Archive. https://cdha.cuny.edu/items/show/4992.

Feaster, Bob. "For Brother George Jackson." *The Paper*, September 30, 1971.

Federici, Silvia. *Wages Against Housework*. Bristol: Falling Wall Press, 1975.

————, and Arlen Austin, eds. *Wages for Housework: The New York Committee 1972–1977: History, Theory, Documents*. Brooklyn: Autonomedia, 2017.

Ferguson, Roderick A. "On the subject of roots: The ancestor as institutional foundation." *Radical Philosophy* 2, no. 10 (Summer 2021). https://www.radicalphilosophy.com/article/on-the-subject-of-roots/.

————. *The Reorder of Things: The University and its Pedagogies of Minority Difference*. Minneapolis: University of Minnesota Press, 2012.

————. *We Demand: The University and Student Protests*. Berkeley: University of California Press, 2017.

Fernandes, Sujatha. "Building Child-Centered Social Movements." *Contexts* 15, no. 1 (2016): 54–59.

Fernández, Johanna. *The Young Lords: A Radical History*. Chapel Hill: University of North Carolina Press, 2019.

Ferretti, Fred. "High School Students of the City, Unite!" *New York Magazine*, April 28, 1969.

Fischbach, Michael R. *Black Power and Palestine: Transnational Countries of Color*. Stanford: Stanford University Press, 2018.

Fish, Cheryl J. "Place, Emotion, and Environmental Justice in Harlem: June Jordan and Buckminster Fuller's 1965 'Architextual' Collaboration." *Discourse: Journal for Theoretical Studies in Media and Culture* 29, no. 2, 2007: 330–345.

Flores Niemann, Yolanda, Gabriella Gutiérrez y Muhs, and Carmen G. González, eds. *Presumed Incompetent II: Race, Class, Power, and Resistance of Women in Academia*. Logan: Utah State University Press, 2020.

Forbes, Jack D. *"Yanga Ya," Selected Poems & The Goals of Education* (Parts I & II). In *Lost & Found: The CUNY Poetics Document Initiative, Series 7*, edited by William Camponovo. New York: CUNY Graduate Center, 2017.

Fortuño Bernier, Francisco J. "'*Cerrar para abrir*': Puerto Rican Student Struggles and the Crisis of Colonial-Capitalism." *Viewpoint Magazine*, April 27, 2017. https://viewpointmag.com/2017/04/27/cerrar-para-abrir-puerto-rican-student-struggles-and-the-crisis-of-colonial-capitalism/.

Francis-Snyder, Emma, dir. *The Takeover*. 2021; Brooklyn: Market Road Films.

Franklin, H. Bruce. *Vietnam & Other American Fantasies*. Amherst: University of Massachusetts Press.

Freeman, Joshua B. *Working-Class New York: Life and Labor Since World War II*. New York: New Press, 2000.

Freire, Paulo. *Education: The Practice of Freedom*. London: Writers and Readers Publishing Cooperative, 1976.

Freund, Sara. "Chicago teachers fight for affordable housing in contract negotiations." *Curbed*, October 16, 2019. https://chicago.curbed.com/2019/10/10/20908479/chicago-teachers-strike-affordable-housing/.

Friedlander, David. Editorial. *The Paper*, September 30, 1971.

Friedman, Zack. "Student Loan Debt Statistics In 2022: A Record $1.7 Trillion." *Forbes*, May 16, 2022. https://www.forbes.com/sites/zackfriedman/2022/05/16/student-loan-debt-statistics-in-2022-a-record-17-trillion/.

Fujino, Diane C. *Yuri Kochiyama: Heartbeat of Struggle*. Minneapolis: University of Minnesota Press, 2005.

Funaroff, Sol. "The Bellbuoy." In *The Spider and the Clock: Poems*. New York: International Publishers, 1938.

Gago, Verónica. *Feminist International: How to Change Everything*. New York: Verso, 2020.

García Peña, Lorgia. *Community as Rebellion: A Syllabus for Surviving Academia as a Woman of Color*. Chicago: Haymarket Books, 2022.

Gardiner, Judith. "What Happened to Socialist Feminist Women's Studies?" *Feminist Studies* 34, no. 3 (Fall 2008): 558–583.

Garza, Alicia. "A Herstory of the #BlackLivesMatter Movement." *Feminist Wire*, October 7, 2014. https://thefeministwire.com/2014/10/blacklivesmatter-2/.

Gaudino, Jenna. "CUNY Adjuncts Dish Out Demands at 'Brunch with Felo.'" *Indypendent*, February 14, 2022. https://indypendent.org/2022/02/cuny-adjuncts-dish-out-demands-at-brunch-with-felo/.

Gay Academic Union. "The Universities and the Gay Experience: Proceedings of the Conference Sponsored by the Women and Men of the Gay Academic Union, November 23 and 24, 1973." New York: Gay Academic Union, 1974.

Gay, Roxane. "The Legacy of Audre Lorde." *The Paris Review*, September 17, 2020. https://www.theparisreview.org/blog/2020/09/17/the-legacy-of-audre-lorde/.

George Washington University's Milken Institute School of Public Health and University of Puerto Rico

Graduate School of Public Health. "Project Report: Ascertainment of the Estimated Excess Mortality from Hurricane María in Puerto Rico." GW Milken Institute SPH, August 27, 2018. http://prstudy.publichealth.gwu.edu/releases-reports.

Geron, Kim, Michael Liu, and Tracy A. M. Lai. *The Snake Dance of Asian American Activism: Community, Vision, and Power*. Washington, DC: Lexington Books, 1994.

Gilich, Yulia, and Tony Boardman. "Wildcat Imaginaries: From Abolition University to University Abolition." *Critical Times* 5:1 (April 2022): 109–120.

Gillen, Jay. *Educating for Insurgency: The Roles of Young People in Schools of Poverty*. Chico: AK Press, 2014.

Giovanni, Nikki. "I Fell Off the Roof One Day (A View of the Black University)." In *The Black Woman: An Anthology*, edited by Toni Cade Bambara, 165–170. New York: New American Library, 1970.

Giwa, Tayo, and Cynthia Gordy Giwa, dirs. *The Sun Rises in the East*. 2022; Brooklyn: Black-Owned Brooklyn.

Glück, Zoltán, Manissa McCleave Maharawal, Isabelle Nastasia, and Conor Tomás Reed. "Organizing Against Empire: Struggles Over the Militarization of CUNY." *Berkeley Journal of Sociology* 58 (2014): 51–58.

Goldstone, Andrew. "For Aijaz Ahmad." *AndrewGoldstone.com* (blog), March 11, 2022. https://andrewgoldstone.com/blog/ahmad/.

Gómez, Alma, Cherríe Moraga, and Mariana Romo-Carmona, eds. *Cuentos: Stories by Latinas*. New York: Kitchen Table: Women of Color Press, 1983.

Gornick, Vivian. *The Romance of American Communism*. New York: Basic Books, 1979.

Gould-Wartofsky, Michael. "When Rioting is Rational." *Jacobin Magazine*, January 2, 2015. https://www.jacobinmag.com/2015/01/when-rioting-is-rational-ferguson/.

Grande, Sandy. "Refusing the University." In *Toward What Justice? Describing Diverse Dreams of Justice in Education*, edited by Eve Tuck and K. Wayne Yang, 47–65. New York: Routledge, 2018.

Greenberg, Irving "Yitz." "Scholarship and Continuity: Dilemma and Dialectic." In *The Teaching of Judaica in American Universities: The Proceedings of a Colloquium*, edited by Leon A. Jick, 115–131. Brooklyn: Ktav Publishing House, 1970.

Greenberg, Irving, and Elie Wiesel. "Letters to the Collective." *The Paper*. December 18, 1975.

Griffin, Farah Jasmine. "Toni Cade Bambara: Free to Be Anywhere in the Universe." *Callaloo: A Journal of African-American and African Arts and Letters* 19, no. 2 (1996): 229–231.

———. *"Who Set You Flowin'?": The African-American Migration Narrative*. Oxford: Oxford University Press, 1995.

The Guardian. "Cubans to open talks about US fugitives including Assata Shakur as ties warm." April 15, 2015. https://www.theguardian.com/us-news/2015/apr/15/cuban-us-fugitives-open-talks-terror-list-ties-warm/.

Gumbs, Alexis Pauline. *"17th Floor*: A pedagogical oracle from/with Audre Lorde." *Journal of Lesbian Studies* 21, no. 4 (2016): 375–390.

———. "Communiqué to White Ally Heaven." *Sinister Wisdom* 87 (Tribute to Adrienne Rich – Fall 2012): 86–100.

———. "Nobody Mean More: Black Feminist Pedagogy and Solidarity." In *The Imperial University: Academic Repression and Scholarly Dissent*. Minneapolis: University of Minnesota Press, 2014.

———. "The Shape of My Impact." *Feminist Wire*, October 29, 2012. https://thefeministwire.com/2012/10/the-shape-of-my-impact/.

———. "This Instant: June Jordan and a Black Feminist Poetics of Architecture." Four-part meditation on Black feminist architecture as informed by the Black feminist poet and architect June Jordan, July 22, 2013. https://www.scribd.com/document/155271148/This-Instant-June-Jordan-and-a-Black-Feminist-Poetics-of-Architecture/.

Gunderson, Christopher. *The Struggle for CUNY: A History of the CUNY Student Movement, 1969–1999*. Master's Thesis, Macaulay Honors College, 2014.

Guridy, Frank Andre. *Forging Diaspora: Afro-Cubans and African Americans in a World of Empire and Jim Crow*. Chapel Hill: University of North Carolina Press, 2010.

Gutfreund, Barbara. "Wednesday Night and Thursday Morn." *The Campus*, November 14, 1968.

Gutiérrez y Muhs, Gabriella, Yolanda Flores Niemann, Carmen G. González, and Angela P. Harris, eds. *Presumed Incompetent: The Intersections of Race and Class for Women in Academia*. Logan: Utah State University Press, 2012.

Gutman, Marta. "Intermediate School 201: Race, Space, and Modern Architecture in Harlem." In *Educating Harlem: A Century of Schooling and Resistance in a Black Community*, edited by Ansley T. Erickson and Ernest Morrell, 183–209. New York: Columbia University Press, 2019.

Hahn, Steven. *A Nation Under Our Feet: Black Political Struggles in the Rural South from Slavery to the Great Migration*. Cambridge: Harvard University Press, 2003.

Hall, Stuart. "Race, Articulation, and Societies Structured in Dominance." In *Essential Essays, Volume 1:*

Foundations of Cultural Studies, edited by David Morley, 172–221. Durham: Duke University Press, 2018.

Hallas, Duncan. "Agitation and Propaganda." *Socialist Worker Review* 68 (September 1984). www.marxists. org/archive/hallas/works/1984/09/agitprop.htm/.

Hancock, LynNell, and Meredith Kolodner. "When high achievers have no place to go." *The Hechinger Report*, January 13, 2015. https://archive.fo/gU9MM/.

Hansberry, Lorraine. "Lorraine Hansberry Discusses Her Play *A Raisin in the Sun*." In *The WFMT Studs Terkel Radio Archive*. https://studsterkel.wfmt.com/programs/lorraine-hansberry-discusses-her-play-raisin-sun/.

Harris, Adam. "The Death of an Adjunct." *The Atlantic*, April 8, 2019. https://www.theatlantic.com/education/archive/2019/04/adjunct-professors-higher-education-thea-hunter/586168/.

Hartman, Saidiya. *Lose Your Mother: A Journey Along the Atlantic Slave Route*. New York: Farrar, Straus and Giroux, 2008.

———. "The Terrible Beauty of the Slum." *Brick: A Literary Journal* 99 (July 28, 2017). https://brickmag. com/the-terrible-beauty-of-the-slum/.

———. "Venus in Two Acts." *Small Axe* 12, no. 2 (June 2008): 1–14.

———. *Wayward Lives, Beautiful Experiments: Intimate Histories of Riotous Black Girls, Troublesome Women, and Queer Radicals*. New York: W.W. Norton, 2019.

Harvard Crimson. "N.Y. Courts Ponder Feinberg Law Act Would Bar Teachers Belonging to Groups on Subversive List." April 20, 1950. www.thecrimson.com/article/1950/6/20/ny-courts-ponder-feinberg-law-act/.

Harvey, David. "The Right to the City." *New Left Review* 53 (September–October 2008). https://newleftreview.org/issues/ii53/articles/david-harvey-the-right-to-the-city/.

Haslip-Viera, Gabriel. Email communication with the author. February 4, 2020.

Heatherton, Christina. *Arise! Global Radicalism in the Era of the Mexican Revolution*. Oakland: University of California Press, 2022.

Heffernan, Ann, and Noor Nieftagodien. *Students Must Rise: Youth Struggle in South Africa Before and Beyond Soweto '76*. Johannesburg: Wits University Press, 2016.

Henderson, David. "Allen Ginsberg & David Henderson at Naropa 1981 (Part One)." January 1, 1970. *The Allen Ginsberg Project* (blog). https://allenginsberg.org/2015/11/allen-ginsberg-david-henderson-at-naropa-1981-part-one/.

———. "Alvin Cash / Keep on Dancing." *Low East*. Berkeley: North Atlantic Books, 1980.

———. "black literature." *Teachers & Writers Collaborative Newsletter* 2, no. 1 (April 1969).

———. Email communication with Ammiel Alcalay, shared with the author. October 22, 2013.

———. Interview with the author. April 2, 2022.

———. "Keep on Pushing." *De Mayor of Harlem*. New York: E.P. Dutton and Co., 1970.

———. Letter to June Jordan. Series IV, Box 35, Folder 5. June Jordan Papers, 1936–2002. Schlesinger Library on the History of Women in America, Radcliffe Institute, Cambridge, MA.

———. "May 19, 1967—Class Observation." *Teachers & Writers Collaborative Newsletter* 1, no. 1, September 1967.

———. "June 9, 1967—Presentation to the Students." *Teachers & Writers Collaborative Newsletter* 1, no. 1, September 1967.

———. "June 16, 1967—Presentation to the Class." *Teachers & Writers Collaborative Newsletter* 1, no. 1, September 1967.

———. "PRE-BACCALAUREATE PROGRAM CITY COLLEGE: Report on the Summer Seminar." Series XXVII, Carton 9, Folder 385. Adrienne Rich Papers, 1927–1999. Schlesinger Library on the History of Women in America, Radcliffe Institute, Cambridge, MA.

———. "Some Impressions: Recorded as a Participant-Observer in the Summer Experimental Program in Deaf Education, Gallaudet College for the Deaf, Kendall Elementary School (for Deaf Children), July 29 to August 4, 1967." In *Journal of a Living Experiment: A Documentary History of the First Ten Years of Teachers & Writers Collaborative*, edited by Phillip Lopate, 76–80. New York: Teachers & Writers Collaborative, 1979.

Hilliard, Tom. "Degrees of Difficulty: Boosting College Success in New York City." *Center for an Urban Future* (December 2017). https://nycfuture.org/research/degrees-of-difficulty/.

History Task Force. *Labor Migration under Capitalism: The Puerto Rican Experience*. New York: Monthly Review Press, 1979.

Ho, Fred, Carolyn Antonio, Diane Fujino, and Steve Yip, eds. *Legacy to Liberation: Politics and Culture of Revolutionary Asian/Pacific America*. Chico: AK Press, 2000.

Hobson, Emily. *Lavender and Red: Liberation and Solidarity in the Gay and Lesbian Left*. Berkeley: University of California Press, 2016.

Hoff, James. "The Economics of Prestige." *Inside Higher Ed*, April 21, 2014. www.insidehighered.com/

views/2014/04/21/essay-what-hiring-paul-krugman-says-about-values-public-higher-education/.

Hoffnung-Garskof, Jesse. *A Tale of Two Cities: Santo Domingo and New York after 1950*. Princeton: Princeton University Press, 2008.

Hogan, Kristen. *The Feminist Bookstore Movement: Lesbian Antiracism and Feminist Accountability*. Durham: Duke University Press, 2016.

Hogness, Peter. "City College teach-in at center of storm." *Clarion*, December 2001. https://archive.psc-cuny.org/PDF/Clarion_Dec_03.pdf/.

———. "Union says no to austerity contract." *Clarion*, September 2004. https://archive.psc-cuny.org/PDF/Clarion%20Sept%2004.pdf/.

Holladay, Hilary. *The Power of Adrienne Rich: A Biography*. New York: Penguin, 2020.

Holmes, Linda Janet. *A Joyous Revolt: Toni Cade Bambara, Writer and Activist*. Westport: Praeger, 2014.

hooks, bell. *Teaching to Transgress: Education as the Practice of Freedom*. London and New York: Routledge, 1994.

Horne, Gerald. *Fire This Time: The Watts Uprising and the 1960s*. Burlington: Da Capo Press, 1995.

Hoskins, Janet Alison, and Viet Thanh Nguyen, eds. *TransPacific Studies: Framing an Emerging Field*. Honolulu: University of Hawaii Press, 2014.

Howe, Florence. "New Curricular Focus in Women's Studies Programs: Trends in Degree-Granting and Minor-Granting Women's Studies Programs." In *Women's Studies Newsletter* 4 (Winter 1976): 1–2.

Hsu, Hua. "The Asian-American Canon Breakers." *New Yorker*, December 30, 2019. https://www.newyorker.com/magazine/2020/01/06/the-asian-american-canon-breakers/.

Hull, Akasha (Gloria T.), Patricia Bell Scott, and Barbara Smith, eds. *All the Women are White, All the Men are Black, But Some of Us Are Brave: Black Women's Studies*. New York: Feminist Press, 1982.

Human Rights Watch. "'Kettling' Protesters in the Bronx: Systemic Police Brutality and Its Costs in the United States." September 30, 2020. https://www.hrw.org/report/2020/09/30/kettling-protesters-bronx/systemic-police-brutality-and-its-costs-united-states/.

Invisible Committee. *The Coming Insurrection*. Los Angeles: Semiotext(e), 2007.

Jackson, George. *Blood in My Eye*. Baltimore: Black Classics Press, 1990.

Jackson, Laura (Riding). *Anarchism is Not Enough*. Edited by Lisa Samuels. Berkeley: University of California Press, 2001.

James, C. L. R., Grace C. Lee, and Cornelius Castoriadis. *Facing Reality*. Detroit: Correspondence Publishing Co., 1958.

James, Joy. "Framing the Panther: Assata Shakur and Black Female Agency." In *Want to Start a Revolution?: Radical Women in the Black Freedom Struggle*, edited by Dayo F. Gore, Komozi Woodard, and Jeanne Theoharis, 138–160. New York: New York University Press, 2009.

James, Winston. *Holding Aloft the Banner of Ethiopia: Caribbean Radicalism in Early Twentieth Century America*. New York: Verso, 1998.

Janae, Brionne. "Against Mastery." *The American Poetry Review* 50, no. 6 (November/December 2021). https://aprweb.org/poems/against-mastery/.

Jean-Charles, Petruce. "LGBTQ Americans are getting coronavirus, losing jobs. Anti-gay bias is making it worse for them." *USA Today*, May 9, 2020. https://www.usatoday.com/story/news/nation/2020/05/09/discrimination-racism-fuel-COVID-19-woes-lgbtq-americans/3070036001/.

Jews for Racial and Economic Justice. "Understanding Anti-Semitism: An Offering to Our Movement." November 2017. https://www.jfrej.org/assets/uploads/JFREJ-Understanding-Antisemitism-November-2017-v1-3-2.pdf/.

Jiménez, Lillian. "Puerto Ricans and Educational Civil Rights: A History of the 1969 City College Takeover (An Interview with Five Participants)." In *CENTRO: Journal of the Center for Puerto Rican Studies Journal* 21, no. 2 (Fall 2009): 159–175.

John Brown Anti-Klan Committee. "Bulletin! Assata Shakur Escapes." *Death to the Klan!* November 1979. http://freedomarchives.org/Documents/Finder/DOC37_scans/37.dttk.nov79.pdf/.

———. "Defeat Operation Snowflake!" *Death to the Klan!* no. 3 (January/February 1980). http://freedomarchives.org/Documents/Finder/DOC37_scans/37.dttk.jan80.pdf/.

———. "Fight White Supremacy at City College." *Death to the Klan!* (November 1979). http://freedomarchives.org/Documents/Finder/DOC37_scans/37.dttk.nov79.pdf/.

———. "Open Forum: Keep Sydenham Open/Stop Operation Snowflake." *The Paper*, September 23, 1980.

———. "Open Forum: Racism at City College." *The Paper*, November 5, 1980.

———. "Operation Snowflake: Urban Genocide at CCNY." *The Paper*, February 19, 1980.

Johnson, Cedric. *Revolutionaries to Race Leaders: Black Power and The Making of African American Politics*. Minneapolis: University of Minnesota Press, 2007.

Jones, Adele, and Group. "Ebony Minds, Black Voices." In *The Black Woman: An Anthology*, edited by Toni Cade Bambara, 227–237. New York: New American Library, 1970.

Jones, Ann. "America's Child Soldiers: JROTC and the Militarizing of America." *TomDispatch*, December 15, 2013. http://www.tomdispatch.com/post/175784/tomgram%3A_ann_jones,_suffer_the_children/.

Jones, Hettie. *How I Became Hettie Jones*. New York: E.P. Dutton and Co., 1990.

Jones, LeRoi/Amiri Baraka. "Black Art." *Liberator* 6 (January 1966).

———. *Black Magic: Collected Poetry, 1961–1967*. Indianapolis: Bobbs Merrill Co., 1969.

Jordan, June. "Black Commentary on White Discussion of Black Studies." Series XI, Box 75, Folder 9. June Jordan Papers, 1936–2002. Schlesinger Library on the History of Women in America, Radcliffe Institute, Cambridge, MA.

———. "The City and City College: an off-campus, off-camera perspective." Series XI, Box 75, Folder 11. June Jordan Papers, 1936–2002. Schlesinger Library on the History of Women in America, Radcliffe Institute, Cambridge, MA.

———. "City College Graduate Poetry Workshop Description." Series XII, Box 76, Folder 15. Schlesinger Library on the History of Women in America, Radcliffe Institute, Cambridge, MA.

———. "Comment on Aptheker's 'The Superiority of the Negro.'" *American Dialog*, October–November 1965. Series VII, Box 58, Folders 24–25. June Jordan Papers, 1936–2002. Schlesinger Library on the History of Women in America, Radcliffe Institute, Cambridge, MA.

———. "The Determining Slum." Paper submitted to the Housing Department, Mobilization for Youth, July 12, 1966. Series XI, Box 75, Folder 2. June Jordan Papers, 1936–2002. Schlesinger Library on the History of Women in America, Radcliffe Institute, Cambridge, MA.

———. "Elegy of Place." *American Dialogue*, October–November 1965. Series VII, Box 58, Folder 24. June Jordan Papers, 1936–2002. Schlesinger Library on the History of Women in America, Radcliffe Institute, Cambridge, MA.

———. "Instant Slum Clearance." *Esquire* (April 1965). Series VII, Box 58, Folder 24. June Jordan Papers, 1936–2002. Schlesinger Library on the History of Women in America, Radcliffe Institute, Cambridge, MA.

———. *June Jordan: "Life Studies," 1966–1976*. In *Lost & Found: The CUNY Poetics Document Initiative, Series 7*. Edited by Conor Tomás Reed and Talia Shalev. New York: The Center for the Humanities, Graduate Center of the City University of New York, 2017.

———. Letter to Audre Lorde. 1973. Series 1, Box 3, Folder 63, Audre Lorde Papers, Spelman College Archives, Atlanta, GA.

———. "Letter to Michael (1964)." In *Civil Wars*, 16–22. Boston: Beacon Press, 1981.

———. "Letter to R. Buckminster Fuller (1964)." In *Civil Wars*, 23–28. Boston: Beacon Press, 1981.

———. "Moving Towards Home." In *Living Room: New Poems*. New York: Thunder's Mouth Press, 1985.

———. *Moving Towards Home: Political Essays*. London: Virago Press, 1989.

———. "Ocean Hill-Brownsville Graduation Speech for IS 55, June 19, 1970." Series VI, Box 55, Folder 6. June Jordan Papers, 1936–2002. Schlesinger Library on the History of Women in America, Radcliffe Institute, Cambridge, MA.

———. "One Way of Beginning This Book." In *Civil Wars*, xv. Boston: Beacon Press, 1981.

———. "An Opinion: June Meyer on Negro Aims." *Mademoiselle*, April 1966. Series VII, Box 58, Folders 24–25. June Jordan Papers, 1936–2002. Schlesinger Library on the History of Women in America, Radcliffe Institute, Cambridge, MA.

———. "Poem about Police Violence." In *Directed by Desire: The Collected Poems of June Jordan*, 272. Port Townsend: Copper Canyon Press, 2007.

———. *Soldier: A Poet's Childhood*. New York: Basic Books, 2000.

———. *Soulscript: Afro-American Poetry*. New York: Doubleday, 1970.

———. "Statement by June Jordan to Board of Higher Ed, on CUNY Retrenchment, End of Open Admissions, Imposition of Tuition; Speaking on behalf of Black Colleagues in English Dept. at CCNY." Series XII, Box 76, Folder 14. June Jordan Papers, 1936–2002. Schlesinger Library on the History of Women in America, Radcliffe Institute, Cambridge, MA.

———. "Visitors and Adult Friends of the Children." Series V, Box 54, Folder 10. June Jordan Papers, 1936–2002. Schlesinger Library on the History of Women in America, Radcliffe Institute, Cambridge, MA.

———. "The Voice of the Children (1967)." In *Civil Wars*, 29–38. Boston: Beacon Press, 1981.

———. "You Can't See the Trees for the School." *Urban Review*, December 1967. Series VII, Box 58, Folder 25. June Jordan Papers, 1936–2002. Schlesinger Library on the History of Women in America, Radcliffe Institute, Cambridge, MA.

———, and Peter Erickson. "After Identity." *Transition* 63 (1994): 132–149.

Joseph, Gloria I., ed. *The Wind is the Spirit: The Life, Love and Legacy of Audre Lorde*. New York: Villarosa Media, 2016.

Joselow, Maxine. "CUNY Considers Free Speech Policy." *Inside Higher Ed*, June 20, 2016. www.insidehigh-ered.com/news/2016/06/20/cuny-considers-free-speech-policy/.

Jules, Jason, and Graham Marsh. *Black Ivy: A Revolt in Style*. London: Reel Art Press, 2021.

Kaminer, Ariel. "Two New York City Colleges Draft Rules That Restrict Protests." *New York Times*, December 10, 2018. http://www.nytimes.com/2013/12/11/education/2-new-york-city-colleges-draft-rules-that-restrict-protests.html/.

Kang, Jay Caspian. *The Loneliest Americans*. New York: Crown Publishing, 2021.

Karagueuezian, Dikran. *Blow it Up! The Black Student Revolt at San Francisco State and the Emergence of Dr. Hayakawa*. Boston: Gambit, 1971.

Kaufman, Alan. *Drunken Angel: A Memoir*. Jersey City: Viva Editions, 2013.

Kay, Philip. "'Guttersnipes' and 'Eliterates': City College in the Popular Imagination." PhD diss., Columbia University, 2011.

Kay-Trask, Haunani. *Eros and Power: The Promise of Feminist Theory*. Philadelphia: University of Pennsylvania Press, 1981.

Kelley, Robin D. G. "Black Study, Black Struggle." *Boston Review*, October 24, 2016. https://www.bostonreview.net/forum/robin-kelley-black-struggle-campus-protest/.

———. *Freedom Dreams: The Black Radical Imagination*, Twentieth Anniversary Edition. Boston: Beacon Press, 2022.

———. *Hammer and Hoe: Alabama Communists During the Great Depression*. Chapel Hill: University of North Carolina Press, 1990.

———. "'This Ain't Ethiopia, But It'll Do': African Americans in the Spanish Civil War." In *Race Rebels: Culture, Politics, and the Black Working Class*, 123–158. New York: Free Press, 1996.

"Kettled in Mott Haven." *Spirit of May 28*, November 29, 2022. https://www.sm28.org/articles/kettled-in-mott-haven/.

Khalid, Asma. "How White Liberals Became Woke, Radically Changing Their Outlook on Race." *NPR.org*, October 1, 2019. https://www.npr.org/2019/10/01/763383478/how-white-liberals-became-woke-radically-changing-their-outlook-on-race/.

King, David Howard. "New York City Interests Given Varied Priority in Three Albany Budget Plans." *Gotham Gazette*, March 16, 2016. www.gothamgazette.com/city/6226-new-york-city-interests-given-varied-priority-in-three-albany-budget-plans/.

Klassen, David. "Cops Off Campus and Out of Our Unions!: A Report from PSC-CUNY's Rank-and-File." *Spectre Journal*, July 1, 2020. https://spectrejournal.com/cops-out-of-our-unions/.

Klein, Naomi. *The Shock Doctrine: The Rise of Disaster Capitalism*. London: Picador, 2008.

Koestenbaum, Wayne. "Adrienne Rich's Poetry Became Political, but It Remained Rooted in Material Fact." *New York Times*, July 15, 2016. https://www.nytimes.com/2016/07/17/books/review/adrienne-rich-collected-poems-1950-2012.html/.

Korsh, Sben. "Brutality." *New York Review of Architecture* 13, July 15, 2020. https://newyork.substack.com/p/brutality/.

Kuppers, Petra. "Crip Time." *Tikkun* 29, no. 4 (Fall 2014): 29–30.

Kwon, R.O. "Your Silence Will Not Protect You by Audre Lorde review—prophetic and necessary." *The Guardian*, October 4, 2017. https://www.theguardian.com/books/2017/oct/04/your-silence-will-not-protect-you-by-audre-lorder-review/.

Kynard, Carmen. *Vernacular Insurrections: Race, Black Protest, and the New Century in Composition-Literacies Studies*. Albany: SUNY Press, 2014.

la paperson. *A Third University Is Possible*. Minneapolis: University of Minnesota Press, 2017.

Langdell, Cheri Colby. *Adrienne Rich: The Moment of Change*. Westport: Praeger, 2004.

Latin American Studies. "Guillermo Morales Correa: Clandestinidad y exilio." 2004. http://www.latinamericanstudies.org/puertorico/morales-entrevista.htm/.

Lavin, David E., Richard A. Silberstein, and Richard Alba. *Right Versus Privilege: The Open-Admissions Experiment at the City University of New York*. New York: Free Press, 1981.

LeBrón, Marisol. *Policing Life and Death: Race, Violence, and Resistance in Puerto Rico*. Berkeley: University of California Press, 2019.

Lebrón Ortiz, Pedro. *Filosofía del cimarronaje*. Toa Baja: Editora Educación Emergente, 2020.

Lee, Sonia Song-Ha. *Building a Latino Civil Rights Movement: Puerto Ricans, African Americans, and the Pursuit of Racial Justice in New York City*. Chapel Hill: University of North Carolina Press, 2014.

Levine, Judith. "Hating Motherhood." *Boston Review*, March 3, 2022. https://bostonreview.net/articles/hating-motherhood/.

Levinson, Ralph. "Onyx: Of Black People, by Black People, for Black People." *The Campus*, November 16, 1967.

Lewis, Sophie. *Full Surrogacy Now: Feminism Against Family*. New York: Verso, 2019.

Lewis, Thabiti. *'Black People Are My Business': Toni Cade Bambara's Practices of Liberation.* Detroit: Wayne State University Press, 2020.

Liberation News Service. "'Veterans Are Still Experiencing the War at Home': VVAW/WSO Holds Forum on Third World Vets." *Liberation News Service* 520–548 (May–August 1973). Available at Wisconsin Historical Society, GI Press Collection, 1964–1977. https://content.wisconsinhistory.org/digital/collection/p15932coll8/id/75664/.

Liechtenstein, Eli B., and Dave Mesing. "Notes on Contemporary University Struggles: A Dossier." *Viewpoint Magazine,* January 19, 2022. https://viewpointmag.com/2022/01/19/notes-on-contemporary-university-struggles-a-dossier/.

Lipsitz, George. *The Possessive Investment in Whiteness.* Philadelphia: Temple University Press, 2006.

Lisnoff, Howard. "The Resegregation of New York City Schools." *Counterpunch,* August 3, 2018. https://www.counterpunch.org/2018/08/03/the-resegregation-of-new-york-city-schools/.

Lopate, Phillip, ed. "Roots and Origins." In *Journal of a Living Experiment: A Documentary History of the First Ten Years of Teachers & Writers Collaborative,* 14–20. New York: Teachers & Writers Collaborative, 1979.

López, Madeleine E. "Investigating the Investigators: An Analysis of *The Puerto Rican Study.*" In *CENTRO: Journal of the Center for Puerto Rican Studies Journal* 19, no. 2 (Fall 2007): 61–85.

Lorde, Audre. "Age, Race, Class, and Sex: Women Redefining Difference." In *Sister Outsider: Essays and Speeches,* 114–123. Trumansburg: Crossing Press, 1984.

———. *Audre Lorde: "I teach myself in outline," Notes, Journals, Syllabi, & an Excerpt from Deotha.* In *Lost & Found: The CUNY Poetics Document Initiative, Series 7,* edited by Miriam Atkin and Iemanjá Brown. New York: The Center for the Humanities, Graduate Center of the City University of New York, 2017.

———. "Between Ourselves." In *Collected Poems of Audre Lorde,* 223–225 and 323–325. New York: W.W. Norton & Company, 2000.

———. "Blackstudies." In *Collected Poems of Audre Lorde,* 153–157. New York: W.W. Norton & Company, 2000.

———. *A Burst of Light: Essays.* Ann Arbor: Firebrand Books, 1988.

———. *Cancer Journals.* New York: Penguin Books, 2020.

———. "Dear Toni Instead of a Letter of Congratulations Upon Your Book and Your Daughter Whom You Are Raising To Be A Correct Little Sister." In *The Collected Poems of Audre Lorde,* 93–95. New York: W.W. Norton & Company, 2000.

———. "Deotha." Series 2.1, Box 17, Folder 88. Audre Lorde Papers, Spelman College Archives, Atlanta, GA.

———. "For Assata." In *The Black Unicorn: Poems,* 28. New York: W.W. Norton & Company, 1978.

———. "I Am Your Sister: Black Women Organizing Across Sexualities." In *I Am Your Sister: Collected and Unpublished Writings of Audre Lorde,* edited by Rudolph P. Byrd, Johnnetta Betsch Cole, and Beverly Guy-Sheftall, 57–63. Oxford: Oxford University Press, 2009.

———. "An Interview: Adrienne Rich and Audre Lorde." In *Sister Outsider: Essays and Speeches,* 81–109. Trumansburg: Crossing Press, 1984.

———. "Journals." Series 2.5, Box 46. Audre Lorde Papers, Spelman College Archives, Atlanta, GA.

———. "Journals." Series 10, Box 83, Folder 26. Audre Lorde Papers, Spelman College Archives, Atlanta, GA.

———. "Journals; History/lit 210." Series 2.5, Box 46. Audre Lorde Papers, Spelman College Archives, Atlanta, GA.

———. "Journals; Hist/lit suggested readings." Series 10, Box 82, Folder 25. Audre Lorde Papers, Spelman College Archives, Atlanta, GA.

———. "The Law is Male and White: Meeting with the Black Author, Audre Lorde." Interview by Dorothee Nolte. In *Conversations with Audre Lorde,* edited by Joan Wylie Hall, 143–145. Jackson: University of Mississippi Press, 2004.

———. "Learning from the 60s." In *Sister Outsider: Essays and Speeches,* 134–144. Trumansburg: Crossing Press, 1984.

———. "Movement Song." *From a Land Where Other People Live.* Detroit: Broadside Press, 1973.

———. "The Poet as Outsider, Session 4, May 17, 1984." In *dream of europe: Selected Seminars and Interviews, 1984–1992,* 88–95. Chicago: Kenning Editions, 2020.

———. "Race and the Urban Situation." Series 2.5, Box 46. Audre Lorde Papers, Spelman College Archives, Atlanta, GA.

———. "Racist society." Series 2.5, Box 46. Audre Lorde Papers, Spelman College Archives, Atlanta, GA.

———. *Selected Works of Audre Lorde.* Edited by Roxane Gay. New York: W.W. Norton, 2020.

———. "The Transformation of Silence into Language and Action." In *Sister Outsider: Essays and Speeches,* 40–44. Trumansburg: Crossing Press, 1984.

———. "Uses of the Erotic: The Erotic as Power." In *Sister Outsider: Essays and Speeches,* 53–59.

Trumansburg: Crossing Press, 1984.

———. *Zami: A New Spelling of My Name.* Watertown: Persephone Press, 1982.

Louis, Errol. "Police Brutality: A Backstory." *NY1*, June 5, 2020. https://www.ny1.com/nyc/all-boroughs/news/2020/06/05/police-brutality—a-backstory-new-york-city/.

Lubin, Alex. *Geographies of Liberation: The Making of an Afro-Arab Political Imaginary.* Chapel Hill: University of North Carolina Press, 2014.

Lugones, María. *Pilgrimages/Peregrinajes: Theorizing Coalition Against Multiple Oppressions.* Oxford: Rowman and Littlefield, 2003.

Luu, Linda. "Comment from the Field: Toward Interdisciplinary Coalitions: Eunjung Kim's *Curative Violence* and Jasbir K. Puar's *The Right to Maim.*" *Journal of Literary & Cultural Disability Studies* 13, no. 1 (2019): 111–115.

———. "Resistance Everywhere We Went: The Fight for Asian American Studies at CUNY." In *The Children of the People: Writings by and about CUNY Students on Race and Social Justice*, edited by Rose M. Kim, Grace M. Cho, and Robin McGinty, 171–187. Lewes: DIO Press, 2022.

M. "A Critique of Ally Politics." In *Taking Sides: Revolutionary Solidarity and the Poverty of Liberalism*, edited by Cindy Milstein, 64–84. Chico: AK Press, 2015.

Maeda, Daryl. *Chains of Babylon: The Rise of Asian America.* Minneapolis: University of Minnesota Press, 2009.

Magid, Shaul. "As Transition Looms, Jewish Studies is Mired in Controversy." *Religion Dispatches*, May 11, 2021. https://religiondispatches.org/as-transition-approaches-jewish-studies-is-mired-in-controversy/.

Mahabeer, Pamela. "13 Black Profs Call Hunger Strike to Protest City U 'Resegregation.'" *The Campus*, May 7, 1976.

Maher, Jane. *Mina P. Shaughnessy: Her Life and Work.* Urbana: National Council of Teachers of English, 1997.

Marcuse, Herbert. *The Aesthetic Dimension: Toward a Critique of Marxist Aesthetics.* Boston: Beacon Press, 1978.

———. *Counterrevolution and Revolt.* Boston: Beacon Press, 1972.

———. *Eros and Civilization.* Boston: Beacon Press, 1955.

Markowitz, Gerald. *Educating for Justice: A History of John Jay College of Criminal Justice.* New York: CUNY Academic Works, 2008.

———, and David Rosner. *Children, Race, and Power: Kenneth and Mamie Clark's Northside Center.* Charlottesville: University of Virginia Press, 1996.

Marshak, Robert. *Academic Renewal in the Seventies: Memoir of a City College President.* Washington, DC: University Press of America, 1982.

Martín, José. "Policing is a Dirty Job, But Nobody's Gotta Do It: 6 Ideas for a Cop-Free World." *Rolling Stone*, December 16, 2014. https://www.rollingstone.com/politics/politics-news/policing-is-a-dirty-job-but-nobodys-gotta-do-it-6-ideas-for-a-cop-free-world-199465/.

Marx, Karl. *The Civil War in France.* New York: International Publishers, 1989 [first published 1871].

———. *The Eighteenth Brumaire of Louis Bonaparte.* Moscow: Progress Publishers, 1937 [first published 1852].

———, and Friedrich Engels. "Manifesto of the Communist Party." In *Marx/Engels Selected Works, Vol. One.* Moscow: Progress Publishers, 1969 [first published February 1848].

Massiah, Louis. "The Authenticating Audience." *Feminist Wire*, November 18, 2014. http://www.thefeministwire.com/2014/11/authenticating-audience/.

Mayor's Advisory Task Force on the City University of New York. Report on "The City University of New York: An Institution Adrift." June 7, 1999. CUNY Digital History Archive. https://cdha.cuny.edu/items/show/2421/.

Mazzei, Patricia. "'Why Don't We Have Electricity?': Outages Plague Puerto Rico." *New York Times*, November 10, 2021. https://www.nytimes.com/2021/10/19/us/puerto-rico-electricity-protest.html/.

MCC Strike Committee. *MCC Strike Committee Bulletin #1.* 1976. CUNY Digital History Archive. https://cdha.cuny.edu/items/show/1691/.

McCaffrey, Katherine T., Christine Kovic, and Charles R. Menzies. "On Strike: Student Activism, CUNY, and Engaged Anthropology." In *The Children of the People: Writings by and about CUNY Students on Race and Social Justice*, edited by Rose M. Kim, Grace M. Cho, and Robin McGinty, 135–164. Lewes: DIO Press, 2022.

McKinley, Jr., James C. "CUNY Protests Spread to More Schools." *New York Times*, April 28, 1989. https://www.nytimes.com/1989/04/28/nyregion/cuny-protests-spread-to-more-schools.html/.

McKittrick, Katherine. "Freedom is a Secret." In *Black Geographies and the Politics of Place*, edited by Katherine McKittrick and Clyde Woods, 97–114. Brooklyn: South End Press, 2007.

McRuer, Robert. *Crip Theory: Cultural Signs of Queerness and Disability.* New York: New York University Press, 2006.

Mejía, Paula. "Fired Brooklyn College Professor Says CUNY Wrongly Seized Decades of His Research."

Gothamist, February 27, 2019. https://gothamist.com/news/fired-brooklyn-college-professor-says-cuny-wrongly-seized-decades-of-his-research/.

Melamed, Jodi. *Represent and Destroy: Rationalizing Violence in the New Racial Capitalism.* Minneapolis; University of Minnesota Press, 2011.

Melani, Lilia. "Oral History Interview with Lilia Melani." May 22, 2019. CUNY Digital History Archive. https://cdha.cuny.edu/items/show/10642/.

Mendelson, Wilfred. *Let My People Know: The Story of Wilfred Mendelson, "Mendy," August 17, 1915–July 28, 1938.* Edited by Joseph Leeds. https://cuny.manifoldapp.org/projects/let-my-people-know.

Mendenhall, Annie S. *Desegregation State: College Writing Programs after the Civil Rights Movement.* Logan: Utah State University Press, 2022.

Meléndez-Badillo, Jorell A. *The Lettered Barriada: Workers, Archival Power, and the Politics of Knowledge in Puerto Rico.* Durham: Duke University Press, 2021.

Merlan, Anna. "City College Lifts Suspensions Against Two Student Protesters, But Criminal Charges Still Stand." *The Village Voice*, November 25, 2013. http://www.villagevoice.com/news/city-college-lifts-suspensions-against-two-student-protesters-but-criminal-charges-still-stand-6681234/.

The Messenger. Don't Shoot the Messenger!: Six Years of Struggle by CCNY's Banned, Stolen, Defunded, Defamed, Award-Winning Student Newspaper, 1998–2004. SLAM! Herstory Project. Philadelphia: SLAM! Herstory Project, 2013. https://slamherstory.wordpress.com/2013/11/08/dont-shoot-the-messenger-download-this-anthology-of-ccnys-activist-newspaper/.

Meyer, Matt. *Let Freedom Ring: A Collection of Documents from the Movements to Free US Political Prisoners.* Oakland: PM Press, 2008.

Meyerhoff, Eli. *Beyond Education: Radical Studying for Another World.* Minneapolis: University of Minnesota Press, 2019.

Michels, Tony. *Jewish Radicals: A Documentary History.* New York: New York University Press, 2012.

Miller, Cheryl. "Underserved: a case study of ROTC in New York City." *American Enterprise Institute*, May 4, 2011. http://www.aei.org/publication/underserved-a-case-study-of-rotc-in-new-york-city/.

Minor, Ethel. "Third World Round Up: The Palestine Problem: Test Your Knowledge." *SNCC Newsletter*, June–July 1967. https://snccdigital.org/inside-sncc/policy-statements/palestine/.

Mironova, Oksana. "'The scythe of progress must move northward': Urban Renewal on the Upper West Side." *Urban Omnibus*, June 10, 2015. https://urbanomnibus.net/2015/06/the-scythe-of-progress-must-move-northward-urban-renewal-on-the-upper-west-side/.

Mitchell, Eve. "I Am a Woman and a Human: A Marxist-Feminist Critique of Intersectionality Theory." *Unity & Struggle*, September 12, 2013. http://www.unityandstruggle.org/2013/09/i-am-a-woman-and-a-human-a-marxist-feminist-critique-of-intersectionality-theory/.

Mitchell, Katie. *Watched.* Portland: Collective Eye Films, 2017.

Mitchell, Nick. "(Critical Ethnic Studies) Intellectual." *Critical Ethnic Studies* 1, no. 1 (Spring 2015): 86–94.

———. "The Fantasy and Fate of Ethnic Studies in an Age of Uprisings: An Interview with Nick Mitchell." *Undercommoning*, July 13, 2016. https://undercommoning.org/nick-mitchell-interview/.

———. "On Audre Lorde's Legacy and the "Self" of Self-Care, Part 1 of 3." *Low End Theory*, February 18, 2013. http://www.lowendtheory.org/post/43457761324/on-audre-lordes-legacy-and-the-self-of/.

———. "On Audre Lorde's Legacy and the "Self" of Self-Care, Part 2 of 3." *Low End Theory*, May 14, 2013. https://www.lowendtheory.org/post/50428216600/on-audre-lordes-legacy-and-the-self-of/.

Mohandesi, Salar. "On the Black Bloc." *Viewpoint Magazine*, February 12, 2012. https://viewpointmag.com/2012/02/12/on-the-black-bloc/.

Molloy, Sean. "A Convenient Myopia: SEEK, Shaughnessy, and the Rise of High-Stakes Testing at CUNY." PhD diss., CUNY Graduate Center, 2016. ProQuest (10165579).

Moraga, Cherríe, and Gloria E. Anzaldúa, eds. *This Bridge Called My Back: Writings by Radical Women of Color.* New York: Kitchen Table: Women of Color Press, 1981.

Morales, Iris, and Denise Oliver-Vélez. "Why Read the Young Lords Today?" In *The Young Lords: A Reader*, edited by Darrel Enck-Wanzer, ix–xii. New York: New York University Press, 2010.

Morales Correa, William. *Desde la sombra la luz: Pasajes de mi vida.* Scotts Valley: CreateSpace Independent Publishing, 2015.

Morefield, Jeanne. "Beyond Boomerang." *International Politics Reviews* 8 (2020): 3–10.

Moreno Pisano, Claudia. *Amiri Baraka and Edward Dorn: The Collected Letters.* Albuquerque: University of New Mexico Press, 2014.

Morrison, Toni. *The Source of Self-Regard: Selected Essays, Speeches, and Meditations.* New York: Knopf, 2019.

Moses, Bob. *Radical Equations: Civil Rights from Mississippi to the Algebra Project.* Boston: Beacon Press, 2002.

Moten, Fred, and Stefano Harney. *All Incomplete.* London: Minor Compositions, 2021.

———. "Studying Through the Undercommons: Stefano Harney & Fred Moten – interviewed by Stevphen Shukaitis." *ClassWarU*, November 12, 2012. https://classwaru.org/2012/11/12/studying-through-the-undercommons-stefano-harney-fred-moten-interviewed-by-stevphen-shukaitis/.

———. *The Undercommons: Fugitive Planning and Black Study*. Brooklyn and London: Autonomedia and Minor Compositions, 2013.

———. "The University: Last Words." In Strike MoMA Working Group of International Imagination of Anti-national, Anti-imperialist Feelings (IIAAF), *Strike MoMA Reader*, 2021. https://www.strikemoma.org/reader/.

Muller, Lauren, and the Blueprint Collective. *June Jordan's Poetry for the People: A Revolutionary Blueprint*. Oxfordshire: Routledge, 1995.

Muñoz, José Esteban. *Cruising Utopia: The Then and There of Queer Futurity*. New York: New York University Press, 2009.

———. *Disidentifications: Queers of Color and the Performance of Politics*. Minneapolis: University of Minnesota Press, 1999.

Murch, Donna. *Assata Taught Me: State Violence, Mass Incarceration, and the Movement for Black Lives*. Chicago: Haymarket Books, 2020.

———. *Living for the City: Migration, Education, and the Rise of the Black Panther Party in Oakland, California*. Chapel Hill: University of North Carolina Press, 2010.

Murrell, George. "SEEK Dorms: Black Culture and Red Carpet." *The Campus*, October 16, 1968.

Myers, Joshua. *Of Black Study*. London: Pluto Press, 2023.

Nadal, Antonio, and Milga Morales Nadal. "Bilingual Education and Puerto Rican Studies: From Vision to Reality." In *Puerto Rican Studies at the City University of New York: The First Fifty Years*, edited by María Pérez y González and Virginia Sánchez Korrol, 73–97. New York: El Centro Press, 2021.

Naison, Mark. *Communists in Harlem During the Depression*. Champaign: University of Illinois Press, 2004.

Nash, Jennifer C. *Black Feminism Reimagined: After Intersectionality*. Durham: Duke University Press, 2019.

———. "The Political Life of Black Motherhood." *Feminist Studies* 44, no. 3 (2018): 699–712.

Nash, Margaret A. *Women's Higher Education in the United States: New Historical Perspectives*. London: Palgrave Macmillan, 2018.

National Center for Education Statistics. *120 Years of American Education: A Statistical Portrait* (January 1993). https://nces.ed.gov/pubs93/93442.pdf/.

Navarro, Mireya. "New Light on Old F.B.I. Fight; Decades of Surveillance of Puerto Rican Groups." *New York Times*, November 28, 2003. www.nytimes.com/2003/11/28/nyregion/new-light-on-old-fbi-fight-decades-of-surveillance-of-puerto-rican-groups.html/.

NYC Students for Justice in Palestine. "The Real Story: The New McCarthyism and Repression of Palestine Activism at CUNY." *NYCSJP* (blog). February 26, 2016. nycsjp.wordpress.com/2016/02/24/the-real-story-the-new-mccarthyism-and-repression-of-palestine-activism-at-cuny/.

Neal, Larry. "Ellison's Zoot Suit: Politics as Ritual." *Black World* (December 1970): 31–52.

Nelson, Maggie. *On Freedom: Four Songs of Care and Constraint*. Minneapolis: Graywolf Press, 2021.

"Never Forget: 10-Year-Old Clifford Glover Shot in the Back By NYPD." *Black Main Street*, July 22, 2016. https://blackmainstreet.net/never-forget-nypd-officer-killed-10-year-old-clifford-glover/.

New York City Board of Education. "Our Children from Puerto Rico: A Report on Their Island Home by the Visiting Puerto Rican Workshop of 1955" (1957). Manuscripts, Archives and Rare Books Division, Schomburg Center for Research in Black Culture, The New York Public Library.

New York Times. "Malcolm X Scores US and Kennedy: Likens Slaying to 'Chickens Coming Home to Roost.'" December 2, 1963. https://www.nytimes.com/1963/12/02/archives/malcolm-x-scores-us-and-kennedy-likens-slaying-to-chickens-coming.html/.

———. "Wilfred Cartey Dies; A Critic and Poet, 60." March 25, 1992. https://www.nytimes.com/1992/03/25/obituaries/wilfred-cartey-dies-a-critic-and-poet-60.html/.

———. "Teenagers Form Protest Parade: 200 High School Students of City Form a Union." September 22, 1968. https://timesmachine.nytimes.com/timesmachine/1968/09/22/89345528.pdf/.

Newt Davidson Collective. *Crisis at CUNY*. New York: Newt Davidson Collective, 1974.

Neyra, Ren Ellis. *The Cry of the Senses: Listening to Latinx and Caribbean Poetics*. Durham: Duke University Press, 2020.

Ngũgĩ wa Thiong'o. *Globalectics: Theory and the Politics of Knowing*. New York: Columbia University Press, 2012.

Nieves, Evelyn. "Protests Are All but Over at CUNY." *New York Times*, April 28, 1991. https://www.nytimes.com/1991/04/28/nyregion/protests-are-all-but-over-at-cuny.html/.

Nocella II, Anthony J., Priya Parmar, and David Stovall, eds. *From Education to Incarceration: Dismantling the School-to-Prison Pipeline*. New York: Peter Lang, 2014.

Nuñez, Louis. "Reflections on Puerto Rican History: Aspira in the Sixties and the Coming of Age of the Stateside Puerto Rican Community." In *CENTRO: Journal of the Center for Puerto Rican Studies Journal* 21, no. 2 (2009): 33–47.

Nyong'o, Tavia. "José Muñoz: Then and There." *The Baffler*, February 10, 2021. https://thebaffler.com/
    latest/jose-munoz-then-and-there-nyongo/.
———. "The Student Demand." *Bully Bloggers*, November 17, 2015, https://bullybloggers.wordpress.
    com/2015/11/17/the-student-demand/.
O'Brien, M.E., and Eman Abdelhadi. *Everything for Everyone: An Oral History of the New York Commune,
    2052–2072*. Brooklyn: Common Notions, 2022.
Odinga, Sekou, Dhoruba Bin Wahad, Jamal Joseph, eds., *Look for Me in the Whirlwind: From the Panther 21 to
    21st-Century Revolutions*. Oakland: PM Press, 2017.
Okechukwu, Amaka. *To Fulfill These Rights: Political Struggle Over Affirmative Action and Open Admissions*. New
    York: Columbia University Press, 2019.
Okechukwu, Amaka, and Suzy Subways (interviewers). "'It Was Electrifying': Organizers Reflect on the
    March 23, 1995, CUNY Protest 20 Years Later." *SLAM! Herstory Project*. Philadelphia: SLAM! Herstory
    Project, 2015. https://slamherstory.wordpress.com/2015/03/23/it-was-electrifying-organizers-reflect-
    on-the-march-23-1995-cuny-protest-20-years-later/.
Opie, Frederick Douglass. *Upsetting the Apple Cart: Black-Latino Coalitions in New York City from Protest to Public
    Office*. New York: Columbia University Press, 2014.
Orr, Daylon. *We Shall Not Be Moved: The CCNY Student Strike of 1949*. Brooklyn: Fugitive Materials, 2022.
Osterweil, Vicky. *In Defense of Looting: A Riotous History of Uncivil Action*. New York: Bold Type Books, 2020.
Ostriker, Alicia. "Her Cargo: Adrienne Rich and the Common Language." *The American Poetry Review* 8.4
    (July/August 1979): 6–10.
Otis, Ginger Adams. "NYC Professor of Black History Says CUNY Illegally Seized $12M Worth of
    Research Materials—Then Lost Most of It." *Daily News*, February 26, 2019. https://www.nydailynews.
    com/new-york/ny-metro-black-history-professor-sues-cuny-over-lost-research-20190225-story.html/.
Ottanelli, Fraser M. "The New York City Left and the Spanish Civil War." In *Facing Fascism: New York
    and the Spanish Civil War*, eds. Peter N. Carroll and James D. Fernandez, 63–69. New York: New York
    University Press, 2007.
Pagan, Teona, Daniel Vazquez, Elizabeth Bazile, Hailey Lam, and Diana Kennedy. "It's Time for CUNY
    to Say Goodbye to Cops: Fighting for a Free University." *Radical History Review*, November 17, 2020.
    https://www.radicalhistoryreview.org/abusablepast/its-time-for-cuny-to-say-goodbye-to-cops-fighting-
    for-a-free-university/.
Painter, Nell Irvin. *The History of White People*. New York: W.W. Norton and Company, 2011.
Palazzo, David P. "The 'Social Factory' in Postwar Italian Radical Thought from Operaismo to Autono-
    mia." PhD diss., CUNY Graduate Center, 2014. ProQuest (3623349).
Palestine Legal. "The Palestine Exception to Free Speech: A Movement Under Attack in the US."
    September 2015. https://palestinelegal.org/the-palestine-exception/.
The Paper. https://www.thepaperccny.online/.
———. "Jewish Studies." December 17, 1970.
———. "Open Forum: Racism at City College." November 5, 1980.
———. "Resolution by the Black Faculty, Department of English." May 6, 1976.
Passerini, Luisa. *Autobiography of a Generation: Italy, 1968*. Middletown: Wesleyan University Press, 1996.
Payne, Charles M., and Carol Sills Strickland, eds. *Teach Freedom: Education for Liberation in the African-American
    Tradition*. New York: Teachers College Press, 2008.
Pérez-Peña, Richard. "At CUNY, Stricter Admissions Bring Ethnic Shift." *New York Times*, May 22, 2012.
    https://www.nytimes.com/2012/05/23/nyregion/at-cunys-top-colleges-black-and-hispanic-fresh-
    men-enrollments-drop.html/.
———. "Amid Protests by Students and Others, CUNY Trustees Vote to Raise Tuition." *New York Times*,
    November 28, 2011. https://www.nytimes.com/2011/11/29/nyregion/cuny-board-approves-tui-
    tion-increases.html/.
Pérez y González, María. Email communication with the author. February 2, 2020.
———. "How a Few Students Transformed the Ivory Tower: Puerto Rican Studies and its ®evolution at
    Brooklyn College." In *Puerto Rican Studies at the City University of New York: The First Fifty Years*, edited by
    María Pérez y González and Virginia Sánchez Korrol, 146–180. New York: El Centro Press, 2021.
Perkins, Linda M. "African-American Women and Hunter College, 1873–1945." *Echo: Journal of the Hunter
    College Archives* (1995): 16–25.
Perkins, Margo V. *Autobiography as Activism: Three Black Women of the Sixties*. Jackson: University Press of
    Mississippi, 2000.
Perlstein, Daniel. "Teaching Freedom: SNCC and the Creation of the Mississippi Freedom Schools."
    History of Education Quarterly 30, no. 3 (Fall 1990): 297–324.
Perspectives Editorial Collective, *Perspectives on Anarchist Theory: Anarcha-Feminisms* 29. Portland: Institute for
    Anarchist Studies, 2016.

Petersen, Glenn. "Viewpoint: ROTC Revival at CUNY Requires Broad-Based Discussion." *Clarion*, September 2013. http://www.psc-cuny.org/clarion/september-2013/viewpoint-rotc-revival-cuny-requires-broad-based-discussion/.

Phelps, Wesley G. "Women's Pentagon Action: The Persistence of Radicalism and Direct-Action Civil Disobedience in the Age of Reagan." *Peace & Change: A Journal of Peace Research* 9, no. 3 (July 2014): 339–365.

Phillip, M. NourbeSe. *Zong!* Middletown: Wesleyan University Press, 2011.

Phillips-Fein, Kim. *Fear City: New York's Fiscal Crisis and the Rise of Austerity Politics*. New York: Metropolitan Books, 2017.

Pinto, Nick. "Under Media Spotlight, City Locates Missing Records of NYPD Political Meddling." *Village Voice*, June 16, 2016. www.villagevoice.com/2016/06/16/under-media-spotlight-city-locates-missing-records-of-nypd-political-meddling/.

Polletta, Francesca. *Freedom is an Endless Meeting: Democracy in American Social Movements*. Chicago: University of Chicago Press, 2002.

———. *It Was Like a Fever: Storytelling in Protest and Politics*. Chicago: University of Chicago Press, 2006.

Prakash, Madhi Suri, and Gustavo Esteva. *Escaping Education: Living as Learning with Grassroots Cultures*. New York: Peter Lang Publishing, 1998.

Prashad, Vijay. *The Darker Nations: A People's History of the Third World*. New York: New Press, 2007.

Primiano, Jillian. "From One Essential Worker to Another: Demanding Safe Working Conditions Could Save My Life." *Left Voice*, April 30, 2020. https://www.leftvoice.org/from-one-essential-worker-to-another-demanding-safe-working-conditions-could-save-my-life/.

PSC-CUNY. "Kristofer Petersen-Overton Gets His Job Back." October 2, 2015. www.psc-cuny.org/about-us/kristofer-petersen-overton-gets-his-job-back/.

Puar, Jasbir K. *Terrorist Assemblages: Homonationalism in Queer Times*. Durham: Duke University Press, 2007.

———. *The Right to Maim: Debility, Capacity, Disability*. Durham: Duke University Press, 2017.

PublicsLab. "All Out for Abortion Access!: Organizing at CUNY and Beyond." October 15, 2022. https://publicslab.gc.cuny.edu/events/all-out-for-abortion-access-organizing-at-cuny-and-beyond/.

Purisic, Ariana. "York College Evacuates After Bomb Threat Hoax." *The Ticker*, March 25, 2022. https://theticker.org/6907/news/york-college-evacuates-after-bomb-threat-hoax/.

Radivojević, Iva. and Martyna Starosta, dirs. *Are You With Me?: Louis Reyes Rivera 1945–2012*. 2021; New York, NY: Occupy CUNY News.

Rankine, Claudia, *Citizen: An American Lyric*. Minneapolis: Graywolf Press, 2014.

Ratcliff, Anthony James. "Liberation at the End of a Pen: Writing Pan-African Politics of Cultural Struggle." PhD diss., University of Massachusetts Amherst, 2009. ProQuest (3372273).

Reed, Conor Tomás. "All Power to the Public Humanities!" *ASAP/Journal*, November 29, 2021. https://asapjournal.com/public-humanities-and-the-arts-of-the-present-all-power-to-the-public-humanities-conor-tomas-reed/.

———. "Black Arts Boomerang," *The New Inquiry*, February 18, 2015. https://thenewinquiry.com/black-arts-boomerang/.

———. "Diving Into SEEK: Adrienne Rich and Social Movements at the City College of New York, 1968–1974." In *Jayne Cortez, Adrienne Rich, and the Feminist Superhero: Voice, Vision, Politics, and Performance in US Contemporary Women's Poetics*, edited by Laura Hinton, 91–116. Washington, DC: Lexington Books, 2016.

———. "The Evolution of Puerto Rican Studies at City College." In *Puerto Rican Studies at the City University of New York: The First Fifty Years*, edited by María Pérez y González and Virginia Sánchez Korrol, 120–145. New York: El Centro Press, 2021.

———. "Intersecting Picket Lines: Free Speech, Palestine, and the CUNY Contract." *Viewpoint Magazine*, June 23, 2016. https://viewpointmag.com/2016/06/23/intersecting-picket-lines-free-speech-palestine-and-the-cuny-contract/.

———. "Long Live Said." *The New Inquiry*, October 25, 2013. https://thenewinquiry.com/long-live-said/.

———. "On the City as University: Occupy and the Future of Public Education." *Tidal Magazine* (2012)/ *The Indypendent*, May 25, 2012. https://indypendent.org/2012/05/the-city-as-university-occupy-and-the-future-of-public-education/.

———. "Race." In *Keywords for Radicals: The Contested Vocabulary of Late Capitalist Struggle*, edited by Kelly Fritsch, Clare O'Connor, and A.K. Thompson, 343–350. Chico: AK Press, 2016.

———. "Radiating Black~Puerto Rican~Feminist Studies from the City University of New York to the Americas and the Caribbean." Event series, Center for the Humanities, City University of New York Graduate Center, New York, November 2020–January 2021. https://www.centerforthehumanities.org/programming/radiating-black-puerto-rican-feminist-studies-from-the-city-university-of-new-york-to-the-americas-and-the-caribbean/.

————. "Realizing the Dream of a Liberation University." *Verso* (blog), September 8, 2020. https://www.versobooks.com/blogs/4848-hot-city-realizing-the-dream-of-a-liberation-university/.

————. "Remembering Jane Marcus: CUNY Prof Was a Tenaciously Brilliant Scholar, Activist." *The Indypendent*, June 9, 2015. https://indypendent.org/2015/06/remembering-jane-marcus-cuny-prof-was-a-tenaciously-brilliant-scholar-activist/.

————. "Remembering Louis Reyes Rivera—The People's Poet & a Fighter for a Free and Open CUNY." *The Indypendent*, March 15, 2012. https://indypendent.org/2012/03/remembering-louis-reyes-rivera-the-peoples-poet-a-fighter-for-a-free-and-open-cuny/.

————. "Seed Foundations Shakin'": Interwar African Diasporic Responses to Fascism and the 1936–1939 Spanish Civil War." *The Volunteer: Veterans of the Abraham Lincoln Brigade*, November 22, 2010. https://albavolunteer.org/2010/11/african-responses-to-fascism-the-spanish-civil-war/.

————. "Solid Ground at Occupy Wall Street." *The Indypendent*, September 26, 2011. https://indypendent.org/2011/09/solid-ground-at-occupy-wall-street/.

————. "Step One. Occupy Universities. Step Two. Transform Them." *Tidal Magazine* (December 2011). https://www.e-flux.com/legacy/2013/05/TIDAL_occupytheory.pdf?b8c429/.

————. "'Treasures That Prevail': Adrienne Rich, the SEEK Program, and Social Movements at the City College of New York, 1968–1972." In *Adrienne Rich: "What we are a part of": Teaching at CUNY, 1968–1974 (Part II). Lost & Found: The CUNY Poetics Document Initiative, Series 4*. Edited by Iemanjá Brown, Stefania Heim, erica kaufman, Kristin Moriah, Conor Tomás Reed, Talia Shalev, Wendy Tronrud, and Ammiel Alcalay. New York: The Center for the Humanities, Graduate Center of the City University of New York, 2014.

Reed, Thomas F., and Karen Brandow. *The Sky Never Changes: Testimonies from the Guatemalan Labor Movement*. Ithaca: ILR Press, 1996.

Reid-Pharr, Robert F. "Speaking through Anti-Semitism: The Nation of Islam and the Poetics of Black (Counter) Modernity." In *Social Text* 49 (1996): 133–147.

Retta, Mary. "Students Across the Country Are Going on Strike." *The Nation*, April 24, 2020. https://www.thenation.com/article/activism/students-across-the-country-are-going-on-strike/.

Revolutionary Student Coordinating Committee. "CUNY students and RSCC confront David Petraeus." YouTube video, 2:23. September 9, 2013. https://www.youtube.com/watch?v=3HHab-ZCnJw/.

Rhodes, Messiah. "The Lumpen Blacks." *{Young}ist*, December 4, 2014. https://youngist.github.io/clean-blog/the-lumpen-blacks#.YmWStPvMLrc/.

Rich, Adrienne. *Adrienne Rich: "What we are a part of": Teaching at CUNY, 1968–1974 (Parts I & II)*. In *Lost & Found: The CUNY Poetics Document Initiative, Series 4*, edited by Iemanjá Brown, Stefania Heim, erica kaufman, Kristin Moriah, Conor Tomás Reed, Talia Shalev, Wendy Tronrud, and Ammiel Alcalay. New York: The Center for the Humanities, Graduate Center of the City University of New York, 2014.

————. "Assignment from English 1.8." Carton 9, Folder 390. Adrienne Rich Papers, 1927–1999. Schlesinger Library on the History of Women in America, Radcliffe Institute, Cambridge, MA.

————. "Beginnings." In *Starting Your Own High School*, edited by Elizabeth Cleaners Street School People, 25–27. New York: Random House, 1972.

————. "Blood, Bread, and Poetry: The Location of the Poet (1984)." *Blood, Bread, and Poetry: Selected Prose 1979–1985*. New York: W.W. Norton and Company, 1986.

————. "The Board of Education Hearings." Carton 9, Folder 390. Adrienne Rich Papers, 1927–1999. Schlesinger Library on the History of Women in America, Radcliffe Institute, Cambridge, MA.

————. "The Burning of Paper Instead of Children." In *The Will to Change: Poems 1968–1970*, 42–44. New York: W.W. Norton and Company, 1971.

————. "The Case for a Drop-Out School." *New York Review of Books*, June 15, 1972. https://www.nybooks.com/articles/1972/06/15/the-case-for-a-drop-out-school/.

————. *A Change of World: Poems*. New Haven: Yale University Press, 1971.

————. "City College SEEK English Course 1.8." April 1969." Carton 9, Folder 388. Adrienne Rich Papers, 1927–1999. Schlesinger Library on the History of Women in America, Radcliffe Institute, Cambridge, MA.

————. *Collected Poems: 1950–2012*. New York: W.W. Norton and Company, 2016.

————. "Compulsory Heterosexuality and Lesbian Existence (1980)." In *Blood, Bread, and Poetry: Selected Prose 1979–1985*, 23–75. New York: W.W. Norton and Company, 1986.

————. *Diving into the Wreck: Poems 1971–1972*. New York: W.W. Norton and Company, 1973.

————. "Endpapers." In *Later Poems: Selected and New, 1971–2012, 511–512*. New York: W.W. Norton and Company, 2012.

————. "English 1-H Fall 1971." Carton 9, Folder 388. Adrienne Rich Papers, 1927–1999. Schlesinger Library on the History of Women in America, Radcliffe Institute, Cambridge, MA.

————. "English 13.3W Images of Women in Poetry by Men." Carton 9, Folder 391. Adrienne Rich

Papers, 1927–1999. Schlesinger Library on the History of Women in America, Radcliffe Institute, Cambridge, MA.

———. "Final Comments on the Interdisciplinary Program, Spring 1972." Carton 9, Folder 387. Adrienne Rich Papers, 1927–1999. Schlesinger Library on the History of Women in America, Radcliffe Institute, Cambridge, MA.

———. "For the Young Anarchists." In *Later Poems: Selected and New, 1971–2012*, 495. New York: W.W. Norton and Company, 2012.

———. *Leaflets: Poems, 1965–1968*. New York: W.W. Norton and Company, 1969.

———. "The muralist." In *What Is Found There: Notebooks on Poetry and Politics*, 43–53. New York: W.W. Norton and Company, 1993.

———. "Note to Mina Shaughnessy, 18 June 1968." Carton 9, Folder 386. Adrienne Rich Papers, 1927–1999. Schlesinger Library on the History of Women in America, Radcliffe Institute, Cambridge, MA.

———. "Notes for English 1.8." Carton 9, Folder 390. Adrienne Rich Papers, 1927–1999. Schlesinger Library on the History of Women in America, Radcliffe Institute, Cambridge, MA.

———. "Notes on Eng 13.3." Carton 9, Folder 392. Adrienne Rich Papers, 1927–1999. Schlesinger Library on the History of Women in America, Radcliffe Institute, Cambridge, MA.

———. "Notes Toward a Politics of Location (1984)." In *Blood, Bread, and Poetry: Selected Prose 1979–1985*, 210–231. New York: W.W. Norton and Company, 1986.

———. *Of Woman Born: Motherhood as Experience & Institution*. New York: W.W. Norton and Company, 2021.

———. "Raya Dunayevskaya's Marx." In *Arts of the Possible: Essays and Conversations*, 83–97. New York: W.W. Norton and Company, 2001.

———. "SEEK Notes." Carton 9, Folder 389. Adrienne Rich Papers, 1927–1999. Schlesinger Library on the History of Women in America, Radcliffe Institute, Cambridge, MA.

———. "Sources: XXII." In *Your Native Land, Your Life: Poems*, 25. New York: W.W. Norton and Company, 1986.

———. "Split at the Root." In *Blood, Bread, and Poetry: Selected Prose 1979–1985*, 100–123. New York: W.W. Norton and Company, 1986.

———. "Statement to C.C.N.Y Faculty Meeting, Wednesday, April 23 [1969]." Carton 9, Folder 389. Adrienne Rich Papers, 1927–1999. Schlesinger Library on the History of Women in America, Radcliffe Institute, Cambridge, MA.

———. "Teaching Language in Open Admissions (1972)." In *On Lies, Secrets, and Silence: Selected Prose 1966–1978*, 51–68. New York: W.W. Norton, 1979.

———. "Tear Gas." In *Poems: Selected and New 1950–1974*, 139. New York: W.W. Norton and Company, 1975.

———. "To: ALL Students in English 1.8 B2 and 1.8 C4." Carton 9, Folder 390. Adrienne Rich Papers, 1927–1999. Schlesinger Library on the History of Women in America, Radcliffe Institute, Cambridge, MA.

———. "Toward a Woman-Centered University." In *On Lies, Secrets, and Silence: Selected Prose 1966–1978*, 125–156. New York: W.W. Norton, 1979.

———. "Transcendental Etude." In *The Dream of a Common Language: Poems 1974–1977*, 72–77. New York: W.W. Norton and Company, 1978.

———. "We have read and talked about LeRoi Jones' essay." Carton 9, Folder 390. Adrienne Rich Papers, 1927–1999. Schlesinger Library on the History of Women in America, Radcliffe Institute, Cambridge, MA.

———. "When We Dead Awaken: Writing as Re-Vision (1971)." In *On Lies, Secrets, and Silence: Selected Prose 1966–1978*, 33–50. New York: W.W. Norton and Company, 1979.

———. "Write a description of a course." Carton 9, Folder 390. Adrienne Rich Papers, 1927–1999. Schlesinger Library on the History of Women in America, Radcliffe Institute, Cambridge, MA.

———. "Write an analysis of your neighborhood." Carton 9, Folder 388. Adrienne Rich Papers, 1927–1999. Schlesinger Library on the History of Women in America, Radcliffe Institute, Cambridge, MA.

Rickford, Russell. *We Are an African People: Independent Education, Black Power, and the Radical Imagination*. Oxford: Oxford University Press, 2016.

Riley, Clayton. "Living Poetry by Black Arts Group." *Liberator* 5, no. 5 (May 1965): n.p..

Rivera, Louis Reyes. "Conrad Attacks Open Admissions Plan." *Tech News*, February 27, 1970.

———. *Jazz in Jail*. East Elmhurst: Blind Beggar Press, 2016.

———. "Student Files for Federal Agent?" *Tech News*, October 23, 1969.

———. "Student-Member of BHE Doubts Scott's Abilities." *Tech News*, October 7, 1969.

———. "Unanswered Questions." *Tech News*, October 23, 1969.

Rivera Cusicanqui, Silvia. "*Ch'ixinakax utxiwa*: A Reflection on the Practices and Discourses of Decolonization." In *Ch'ixinakax utxiwa: On Practices and Discourses of Decolonization*, 46–70. Cambridge:

Polity Press, 2020.

Roberts, Neil. *Freedom as Marronage*. Chicago: University of Chicago Press, 2015.

Robin, Corey. "The Pandemic is the Time to Resurrect the Public University." *New Yorker*, May 7, 2020. https://www.newyorker.com/culture/cultural-comment/the-pandemic-is-the-time-to-resurrect-the-public-university/.

Roediger, David R. *The Wages of Whiteness: Race and the Making of the American Working Class*. New York: Verso, 2007.

Rojas, Fabio. *From Black Power to Black Studies: How a Radical Social Movement Became an Academic Discipline*. Baltimore: Johns Hopkins University Press, 2007.

Romney, Patricia. *We Were There: The Third World Women's Alliance & The Second Wave*. New York: Feminist Press, 2021.

Rosenau, William. *Tonight We Bombed the US Capitol: The Explosive Story of M19, America's First Female Terrorist Group*. New York: Atria Books, 2020.

Rosenfeld, Seth. *Subversives: The FBI's War on Student Radicals, and Reagan's Rise to Power*. New York: Farrar, Straus and Giroux, 2012.

Rudy, S. Willis. *The College of the City of New York: A History: 1847–1947*. New York: City College Press, 1949.

Rugh, Peter. "The CUNY Wars: How David Petraeus Turned America's Most Diverse University Into a War Zone." *Alternet*, December 10, 2013. http://www.alternet.org/education/cuny-wars-how-david-petraeus-turned-americas-most-diverse-university-war-zone/.

Rustin, Bayard Papers. Microfilm reels #11–12. Manuscripts, Archives and Rare Books Division, Schomburg Center for Research in Black Culture, The New York Public Library.

Sánchez Korrol, Virginia E. *From Colonia to Community: The History of Puerto Ricans in New York City, 1917–1948*. Westport: Preager, 1983.

Sartre, Jean-Paul. "Preface." In Frantz Fanon's *Wretched of the Earth*, 7–31. New York: Grove Press, 1963.

Sasmor, Ken, and Tom Foty. "It May Not Be the Place You Knew." *The Campus*, May 6, 1969.

Save KCC Urban Farm. "Say NO to budget cuts at the urban farm!" *The Action Network*. https://action-network.org/petitions/say-no-to-proposed-budget-cuts-to-kingsborough-community-colleges-urban-farm/.

Savio, Mario. "Mario Savio's Speech before the FSM Sit-in." December 3, 1964. *Free Speech Movement Archives*. http://www.fsm-a.org/stacks/mario/mario_speech.html/.

Schell, Eileen. *Gypsy Academics and Mother-Teachers: Gender, Contingent Labor, and Writing Instruction*. Portsmouth: Heinemann, 1997.

Schirmer, Eleni, Jason Wozniak, Dana Morrison, Joanna Gonsalves, and Rich Levy. "Making the Invisible Visible: Organizing against the Instructionally Harmful, Antidemocratic Effects of Institutional Debt." *AAUP Journal of Academic Freedom* 12 (2021). https://www.aaup.org/sites/default/files/Schirmer_et_al_.pdf/.

Schonberger, Benjamin. "Student Protests Over State Budget Cuts Spread to 8 CUNY Campuses." *The Chronicle of Higher Education*, April 17, 1991. https://www.chronicle.com/article/Student-Protests-Over-State/86937/.

Schrader, Stuart. *Badges Without Borders: How Global Counterinsurgency Transformed American Policing*. Oakland: University of California Press, 2019.

Schrecker, Ellen. *No Ivory Tower: McCarthyism and the Universities*. Oxford: Oxford University Press, 1986.

Schulman, Grace. "*Diving into The Wreck: Poems 1971–1972* by Adrienne Rich." *The American Poetry Review* 2.5 (September/October 1973): 11.

Schulman, Sarah. "Today I Testified Before the CUNY Task Force on Anti-Semitism." *Jadaliyya*, March 24, 2016. http://jadaliyya.com/Details/33117/Today-I-Testified-Before-the-CUNY-Task-Force-on-Anti-Semitism/.

Schultz, Dagmar, dir. *Audre Lorde: The Berlin Years 1984 to 1992*; 2012. New York: Third World Newsreel.

Schwartz, Claire. "Reading Otherwise: On kinship, racial pedagogy, and reading as revision." *Jewish Currents*, March 21, 2022. https://jewishcurrents.org/reading-otherwise/.

Scott-Heron, Gil. "Running." *I'm New Here*. XL Recordings, 2010, CD and LP.

Seamster, Louise, and Raphaël Charron-Chénier. "Predatory Inclusion and Education Debt: Rethinking the Racial Wealth Gap." *Social Currents* 4, no. 3 (2017): 199–207.

Serrano, Basilio. "¡Rifle, Cañón, y Escopeta!: A Chronicle of the Puerto Rican Student Union." In *The Puerto Rican Movement: Voices from the Diaspora*, edited by Andrés Torres and José E. Velásquez, 124–143. Philadelphia: Temple University Press, 1998.

Shakur, Assata. *An Autobiography*. Brooklyn: Lawrence Hill Books, 2001.

———. "Black Liberation: A Reminder." *The Paper*, February 20, 1975.

———. "Women in Prison: How We Are." *The Black Scholar* 9, no. 7 (April 1978).

Shapiro, Eliza. "'I Love My Skin!' Why Black Parents Are Turning to Afrocentric Schools." *New York Times*, January 8, 2019. https://www.nytimes.com/2019/01/08/nyregion/afrocentric-schools-segregation-brooklyn.html/.

Sharpe, Christina. *In the Wake: On Blackness and Being.* Durham: Duke University Press, 2016.

Shaughnessy, Mina P. "Diving In: An Introduction to Basic Writing." *College Composition and Communication* 27 (October 1976): 234–239.

———. *Errors and Expectations: A Guide for the Teacher of Basic Writing.* Oxford: Oxford University Press, 1977.

Sherwin, Wilson. "Working for Abolition Means Abolishing Work." *Spectre Journal,* June 1, 2022. https://spectrejournal.com/working-for-abolition-means-abolishing-work/.

Sherwood, Daniel A. "Civic Struggles: Jews, Blacks, and the Question of Inclusion at The City College of New York, 1930–1975." PhD diss., New School University, 2015. ProQuest (3707753).

Shor, Ira. Interview with the author. January 28, 2022.

———. "Our Apartheid: Writing Instruction and Inequality." *Journal of Basic Writing* 16, no. 1 (Spring 1997): 91–104.

Showalter, Elaine. "Introduction: Teaching about Women, 1971." In *Female Studies IV*, edited by Elaine Showalter and Carol Ohmann, 3–14. Pittsburgh: KNOW, Inc., 1972.

Sickels, Amy. *Adrienne Rich.* Philadelphia: Chelsea House Publishers, 2005.

"The Siege of the Third Precinct in Minneapolis: An Account and Analysis." *CrimethInc,* June 10, 2020. https://crimethinc.com/2020/06/10/the-siege-of-the-third-precinct-in-minneapolis-an-account-and-analysis/.

Siegel, Jacob. "Eric Garner Protesters Have a Direct Line to City Hall." *Daily Beast,* January 11, 2014. https://www.thedailybeast.com/eric-garner-protesters-have-a-direct-line-to-city-hall/.

Sigal, Brad. "Interview by Suzy Subways: Brad Sigal on SLAM! at City College from 1996 to 2000." *SLAM! Herstory Project.* Philadelphia: SLAM! Herstory Project, 2012. https://slamherstory.wordpress.com/2014/04/07/first-audio-segments-from-the-oral-history-interviews/.

Simms, Paul B. "Black Athletes Defend Olympic Action." *Tech News*, October 30, 1968.

———. "Black Comic Turned Politician: An Interview with Dick Gregory." *Tech News*, October 31, 1967.

———. "Dan Watts on Powell and on Black Rights and the White Man." *Tech News*, February 14, 1967.

———. "From a Black Chair: Institute for Black Students." *Tech News*, December 16, 1968.

———. "From a Black Chair: The Three Lies." *Tech News*, October 23, 1968.

———. Interview with the author. May 22, 2012.

———. "McKissick Accuses Miseducation in Schools." *Tech News*, April 18, 1967.

———. "Minister [Farrakhan]: Black Muslims Don't Exist." *Tech News*, May 9, 1967.

———. "The U.A.A.A.; Black Politics: An Interview with William Wright." *Tech News*, October 3, 1967.

———. "What Was Behind the CCNY Takeover?" *Harvard Crimson,* July 7, 1969. https://www.thecrimson.com/article/1969/7/22/what-was-behind-the-ccny-takeover/.

Simms, Paul B. and Denise Adams. "Paul and Denise Adams Simms: An Oral History." YouTube video, 48:44. August 22, 2021. https://www.youtube.com/watch?v=bq5qdE1vd4c/.

Simms, Paul B., and Louis R. Rivera. "Volpe Throws Light on Cartey Mystery, Faculty Cited as the Deciding Factor." *Tech News*, September 25, 1969.

Sitrin, Marina. "The Anarchist Spirit." *Dissent Magazine* (Fall 2015). https://www.dissentmagazine.org/article/anarchist-spirit-horizontalism/.

Sivanandan, A. *Catching History on the Wing: Race, Culture and Globalisation.* London: Pluto Press, 2008.

Smith, Barbara, ed. *Home Girls: A Black Feminist Anthology.* New York: Kitchen Table: Women of Color Press, 1983.

Smith, Carol. Interview with the author. October 2021.

———. *The Struggle for Free Speech at CCNY, 1931–42.* https://virtualny.ashp.cuny.edu/gutter/panels/panel1.html/.

Smith, Eric R. "New York's Aid to the Spanish Republic." In *Facing Fascism: New York and the Spanish Civil War*, edited by Peter N. Carroll and James D. Fernandez, 47–48. New York: New York University Press, 2007.

Smith, Neil. "Contours of a Spatialized Politics: Homeless Vehicles and the Production of Geographical Scale." *Social Text* 33 (1992): 55–81.

Smolarski, Chloe, and Irwin Yellowitz. "CUNY Adjunct Labor." CUNY Digital History Archive. https://cdha.cuny.edu/collections/show/292/.

Solomon, Mark. *The Cry Was Unity: Communists and African Americans, 1917–36.* Jackson: University Press of Mississippi, 1998.

Spencer, Robyn C. Email communication with the author. September 20, 2017.

———. *The Revolution Has Come; Black Power, Gender, and the Black Panther Party in Oakland.* Durham: Duke University Press, 2016.

Spring, Joel. *A Primer of Libertarian Education*. Montreal: Black Rose Books, 1975.

Springer, Kimberly. *Living for the Revolution: Black Feminist Organizations, 1968–1980*. Durham: Duke University Press, 2005.

———. "Radical Archives and the New Cycles of Contention." *Viewpoint Magazine*, October 31, 2015. https://viewpointmag.com/2015/10/31/radical-archives-and-the-new-cycles-of-contention/.

Srilangarajah, Virou. "We Are Here Because You Were with Us: Remembering A. Sivanandan (1923–2018)." *Verso* (blog), February 7, 2018. https://www.versobooks.com/blogs/3608-we-are-here-because-you-were-with-us-remembering-a-sivanandan-1923-2018/.

Srinivasan, Amia. *The Right to Sex: Feminism in the 21st Century*. New York: Farrar, Straus and Giroux, 2021.

Stansell, Christine. "Review." *Off Our Backs* 4.3 (February 1974): 15.

Starr, Meg. "Hit Them Harder: Leadership, Solidarity, and the Puerto Rican Independence Movement." In *The Hidden 1970s: Histories of Radicalism*, edited by Dan Berger, 135–154. New Brunswick: Rutgers University Press, 2010.

Staudenmaier, Michael. *Truth and Revolution: A History of the Sojourner Truth Organization, 1969–1986*. Chico: AK Press, 2012.

Stewart, Sean, ed. *On the Ground: An Illustrated Anecdotal History of the Sixties Underground Press in the U.S.* Oakland: PM Press, 2011.

Stern, Michael. "Teen-Age Revolt: Is It Deeper Today?" *New York Times*, October 7, 1968. https://timesmachine.nytimes.com/timesmachine/1968/10/07/77180873.pdf.

Strong, Lynn Steger. "How Adrienne Rich Changed Her Mind." *The New Republic*, May 13, 2021. https://newrepublic.com/article/162365/adrienne-rich-changed-mind-biography-review/.

Sullivan, Mecca Jamilah. *The Poetics of Difference: Queer Feminist Forms in the African Diaspora*. Chicago: University of Illinois Press, 2021.

Svetlovsky, June, and Ben Chitty. "Vietnam Era Ends at the City University of NY." *The Veteran: Vietnam Veterans Against the War* 26 (Fall 1996): 1, 7, 13. http://www.vvaw.org/pdf/v26n1.pdf/.

Táíwò, Olúfẹ́mi O. *Elite Capture: How the Powerful Took Over Identity Politics (And Everything Else)*. Chicago: Haymarket Books, 2022.

Tarì, Marcello. *There is No Unhappy Revolution: The Communism of Destitution*. Translated by Richard Braude. Brooklyn: Common Notions, 2021.

Tarlau, Rebecca. *Occupying Schools, Occupying Land: How the Landless Workers Movement Transformed Brazilian Education*. Oxford: Oxford University Press, 2019.

———. "Prefigurative Politics With, In, and Against the State: The Brazilian Landless Workers Movement and Latin American Philosophies of Education." In *Schooling in the Caribbean and Latin America: Reproduction, Resistance, Revolution, LÁPIZ* 5 (2020). https://www.lapes.org/_files/ugd/c3ccc5_6a9a7edb380e4d-deb6cb04b166a37717.pdf/.

Tarleton, John. "NYPD Spy Scandal Hits CUNY: Muslim Students Target of Profiling." *Clarion*, November 2011. http://www.psc-cuny.org/clarion/november-2011/nypd-spy-scandal-hits-cuny-muslim-students-target-profiling/.

Taylor, Astra, and Todd Wolfson. "Beyond the Neoliberal University." *Boston Review*, August 4, 2020. http://bostonreview.net/class-inequality/todd-wolfson-astra-taylor-beyond-neoliberal-university/.

Taylor, Keeanga-Yamahtta. "Joe Biden, Kamala Harris, and the Limits of Representation." *New Yorker*, August 24, 2020. https://www.newyorker.com/news/our-columnists/joe-biden-kamala-harris-and-the-limits-of-representation/.

———. *Race for Profit: How Banks and the Real Estate Industry Undermined Black Homeownership*. Chapel Hill: University of North Carolina Press, 2019.

Team Colors Collective. *Uses of a Whirlwind: Movement, Movements, and Contemporary Radical Currents in the United States*. Chico: AK Press, 2010.

Tech News. "B.H.E. Is Also Dirty." March 5, 1970.

———. "Copeland Style Moderation." September 25, 1969.

———. "Jackson State, Augusta, Orangeburg, Texas Southern, and on, and on, and on." May 15, 1970.

———. "Scott Develops New Courses: Curriculum to be Expanded." October 30, 1969.

———. "Unanswered Questions." October 23, 1969.

Theoharis, Jeanne. "'I Feel Like a Despised Insect': Coming of Age Under Surveillance in New York." *The Intercept*, February 18, 2016. https://theintercept.com/2016/02/18/coming-of-age-under-surveillance-in-new-york/.

———, Alan Aja, and Joseph Entin. "Spare CUNY, and Save the Education our Heroes Deserve." *City Limits*, May 13, 2020. https://citylimits.org/2020/05/13/opinion-spare-cuny-and-save-the-education-our-heroes-deserve/.

Thomas, Lorenzo. "The Shadow World: New York's Umbra Workshop & Origins of the Black Arts Movement." *Callaloo* 4 (October 1978): 53–72.

Thompson, Ahmir "Questlove," dir. *Summer of Soul*. 2021, Los Angeles, California: Searchlight Pictures.

Tillman, Linda. "Jewish Studies Threatened." *The Campus*, September 29, 1978.

Tinajero, Araceli. *El Lector: A History of the Cigar Factory Reader*. Austin: University of Texas Press, 2010.

Tinson, Christopher M. *Radical Intellect: Liberator Magazine and Black Activism in the 1960s*. Chapel Hill: University of North Carolina Press, 2017.

Toupin, Louise, and Käthe Roth. *Wages for Housework: The History of an International Feminist Movement, 1972–77*. London: Pluto Press, 2018.

Traub, James. *City on a Hill: Testing the American Dream at City College*. Burlington: Da Capo Press, 1994.

Treitler, Vilna Bashi. *The Ethnic Project: Transforming Racial Fiction into Ethnic Factions*. Stanford: Stanford University Press, 2013.

Tucker, Daniel, and Anthony Romero, eds. *Organize Your Own: The Politics and Poetics of Self-Determination Movements*. Chicago: Soberscove Press, 2016.

Umoja, Akinyele Omowale. *We Will Shoot Back: Armed Resistance in the Mississippi Freedom Movement*. New York: New York University, 2013.

The United Federation of College Teachers. "Draft of an Appeal to the City University Community." CUNY Digital History Archive. https://cdha.cuny.edu/items/show/3112/.

Unity and Struggle. "Big Brick Energy: a multi-city study of the 2020 George Floyd uprising." July 20, 2022. http://www.unityandstruggle.org/2022/07/big-brick-energy-a-multi-city-study-of-the-2020-george-floyd-uprising/.

UCSC COLA Agitation Committee. "Time to Strike: Academic Workers and the Tactic of Withholding Grades." *Jadaliyya*, August 20, 2020. https://www.jadaliyya.com/Details/41578/Time-to-Strike-Academic-Workers-and-the-Tactic-of-Withholding-Grades/.

Valburn, Marjorie. "Lives and Livelihoods." *Inside Higher Ed*, June 23, 2020. https://www.insidehighered.com/news/2020/06/23/cuny-system-suffers-more-coronavirus-deaths-any-other-higher-ed-system-us/.

Van Nort, Sydney. *The City College of New York*. Charleston: Arcadia Publishing, 2007.

Velásquez, José E. "Another West Side Story: An Interview with Members of El Comité-MINP." In *The Puerto Rican Movement: Voices from the Diaspora*, edited by Andrés Torres and José E. Velásquez, 88–106. Philadelphia: Temple University Press, 1998.

Vera Institute. "People in Jail and Prison in Spring 2021." https://www.vera.org/downloads/publications/people-in-jail-and-prison-in-spring-2021.pdf/.

Villarosa, Linda. "'A Terrible Price': The Deadly Racial Disparities of COVID-19 in America." *New York Times*, April 29, 2020. https://www.nytimes.com/2020/04/29/magazine/racial-disparities-COVID-19.html/.

Wallis, Hanna. "Nurses Say They Don't Want to Be Called Heroes During the Coronavirus Pandemic." *Teen Vogue*, April 28, 2020. https://www.teenvogue.com/story/nurses-dont-want-to-be-called-heroes/.

Washington Post. "Fatal Force: Police Shootings Database." Last updated March 21, 2023 [originally published May 30, 2015]. https://www.washingtonpost.com/graphics/investigations/police-shootings-database/.

"'We All Float Down Here': RAM's 'Floating Tactics' and the Long Hot Summer of 1967." In *Movement for No Society*. Seattle: Contagion Press, 2018. Out of print; available at https://theanarchistlibrary.org/library/movement-for-no-society-movement-for-no-society.

Weaver, James. "The Student as Worker." In *The University and Revolution*, edited by Gary Weaver and James Weaver, 59–65. Englewood Cliffs: Prentice-Hall, 1969.

Wei, William. *The Asian American Movement*. Philadelphia: Temple University Press, 1993.

Weinberg, Meyer. *A Chance to Learn: The History of Race and Education in the United States*. Cambridge: Cambridge University Press, 1977.

Weissman, Sarah. "HBCU Bomb Threats Take a Toll on Mental Health." *Inside Higher Ed*, April 8, 2022. https://www.insidehighered.com/news/2022/04/08/hbcu-bomb-threats-take-toll-mental-health/.

———. "Racist Graffiti Creates Months of Tension at Queens College." *Inside Higher Ed*, May 25, 2022. https://www.insidehighered.com/news/2022/05/25/racist-graffiti-creates-months-tensions-queens-college/.

Whalen, Carmen. "Radical Contexts: Puerto Rican Politics in the 1960s and 1970s and the Center for Puerto Rican Studies." In *CENTRO: Journal of the Center for Puerto Rican Studies Journal* 21, no. 2 (2009): 221–255.

Wilder, Craig Steven. *Ebony and Ivy: Race, Slavery, and the Troubled History of America's Universities*. New York: Bloomsbury Press, 2013.

Wilderson III, Frank. *Afropessimism*. New York: W.W. Norton and Company, 2020.

Williams, Bianca C., Dian D. Squire, and Frank A. Tuitt, eds. *Plantation Politics and Campus Rebellions: Power, Diversity, and the Emancipatory Struggle in Higher Education*. Albany: SUNY Press, 2021.

Williams, Evelyn. *Inadmissible Evidence: The Story of the African-American Trial Lawyer Who Defended the Black Liberation Army.* Brooklyn: Lawrence Hill Books, 1994.

Williams, Heather Andrea. *Self-Taught: African American Education in Slavery and Freedom.* Chapel Hill: University of North Carolina Press, 2005.

Wilson Gilmore, Ruth. *Golden Gulag: Prisons, Surplus, Crisis, and Opposition in Globalizing California.* Berkeley: University of California Press, 2007.

Winston, Celeste. "'How to Lose the Hounds': Tracing the Relevance of Marronage for Contemporary Anti-Police Struggles." PhD diss., CUNY Graduate Center, 2019. ProQuest (13863975).

———. "Maroon Geographies." In *Annals of the American Association of Geographers* 111, no. 7 (2021): 2185–2199.

Wong, Ryan Lee. "Basement Workshop: The Genesis of Asian American Resistance Culture," n.d. https://www.ryanleewong.com/essays-and-criticism/project-five-wwka6/.

Woodbine. "Urgent Pedagogies and Autonomous Infrastructure with Sandi Hilal and Pelin Tan." September 22, 2021. https://www.patreon.com/posts/56492881/.

Wright, Michelle. *Becoming Black: Creating Identity in the African Diaspora.* Durham: Duke University Press, 2004.

Wright, Steve. *Storming Heaven: Class Composition and Struggle in Italian Autonomous Marxism.* London: Pluto Press, 2002.

Wu, Ernest. "Scott Calls Proposal to Disband Dept 'Political Expedient.'" *The Campus,* March 26, 1971.

Yamashita, Karen Tei. *I-Hotel.* Minneapolis: Coffee House Press, 2010.

Yanagida, R. Takashi. "Asian Students vs. University Control: The Confrontation at C.C.N.Y." *Bridge* 1.5 (May/June 1972).

Young, Douglas. "Working Alone: Atomized and Desocialized Production as an Obstacle to Power." *Spectre Journal,* April 21, 2022. https://spectrejournal.com/atomized-and-desocialized-production-as-an-obstacle-to-power/.

Zeemont, Anna. "'The Act of the Paper': Literacy, Racial Capitalism, and Student Protest in the 1990s." PhD diss., CUNY Graduate Center, 2022. ProQuest (29252779).

Zibechi, Raúl. *Territories in Resistance: A Cartography of Latin American Social Movements.* Chico: AK Press, 2012.

Zinn, Howard. *A People's History of the United States.* New York: Harper, 2017.

———. *SNCC: The New Abolitionists.* Boston: Beacon Press, 1964.

INDEX

This index groups countries within continents and hemispheres, states within countries, cities within states, and boroughs within cities. In entries for City University of New York and New York City, readers will find respective subentries according to the college or borough, followed by CUNY-wide or NYC-wide references. In entries for Black, Jewish, and Puerto Rican Studies, readers will find general references, followed by respective references to educators, students, and women, followed by references to these Studies. This index references citations only in the body of the book. Please consult the footnotes for additional citations of people, organizations, places, and concepts.

Lomax, Louis, 67
López, Iris, 172
Lorde, Audre, 3–5, 12, 16–17, 39, 70, 76, 78, 85, 88, 91–96, 98–99, 101, 107 119, 117–120, 143, 149, 177–178
Luciano, Felipe, 128
Lumumba, Patrice, 42
Luu, Linda, 52

M

Madame Binh Graphics Collective, 146
Maeda, Daryl, 5, 35
Mailer, Norman, 30
Malraux, Andre, 72
Maoism, 102, 163; *see also* Mao Tse-Tung
March on Washington for Jobs and Freedom, 8, 33–34
Marcus, Jane, 3
Marcuse, Herbert, 117
Martínez, Antonia, 44
Marx, Karl, 13, 109, 140, 176
Marxism, Marxists, 6, 102, 117, 184; Autonomists [Marxists], 6
Marxist Feminist Group 1 (MF1), 49
Massiah, Louis, 88
Matos-Rodríguez, Félix V., 172, 177
May 19th Organization, 144, 150
Mbande, Nzinga, 149
McCarthy, Joseph, 29–30; McCarthyism, 28–32, 40, 168–169
McClain, James, 142
McDade, Tony, 173
McKissick, Floyd, 129
Michaux, Lewis, 63
Middle East, 6; Cyprus, 103; Iraq, 1, 18, 156, 159–160
militant research, 12
Miller, Arthur, 164
Miner, Myrtilla, 21
Mitchell, Nick, 16, 91, 186
Miyamoto, JoAnne, 48
Mohandesi, Salar, 11
Molloy, Sean, 150
Morales, Guillermo, 4, 8, 17, 43, 56–57, 124, 139, 141–146, 150–151
Morales, Iris, 128
Moreno, Cenen, 75
Morgan, Robin, 49
Moten, Fred, 77, 146
Muñoz Marín, Luis, 30
Muñoz, José Esteban, 12, 184
Muslims 63, 159, 166–167
Mussolini, Benito, 26
Myers, Joshua, 74

N

Nash, Jennifer C., 115
Nation of Islam (NOI), 37, 129
National Association for the Advancement of Colored People (NAACP), 33, 144
National Committee for the Defense of Political Prisoners, 143
National Endowment for the Arts (NEA), 94
National Student League (NSL), 25
Neal, Larry, 39, 165
neoliberalism, neoliberals, 8, 10, 18, 54, 86, 158, 169, 176–177, 184
New York City, 1–4, 8,14, 17, 21–23, 25–26, 30–31, 33–34, 38, 44, 47, 49–50, 52, 54, 56, 58, 62–63, 67, 72, 76, 78–79, 81, 86–88, 102–103, 107, 112, 131, 141, 146, 153, 157, 160, 164, 173–174, 179–180, 185, 187; Board of Education, 31, 36; Municipal Assistance Corporation (MAC), 55; New York Police Department (NYPD), 14, 18, 23–25, 29, 34–35, 41, 43, 47, 49, 57, 66–67, 81, 88, 107–108, 110, 112–113, 126, 136, 142, 144–145, 150, 155, 157, 161–167, 169, 174, 176, 178–179, 186; Bronx, 2, 31, 34–36, 42, 48, 66, 79, 84, 131; Bronx Social Center, 158, 187; North Bronx Collective, 179–180; Take Back the Bronx, 174; United Bronx Parents, 33; Brooklyn, 23, 31, 34, 35–36, 48, 61, 66–67, 69, 71, 79, 130, 149; Afro-American Teachers Association, 47; Brooklyn Commons, 187; Crown Heights, 164; Crown Heights Tenant Union, 158; Friends of the TENTS, 187; Interference Archive, 187; Lesbian Herstory Archives, 187; Ocean Hill-Brownsville, 8, 36, 48, 79–80, 97, 130, 141; SUNY Downstate Medical Center, 127; *Uhuru Sasa Shule* (Freedom Now School), 48; Weeksville Heritage Center, 187; Wendy's Subway, 178; Manhattan, 29, 34, 180; 16 Beaver Street, 187; American Indian Community House, 49; Apollo Theater, 125; Barnard College, 144; Bellevue Hospital, 145; Brecht Forum, 187; Chinatown, 49, 52; Basement Workshop, 49; Columbia University, 5, 8, 24, 30, 37, 41, 47–49, 65, 70, 93, 135, 148; Cooper Union, 159; East Village, 126; Elizabeth Cleaners Street School, 106; Gathering of the Tribes, 187; Harlem, 1–3, 6, 23–24, 31, 34–36, 38–39, 43–44, 48–49, 57, 61–71, 73, 79, 84, 94, 109, 118, 124–125, 127–132, 137–138, 140–141, 144, 147, 163, 165; Intermediate School (IS) 201, 35–36; Lower East Side, 23, 31, 35, 48, 61, 64–66, 68, 79, 84, 118, 131, 140; Mobilization for Youth (MfY), 68, 85; New School for Social Research, 64, 157; New York University (NYU), 24, 125, 157; Page Three, 113; Schomburg Center for Research in Black Culture, 187; School of Visual Arts (SVA), 141, 145–146; Sea Colony, 113; Speaker's Corner, 21, 63; St. Vincent's Hospital, 2; Wall Street, 110; Upper West Side, 140; Washington Heights, 57 World Trade Center (WTC), 155; Young Men's/ Young Women's Hebrew Association, 93; Queens, 34, 66, 103, 136, 140, 144; 5Pointz, 187; Staten Island, 161; Asian Americans for Action, 41; Can't Touch This NYC, 166; *Círculo de Tabaqueros* [Circle of Cigar Makers], 22; College Teachers Union, 26–27; Comité Boricua En La Diáspora, 174; Cop Watch NYC, 174; Decolonize This Place, 158, 169, 174; Direct Action Front for Palestine, 158, 166; *Ejemplo, El* (The Example), 22; Fuck the Police / Free the People / Fight the Power (FTP), 174; High School Student Union, 130; Making Worlds, 158; NYC for Abortion Rights (NYCFAR), 179; NYC Shut it Down, 174; Occupy Wall Street (OWS), 157–159, 170; Occuprint, 157; Occupy CUNY, 157;

ABOUT THE AUTHOR

Conor 'Coco' Tomás Reed is a Puerto Rican/Irish gender-fluid scholar-organizer of radical cultural movements at the City University of New York. Conor is codeveloping the quadrilingual anthology *Black Feminist Studies in the Americas and the Caribbean*, is the current comanaging editor of *LÁPIZ Journal*, and is a contributing editor of *Lost & Found: The CUNY Poetics Document Initiative*. Conor is a cofounding participant in Free CUNY, Rank and File Action, and Reclaim the Commons; and is a member of CUNY for Abortion Rights.

ABOUT COMMON NOTIONS

Common Notions is a publishing house and programming platform that fosters new formulations of living autonomy. We aim to circulate timely reflections, clear critiques, and inspiring strategies that amplify movements for social justice.

Our publications trace a constellation of critical and visionary meditations on the organization of freedom. By any media necessary, we seek to nourish the imagination and generalize common notions about the creation of other worlds beyond state and capital. Inspired by various traditions of autonomism and liberation—in the US and internationally, historical and emerging from contemporary movements—our publications provide resources for a collective reading of struggles past, present, and to come.

Common Notions regularly collaborates with editorial houses, political collectives, militant authors, and visionary designers around the world.

commonnotions.org
info@commonnotions.org

MORE FROM
COMMON NOTIONS

Abolishing Carceral Society
Abolition Collective

978-1-942173-08-3
$20.00
256 pages

Beyond border walls and prison cells—carceral society is everywhere. In a time of mass incarceration, immigrant detention and deportation, rising forms of racialized, gendered, and sexualized violence, and deep ecological and economic crises, abolitionists everywhere seek to understand and radically dismantle the interlocking institutions of oppression and transform the world in which we find ourselves. These oppressions have many different names and histories and so, to make the impossible possible, abolition articulates a range of languages and experiences between (and within) different systems of oppression in society today.

Abolishing Carceral Society presents the bold voices and inspiring visions of today's revolutionary abolitionist movements struggling against capitalism, patriarchy, colonialism, ecological crisis, prisons, and borders.

In the first publication of the series, the Abolition Collective renews and boldly extends the tradition of "abolition-democracy" espoused by figures like W. E. B. Du Bois, Angela Davis, and Joel Olson. Through study and publishing, the Abolition Collective supports radical scholarly and activist research, recognizing that the most transformative scholarship is happening both in the movements themselves and in the communities with whom they organize.

Abolishing Carceral Society features a range of creative styles and approaches from activists, artists, and scholars to create spaces for collective experimentation with the urgent questions of our time.

MORE FROM
COMMON NOTIONS

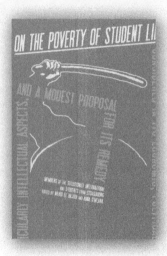

On the Poverty of Student Life
Members of The Situationist
International and Students from Strasbourg

Edited by Mehdi El Hajoui and Anna O'Meara

978-1-942173-57-1
$24.00
376 pages

When the Situationist International was a little known revolutionary art group, before Guy Debord's philosophical masterpiece *The Society of the Spectacle* was published, and before Paris' universities were occupied in May '68, a pamphlet titled *On the Poverty of Student Life* spurred a scandal that would turn into a global revolt.

On the Poverty of Student Life was a match that recognized and described student and youth alienation, and the way it was printed and distributed spread that fire. For the first edition, supporters of the SI (mis)appropriated school funds to create and distribute 10,000 copies of the pamphlet. From there, dozens of editions were produced by worker- and student-run printing presses around the world, from Paris to East London, from Tokyo to Detroit. This new edition highlights this global underground circulation and brings attention to the common conditions of students, workers, and internationalist resistance in the world of the sixties—bringing that historic reckoning to the present.

Featuring the original English adaptation by former SI member and celebrated translator Donald Nicholson-Smith, an interview with primary author Mustapha Khayati where he traces his map from colonial Algeria to imperial France to the university and the streets, and essays about the political relevance of the manifesto (then and now)—an edition like this has never before existed. With beautiful photographs of nearly one hundred different editions this book provides a cartography of an uprising.

MORE FROM
COMMON NOTIONS

Wages for Students
Written by the 'Wages for Students'
Students

With an Introduction by George
Caffentzis, Monty Neill, and
John Willshire-Carrera
Edited by Jakob Jakobsen, María
Berríos, and Malav Kanuga

978-1-942173-02-1
$13.95
224 pages

Wages for Students was published anony-
mously by three activists in the fall of 1975. It was written as "a pamphlet
in the form of a blue book" by activists linked to the journal *Zerowork*
during student strikes in Massachusetts and New York.

Deeply influenced by the Wages for Housework Campaign's analysis of
capitalism, and relating to struggles such as Black Power, anticolonial
resistance, and the antiwar movements, the authors fought against the
role of universities as conceived by capital and its state. The pamphlet
debates the strategies of the student movement at the time and denounc-
es the regime of forced unpaid work imposed every day upon millions of
students. *Wages for Students* was an affront to and a campaign against the
neoliberalization of the university, at a time when this process was just
beginning. Forty years later, the highly profitable business of education
not only continues to exploit the unpaid labor of students, but now also
makes them pay for it. Today, when the student debt situation has us
all up to our necks, and when students around the world are refusing to
continue this collaborationism, we again make this booklet available "for
education against education."

This trilingual edition includes an introduction by George Caffentzis,
Monty Neill, and John Willshire-Carrera alongside a transcript of a collective discussion organized by Jakob Jakobsen, Malav Kanuga, Ayreen
Anastas, and Rene Gabri, following a public reading of the pamphlet
by George Caffentzis, Silvia Federici, Cooper Union students, and other
members and friends of 16 Beaver.

BECOME A COMMON NOTIONS MONTHLY SUSTAINER

These are decisive times, ripe with challenges and possibility, heartache and beautiful inspiration. More than ever, we are in need of timely reflections, clear critiques, and inspiring strategies that can help movements for social justice grow and transform society.

Help us amplify those necessary words, deeds, and dreams that our liberation movements and our worlds so need.

Movements are sustained by people like you, whose fugitive words, deeds, and dreams bend against the world of domination and exploitation.

For collective imagination, dedicated practices of love and study, and organized acts of freedom.

By any media necessary.

With your love and support.

Monthly sustainers start at $12 and $25.
Join us at commonnotions.org/sustain.